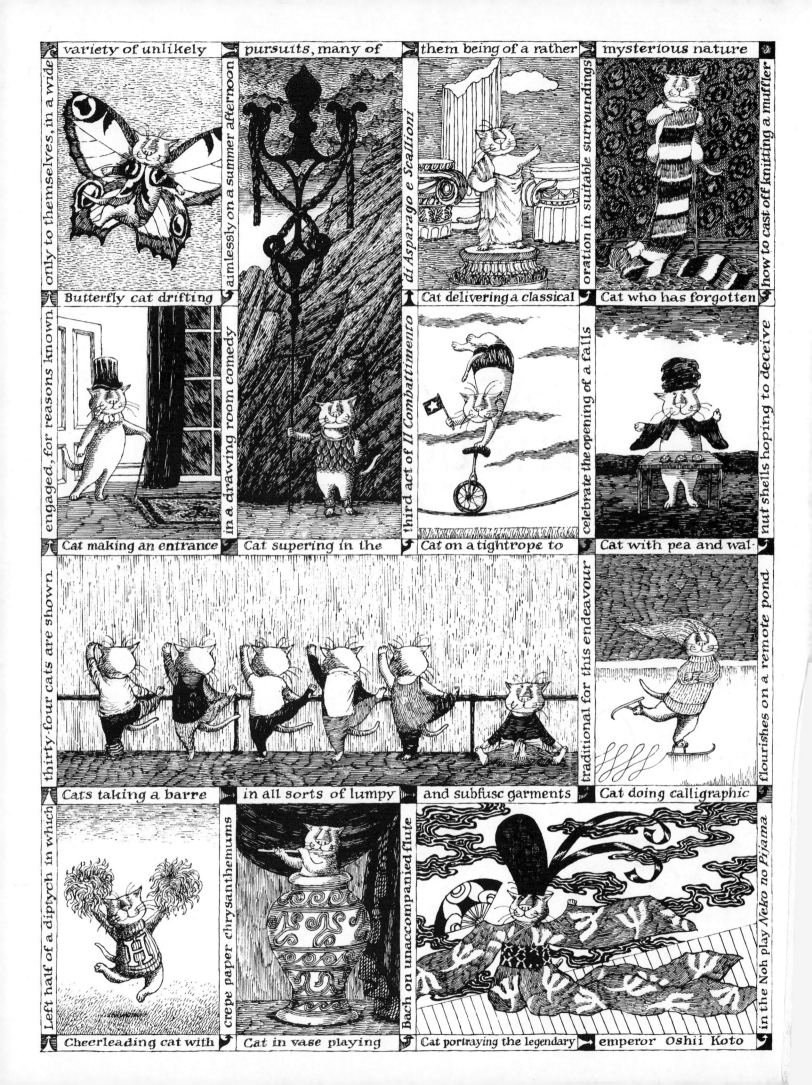

variety of unlikely pursuits, many of them being of a rather mysterious nature

only to themselves, in a wide

aimlessly on a summer afternoon

di Asparago e Scallioni

oration in suitable surroundings

how to cast off knitting a muffler

Butterfly cat drifting

Cat delivering a classical

Cat who has forgotten

engaged, for reasons known

in a drawing room comedy

third act of Il Combattimento

celebrate the opening of a falls

nut shells hoping to deceive

Cat making an entrance

Cat supering in the

Cat on a tightrope to

Cat with pea and wal-

thirty-four cats are shown

traditional for this endeavour

flourishes on a remote pond

Cats taking a barre

in all sorts of lumpy

and subfusc garments

Cat doing calligraphic

Left half of a diptych in which

crepe paper chrysanthemums

Bach on unaccompanied flute

in the Noh play Neko no Pijama

Cheerleading cat with

Cat in vase playing

Cat portraying the legendary

emperor Oshii Koto

CAT CATALOG

THE ULTIMATE CAT BOOK

CAT CATALOG

THE ULTIMATE CAT BOOK

EDITED BY JUDY FIREMAN

WORKMAN
PUBLISHING CO.
NEW YORK

Library of Congress Cataloging in Publication Data
Main entry under title:

Cat catalog.

Includes index.
1. Cats. I. Fireman, Judy.
SF442.C38   636.8   76-25473
ISBN 0-911104-81-X
ISBN 0-911104-82-8 pbk.

Cover painting: Paul Hanson
Jacket and book design: Paul Hanson

Workman Publishing Company, Inc.
231 East 51 Street
New York, New York 10022
Manufactured in the United States of America
First printing September 1976
10 9 8 7 6 5

We wish to thank the following for permission to include copyrighted material.

Jerry Abramowitz, photo, page 235. Copyright © 1976 by Downe Publishing, Inc. Reprinted with permission of *Ladies' Home Journal.*

Hilaire Belloc, verses, page 275. From THE BAD CHILD'S BOOK OF BEASTS as included in CAUTIONARY VERSES. Reprinted with permission of Random House, Inc.

Louis J. Camuti, "Euthanasia: A Deadly Vital Subject," pages 233–34. Reprinted with permission of *Feline Practice.*

"Cat Shows in the United States and Canada," page 142. Reprinted with permission of *Cats* magazine.

Robert Cooke, "Boston is Foothold of Cats with Extra Toes," page 168. Reprinted with permission of *The Boston Globe.*

T.S. Eliot, "The Naming of Cats," pages 272, 275. From OLD POSSUM'S BOOK OF PRACTICAL CATS, copyright © 1939 by T.S. Eliot; renewed 1967 by Esme Valerie Eliot. Reprinted with permission of Harcourt Brace Jovanovich, Inc.

Liselotte Erlanger, "The Story of Gottfried Mind," pages 82–83. Reprinted with permission of *Cats* magazine.

J.K. Frenkel, diagram, page 242. From "Toxoplasmosis" in R.A. Marcial-Rojas (ed.), PATHOLOGY OF PROTOZOAL AND HELMINTHIC DISEASES WITH CLINICAL CORRELATIONS, pages 254–290. Baltimore: William & Wilkins, 1971. Reprinted with permission of the author.

Robert Graves, "The Cat-Goddesses," page 275. In COLLECTED POEMS 1955 copyright © 1955 by Robert Graves. Reprinted with permission of Curtis Brown, Ltd.

Dick Gregory, "Another Voice," page 212. From pages 150–151 "A seven-day streamlining and realigning menu" and paraphrased from pages 145, 151 in DICK GREGORY'S NATURAL DIET FOR FOLKS WHO EAT: COOKIN' WITH MOTHER NATURE by Dick Gregory. Edited by James R. McGraw with Alvenia M. Fulton. Copyright © 1973 by Richard Claxton Gregory. Reprinted with permission of Harper & Row, Publishers, Inc.

Benjamin L. Hart, "Learning Ability in Cats," pages 236–37. Reprinted with permission of *Feline Practice.*

Vicky McMillan, "Groovy Catnip," page 199. Reprinted with permission of *Cat Fancy* magazine.

Paul Rowan, "You Can't Declaw With Love," pages 192–93. In CATS PREFER IT THIS WAY, copyright © 1976 by Carole Wilbourn and Dr. Paul Rowan. Reprinted with permission of Coward, McCann & Geoghegan.

John Voight, "The Black Death Plague and the Cat," pages 17–19. Reprinted with permission of *Cat Fancy* magazine.

Leon F. Whitney, charts, pages 215, 217, 219. From THE COMPLETE BOOK OF CAT CARE copyright © 1953 by Leon F. Whitney. Reprinted with permission of Doubleday & Co., Inc.

Robley Wilson, Jr., "Cat Watching," pages 67–68. Copyright © by University of Tulsa. Reprinted with permission of the author.

William Butler Yeats, "The Cat and the Moon," page 59. From THE COLLECTED POEMS OF W.B. YEATS copyright © 1919 by Macmillan Publishing Co., Inc., renewed 1947 by Bertha Georgie Yeats. Reprinted with permission of M.B. Yeats, Miss Anne Yeats and the Macmillan Co. of London & Basingstoke.

The *Cat Catalog* Paw Print Award goes to the following for their special help:
Edmund Blair Bolles, Thomas Dent, Paul Hanson, Patrick Oliver, Jennifer Rogers, Raymond Smith, Will Thompson, Suzanne Weaver, and everyone at Trade Composition.

CONTENTS

I. THE HISTORICAL CAT

II. THE MYSTICAL CAT

III. THE ARTISTIC CAT

IV. THE WELL BRED CAT

V. THE PUBLIC CAT

VI. THE PHYSICAL CAT

VII. THE PASSIONATE CAT

VIII. THE HEALTHY CAT

IX. THE WELL FED CAT

X. THE MEDICAL CAT

XI. THE PERFORMING CAT

XII. THE PRIVATE CAT

XIII. THE LEGAL CAT

XIV. THE CONSUMING CAT

INTRODUCTION

THE ALLEY CAT slinks around corners and howls on a back fence. The tabby, always cute and kittenish, is forever chasing balls of yarn and swatting at string. The elegant Siamese stands poised and graceful. The longhaired Persian relaxes, puffed and purring. All of them secretive, allowing intimacies only on terms they define and at times they designate.

First came the cats, allusive, mysterious and beautiful. Then came the questions. Do cats really see in the dark? Do they, in fact, have nine lives and how was the number determined? Why do cats slink when they walk? What is so special about pedigreed cats? The world is full of cat mysteries needing a very special book to illuminate them.

It is to the marvelous cat that the *Cat Catalog* is dedicated. This book is meant to be a valuable reference guide which will help you know how to take care of your cat, how to appreciate it, how to understand it. Written by professionals in a wide range of fields, the *Catalog* covers history, health, art, music, breeds, products, folklore and legend. Veterinarians, psychologists, researchers, breeders, trainers, all of them cat lovers, share their expertise to bring you a little closer to your quintessential pet.

This book tells you how to adopt a raggedy stray, recognize which of thirty-two breeds it is, bathe it, attend to its medical needs, feed it, photograph it, train it, give it a sanity and an I.Q. test, tell whether or not it is psychic, and leave it a legacy. Basic or frivolous, your cat's needs will be taken care of by the *Cat Catalog*.

As well as care and love, the cat needs admiration — for its grace, its beauty, its style. In the house or in the alley, it keeps itself clean and neat, and the effort is not in vain. No book would dare commit itself to exploring the world of the cat without honoring the cat's sense of form and beauty. Hundreds of photographs make this book handsome and pleasing to the eye and some of America's best known artists have rendered illustrations for the *Cat Catalog* in homage to the ultimate feline.

Worshiped by the Egyptians as a god, brought to Europe by the Romans, an outcast and a symbol of evil during the Middle Ages, respected by the Victorians as a practical domestic companion, the cat has recently made a big comeback as a favorite pet. It takes more than an ordinary book to honor the cat — I hope you find the *Cat Catalog* more than you imagined a cat book could be.

J. F.

I. THE HISTORICAL CAT

THE CAT IN EGYPT

Jean Cantin

ANCIENT EGYPT HAS been credited with being the first country to domesticate the cat and the only country to deify the cat to such an extent that eventually cats as gods outnumbered their human counterparts.

Contradictory speculation aside, credit for the cat's arrival in Egypt is generally given to the Ethiopians — particularly to Sesostris, who reportedly brought a few cats into Egypt after his conquest of Nubia. Some authorities claim that the cat was tamed by 3500 B.C. and deified by c. 3000 B.C.; the earliest portrait of the cat goddess Bastet was found in a temple of the Fifth Dynasty (c. 3000 B.C.).

Whatever their means of arrival, cats were immediately accepted into Egyptian families and loved for the same reasons we love them today — for their beauty, grace, suppleness and mysterious aloofness. They quickly became the adored members of the household and were as spoiled and pampered as cats are now. Their food was cut into little pieces lest they choke, and often they were encouraged to eat off of their master's plate. Even strays were treated to a feast of bread soaked in milk. In addition, cats were extremely useful animals and kept the Egyptian homes free of rats, mice and snakes.

There is no question that the first domesticated cats were not nearly as pretty as those of the modern world. There were two types of Egyptian cats depicted in paintings and sculpture: short-eared and blunt-nosed; long-eared and sharp-nosed. Both types were usually ginger-colored with black markings, and all were, to some extent, striped and short-haired. In ancient Egyptian art all cats were shown ritually, in a stately, dignified manner and always with their tails curled to the right. There is no information available explaining the right-side positioning of the tail nor on how they carried them when not posing for pictures.

Cats Become Gods

Scholars differ on the subject of how these ordinary house pets came to be worshiped as gods. The least imaginative explanation is the high esteem they earned by protecting the storage bins of grain from rodents. Some historians claim the cat became a god image because of its beauty. Occultists say it was because of the cat's magic properties.

One of the magic qualities attributed to cats was the ability to see in the dark. Egyptians feared the night, and most of their other animals rested when the sun set. But the cat seemed to make no distinction between day and night. Cats' eyes behaved strangely when compared to man's, and this brought about a certain amount

Bastet, shown on this papyrus scroll (XXI Dynasty), bears the cross of life while presiding at a funeral.

A bronze cat with kittens shows that the Egyptian interest in cats included a concern for realistic details as well as for the mythological symbolism of fertility.

Wooden carvings of cats were sometimes made in fulfillment of pledges given to the Egyptian goddess Bastet.

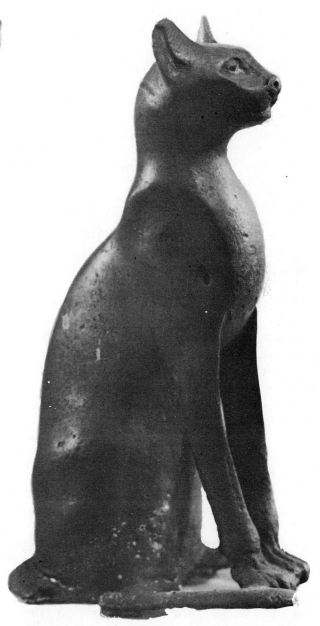

The Greek conquest of Egypt did not end the Egyptian worship of cats, as a bronze figure from the Ptolemaic period shows.

In the fertile valley of the Nile stone carvings of cats representing Bastet, goddess of fertility, began to appear very early in Egyptian history.

of fear. The widening and narrowing of their eyes with the waxing and waning of light was interpreted as evidence of a direct relationship, even kinship, between cats and the sun and moon. The fact that a cat slept curled up in a moonlike circle was also considered significant, if not conclusive proof of a heavenly connection. To the Egyptians, this curled position of the sleeping cat, with its head touching its tail, symbolized eternity as well.

By 2000 B.C. the moon concept had gotten out of hand: the Egyptians decided the cat was saving the world from darkness. They reasoned that since the moon reflects the light of the solar system, the cat's eyes, which looked phosphorescent in the dark, were mirroring the rays of the sun. Therefore, the cat kept the Egyptians protected from total darkness during the night. Because of its connection with the moon, the cat was also invested with the power to control tides, weather and growth of crops. The eyes of the cat remained a fascination for the Egyptians, who thought its strange gaze could penetrate the mind and soul, and thus regulate one's life to some degree; indeed, the Egyptian word for cat is *mau*, which means "to see."

No one knows when the Egyptian cat achieved sanctification. There was no official act proclaiming it divine, but Egyptian art testifies to the fact that the cat was considered sacred for over two thousand years. When considering the myths and legends of the Egyptians, it is important to remember that all their gods and goddesses had a confusing way of merging with one another; one god easily and often took on the properties of another.

At the earliest stage of worship, the cat was recognized as sacred to the Egyptian goddess of motherhood and fertility, Isis. According to legend, the cat goddess Bastet was the daughter of Isis and her sun god husband Osiris, also called Ra. (Osiris, Horus, Ra and Ptah were all different forms of the sun god.) Bastet's father had the distinction of being not only the sun god, but god of the underworld besides; thus he was responsible for the protection of the souls of the dead. Bastet's mother was content to be the sun, moon and earth goddess. She also merged with the goddess of pleasure, Hathor, who was cow-headed, and with the Theban mother goddess, Mut. The worship of Bastet at various times overlapped the worship of Isis, Mut and Hathor, as well as that of the lion goddesses, Sekhmet and Tefnut.

Bastet Worship

It must have been a great relief to all when things became simplified around 950 B.C. with the emergence of Bastet as the primary goddess. But perhaps not too simplified. The goddess Bastet was also referred to as Bast or Pasht, depending on what region you came from. Historians believe that our word "puss" is derived from the Egyptian word *Pasht*.

The goddess Bastet was usually depicted in bronze sculpture. The earlier sculptures show her as lion-headed, but gradually she took the shape of a human body with the head of a cat — the human form occasionally being replaced by a cat's limbs and tail. She always wore a long dress, sometimes of V-neck design, elaborately embroidered. Often she carried three symbols: a basket, a sistrum (the musical rattle used in the worship of Isis) and a small shield, or aegis.

As representatives of Bastet, Egyptian cats had an awesome responsibility. Bastet was not only goddess of sexuality and fertility, but she was also the embodiment of the time-honored ideal of virgin motherhood. How the Egyptians managed to combine these two concepts is hard to imagine, but they worked it out. Bastet gradually assumed the qualities originally bestowed on Isis and Osiris. Besides being the sun, moon, motherhood and love goddess, she was further charged with the protection of the dead, the success or failure of crops and the making of rain.

Cats also had something to do with the healing of the sick, though their role in this service was indirect at best. When the child of a wealthy Egyptian became seriously ill, the family wasted no time in seeking the help of Bastet. All the relatives of the child immediately shaved the hair off their head and sold it for gold or silver. The money was delivered to the temple and used by the keeper to purchase milk and fish for the cats held there for the sole purpose of worship. The family gathered in the temple, and while the priests chanted the cats devoured the food. The relatives of the sick child found great significance in looking into the eyes of the cats and determining from their strange gaze whether or not the child would recover.

Egyptian worship of the cat reached such intensity that the penalty for taking a cat's life was death. It was also very unlucky to come upon a dead cat in the street; if seen, you ran the risk of being held responsible for its demise. When this situation arose, the passer-by would start to cry aloud with grief, beating his breast and lamenting the loss — regardless of whose cat it was.

The eventual death of the family cat was inevitable and must have been a painful experience for those Egyptians who considered their pet divine. The bereaved went immediately into mourning and displayed their grief by shaving off their eyebrows as a token of affliction. The length of the formal mourning period has not been recorded, but no doubt it lasted at least until the eyebrows grew back.

The actual funeral varied with the degree of importance achieved by the cat. Temple cats were given the most elaborate service and were ultimately laid to rest in a true sarcophagus or tomb. Milk was often placed in the sacred vault, and though not literally replenished it was believed that the incantations of the temple priests kept the bowls constantly filled. While the service was less elaborate for house cats, crying, breast-beating and wine-drinking always accompanied their funerals. Neighborhood collections were often taken up to help a middle-income family bury their pet. Even the very poor interred their cats in cemeteries. It has been estimated that first-class funerals cost as much as the modern equivalent of $1,200, whereas second-class funerals could be as cheap as $200.

During the middle of the nineteenth century, an entire cemetery of embalmed cats was discovered in Beni-Hassan, Egypt. Over 300,000 mummies were uncovered. Unfortunately, not one archaeologist was on hand to prevent the authorities from destroying the remains. The mummified cats, totaling twenty tons, were loaded on cargo boats and shipped to Liverpool, England. There they were broken down and sold to farmers at $18 a ton to be used as fertilizer. According to a contemporary newspaper account, the auctioneer used the body of an embalmed cat for his gavel. Only a few mummified cats have been discovered since.

The Bubastis Festival

The worship of the cat reached its peak around 950 B.C., with the cultural center for cat worship located in the city of Bubastis, situated east of the Nile Delta. King Osorkon II constructed a magnificent hall surrounded by canals from the Nile. An inscription in the sanctuary reads, *"I give thee every land in obeisance, I give thee all power like Ra."*

CAT MUMMIES

Funeral arrangements were elaborate for cats of the aristocracy, and great care was taken to give them a really big send-off. Precise rules governed the laying-out ceremony. The cat's master wrapped the animal in clean linen and then carried it through the streets, lamenting bitterly until he reached the mortician's office. There it was carefully embalmed and treated with drugs and spices before being wrapped again in colorful strips of cloth for mummification. The cats were embalmed because of the Egyptian belief in immortality, a doctrine which they originated. When the wrapping process was completed, cloth was laid over the eyes and carefully painted to match the original eyes. Perky artificial ears were put in place at a jaunty angle; as a final touch a collar, usually of turquoise, was positioned around the cat's neck before it was deposited in a specially prepared case. The case, which measured up to three feet high, was hollowed out in the shape of a seated or standing cat. Sometimes mouse mummies were buried with the cat so it would have food during its afterlife.

ALICE SU

Wooden tomb for a mummified mouse (c. 600 B.C.).

Enthusiastic pilgrims traveled by boat in April and May from the twenty major cities lining the Nile to a yearly festival in honor of Bastet. It is estimated that more than 700,000 people made this trip each season to celebrate the great festival of Bubastis.

PERSIAN CAT COUP

Cats also played a role in Egyptian military life. One of the most unusual battles in history took place in 500 B.C., during a time when the Egyptians were under siege by the Persians at the city of Pelusium. Things were not going well for the Persians; they were met by fierce resistance and it looked as though the battle would go to the Egyptians. Finally all seemed lost, and the Persians appeared to abandon the fight. The troops disappeared for eight days. Under cover of darkness, they searched the cities and towns, rounding up as many cats as they could find. When the battle resumed, and the Egyptians were ready to finish things off, the Persians released most of the cats, who promptly ran in panic over the battlefield. Then, with each soldier carrying a live cat in his arms, the Persians attacked. One can only assume that the weapons must have been the kind that can be wielded with one hand, although even that would have been difficult while holding a struggling cat. (Picture a modern-day soldier trying to fire an M-16 rifle while carrying a cat.) Not one Egyptian dared to risk the injury of one cat, as such a sacrilege could not be considered. Not a single blow was exchanged, and the defeat was devastating for the Egyptians.

All historians agree that many people went to Bubastis, but there is great discrepancy among scholars regarding exactly what happened once they got there. The more conservative accounts concede that there might have been some intoxication other than religious zeal, while others describe the entire festival as one drunken sexual orgy, with a great consumption of grape wine. There was much marching around, playing of musical instruments and general frenzy, very like our Mardi Gras Festival. The women used a type of cymbal called the *crotala*, while the men played flutes.

There is some evidence that the festival started while the participants were still traveling toward Bubastis in their boats. As they approached each city along the way, the boats would be rowed to the banks. The women would scream off-color jokes and lewd suggestions at the gathering crowd and finally fling their clothes over their heads. This was repeated at every city and was a sign for those on shore, unable to make the trip, to start their own orgy at home.

Upon arrival at Bubastis, food and wine were served and the orgies that followed were looked upon with approval by the authorities. They were believed to directly increase the fertility not only of the crops, but of the animals and women, too.

The Party's Over

During the two-thousand-year reign of Bastet, cats were jealously protected and means were taken to prevent them from being exported to other countries. Historians speculate that Egyptians looked upon their cats as a secret weapon upon which the security and greatness of the country depended. It was a serious crime to smuggle them out of the country.

The decline of the cat cult in Egypt was very gradual, but by the year 100 B.C. it was on its way out. Phoenician traders are credited with being partly responsible for this. Word had spread throughout the world about the cat's talent as a rodent-catcher. Everybody wanted one — particularly in Europe, where rats were an increasing problem. The Phoenicians, who for years had been trying to sneak them out, finally managed to export them in quantity. Once the cat became common to other parts of the world it ceased to be a god. For cats, it had been the best of times.

Jean Cantin, a cat lover and free-lance writer, lives in Stamford, Connecticut.

The Egyptian reverence for cats continues to inspire people.
This memorial to a living cat, Theo,
was designed by artist Barton Beněs
and commissioned by Theo's owner, Jimmy Newcomer.
This memorial is made of wood and glass; the cat is fabric.
Upon his death, Theo will be cremated
and his remains placed inside the fabric cat
which will be sewn shut and then serve as an eternal memorial
to Theo.

COURTESY OF JIMMY NEWCOMER.

PHOTO BY ALICE SU.

THE SOCIAL HISTORY OF THE CAT

Timothy Bay

GIB, TOM, PYEWACKET, Pasht, Grizel, Grimalkin, Puss, Tabbald. Throughout the ages, the cat has gone under a variety of names, while its pawprints have appeared in a wondrous diversity of lands. A god in Egyptian times, a companion of sorceresses at the Sabbath, a muse in French literature, a sometime member of royalty in the Orient, a showpiece in the Victorian era, the cat has moved with ease and authority through salons and temples, palaces and alleyways.

The Birth of Cat History

It is generally assumed that the Egyptian cat, descended from the African wildcat (*Felis libyca*), slinked its way into history about 3500 B.C. The modern house cat, *Felis catus*, in turn, is a hybrid — a crossbreed of the *Felis libyca* with the European wildcat, *Felis sylvestris*, who inhabits southern and central Europe. The roots and evolution of this ancestry, however, are only dimly understood, although scientists believe that the cat developed from the *Miacidae*, a family of carnivores which lived during the Eocene epoch, some fifty million years ago. In fact, the cat, the weasel and the dog, share a common prehistoric forebear, since they are all distant relatives of this carnivore.

In Egypt, rats were the classic plague, along with snakes and smaller vermin; following each inundation of the Nile, every farm became an island on which these pests would congregate. The farmer would rely on the cat to rid him of these invaders, and for his help, the cat became a protected and revered member of society.

While Greeks had a much less exalted view of the cat (although a good ratter had a high marketplace value in fifth-century Greece), the animal figured significantly in their mythology.

According to legend, Apollo, the sun god, created the lion to frighten his sister, Artemis, the moon goddess. Artemis, in turn, retaliated by creating the cat, thereby establishing the belief that the cat is a child of the moon.

In the sixth century B.C., Aesop acknowledged the popular identification of cats with women. In one fable, Venus, solicited by a cat who had fallen for a handsome young man, agreed to turn the cat into a woman. Despite her new appearance, the transformed feline retained vestiges of her old identity: when she saw a mouse scamper through the bedroom, she leaped out of her bed in excitement.

The Romans were even less reverent of Egypt's four-legged icons; as a result, problems occasionally arose between the two cultures. Once, when the Nile area was occupied by Caesar and his army, a Roman soldier was mobbed and murdered savagely in an Alexandria street for the crime of accidentally killing a cat.

By the first century of the Christian era, Phoenician traders were bringing cats into various ports of the Mediterranean, thus establishing a European beach head for the animal. There is evidence to document the existence of cats in Scotland and the Netherlands by the fifth century A.D., and in Saxony and Wales by the ninth century.

One account of the cat's settlement in northern Europe is very romantic. When the Greek General Galsthelos, who commanded the Pharaoh's army, was defeated by the miracle of the parting of the Red Sea waters, he fled to the far end of the Mediterranean. He settled in Portugal with his wife Scota, a pharaoh's daughter. Here he founded the kingdom of Brigantium. As the story goes, Scota brought with her a number of cats. Centuries later, Fergus I, a descendant of this royal line, became a ruler of a great northern kingdom which he named Scotland, after his famous forebear. The descendants of Scota's Egyptian mascot cats were then brought over to Scotland, where they started a new life and lineage.

By the fifth century, the age of the ratting cat — the millennium of the mouser — had arrived. Barbarian invasions sweeping across Europe brought with them rats and the plague. From the North Sea to the Adriatic, countries passed laws sanctioning the cat and fixing its marketplace value. In 936, Howell the Good, in Wales, created a series of laws which were incorporated in the kingdom's legal code, establishing the cat's worth and mandating penalties for those who would wound or mistreat the animal.

The cat's value as a rat-catcher was cemented by the eleventh century, when the

Crusaders returning from the Holy Land brought with them the disease-bearing black rats. Fortunately, they also brought with them hundreds of cats from Palestine. These émigrés from the Middle East intermingled with their domestic cousins in Europe to create new distinctive breeds of felines.

The Cat Falls from Grace

The cat's glory turned out to be short-lived; it would soon become an outcast in Christendom. Its loss of status is traceable in part to its pagan associations and mythological background. At the same time, the cat's mysterious habits and inexplicable features would also help cast it beyond the pale in the role of consort of witches and warlocks, an enemy of the Church.

During the Middle Ages, the Norse goddess of love, Freya, chose the cat as her symbol; two black cats drove her chariot. A small religion developed around this goddess, but by the fifteenth century it had deteriorated into a Bacchanalian cult. In the Church's backlash against such paganism, thousands of cats were destroyed. Throughout the early Middle Ages, the cat had figured in pagan rites in the Highlands and western isles of Scotland; as these cults were exorcised, the cat became a scapegoat.

Now hundreds of thousands of cats were destroyed in ceremonies presided over by priests, and hundreds more were crucified and flayed. In Vosges, they were burned on Shrove Tuesday; in Alsace, they were tossed into the Easter bonfire; in Belgium, once a year, they were thrown from the tops of towers. The cat had become a favorite sacrificial victim in religious observances. In 1484, Pope Innocent VIII, by denouncing the cat and all who were its friends, made official this reign of terror.

The Egyptians had made the cat a god, but now the Church made it a disciple of Satan. The association of cats with witchcraft, however, was an old one, deeply rooted in mythological soil. Artemis, the moon goddess and protector of cats, according to the Romans, sent the first witch, Aradia, to earth to teach human beings magic and witchcraft. Cats as the offspring of the moon and companions of Diana (called Artemis by the Greeks) became the living embodiment of all kinds of mysteries.

The ancient Britons, for example, believed that if you gazed deeply into a cat's eyes, you would be able to see exactly what was happening in the spirit world. And old folklore of Finland

> In the Middle Ages, people believed that cats sucked the breath of babies or stole their blood, the obvious inference being that the cat was the Devil himself and intended to use the blood in his Black Mass.

tells that black cats were messengers of death and would carry the souls of dead people to the other world.

Physically and temperamentally, the cat was perfectly cast for this otherworldly role. Its stealth, independence and uncanny habits, luminous eyes, nocturnal life style — all gentle reminders of the untamed primal power of the jungle — helped create this aura of self-contained mystery.

The cat also suffered guilt by association, since many of the witches were lonely old women who valued very highly its companionship. Unfortunately, the witches themselves were not always kind to their allies and familiars. In the old remedies devised by the hags, cats were often an important ingredient: cats' brains, eyes and grease were staples of their elixirs. Moreover, the cat was a victim of man's terrible ignorance in everyday matters. Primitive farmers discovering that their barns were ruined — usually by rats or dampness — would jump to the conclusion that the cat, which often prowled around the barns, was a witch responsible for the damage.

Ironically, at the same time that the Church was publicly persecuting Grimalkin, cats were entrenched in convents and abbeys, performing their ancient role as rat-catchers. But this contradiction is typical of the dual role of the cat throughout the Middle Ages. While cats were being burned in the streets, many people privately looked upon the household cat as a guardian spirit and talisman.

The Fireside Sphinx Reigns

Despite many vicissitudes throughout history, the cat remained the patron saint of the hearth. Early on, the Romans looked upon the cat as a household god, a tutelary presence whose spirit was invoked at marriages and funerals. Tributes were paid to the cat at funerals to ensure that its protection would extend to the future life of the deceased. At marriages, the bride made a sacrifice to it and gave money as she crossed the threshold of her new home.

In Scotland, during the Middles Ages, if a white cat entered a house, it was regarded as an omen of sickness or trouble; if a black cat entered, it was seen as a harbinger of good luck.

To propitiate the cat's domestic blessings, the arrival of a new cat in the home was celebrated with a special ceremony. The ritual was to carry the animal three times around the pot hanger, then rub its paws against the wall of the chimney. It was believed that if this procedure were properly performed, the cat would never leave. The cat at no time was allowed to be carried far away from the house for fear of some calamity; the only safe way to move the animal was to repeat the ritual connected with its arrival.

COOPER-HEWITT MUSEUM OF DESIGN, NEW YORK

A serenely napping cat is stalked by a rat in this engraving by Cornelius Visscher (1610–1670).

This need to have the cat's protective presence gave rise to a particularly barbaric medieval custom: a live cat, serving as guardian spirit, was bricked into the façade when a house was being built. In Denmark, as late as the nineteenth century, peasants of Jutland would bury a live cat at the threshold of their cottage. The fourteenth-century Italian poet Petrarch took the dead cat of his beloved Laura, embalmed it in the Egyptian manner, and placed it over his doorway, where it was to remain in protective vigil until his death.

Sexual Politics

Cats also have a special place in the affairs of the heart. Ever since its day of deification, the cat has been a female symbol, closely bound up with the feminine sensibility and the spirit of romance. In Flanders, during the Middle Ages, a cat sitting by the door before a wedding was a sign of bad luck;

in France, any girl who trod carelessly on a cat's tail was advised to delay her wedding for a year.

At the same time, cats would assume the form of women, or women, particularly witches, would metamorphose into cats. This mystical pact between cat and woman was particularly strong in the Orient, where dozens of legends have been handed down in which cats take on the shapes of old women, courtesans and young girls.

But there is a larger meaning involved. The cat's nature, as several French writers have noted, is symbolically linked to a frequently neglected element in our society: the world of the senses, the female sensibility, the life of the imagination. Cats have for centuries been associated with love and devotion — two qualities always revered by men in their women.

By the end of the Renaissance, the cat was comfortably residing in working-class homes. Nevertheless, the cat had some friends in high places. Cardinal Wolsey, a formidable man in sixteenth-century England, took his cat to the dinner table, to audiences, and to the cathedral when he was officiating at services. The French statesman Cardinal Richelieu was constantly surrounded by his adoring cats; he made provisions for all fourteen of them in his will, but when he died his Swiss guards rounded up the poor creatures and burned them.

During the eighteenth and early nineteenth centuries, the cat became a darling of the beau monde of the French bourgeoisie. Mme. de Staël, Mme. Récamier and the Duchesse de Bouillon were all cat fanciers, and Mme. Helvetius decked out her cats like fine ladies, swaddling them in fur robes and silk costumes.

A Persian cat with bird appeared on this French wallpaper panel (c. 1830).

COOPER-HEWITT MUSEUM OF DESIGN, NEW YORK

Modern Times—Reevaluating Virtues

The real turning point in the rehabilitation of *Felis catus* came in the eighteenth century in the form of its old enemy, the rat. In 1799, the first cases of the plague appeared in Napoleon's expeditionary army in Egypt, and the cat, still partially in eclipse since the Middle Ages, once more became a valuable commodity.

Earlier, in 1749, the new colonies of America were invaded by an army of black rats, and domestic cats imported from Europe helped turn the tide in the battle between colonist and rodent for control of the grain supplies. Reportedly, cats had come over on the *Mayflower*, but they did not emerge as true members of the colonial community until this showdown over a valuable food source.

In the early 1700's, cats had accompanied Spanish friars and soldiers who were attempting

PHOTO. BIBL. NAT. PARIS

The wife's penalty for adultery in Turkey was to be drowned with a cat.

A stylized cat in profile by Coypel from Moncrif's Les Chats *(Paris, 1727), one of the earliest books about the cat.*

cat had become a highly fashionable and venerated pet, while the more exotic varieties of the animal were considered status objects. In 1884, Owen Gould, the British consul general at Bangkok, was given a pair of Siamese cats by the King of Siam as a farewell present. Gould shipped his cats to England, where they became princes of high society.

The cat had also found its home in belleslettres. In the nineteenth century, the cat strolled into French literature, captivating many of the literary luminaries of the period, including Baudelaire, Gautier, de Maupassant and Anatole France. This kinship between cat and scribe would become a tradition in France which reached its apotheosis with Colette, poet laureate of the cat.

The Victorian Age was the cat's Belle Epoque. Partly, it was the spirit of the age itself, an age of gingerbread artifice and sentiment, which led to this ascendancy. In this decorous and decorative epoch, there was a new awareness of the rich variety, stylish grace and formal beauty of the cat, a heightened appreciation of the creature as a domestic *objet d'art.* Venerated as a guardian of the home, honored as a mouser, the cat was now celebrated as a thing of beauty.

In 1871, the first cat show, organized by Harrison Weir, was held at the Crystal Palace in London. This event represented the glittering centerpiece of the cat revival. In 1895, another

to convert the Indians while building civilizations in the wilderness of the Southwest. As the Jesuit Brothers moved up the west coast of Mexico founding missions, the domestic cat provided protection for the grain and rode shotgun against disease-carrying rodents.

The work of Louis Pasteur in the midnineteenth century helped in the rehabilitation of the cat's position in society. Pasteur's discoveries sparked a whole new wave of hygiene conscientiousness among Europeans. Suddenly, many animals were avoided because they were believed to be unclean, potential disease-carriers. Whereas nobody would touch a dog during this period without wearing white gloves, the cat, a model of cleanliness, was given a clean bill of health; the good news paved the way for its triumphant return to popular favor.

By the end of the nineteenth century, the

A Victorian cat fancier, Mrs. Roberts Locke, with her cats Calif, Siam and Bangkok.

The cat surveys the wonders of the city in Marc Chagall's Paris Through the Window *(1913).*

Englishman, J. T. Hyde, organized an American version at Madison Square Garden. Both shows were big successes, and they bred a new generation of cat fanciers and a whole tradition of club-sponsored cat shows.

The cat now entered the twentieth century once again a mascot and sovereign of the home, esteemed for its companionship, aesthetic grace and mousing wizardry.

As a civic-minded citizen, the cat performs valuable service to the state. In France, America, Denmark and many other countries, the ratting cat maintains a vigil in post offices, museums, libraries, butcher shops and warehouses. The most dramatic recent example of its utility in this area occurred in 1961. At that time, the rice fields of Borneo were so saturated with rats that an emergency airlift was created: all the stray cats of Singapore were rounded up and parachuted by the hundreds into the fields. They routed the rats and saved the crops.

Domestic cats now outnumber dogs in many places of the world. In France, cats reportedly outnumber their four-legged fellow travelers, 7.5 million to 6 million. In Great Britain, 4.2 million cats have won the affection of their countrymen, compared to 4 million canines.

Besides those cats who enjoy domestic bliss,

The wild cat existed in America before its discovery by the Europeans. A hunter brought one of them to Christopher Columbus, which was of an ordinary size, of a brownish gray colour, and having a very long and strong tail. *From Count de Buffon's* Natural History *1767, English translation by William Smellie.*

there are also the hordes of the homeless, the gypsies who inhabit the back alleys, docks, public squares and abandoned tenements in Europe and America. Colette once called Paris the "Buchenwald of Cats" because of that city's rag-tag army of the street-wise. In Rome, cats ricochet through the streets and alleys, indifferent to politics and the elements, and congregate at night in the back streets and historic ruins. Animal protection societies have sprung up throughout the world, offering a support system for these strays and other wayward animals. There is the Association des Amis des Bêtes in France, the Royal Society for the Prevention of Cruelty to Animals in England, the American Society for the Prevention of Cruelty to Animals, as well as many other groups.

Socially, the cat-as-symbol has moved upward into the high reaches of fashion as the ideal of feline beauty has become assimilated into the canons of stylish taste. The sleekness, subtle sensuality, grace and elegance associated with cats have become an advertising totem and an ideal peddled by merchants and arbiters of couture.

The cat has also created an enduring persona in the media, a folk hero of our time. From "Crazy Cat" to "Felix" to "mehitabel," the cat has been endearingly portrayed as a wily, street-smart operative on the eternal prowl for canaries, mice and the good life. Musing on her own destiny, mehitabel, Don Marquis' poet-princess of the alley cat, gives a final philosophical comment on the independent life style of the alley cat.

> "do you think that i would
> change
> my present freedom to
> range
> for a castle or moated grange
> wotthehell, wotthehell . . ."

Individual cats have made their own contributions to history in the twentieth century. In the 1930's, a cat did his bit to help in the building of Grand Coulee Dam. It carried a string tied to its tail through a winding drainpipe during the construction. The string was tied to a rope and the rope to a cable that the engineers had been unable to get through the pipe. And in 1950, as reported in the London *Times,* a four-month-old cat scaled the Matterhorn. The cat kept pace with a group of mountaineers, although it managed to make its own ascent to the 14,780-foot summit without the benefit of ropes or equipment.

Another famous cat was involved in a White House romance in the 1920's. The cat, Timmie, belonged to a Washington newspaperman, Bascom Timmons; its paramour, Caruso, was a canary belonging to President Calvin Coolidge. The romance began when the newspaperman took his pet to the White House on his rounds. Eventually, Coolidge sent the canary to Timmons' home to live with the cat. The canary would often walk up and down the back of his feline friend or rest between his paws. According to Timmons, the poignant fade-out finally came when Caruso fell over dead one day while singing to the cat.

The romance between cat and human, however, continues to grow. More and more people are falling under the spell of these beautiful, independent and unfathomable creatures. Cats are special, and apparently they are irresistible.

As Colette once wrote, "There are no ordinary cats."

Timothy Bay is free-lance writer whose work has appeared in newspapers and national magazines. He lives on the Upper West Side of Manhattan, where he shares a refrigerator with a cat named Lilly.

THE BLACK DEATH PLAGUE AND THE CAT

John Voight

CAT FACT IS stranger than cat fiction. Amazing as it seems, six hundred years ago the house cat literally saved European civilization from destruction. It was during the fourteenth century that men, cats, rats and the Black Plague entered into a historical interplay that would determine the fate of Western civilization. The central actor and hero in this drama of life and death was the cat.

Before the fourteenth century, during the Dark Ages, man had clearly divided the universe into that which was thought good and that which was thought evil. At the beginning of the fourteenth century, man added the cat to Satan's portion of the universe. It was then, for the first time in history, that people claimed that witches, demons and Satan himself could appear in the shape of a cat. It was also believed that any creature under Satan's control would inevitably own a cat. People became suspect of cat and cat owner alike.

It was said that when Satan appeared at the mysterious witches' sabbath, the time for witches and their cats to meet their sovereign, he showed himself in the form of a huge green cat with fiery red eyes and sparkling fur. Carvings of witches, each with a cat, began to appear on cathedral walls. The first of such carvings was made on the western doorway of the cathedral of Lyons. It shows a naked witch riding a goat. Her right hand clutches one of the goat's horns; her left hand holds a cat.

Strangely enough, even the children in their own way saw the cat as an evil creature. In the streets of Europe, a new children's song was sung at every cat the children saw. The lyrics were short and simple: "Grimalkin the foul Fiend's cat — Grimalkin the witches' brat."

All of these false assumptions about the evil nature of the cat led to one of the stupidest and cruelest series of acts in the history of man: the persecution of the cats. Because it was thought cats were the Devil's creatures, cats were hunted down and killed in every European country. Cats were crucified or thrown howling into ovens.

Now was the time of the autos-da-fé, the bonfires of the unholy cats. It was the time of the fires of St. John, when in the presence of priests and mayors baskets of live cats were annually burned in hilltop bonfires. To justify these sentences of torture and death, cat trials were held in local civil and religious courts. The officials always handed down sentences of death, clothing them in such high-sounding clichés as the "nobility of mind," or the "fight against evil."

The religious and legal establishments were supported in their crimes against the cats by the majority of the people — but not by all the people. Here and there, scattered about the towns and countrysides, cat owners would guard their pets against the monstrous crimes that were

A harmless necessary cat.

SHAKESPEARE

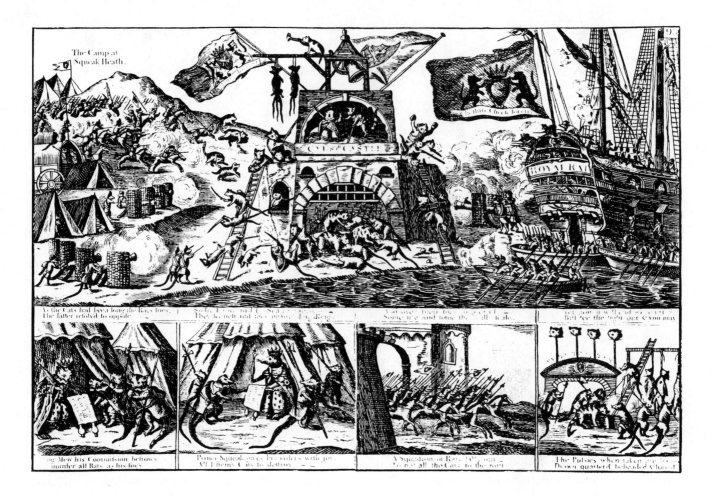

being committed. And this was indeed a bold thing to do, for the mere owning of a cat was a cause of suspicion. Cat owners as well as their cats faced the fires of the inquisitions.

But the persecutors of the cats would soon pay for their folly. In the fourteenth century, the knights returning home from the Crusades in the Holy Land did not return alone. In their brightly pennanted ships deep in the dark holes lurked the fierce Asiatic black rat. In the blood of these creatures was the bubonic plague — the Black Death. It was these rats, and not the cats, who were the true enemies of mankind.

With so few cats in Europe and more cats killed each year, the black rats quickly overran the entire continent. Crops, stored grains, and property were destroyed by these vermin. Swarms of rats attacked the children on the streets and the babies in their cradles. No longer was the song "Grimalkin the foul Fiend's cat" heard. Epidemics of typhus broke out. But a thousand times worse than any of this was the terror of the Black Plague.

The plague, carried to man from the fleas on the rats, struck in the middle of the four-teenth century. The symptoms were always the same: high fever, chills, prostration, delirium, black hemorrhages, and death.

Because of the plague, in only two years, three out of every four people in Europe died. This amounted to twenty-five million human lives. European civilization was in the balance. Never before or since has mankind suffered so much death in so short a time. The only solution to the problem was the cat. Only the cat could destroy the Asiatic rat — but the cat had almost been killed off by the very men who were now dying of the plague. Cat owners fared better than their cat-hating neighbors. For those few who had risked their lives by owning cats, the black rats were not so great a problem. When the towns and farms that had no cats swarmed with the black killers and the plague they carried, the homes with cats were relatively free of the rats. It was to their cats that the cat owners owed their lives.

The officials of church and state slowly saw the mistake of their past inquisitions against the cats. Even the most fanatical cat hater knew that a cat would rid his home of the black rats. Sadly enough, it would be centuries before the cat would gain the status of a beloved household pet, but in the late fourteenth century the inquisitions against the cats were stopped.

First the churches stopped the practices of the fires of St. John and the autos-da-fé. Then even the monastic rules that had forbidden animals in monasteries and nunneries were changed. The *Ancren Riwle* of England for nunneries that read, "Ye, my dear sisters, shall have no beast but a cat," became the new rule in both nunneries and monasteries on the Continent. From their prosecutions, the churches turned toward saving the cats.

Countries also ended their support of the killing of cats. Laws that aided cats and cat owners were passed. With the menace of the black rats, the cat became a valuable object. In the past, there had been laws forbidding the stealing or killing of cats. These laws were once again put into practice. In one such Welsh law, anyone who stole or killed a cat would have to pay a fine of one sheep, including all her fleece and lambs.

Even though the cat was not yet fully accepted as a household pet, she had at least gained a measure of safety in European society. And a well-deserved place: with the cat inquisitions over, the added numbers of cats destroyed the swarms of black rats. The plague ended. As

It is better to feed one cat than many mice.

NORWEGIAN PROVERB

English poet laureate John Skelton wrote, "These vylanous false cats / Were made for mice and rattes."

The ways of history are strange indeed. When Europeans began to destroy their innocent cats, they left themselves no protection against the newly invading Asiatic black rat and Black Plague. Europe suffered heavily for its crime against the cats. Three-fourths of the entire population died of the plague. When the cats showed their ability in destroying the Asiatic vermin, people's opinions changed. Both the church and the state ceased their senseless killing of the cats. Men slowly came to see the cat not as an agent of evil, but as an agent of good.

Abridged from Cat Fancy *(December, 1975).*

THE CATS OF CHINA AND JAPAN

Barbara Nixon

CATS IN JAPAN and China have had as checkered a career of acceptance as anywhere in the world. They were pampered and adored as favorites of court, figured importantly in the mythology, folklore and legends of both countries, and have made for themselves a revered nook in the annals of Chinese and Japanese history. Modern attitudes toward the cat in the Orient parallel closely those of the West, although indigenous folk customs survive in varying degrees in China and Japan.

To trace the domestication of the cat in China and Japan it is necessary to return to ancient Egypt, the cradle of civilization and, seemingly, of cats. It was from Egypt that cats were smuggled — under penalty of instant death to the brigand — into Western Asia as efficient ratters. Next, Central Asia imported cats, and from there they were brought into China.

The Domestication of Cats in the Orient

The arrival of the domesticated cat in China is generally accepted as having occurred early in the Han era (206 B.C.–A.D. 221), a thesis confirmed by many references to cats in ancient texts. The Book of Rites, dating from the second century A.D., advises continuation of certain sacrificial and theatrical ceremonies performed for the cat god because of services rendered by cats to man. The renowned historical work of China, Toho-Saku-Den in Shiki, refers to a fine charger as being much inferior to a lame cat in catching mice. The animal's solid position in the daily life of the Chinese by that time is affirmed by its popularity as a subject of poems written during the Tang dynasty (A.D. 618–907). It is described as a beast of prey, a creature of darkness and cunning, which has a body like a wild cat and a face like a tiger.

The domesticated cat is assumed to have been introduced into Japan through Manchuria and Korea in the early sixth century, about the same time as the introduction of Buddhism. While a custom of the time dictated that two cats be kept in every Buddhist temple to protect sacred documents from damage by rodents, it appears that cats were originally accepted into Japanese life to be revered as objects of great beauty. A famous ancient Japanese reference to cats in Kokon Chobun Shu: A Collection of Famous Anecdotes relates, "The Abbott Kwankyo at his mountain cottage found a very fine cat astray, from where it was not known, and he caught it and tamed it . . ." From this mention it can be concluded that the cat was domesticated

The mood of sheltered innocence in this scene of Cat, Rock, and Peonies *(Ch'ing Dynasty) is typical of Chinese cat art.*

among the people and the Imperial Court sometime in the Heian (A.D. 794–1192) or Nara (A.D. 710–794) period. Another Imperial reference, found in Classified Annals of Japan, states, "On September 19, 999, in the reign of Emperor Ichijo, kittens were given birth at the Imperial Palace." The pure-white mother cat gave birth to five beautiful white kittens in Kyoto, so delighting the Emperor that he decreed the animals be brought up with the care usually given infant princesses.

The original cats imported from China and Korea were predominantly pure-white; some were black and a very few were tri-colored. Later importation of Southeast Asian cats and subsequent cross-breeding produced the Japanese "three colors" cat, still regarded as lucky even today. Fishermen particularly favor them, believing them able to foresee the approach of tempests. Cats are taken on fishing voyages to assure safety and a good catch. Black cats are also considered good-luck cats, and are believed to cure various diseases. White cats are less rare than black or tri-colored cats, are loved for their beauty, but are not considered good or bad luck.

While the cat certainly enjoyed centuries of luxurious care in Japan, the time finally came when it had to start earning its keep. Between the thirteenth and fifteenth centuries, the production of silk became one of Japan's most important industries, and mice were attracted in droves to the silkworms. The cat was the logical solution to the problem, but the Imperial Court was reluctant to consign their pampered pets to such menial work. Amazingly, they thought it would be sufficient for the mice just to know cats were around, so instead of their pets they used drawings and statues of cats to repel mice. When this stratagem didn't work, the cat was blamed and banished from favor. By this time the silk industry and grain harvest were severely threatened. The government passed decrees stating that all cats were to be set at liberty, and it was forbidden to give, buy or sell cats. As a result, the freed cats set about their natural business of catching mice, thereby saving the silk industry and the harvest from hordes of rodents.

Predators and Princesses

The choosing of one's personal cat in China and in Japan points up a major difference in the attitudes of the two countries toward the animal. While in Japan a man would likely choose a cat on the basis of physical beauty or a winning per-

Japanese drawings like Girl and Cat *(18th century) were often inspired by the classic romance* Tales of the Genji *in which a cat was instrumental in bringing love to the heroine.*

sonality, the Chinese prime consideration is more utilitarian: the ability to hunt. This is not to say that the Chinese don't love their cats or appreciate their beauty. There can be no doubt of this, as the animals can be seen being prized and petted. The Chinese comment freely on the cat's grace of movement, the softness and beauty of its coat, the rare flexibility of its muscles and the agility with which it catches its prey. But beautiful cats, rare kinds and fancy breeds, are all classed as inferior if deficient in ability to hunt.

The differences between Chinese and Japanese attitudes toward the cat are also reflected in the development of the words for "cat" in the two cultures. As in many languages throughout the world, the Chinese words for "cat" — *mio, mauk* and *miu* — all are derived from the meowing sound made by the animal. But in Japanese, which takes its ideographic alphabet from the Chinese, the word for "cat" is *neko.* Thus, proposes one school of thought, the Chinese *mio* has metamorphosed into Japanese as *neko.* The more popular theories state that the name *neko* was derived from corrupted forms of words meaning "sleeping young," "resembling a tiger" or "waiting for a rat" — all of which seem appropriate designations for the cat and are in

The delicate lines in a detail from Cat and Butterfly *(18th century) show the sophisticated tastes of the general Japanese public which bought many such prints.*

This Ming Dynasty (1368–1644) bronze exemplifies the Chinese respect for the cat's toughness.

keeping with the Japanese emphasis on the cat's beauty and extraordinary powers.

The Chinese, however, are very practical about their cats and fetch a high price for them on the open market. The necessity for cats assures this, as there are always many rats to be dealt with. To keep rats down is the chief function of cats in China. It is said that the Chinese hate rats as they hate thieves and that they consign them to the same fate.

Securing a good cat in China is not a matter to be taken lightly, and one would be wise to consult a cat dealer. Such a man is often to be seen with a number of cats of various ages in basket cages at market or hawking them on the street. The Chinese cat expert can see qualities in a cat that are lost to the average Western eye, such as which cats are the best hunters and which will not wander from home. The Chinese have detailed sets of specifications they use when purchasing a cat to assure that it is the finest hunter available.

A fine hunting cat will have a short, compact, well-proportioned body and a round head, with the looks of a tiger. Such a cat has a solid, agile, businesslike look about him, as contrasted to the loose, long-bodied cats regarded as wanderers, or to the long-faced kind that prefers stealing chickens to its legitimate work of hunting rats. The tail must be at least as long as the body, and the tail should rise straight up when the cat is stroked. At the scent of prey, the tail will wag slowly and definitely. Too thick a tail or one with no curve indicates a lazy cat. The eyes, said one Chinese poet, should be "yellow as gold and clear as silver with the brightness of spar-

kling water." Ears should be long and thick. Thin ears are a sign that the cat can't stand cold. When walking, the proper cat will keep its ears gently moving as if on the alert for prey. The whiskers must be stiff and plentiful. The cats of China come in many colors, and a pure color of any description is prized. A particularly sought-after combination is a white throat and chest with black neck and back; this cat is called colloquially "the dark cloud over the snow."

One of the most relied-upon methods by which the Chinese determine the quality of a cat is the counting up of the ribbed lines on the roof of its mouth. The very best cats have nine lines, an indication that they will hunt all year round. A cat with only seven lines is proficient for six months; the undesirable animal with a mere five lines is good for only three months. The trick is to get the animal to cooperate while you peer into its mouth to count lines. Usually the word of the cat dealer must be taken in this matter.

Other points the Chinese watch for when selecting a cat are spotted or patched legs and long hair on the feet: these are interpreted as warnings that the subject loves to go on wide, prodigal expeditions. Black patches inside the mouth are ominous signs — better to have uniform red color. Black footpads are preferable to white or blotched. When standing, claws should not show; if they do, it indicates the cat goes prowling over housetops, upsetting your own and your neighbors' roof tiles. The bend of the foot should be free from long hairs, but if you find three long hairs the cat will not return until late; four hairs, even later, and so on. Also, an expert hunter snores in its sleep!

Chinese Practicality

The cat *par excellence* is acknowledged when all rats disappear from the house as if by magic. The Chinese assert that rats can distinguish between safe cats and dangerous cats. Rats will stay around when only second-rate cats, are there, but will flee immediately at the scent of a first-rate ratter.

Having finally found the best cat available, the Chinese owner will go to all lengths to keep the cat safe. Each family carefully guards its pet.

SPIDER HUNTING

While living in the southern part of Japan, where spiders outnumber people eighty-six to one, I came to fully appreciate the hunting abilities of my four cats. They were never allowed outside, but there was more than enough wildlife inside to compensate, as the house backed onto a bamboo rain forest replete with spiders in assorted styles and sizes.

The two male cats were more enthusiastic hunters than the females, but all truly earned their cat food. Every night they would start making the rounds of suspected spider hangouts, places where spiders had been seen or caught before. There would be the sound of a terrific scuffle with ferocious growling and spitting. Then silence, as the ever-victorious cats would circle their prey, making sure it was quite finished, congratulating each other on a battle well-fought.

Sentry duty continued after lights out, in shifts. One cat on, three off and sleeping until awakened by the returning scout to change shifts. In the morning, the living room battleground would be littered with casualties from the night before — round buttons, varying in diameter, hairiness and hue, each surrounded by eight stray detached legs.

And so it continued every night for a year, as the four cats methodically decimated the spider population of southern Japan. They have my everlasting gratitude. B.N.

In cities and towns, the cat is often tied up by a cord or has a weight attached to it which is sufficiently heavy to prevent it from wandering. A fine hunting cat is a prized possession in any Chinese home.

Caring for the cat means keeping it fit to perform its duties. The cat is fed soft rice mixed with boiled fish or raw meat, and is slightly underfed to keep its hunting instincts sharp. During the winter, the animal receives a heat-producing diet, and is fed only in the morning and at noon: feeding it at night would impair the desire to hunt. And the cat is kept away from the fireplace because too much heat creates a stupor and promotes lethargy. An occasional bath is called for, and to lessen danger to oneself the Chinese feel it is necessary to render the cat drunk before bathing. A dose of peppermint usually makes even the feistiest cat docile. Fresh peach tree leaves mixed with hay bedding keep fleas away.

All this fine care is richly deserved by the skilled ratter, but what about less lucky, less talented felines? Well, black cat skins are tanned and made into fur garments. And while the wild cat is considered good to eat and very wholesome, the poor of China also eat house cat. Some provinces even regard the flesh of blacks cats as especially nutritive.

The cat also has its place in Chinese folk medicine. Bronchitis is treated by mixing alcohol with cat's skull burned to powder. Mixed with oil and applied externally, burned and powdered skull cures ratbite. Soup of cat flesh is good for a deep-running sore, but only if it is taken on an empty stomach, which shouldn't be difficult to manage if you think about it.

Japanese Veneration of Cats

In Japan, the cat enjoys a more revered position. Japanese people believe in a sense of brotherhood between men and all living things. Sometimes this is inspired by religious faith, sometimes by superstition. Often it manifests itself as homage to unseen powers, as in the Japanese veneration of animals after their death. This special devotion, Buddhist in origin, is to remind followers of their duty to pray, work and be selfless. To attain ultimate Buddhist perfection, Nirvana, one's life must be lived beyond self and senses, suffering and existence. If an individual falls down in his striving for Nirvana, his soul will come back to life as a lower being — such as a cat or other animal, or even an insect. However,

THE MYTH OF THE CLEAN CAT DEBUNKED

Cats are clean pets, immaculate by nature, right? Wrong! All that paw-licking, wiping-of-the-face routine is for our benefit, furthering their perfect-pet image. What pet owner would tolerate a cruddy cat stomping around the place? Cats know this, and lick and fuss accordingly.

But when they think they are not being observed, they let their crummier instincts take over. The joy of a tom cat rolling in the dust and covering himself until he is unrecognizable must be seen to be believed. Or observe the dainty little feline who likes nothing better than to curl up for a nap in the fireplace ashes — and there has not been a fire for days, so it is not the heat she is after. It is the joy of dirt!

When discovered filthy, the cat exhibits nonplussed (nonpussed?) embarrassment at being caught with his kitty-britches down. The *real* cat is out of the bag when these things happen — and the human knows he has been had. B.N.

if he has been successful in his quest for eternal perfection, he will not be reincarnated at all, but will attain Nirvana. Thus every animal houses a not-too-successful soul working toward this state. Even the death of a cat, therefore, is an occasion requiring gravity and respect. A special Buddhist temple in Tokyo is devoted to the veneration of cats, and here the faithful present likenesses of their pets after the animals' death. The statues or paintings are placed on the altar, and the cats are buried in or near the temple grounds. This practice assists the cat on its journey to Nirvana; it frees the human soul that was contained within the animal form on earth and allows it to attain eternal perfection. As a side benefit to the owner, homage to his cat assures him good luck and happiness in his own life.

In animal cemeteries in Japan, impressive services are held for the souls of dead cats and dogs and other animals, sometimes including insects. On such occasions, many people visit the graves of cats who became famous by saving their master's life, often in dramatic circumstances. There is a bridge in Tokyo dedicated to a cat that tried to relieve the poverty of its sick mistress by stealing small gold objects from a neighboring money lender; this bridge, the Nekomatabashi, is visited by the faithful in veneration.

Cats in Oriental Folklore

The cat also figures prominently in both Japanese and Chinese folklore, new and old. While there are a few horror tales involving malevolent cat beings, including one Japanese tale of a monstrous vampire cat, most stories are about cats that are sympathetic to man. One Japanese account tells of a poor old couple who loved a black cat which they owned. When overwhelming hardship set in, the cat, out of affection and gratitude for years of good care, turned into a geisha. The money she earned was given to the couple, and although she was unhappy performing the duties expected of her, she be-

ALICE SU

A Japanese good luck statue; the paw beckons prosperity.

came famous for her dancing. Then came the day when a client, a boatman, caught a glimpse of her in cat form. She made him promise not to reveal her identity, but the secret proved too hard for him to keep and he couldn't resist telling a boatload of passengers the truth about the famous dancing geisha. At that moment, a dense cloud appeared and from it a huge black cat reached down and snatched him away. This popular story is repeated often and is the subject of plays and dances.

Probably the most widely acknowledged good-luck cat in Japan is the *maneki neko*, or "beckoning cat." Statues of this attractive female tri-colored cat show her sitting with one paw raised to her ear, beckoning as if to welcome. "With the beckoning of a cat comes the beckoning of prosperity" goes the ancient saying. *Maneki neko* figurines can be found in many shops and particularly in restaurants, where they are thought to attract customers. The origin of the figurine is said to be the tale of a famous woman of Yoshiwara whose favorite cat was killed as it tried to warn her of a dangerous snake. She had a copy of the cat carved in wood, and this became the famous charm. In her other paw, the cat often holds an ancient gold coin, indicating she will bring riches to her owner. It is a common proverb in most parts of the Orient, including China and Japan, that a cat wiping its paw over its ear means distinguished visitors will soon arrive.

Other popular Japanese adages about cats include the one which claims that cats with long tails will take human form and bewitch people. This probably came about as an explanation of why the native cats of Japan have very short tails. The classic name for the cat, *neko*, is sometimes given to geisha girls, because to charm their guests these artful young women play the *shamisen*, a stringed musical instrument made partly from cat skins and from which the geisha extract soft meowing sounds.

Chinese maxims about cats cover many diverse aspects of an animal obviously loved by the people. It is said that a cat's eyes are an accurate indicator of the time of day. At noon, the pupils are mere lines; mornings and afternoons, they resemble slivered almonds; night pupils are perfectly round. The edges of the ears of a cat that has eaten rats, and the ears of a tiger that has

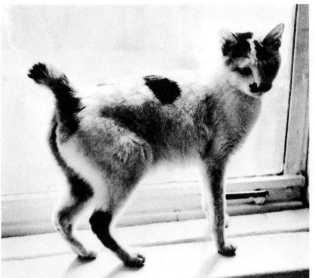

A Japanese Bobtail — the national cat.

eaten a man, will be sawlike. If you brush the fur of a lone cat with a bamboo scrubber, it is quite possible for it to have kittens — just as it is possible to hatch a chick merely by keeping an egg in a warm place. It is even maintained by the Chinese that the more clever cats can calculate the whereabouts of a rodent by means of arithmetical scratches on the ground. As in Japan, the domestic cat is sometimes spoken of as guardian of silkworms because it keeps away rats which devour the insects. But the advent of a strange cat in a household is believed to be a portent of approaching poverty. And robbers and rebels are called rats, while soldiers and their officers are called cats, for obvious reasons.

It is clear that the cat in China and in Japan is a highly regarded, closely observed animal. Whether it be the solid, compact-bodied ratter preferred in China or the tri-colored good-luck cat of Japan, each is kept and wondered about and cared for just as cats are throughout the Western World. The Oriental ideas and attitudes toward the cat are no more or less curious than those of the West, but they are alien enough to the Western mind to make them fascinating. For, underlying the differences of cultural outlook between East and West, is a common respect and love for a unique animal — the cat.

Barbara Nixon, a free-lance writer in New York, has lived in the Orient with her four cats.

THE VICTORIAN SENSIBILITY AND CATS

Carl T. Burton

IF THE VICTORIANS didn't exactly invent household pets, they had much to do with popularizing them — especially "man's best friend," the dog. Queen Victoria kept dogs by the score, and in nearly every informal photograph of her, two, three or a dozen of these pets surround her, obviously on their best behavior, awed, perhaps, by the Imperial Presence. Famous writers had their dogs, too, and Elizabeth Barrett Browning's Flush — the subject of one of Virginia Woolf's novels — is the best-known and probably most insufferable of its kind. But Mrs. Browning and the widowed Queen were only typical. Everyone loved dogs, and this affection had something to do with the English love of sports, especially horses and hunting, which, in turn, required dogs — lots of them.

What was an autumn morning in the country without the local hunt, thundering after some poor fox, beagles in full cry? What was shooting on the moors without a pack of dogs to do the work? And dogs did more than merely help gentlemen slaughter small game: they herded sheep, and if the paintings of sheep dogs are a true indication, they were a race of animal unfailingly noble, loyal, kind and true.

In general, the Victorians sentimentalized animals, attributing to them human feelings and attitudes — something that shouldn't happen to a dog. One good thing came out of the new Victorian interest in animals, both large and small: the Society for the Prevention of Cruelty to Animals. For the first time in Western history, people began formally to question the inhumane treatment meted out so casually to animal life. It became everyone's business if a cabby beat his horse to death; slowly, people began to realize that animals had feelings and rights.

But what about cats? They were there, all right, in nearly everyone's house, prowling about in barnyards, rubbing up against the legs of milkmaids in the dairy, hunting for rodents in the dark reaches of Victorian cities. As we look over the surviving cultural artifacts, however, we find that cats are often ignored or taken for granted. Strangely enough, they escape most of the extreme sentimentalization that afflicts the dog. For the most part, the Victorians paid cats the compliment of taking them seriously. People

A pampered Victorian from The Cat Picture Book *by Mrs. H. B. Paull (London, 1880).*

tended to regard cats as useful animals with their own lives to lead — not as failed human beings. Nevertheless, painters and writers realized that cats were powerful symbols. They always have been.

In picture after picture, cats lie on the hearth, curl up at the feet of little girls and sit in house windows, looking out on the passing scene. In nearly every instance, the cat symbolizes the happy home. One piece of very minor popular art typifies this view of cats. In *The Happy Home*, an illustrated religious tract, a solidly middle-class father sits surrounded by his modestly dressed wife and four very young children. Obviously, he is reading from some kind of devotional book, as the accompanying verse leads us to believe. Standing there in the foreground of the illustration, though, is a cat — an ordinary, striped domestic short-hair — watching the prayer-reading with grace and obvious interest. Keeping this picture in mind, and all the others like it, one might amend the verse to read: *Happy is the home where cats are wont to live.* Since the Victorians placed such a high value on home and hearth, the domestic animal that sits by the fireplace assumes the status of a minor but

THE HAPPY HOME.

Happy the home, when God is there,
  And love fills every breast;
Where one their wish, and one their prayer,
  And one their heavenly rest.

Happy the home where Jesus' name
  Is sweet to every ear;
Where children early lisp His fame,
  And parents hold Him dear.

Happy the home where prayer is heard,
  And praise is wont to rise;
Where parents love the sacred Word,
  And live but for the skies.

Lord, let us in our homes agree,
  This blessed peace to gain;
Unite our hearts in love to Thee,
  And love to all will reign.

The cat is the companion of the fireside.

EDWARD E. WHITING

important god. Cats and happy homes go together.

Cats, kittens and little girls go together, too, and this is about as sentimental as the Victorians ever got about their cats. Even Lewis Carroll's Alice loses some of her charm when she scolds her cat, Dinah, and her kittens. There may be a good reason for the quantity of pictures showing little girls nursing kittens and playing dolls. Cats make good mothers. They are clean, loving and, at the same time, thoroughgoing disciplinarians. Thus they furnish lovely role models for little Victorian girls, who have only one career to look forward to: marriage and all that it entails. Mothering kittens, like mothering dolls, provides good practice.

But the Victorians were perfectly aware that there was another side to cats. After all, cats like to mouse and to hunt birds. Lady Jane, a cat in Dickens' *Bleak House,* is a ferocious beast. She tears furniture, scratches, and menaces all bird life. Even Alice's beloved Dinah does more than merely wash her kittens and amuse little girls. As Alice, newly fallen down the rabbit hole into Wonderland, tells the mouse (they are swimming together in a lake of Alice's tears), Dinah "is such a dear quiet thing . . . and she sits purring so nicely by the fire, licking her paws, and washing her face — and she is such a nice soft thing — and she's such a capital one for catching mice —

"Oh I beg your pardon!" she then says, realizing that she has sorely distressed her listener.

"Would *you* like cats if you were me?" replies the mouse.

Everyone likes Carroll's Cheshire Cat, probably better known than the cat member of that odd couple, the Owl and the Pussy Cat who went sailing in a pea-green boat. The Cheshire Cat is the cat of the century. Tenniel's illustrations have been copied and reproduced everywhere. No such breed of cat ever actually existed, as Carroll's critics like to point out. The author probably got the idea of the grinning cat from inn signboards in Cheshire or from the

AN AILUROPHOBE ON CATS

REPRINTED FROM THE LONDON EDITION, 1791,

TRANSLATED BY WILLIAM SMELLIE.

The traditional, pre-Victorian attitude toward cats was summed up in the Count de Buffon's *Natural History* (1767):

The cat is an unfaithful domestic, and kept only from the necessity we find of opposing him to other domestics still more incommodious, and which cannot be hunted; for we value not those people, who, being fond of all brutes, foolishly keep cats for their amusement . . . Even the tamest cats are not under the smallest subjection, but may rather be said to enjoy perfect liberty; for they act to please themselves only; and it is impossible to retain them a moment after they choose to go off. Besides, most cats are half wild. They know not their masters, and only frequent barns, offices, or kitchens, when pressed with hunger.

Cheshire cheeses once molded into the shape of such cats. But somehow, in this creature, Carroll managed to combine many of the characteristics of cathood and call them to our attention by sheer exaggeration.

The Cheshire Cat is independent, able to get around better than any other creature in Wonderland. Its uncanny ability to appear and disappear at will suggests feline skill at moving unobtrusively through all environments. Moreover, it is beholden to no one, not even to kings. The Cheshire Cat disdainfully staring down the King of Hearts proves that cats can indeed look at kings, and Alice cannot resist pointing out this fact to the irate monarch. It is a menacing creature, too, and as we look at its great face, floating in space, we can sympathize with the mice who must confront those eyes and all those teeth. Finally, the Cheshire Cat, like all the best cats, is smart, witty and sane:

". . . we're all mad here, I'm mad. You're mad," said the Cat.

"How do you know I'm mad?" said Alice.

"You must be," said the Cat, *"or you wouldn't have come here."*

Alice didn't think that proved it at all: however, she went on: *"And how do you know that you're mad?"*

"To begin with," said the Cat, *"a dog's not mad. You grant that?"*

"I suppose so," said Alice.

"Well, then," the Cat went on, *"you see a dog growls when it's angry, and wags its tail when it's pleased. Now I growl when I'm pleased, and wag my tail when I'm angry. Therefore, I'm mad."*

"I call it purring, not growling," said Alice.

"Call it what you like," said the Cat.

Carl T. Burton, a Victorian scholar, lives in New York without a cat.

II. THE MYSTICAL CAT

LORE AND LEGENDS OF THE CAT

Lily Groover Jackson

In The Belling of the Cat, *an anonymous 17th century Dutch painting, a dignitary ties a bell around a cat's neck to lessen the danger from the cat's predatory instincts.*

HE SLEEPS so peacefully, there on the best chair in the house. Could that sleek, contented creature be privy to dark, malevolent secrets from an alien domain? Is there a psychic spirit emanating from within his graceful body, beaming magical rays? Is he in consortium with witches, warlocks and demons? Does he maintain contact with those ancients who exalted him to deification? Can he make transitory leaps from the occult world back to the easy and comfortable life of the family pet?

He knows something, for sure. After all, he's been around for a long time — some five thousand years.

Salad Days in Ancient Times

The Egyptian cat goddess, Bastet (known alternately as Bast or Pasht), was a major figure in the Egyptian pantheon, and the Egyptians placed great faith in the power of a living cat to protect them from all kinds of evil. Failing a living cat, one could ask for protection through the use of an amulet, many examples of which, showing the eye of Horus, in conjunction with cats, have been preserved.

If the Egyptian had no cat or amulet, he could resort to charms and spells or invocation of gods. Since he was virtually unprotected and subject to annoyance by any demon who might happen along, he called on the powerful sun god Ra, who in the form of a cat had destroyed the wicked Apep to ward off evil spirits.

As every limb of the cat contained powerful potential spirits, small ivory wands ornamented with the head of a cat were buried with the dead to enable them to combat any demons or devils they might encounter on the journey to the Jalous fields, where dwelt the dead.

As civilization spread, the popularity and fame of the cat traveled with the Phoenician traders. The Romans took to the cat with enthusiasm. He was the only animal admitted to their temples, where he received the same glorification that had been his due in the earlier Egyptian culture.

The sly and stealthy qualities of the cat were often incorporated into Roman mythology. The famous goddess Diana assumed cat form to escape Typhon, that fearsome creature whose fiery breath destroyed everything in his path as

European folklore claims that a cat twenty years old turns into a witch and a witch a hundred years old turns back into a cat.

The cat is the only domestic animal that can look a man straight in the eye without flinching. This ability gave rise to the ancient superstition that cats can read human minds.

he roared over land and sea. To thwart his tyrannical ambition to attain sovereignty, the gods and goddesses hid themselves from him by assuming the form of animals. Likewise Hecate, a mysterious divinity who was identified with night, demons and magic, adopted a catlike mien until Zeus finally destroyed Typhon with a thunderbolt; thereafter, though Hecate resumed her proper form, she had a special affection for cats and became their patron saint.

Thus the cat rose to demonic proportions as he roamed at will through these opulent civilizations, metamorphosing his sleek, graceful body into divine effigies with complete aplomb.

Mohammed and Christian Cats

Curiously, for all his vaunted sanctity, the cat fails to make any more impression in the Bible than a passing reference in the Apocrypha. Feeling this omission at best an oversight, at worst a dastardly slight, the Mohammedans tried to temper this neglect not only with a reverence for the feline, but with an explanation for his creation. The Mohammedan version of the cat's origins states that the mouse duo aboard Noah's Ark kept increasing their family so prolifically that Noah felt disposed to take drastic action. He passed his hand three times over the head of the lioness and she sneezed forth the cat, who promptly took care of the mouse overpopulation. Or, if you prefer, according to Arabian legend, while on the Ark the kingly lion was tempted out of stately seclusion by the wiles of an amorous monkey. The result of this transgression of natural law was the birth of a cat.

The love and respect given to the cat by the Mohammedans is best illustrated by an oft-repeated tale about the revered prophet Mohammed, a dedicated ailurophile if ever there was one. Mohammed was deep in

Good and Evil vie for the hand of a young lady cat in Grandville's symbolic and humorous drawing.

contemplation one day with his favorite cat Muezza dozing in his arms. When the time came for the great leader to arise and go to his devotions, he cut off his sleeve rather than disturb the snoozing cat.

The cat finally awakened and arched its back to show appreciation for the prophet's thoughtfulness. Mohammed administered his blessing by passing his hand over Muezza's back three times, thus granting the cat perpetual immunity from the danger of falling and ensuring it a permanent place in Islamic paradise. Forever after, the cat was assured the ability to land on its feet.

The Inscrutable Orient

The cat seems to have settled with ease into Oriental folklore about the fifth century A.D. In both China and Japan, he generally plays a mischievous part in popular tradition. He steals precious objects, perniciously produces dancing balls of fire and sometimes grows a forked tail thereby becoming a demon. In Chinese folklore he was employed by old women to perform perverse deeds; in Japan, he destroyed these hags. The cat's spiritual strength increases with maturity, and he is able — if he reaches a certain age — to effect certain transformations.

The most fascinating belief in Oriental lore connects the cat with the doctrine of reincarnation. There are countless incidents recalled of a long-deceased relative or friend returning in the form of a pampered cat. Becoming a cat after death is one step in the striving for Nirvana. Therefore, cats are revered as the embodiments of former human souls.

The Middle Ages — The Tide Turns

The Middle Ages brought hard times to the cat. His years of demanding and receiving respect were at an end. His close relationship with the occult in the nether world of black magic became a liability. Witchcraft was called the old religion; ergo, those who practiced it were denouncing Christianity, the new religion. With fear and suspicion prevailing, the witch's familiar, the cat, was doomed to share the fate of his patron. The cat was tried with master or mistress, found guilty and made to suffer the tortures prescribed for sorcerers — burning alive to excoriate those wicked spirits lurking within.

The animal familiar seems to have been originally an English phenomenon. British witches had a magical servant to run their er-

A very weird cat-bat engraving by Kirchner, 17th century.

rands and carry out their devious wishes. Though this servant took other animal forms, the cat image is the one that has remained in the popular imagination the longest.

Throughout Europe, the persecution of witches and their alter egos — the cats — was perpetuated. Convinced that destruction, usually by fire or some other hideous means, was the only way to be free of these devils, superstitious people in medieval times continued an unparalleled and wanton killing of cats, generally in a sacrificial manner. Paradoxically, these devout Christians used pagan rites, such as living sacrifice, to eradicate the presence of pagan spirits in their midst. Killing cats was justified as a means of preventing them — and witches, as well — from practicing horrible deeds.

Cats were thought to turn beer sour, wreck ships, spread disease, lead armies and desecrate crucifixes. One theologian maintained that every cat served seven masters, each for seven years, and then carried the soul of the last into hell. The Protestant reformers held these beliefs with equal fervor; they elaborated the fears by suggesting that the Pope traveled in the form of a black cat to confound honest Christians.

The black cat, long labeled a particular harborer of devilish spirits, became the object of intense hatred. When Pope Clement V suppressed the Order of Knights Templar at the beginning of the fourteenth century, its members confessed under torture that they worshiped the devil in the form of a black cat.

Another black cat was the pivotal figure in an eerie tale bruited throughout France. A

MARTHA JAFFE

The superstition about a black cat crossing one's path derives from the belief that the cat was marking a path to Satan.

knight arrived at a little town called Metz during the peak of an epidemic of St. Vitus's dance. As he was about to fall asleep, he saw an enormous black cat staring at him. He quickly made the sign of the cross and drew his sword. The cat disappeared, leaving behind the sound of hissed blasphemies. The next day, not a citizen of the village seemed to be affected with any twitching and dancing. The epidemic was over. For hundreds of years thereafter, the people organized a ceremonial burning of cats in the esplanade of Metz.

The folklore of the world is full of stories of women who turn into cats. Usually they are surprised in their cat form or attack someone who then wounds or mutilates them in some easily recognizable way. There are stories of wives who turn into cats to steal out at night to visit their lovers. Or, conversely, there are cats who are so enamored of young men that they turn into women so they can become their lovers.

The Paradoxical Cat

The periods of persecution of the cat — believed to be the precursor of practically all the evil and devilment around — strangely did not save man from a very real and definite danger: the plagues that swept across Europe throughout the Middle Ages. Still-primitive medical knowledge could not make the connection between the hordes of rats and the continuing eradication of cats. As the cats were destroyed, the plagues continued. It was never recognized that the cat's practical qualities as a ratter might have served to alleviate much of the human suffering.

In the paradoxical way that symbolism and the supernatural sometimes operate, the cat, for whom so much animosity was felt, could also

Most witches were brought to trial when they were accused of casting a magic spell for evil over a person. One such accused came into court and detailed her confession. She proudly claimed to have the power to change her shape as she chanted:
"I shall goe intill ane catt,
With sorror, and sych, and a blak shott;
And I shall goe in the Divellis nam
Ay gun guhill I com hom againe.
Tio turn back again, she had to say:
Catt, catt, God send thee a blak shott,
I am in a cattis likness just now,
But I sal be in a womanis liknes ewin now.
Catt, catt, God send thee a blak shott."

bring good luck. Perhaps this was a harkening back to the feelings of awe and reverence he inspired in the early Egyptians.

In the Orient, Buddhist tradition says that a light-colored cat will always ensure silver in the house and that the home with a dark-colored cat will never lack for gold. In the South of France there was widespread belief in magician cats, called *matagots*, who could bring prosperity to a house where they were loved and well cared for.

The most famous of *matagots* is perhaps the cat belonging to Dick Whittington, who was three times Lord Mayor of London in the early fifteenth century, and who, according to a folk tale, owed his good fortune to a lucky cat. There are several versions of the story, but one of the most popular tells how young Dick was a poor boy from Gloucestershire who walked the streets of London in search of fame and fortune. Unfortunately, he did not find the streets paved with gold as he had been led to believe. Indeed, he thought himself quite fortunate to have found a job as scullion to a wealthy merchant. With his first wages he bought a cat to keep down the rats in his tiny garret. When the other servants of the house invested money in a trading vessel to be outfitted by their employer, Dick put up the only thing he had: his cat.

The ship arrived at a spice island in the Orient where the palace of the king was said to be overrun with rats. Puss soon vanquished them, earning the king's gratitude in the shape of a princely fortune for its owner, young Dick Whittington.

The cat's eminence in the scheme of things was rising — reinstating him, if not to deification status, certainly to fairly good graces. He even became a companion to holy folk, notably St. Ives and St. Gertrude. No longer was he officially suspected of consorting with the likes of devils and witches or bringing down supernatural ire on the populace at hand. Still, the prejudice continued, not as public policy, but definitely as local lore, more often repeated with a smile than with a shudder.

In modern times, the cat reassumed his good reputation as cat owners recognized his virtues, catered to his desires, became intimidated by his tyranny or just settled for worship from a respectful distance of his unique charms. Yet as he sleeps serenely, with his sly smile and eyes closed to the merest of slits, is there not still an aura of mystery? Does he know of witches and things? Isn't that front tooth looking a little like a fang?

Lily Groover Jackson is a feature writer for The Times-Picayune *in New Orleans.*

Henriette Ronner's depiction of cats all over the world.

CATS AND THE STARS

Margery Bihari

THE RENAISSANCE OF INTEREST in astrology is an exciting phenomenon in an age of increasing technology and specialization. Most people are willing to believe that cosmic influences on human affairs have some validity — if only in affecting the weather, which in turn affects our emotions and life styles. Most of us are at least aware of our sun signs. We may not believe in astrology, but we may be intrigued enough by its mysterious possibilities to want to have our chart done. Many people are becoming more interested in the concept of the biological influence of the cosmos and have investigated their birth charts. Now we are to look at our cat's horoscope. Unfortunately, the idea of trying to understand cats through astrology seems to be stretching an already misunderstood occult science.

Astrology is a science based on the intersection of astronomy, mathematics and psychology. Therefore, the birth chart is a tool for discovering and helping an individual actualize his potential. It takes years of study and observation to understand the complexities of the planetary interactions on human life. Newspaper and magazine horoscopes can never do justice to this complexity of relationships for a cat, much less a human being. The popularization of astrology by the media is detrimental to the valuable information the heavens can give us if we go beyond mere sun sign knowledge. Unfortunately, most people are unwilling to take the time to understand astrology thoroughly.

Complicated astrological analysis of a cat's potential is not needed because it is quite probable that cats, being lower than humans on the intelligence scale and less complicated in their emotional and physical needs, reflect fewer planets in their astrological charts. For humans, it is necessary to determine the relationships between all the planets; the way in which a person uses the energy set up by the planets tells us

about a person's individuality. But cats are not humans (although Buddhists, among others, believe cats are humans in an earlier or later incarnation), and they probably utilize only their sun, moon, Venus and Mars signs.

The sun sign of a cat would reveal its vitality, its sense of itself. The sign the moon was in at a cat's birth would express its instincts, cravings and emotions. Venus reflects the loves and desires, and Mars expresses aggressions. Since the full impact of a planet on an individual is not only by sign but even more by the sign's placement and interaction with the other planets in the chart, it is convenient that the sun sign types seem adequate in fully understanding the cat's personality and psychological make-up. It would be quite difficult to draw up adequate birth charts for cats: even if the correct date and place are known, the chart changes noticeably every few minutes and we would have to be positive as to which cat we picked from the litter and exactly when each kitten was born.

Although some cats are more appealing than others, it is a mistake to ascribe value judgments to their signs, just as it is unfair to do this with human astrological readings. Contrary to popular belief, there are no good or bad aspects, or relationships of the planets; it just feels as if there are. What makes an individual person or cat misuse his energy or use it creatively is a still-unanswered question. The heavens present us with the opportunities; whether or not we take advantage of them is up to us.

Each sign is ruled by a planet and takes on the qualities of that planet. Thus Aries, ruled by Mars, is characteristically rash, dynamic and an initiator. Virgo, ruled by Mercury, characteristically has a mind for detail and a quiet nature, and is concerned with service to others. But it is too simplistic to say all Aries and Virgo cats are alike. Certain qualities are more or less predominant in each sign, and naturally we as humans have preferences. We cannot assume from knowing a cat's sign whether or not it will be good at climbing trees, loving children or being neat at the litter box. Cats are more complicated than that, and there are simply too many unknowns about feline psychology and history. Until more is known, we cannot professionally chart a cat's horoscope.

Margery Bihari, a painter studying astrology, has three cats, two Capricorns and one Taurus.

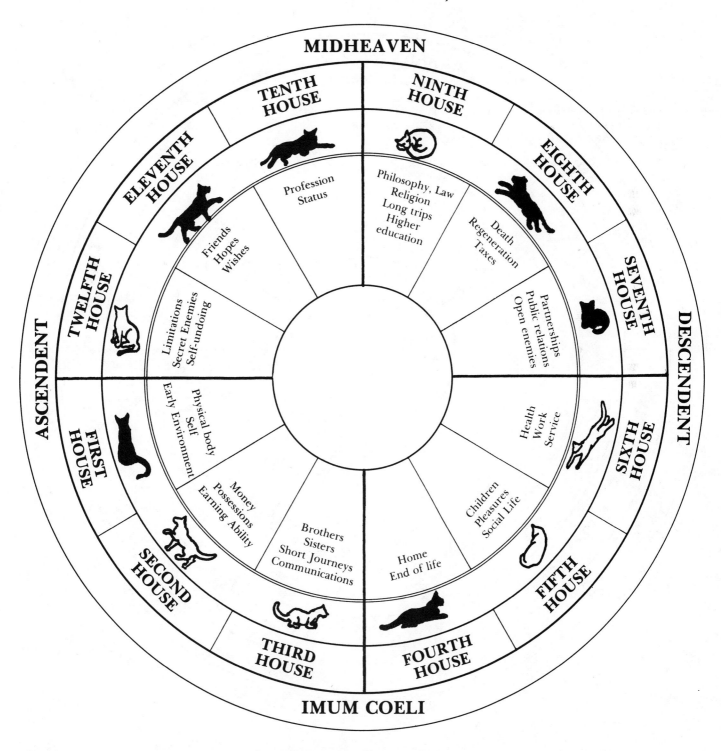

The Astrological Houses

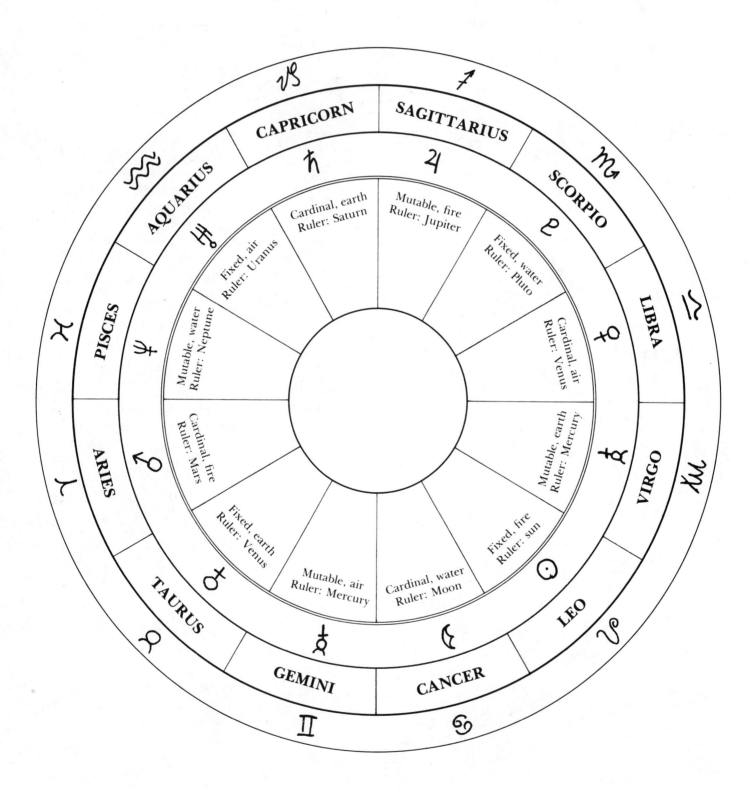

The Astrological Signs

THE WITCH'S CAT

Marion Weinstein

WHEN YOU THINK of a witch, what animal comes to mind first? Or if you happen to *be* a witch, what animal are you most likely to have around the house? It's not only a popular tradition, it's a popular fact: cats and witches are compatible.

In witchcraft, and in other positive occult work, animal life is appreciated as all of nature is revered. Witches and other positive magicians and sorcerers frequently keep many animals in their homes and communicate with others in the wild. However, there are certain other branches of occultism that place an emphasis on destruction, death and animal sacrifice. And in such negative work (for example, so-called "black magic") an animal is often killed as a symbolic means of causing the death of a person far away, or as a means of summoning up an evil spirit. That destructive type of occultism is *not* in the nature of witchcraft; it is to the field of magic what malpractice is to medicine. In the occult, cats are special and their inherent talents are most useful.

Even the predatory nature of cats is considered helpful to witches. It serves as a constant reminder of the dark side of the human and animal spirit, of the workings of life, death and rebirth on this planet. And this predatory instinct can be kept remarkably under control if the cat chooses to do so. According to an ancient Celtic belief, if you ever entered a house and saw a cat and mouse drinking milk out of the same bowl, you could be sure it was a witch's house. Yes, the witch's cat can transcend its darker, instinctive nature and choose to live in perfect harmony with a pet mouse, toad or any small animal. And this transcendent choice illustrates for the witch the essential harmony of all life. It is the cat's way of enacting an important witchcraft principle: the informed choice of Light over Dark, Life over Death.

The cat has often served in the role of witch's familiar. A familiar is a non-human creature that helps the witch in most magic and occult work. The role of familiar goes far beyond the role of a pet animal, because the familiar is both helper and companion to the witch; it is considered an equal.

The cat has always been a favorite choice for a familiar; this tradition can be traced back to the ancient Egyptian mystery schools, in which cats were revered for their psychic powers. Actually, the familiar can be an invisible being or any small animal (toad, mouse, rabbit, small dog, etc.), but cats are particularly good familiars. They have all the qualities that a witch could ever hope to find in an animal helper. A familiar is never "trained;" it must meet the witch on equal ground. Any cat who becomes a familiar inevitably does so of its own free will. It literally volunteers for the work. This is very important in witchcraft, a field of occult work where there is so much emphasis on free will. An independent spirit and voluntary contribution are the only kinds of help a witch can use from an animal.

The witch's work includes E.S.P., telepathy and spirit contact. Cats have a natural talent in all these areas. When a cat wants to read your mind, it can usually do so. Have you ever thought about stepping into the kitchen for a snack and suddenly found your cat at your side? This is not "coincidence" (especially if you're in the habit of giving the cat a handout when you eat something). The cat has actually picked up the image of food from your thoughts. This talent is handy for witches, who often work through their minds. Some things must be said in images and cats have a natural talent for picking up these images.

Every black cat is not a witch.

FRENCH SAYING

Furthermore, cats are not afraid of the unseen world, nor are they afraid of unseen beings. Not only are cats unafraid of spirits, but they usually *like* them. Even in non-witch homes I have seen many a cat staring intently at a portrait of someone who has departed this life. Haunted houses are often frequented — or inhabited — by cats. And mediums often attest that they cannot keep their cats out of the room during a séance; in fact, even neighboring cats have been known to show up, eagerly, the moment that lights are dimmed and the table, or ouija board, is set up. This affinity helps not only the witch but any participating spirits. Spirits like to feel welcome when they enter this plane, and when a cat is present and happy to see them, the contact is easier and more friendly for all concerned.

Witches respect all the animal kingdom. They are interested in what is going on in nature. Animals know about approaching weather conditions, impending dangers, the approach of storms, floods and fires. In the days before radio and television, it was especially important to be in contact with these natural forces, to know about them beforehand. The cat was an excellent helper in this area because of its telepathic talent — the cat can communicate mind-to-mind with a human. The cat could, for example, receive the image of a gathering thunderstorm and then mentally project it to the witch. Many people know how to communicate to their animals, but witches know how to listen when their animals do the communicating.

Cats have always been welcome in homes because they keep away rats and other pests. The cat is by nature a predator, and in a domestic situation where it is cared for, its psychic energy is freed for other matters. Psychic powers are inherent in all animals, but cats have developed these powers to a heightened level. Domestication allowed generations of cats the luxury of being able to sit by the fireside and dream, think, muse, meditate and generally develop their natural psychic powers. The witch appreciates

A woman hath nine lives like a cat.

OLD ENGLISH PROVERB

having an animal around that is always on the psychic lookout. If a witch sees something in a crystal ball, for example, the cat can confirm the vision by "tuning in" on the same area. This process is similar to two mediums looking into the same psychic area — except that, in this case, one medium is human (the witch) and one is animal (the cat). In addition, the cat does not need a triggering device like the crystal ball; unlike humans, animals can focus their psychic gifts by sheer intuition. If you can accept the idea that an animal may function as a psychic reader, then you may further note that the cat's independent personality precludes trying to "please" the witch by coming up each time with a confirming vision. The cat always sees its own vision, and relays this mentally to the witch. If the two mesh, the witch knows that the vision is accurate.

Sometimes, when a witch is doing really difficult psychic work, such as a healing, additional pure animal energy is needed. When witches work in a coven, there are human helpers around to lend their energies to the common cause. But what does the witch do if she happens to be all alone with some psychic task? Whose energy will "plug in" with hers to give that extra boost? The cat comprehends this situation via telepathy and stands by to lend a helping paw.

Witches have been misunderstood and persecuted for centuries; whenever they went anywhere, they had to be careful. Their lives were often in danger, and the silent cat made an ideal traveling companion. A witch who went out — to a meeting, on an herb-gathering expedition or simply for a stroll — would find herself in trouble if her comings and goings were heralded by a noisy pet.

Another advantage of the cat's role as familiar is that occult work is traditionally done at night. When the rest of the world is sleeping, one's psychic energies are least likely to be disturbed. Cats are usually wide awake and energetic at night, so they can join right in on the work with ease.

There are superstitions about cats turning into witches and witches turning into cats. Most of these are untrue. The cat and the witch are simply very quiet. In dark, shadowy places, in times before there were streetlights or any electricity, one minute the cat would be visible, the next minute the witch, and imagination filled in the rest.

Superstition has it that the black cat is the witch's favorite. This is not true. It is true that light colors, such as white, were not favored in a familiar because they were too likely to be seen at night. But the brindle, tortoise shell or dark-grey cat was as popular as the black cat because of its natural camouflage.

People who fear the occult associate black with all witchcraft. And people who believe that the witch can turn into a cat consequently feel that if a black cat crosses their path it could just as easily be the witch herself in the guise of a cat. This is mere superstition. In my opinion, there's no bad luck involved in having a witch — or a cat of any color — cross one's path.

Cats are said to have nine lives. This actually is an extension of the Threefold Law in witchcraft, which states that when you do magical work all good comes back to you three times and all harm comes back to you three times. Because the cat has long been a helper in occult work, it is associated with this essential multiple of the number three ($3 \times 3 = 9$).

There are also superstitions about witches of the past suckling their familiars with human milk. These led to the weird belief that witches have an extra "witch's teat." No, witches do not have this, but they often did suckle kittens or other animal familiars from their own human breasts. (The suckling of favored baby animals, incidentally, is not unique to the witch culture; it was practiced in ancient China and occasionally within American Indian and Eskimo tribes.) This act of love brings the animal and the witch into close contact. The final and most powerful bond between witch and familiar, between human and cat, is just that — *love*. It is the feeling which transcends the barrier between one species and another on this planet. When this barrier is crossed, all kinds of psychic powers are doubled and more readily available. Both witch and cat know this. And if you and your cat love each other, you probably know this too.

Marion Weinstein, a practicing witch, has a New York City radio show, and is the author of a forthcoming book on occult self-help.

One of the most striking differences between a cat and a lie is that a cat has only nine lives.

MARK TWAIN

THE STORY OF THE CAT WHO INVENTED YOGA

Sally Ellyson

I first became interested in Yoga when I traveled in India six years ago. There I met Da Mesudian, an Indian who had been educated in England and who shared my interest in early Sanskrit writings. One evening, my friend and I were sitting in the courtyard of his home, sipping herbal tea and eating mangoes when his old master, the Yogi Sri Subir Chilingarian, came by to welcome me to their country. Having never met a Yogi before, I was fascinated. After we exchanged pleasant formalities, I asked him to tell me about Yoga and its history.

"Yoga is a method of self-realization and spiritual awareness," he said. "There are several different systems of Yoga, but they are really only different paths to the same goal — self-knowledge. Some Yogas concentrate directly on the spiritual aspect of being — Raja Yoga, Jnana Yoga and Karma Yoga. The most well-known Yoga to the Westerner, however, is Hatha Yoga, and Hatha Yoga concentrates on the body as a path to spiritual awareness."

"How did Hatha Yoga come about?" I asked.

And this is the Yogi's story.

"**M**Y MASTER told me," he said, "that he had learned from his master, and he from his master, and on back for several hundreds of years, that an Indian boy of royal birth had once been attempting to learn Karma Yoga, the most advanced of the spiritual Yogas. He was trying to meditate, but his mind kept wandering. After several hours of frustrating failure, the prince decided to go for a walk in the nearby woods instead.

"Walking along the path, kicking stones, the boy chanced to look up at a tree stump on which a large cat was sitting. The cat sat straight up with her paws precisely in front of herself and her tail wrapped around her body. She was purring softly.

" 'Oh, Cat,' said the prince. 'Why is it that you can meditate so peacefully, and try as I do, I cannot meditate. My thoughts keep wandering.'

"The cat opened her eyes, blinked, and yawned at the prince. Then she jumped down from the tree stump and landed on the path in front of the boy. She stretched her paws out in front of herself and wiggled each individual toe, while balancing on her haunches. Then she moved her weight forward onto her front shoulders and smoothly shifted the movement to her back, which she arched more than seemed possible. Just at the top of the arch she yawned again, long and loud, and started the process of slowly reversing each and every movement she had just performed. At the end of the complete cycle, she lay down, turned over on to her back, stretched her paws, neck and tail in all directions, and turned back over.

"She got up to face the prince. 'That, my friend, is how I meditate,' she replied to his earlier question. 'I have learned to prepare myself for meditation by practicing relaxing exercises. I tense and release my muscles and all parts of my body, both inside and out. Then, when my body is completely satisfied, I can meditate without distraction. Here, I will show you some relaxation poses.'

"And the cat then taught the prince a few postures such as the Spinal Twist, in which, in a seated position, the prince learned how to turn the top of his body around to face backward. And she taught the son of royal birth how, also in a seated position, to sit on his hips and raise one leg directly in front of him and lift it to his face (in order to wash his leg, of course). She taught him other exercises as well that day, and when he was through, the prince sat down in the path, crossed his legs and imitated the cat's purring sound by saying 'Om' over and over to himself.

"After fifteen minutes or so, the cat rubbed her head up against the boy's knee. The prince opened his eyes, blinked, and yawned at the cat.

" 'Thank you, Cat,' he said. 'I have finally learned to meditate.'

"And every day the prince returned to the woods to find the cat. And the cat taught him all she knew, and when the prince knew all the cat knew, he went out into the world to teach others the secrets of Hatha Yoga.

"And that," said the old Yogi master, "is how Hatha Yoga came to be."

Sally Ellyson is an editor in a New York publishing house.

The cat always leaves her mark upon her friends.

SPANISH SAYING

THE PSYCHIC CAT

Paulette Cooper

BELIEF IN THE notion that cats possess psychical powers goes back at least as far as the ancient Egyptians, whose word for cat, *mau*, literally meant "to see." Throughout history, cats and their supposedly all-seeing eyes have been consulted as oracles. It was just one step from the belief that cats had psychical powers to the notion that such powers could be transferred to people by their pets. English children were once encouraged to play with cats to help develop clairvoyant powers, and some people have tried to become clairvoyant by the use of cat witchcraft such as mixing the eye of a black cat with human gall, or burning the placenta of the first litter of a black cat to create a magic potion for human eyes.

Today, the common tendency is to dismiss stories that suggest the reality of psychic phenomena and, if plausible scientific explanations are lacking, to attribute the mysterious events to chance or luck. This attitude has discouraged serious research and encouraged unverified anecdotes, hyperbole and charlatanism — the very things that led to a dismissal of psychic phenomena in the first place. But not every unverified "happening" can be laughed away or sneered at.

Some of the tales do have clear sources of truth and therefore pose real questions. The French author Claude Farrère told of a time his usually docile cat, Kare Kedi, suddenly awoke in the middle of the night. Her hair went as rigid as an Indian bed of nails; she riveted her eyes on the left wall in the room, and then began to howl. Farrère could see or hear no reason for her excitement. There were no sounds coming from behind the wall and there was nothing on the wall to account for the cat's sudden bizarre behavior. After a minute or two, her muscles began to jerk; she leaped up, tumbled backward in a somersault, and finally lurched forward into the arms of her amazed and terrified owner. The next morning Farrère learned that at the time of

Kare Kedi's fit, his neighbor, who lived just on the other side of the wall that had so excited the cat, had been murdered.

Accounts like this one have inspired a few resolute scientists to perservere in their investigation of the question of cats and psychic powers. Dr. J.B. Rhine, now at the Institute of Parapsychology in North Carolina, conducted experiments on the extrasensory powers of cats while he was at Duke University. Dr. Karlis Osis of the American Society for Psychical Research in New York City also conducted tests on cats while he was at Duke with Dr. Rhine. Osis tested cats for telepathic and clairvoyant powers, and reported positive confirmation on both. In his first test, he tried to learn if a person could transfer what was on his mind to a cat. The sender (usually Osis himself or Rhine's daughter) was in a booth which the cat could neither see or hear. The cat was released at a spot equidistant from two bowls of food, each of which contained identical portions. The sender would try to get the cat to choose one of the bowls simply by wishing the cat to select the "preferred" one. Osis found that the incidence of cats going to the wished-for bowl was significantly higher than chance, which would have been 50-50.

In a more complicated experiment Osis tested cats' powers of clairvoyance to see if they could determine which of two dishes contained food. This time, one of two randomly selected dishes was empty and the cat was tested to see if

It has been the providence of nature to give this creature nine lives instead of one.

PILPAY

it would approach the full dish. So that the cats had more reason to avoid the empty dish than just worrying about whether or not they would be fed, an electric shock was given if the cat approached the empty bowl. Additionally, Osis controlled for scent by placing a powerful fan deep down in the dish to suck away any smell of food. Here, too, Osis got better-than-chance results; the cats seemed to know which dish would be empty and which one would have food.

Speaking now about the experiments, conducted twenty years ago, Dr. Osis added an interesting postscript: "Only with those cats where I established a nice relationship did I get results," he said. "I could never get E.S.P. out of a cat if he was not my friend. Furthermore, if I had to give a cat worming medication or flea powder one day, the next day there was no E.S.P."

Dr. Osis also believes that cats prefer people who have E.S.P. themselves. He recalled a very shy cat named Chippy who never let anyone outside of his own family touch him. Osis then received a visit from Olaf Jonsson, a psychic who later became astronaut Edgar Mitchell's best subject while Mitchell was conducting E.S.P. experiments from outer space. Chippy, who had rejected the advances or friendship of all other visitors, took one look at the psychic Jonsson, arched his back, and the two became friends immediately.

Osis, who has owned more than two dozen cats, also believes that cats use their psychic abilities to establish who likes and dislikes them. "I am not saying that cats understand what you are thinking if it is a philosophical or abstract concept," he explained, "but cats know what you are thinking when it applies to them, such as whether you like them or not." Few cat owners will deny that cats do sense immediately who likes them and who should be avoided.

An area of special interest to psychic research is the cat's power that has come to be called "psi-trailing" — the ability of a cat to travel far distances through unknown territory in order to reach a specific destination. There are numerous stories — many which cannot be dismissed as luck — about cats who have journeyed great distances to find their owners or return to their original homes. For example, an army sergeant in Kokomo, Indiana took his large yellow tomcat with him when he was transferred to a base in Augusta, Georgia. The cat apparently decided that life in Indiana was preferable and made the 700-mile trip back to his old home in only three weeks. The cat could not have simply remembered the route back to Indiana because he had made the original trip to Georgia in an express train.

The cat's ability to head for home was tested by Presch and Lindenbaum of Germany. They took a number of cats in boxes, several miles from their home and then released them in labyrinths containing twenty-four exits. Eight out of ten of the cats emerged from an exit pointing in the direction of their homes. If simple luck had been involved, the success rate would have been closer to eight out of two hundred.

It is recognized that many animals, cats

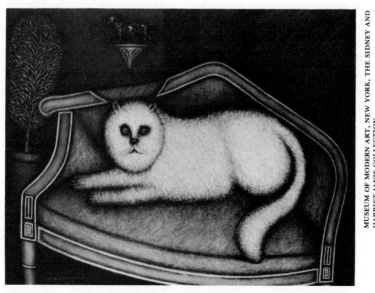

Morris Hirshfield's Angora Cat *(1937–39) must have had psychic powers.*

NIGHT SIREN

MARGARET BALDWIN

It was a Missouri spring, filled with gloomy nights and severe thunderstorms, but this particular night was calm. My blue-point Siamese, Mao, always sleeps soundly beside me throughout the night. That night, however, she awoke and suddenly pawed my hair. I shoved her away, telling her to go back to sleep. She pawed again. I pitched her out of bed; she jumped back up, pawed violently and began licking my face. By then, I was awake enough to see that she was exceptionally nervous: I checked the baby (whom Mao adored). He was all right, then the house — no prowlers. As I was returning to bed, Mao became frenzied; then I heard the first wail of the siren. A tornado struck less than a block away. The storm ended as quickly as it had come. When we returned to bed, we found Mao was already fast asleep. Since then, Mao has never awakened me; nor have we ever had a tornado strike so close to our house. I watch her now during storms. If they don't bother her — I try not to let them bother me.

Margaret Baldwin works in publishing in Independence, Missouri.

included, mark territory with scents; and it has been suggested that psi-trailing may actually be scent-trailing. Some cats, however, have taken so long to make the voyage back home that it is extremely unlikely such scent traces could have remained to guide the cats headed for "home." For example, a cat named Monmousse was once lost in Maine-et-Loire, France, where his owner had taken him for the family holiday. Ten months later, Monmousse appeared at his master's home in Doubs, 465 miles away. Furthermore, the scent-trail theory is no help at all in explaining how cats can find their way to places they have never been. No scent-trailing is possible in the case of Smoky, a Persian cat who got lost at a roadside stop in Oklahoma while his family was moving to Tennessee. Smoky appeared at the new home in Tennessee — although he had never seen it before — exactly one year later.

Some of these reports should be treated skeptically. Consider the experience of Dr. Michael Fox, a veterinarian and author who "lost" his Siamese when moving six miles from his original home. He was naturally pleased when what appeared to be his beloved cat showed up at his new home a few weeks later. Then his original Siamese was found still wandering about in its old neighborhood. The cat that had "moved" to the new home was just another Siamese cat who looked like Dr. Fox's original cat. If a veterinarian could be fooled, it is possible that other people who claim their cats have made incredible journeys may have also been taken in by imposters.

Luck, smell, mistaken identity — there is often an excuse to be clutched at by the doubters, but not always. Sugar was a cream-colored, semi-Persian living with a family in Anderson, California. In 1951, her family decided to move to Oklahoma and, although they wanted to take Sugar with them, they felt that Sugar was just too afraid of cars to be subjected to such an ordeal. Sugar was therefore left behind with a neighbor. Fourteen months later, in Oklahoma, a cream-colored, semi-Persian leaped on the shoulder of the woman from Anderson while she was working outside of her new home. Although the woman thought the cat looked like Sugar, she had her doubts that it could be Sugar. Still a stray would be unlikely to jump onto the shoulder of a stranger, it also seemed unlikely that a cat could cross half a continent of desert and mountain ranges. All doubts were ended however, when she petted the cat and felt the unique bone deformity on the left hip joint — one of Sugar's unique characteristics. The identification was soon verified by the neighbor to whom Sugar had been given in Anderson. Not only did the neighbor identify and remember Sugar's unique bone protrusion, but she also informed the Anderson family that Sugar had stayed with her for only about two weeks before disappearing. Psi-trailing had taken Sugar more than 1,500 miles through land a mountain lion would find harsh to a place she had never been — back to the family she had missed.

Paulette Cooper is a free-lance writer and the author of four books, including The Medical Detectives.

III. THE ARTISTIC CAT

LE PEINTRE PUSS

LE CHAT HEP

L'ECREVAIN FELINE

THE CAT IN LITERATURE 1570-1976

Claire Necker

IF YOU ARE looking for an easy way to kick a bad habit, start cat book collecting and you'll soon find yourself hooked on a harmless substitute with unlimited possibilities for enjoyment. Centuries of time travel through art, history, science, religion, fantasy, folklore, poetry — almost any topic you can name — are yours to explore in the world of cat literature. It is a big world, so big that only a brief summary of what it contains can be covered here, therefore an abbreviated history of cats in literature is presented. Except where noted, these books are out of print and can therefore become the objects of your browsing and searching in attics, bookstores and wellstocked libraries. A detailed reference guide to cat literature is included in my annotated bibliography, *Four Centuries of Cat Books* (1972, in print).

Cats entered English print in a satire on the Roman Church published in 1570. Called *A marvelvos hystory intitulede, Beware the cat*, the text was patterned after the well-known beast epic *Reynard the Fox.* Satirical writing was prevalent at this time and through the next two hundred and fifty years, and cats found their way into it more and more often. The deep contempt felt for them by the general public is reflected in this work: cats were used principally in a disparaging sense, and the animals themselves or the people they were compared to were always the villains. Even the cats of modern satire, though usually anthropomorphic, are often presented in a pejorative light.

Not until the mid-1600s did the cat in print emerge in other roles. The history of Dick Whittington and his cat came out in broadsides and chapbooks, small pamphlets hawked in the streets by peddlers. Short summaries about the cat, still derogatory yet less malicious, filled empty spaces in chapbooks on any subject. Over the next century and into the early 1800s, Puss in Boots arrived along with Dame Trot, Dame Wiggins of Lee and others. Most of the woodcuts of cats appearing in these chapbooks are delightfully rendered.

Gradually, long moral tales took the place of chapbooks, most of them directed to a juvenile audience. Anthropomorphic cats with undesirable traits suffered for their sins in page after page of dreary moralistic reading. But there was also the tale that advised being good to poor puss or suffer the consequences, even though she was merely a "dumb brute." The tide was turning toward humane treatment of cats and other domestic animals. *Felissa*, published anonymously in 1811 but attributed to Charles Lamb, is a palatable example of these usually mournful narratives; it was even reprinted in 1903.

Mrs. Surr and Harrison Weir published their book in 1882.

The humanitarian theme continued where the moralizers left off, declining in the early 1900s but never dying out completely. Susanna Patteson's *Pussy Meow* is the classic be-kind-to-cats book; published in 1901, it is frequently referred to as the cat's *Beautiful Joe* or *Black Beauty*.

As the cat gained status over the years, people naturally became more aware of its needs. Still, when the first English book on cat care, by Lady Cust, was published in 1856, it was considered presumptuous. Its popularity, however, elicited a second printing and, in 1870, a second edition.

In contrast to Lady Cust's brief thirty-one-page work, William Gordon Stables' pioneering book entitled *Cats,* printed in 1874 was five hundred pages long. Half the contents covered care and breeds; the other half was devoted to anecdotes. The make-up of cat books had become diversified, and cats themselves were beginning to be regarded not only as pets but as status symbols. All that was needed to complete the metamorphosis was the publication, in 1889, of *Our Cats and All About Them* by Harrison Weir. The author's prestige as a painter and illustrator went a long way in selling the idea of cats to the public, and cat shows and cat books blossomed. Although *Our Cats* is a general book, a good portion of its contents is devoted to care and breeds, a format similar to the many popular general cat books being published today.

Since the turn of the century, knowledge about cats has increased so rapidly that books covering only a single relevant topic have grown proportionately. The cat book fancier therefore has a chance to limit his library by subject.

Of course, the greatest number of cat books is for children, and a collection of juveniles, in spite of selective choosing, can soon grow into hundreds of volumes. These books are usually divisible by story type, such as cat and dog, cat biography, cats looking for a home. Fairytale and folktale cats alone form a large segment, but properly speaking they belong to people of all ages and not solely to the child.

Juveniles can also be divided into genres as opposed to themes: chapbooks, moral tales, the toy books that followed the moralizers, the varied modern children's books — almost all with distinctive illustrations ranging from horrible to heavenly, and some heavenly horrible. Potential classics are Wanda Gag's *Millions of Cats*, Elizabeth Jane Coatsworth's *The Cat Who Went to Heaven*, Robinson's *Buttons* and A. Birnbaum's *Green Eyes*. Lowery Wimberley's *Famous Cats of Fairyland* contains a good selection of folktales.

Predictably, the second greatest number of cat books treats the care of the cat, including breeds and the "fancy" (the general term for the various organizations devoted to the breeding and advancement of purebred cats). Pioneers in the field have been followed by scores of writers whose efforts are sometimes estimable but more often mediocre hack work. Frances Simpson's *The Book of the Cat* (1903) must be regarded as the best of its kind; though no other book treats cat varieties so exhaustively, only in the last few years have attempts been made to produce an updated version. Cat care books covering a specific breed are also gaining in popularity.

Full-length books about a cat or cats, fictional or real, are surprisingly common. This segment of cat literature contains much good reading and great collecting possibilities. William Gordon Stables' *Shireen and Her Friends* and Violet Hunt's *Loki* (also published as *The cat*) are the best-known older fictional works. More recent titles of undisputed merit are Svend Fleuron's *Kittens, a Family Chronicle,* Maurice Genevoix's *Rrou,* Agnes Rothery's *Into What Port?* and, of course, Colette's *The Cat.* Fiction in which cats find a place continues to appear, as exemplified by George's *Blind Alley* and the Lockridges' Mr. and Mrs. North mysteries. Loving tributes to real cats include Charles Dudley Warner's "Calvin," Carl Van Vechten's *Feathers* and Michael Joseph's *Charles.* Recent years have seen numerous books about other authors' cats.

Cat anthologies comprise poetry, stories or essays, a mixture of all these or a potpourri of almost anything that happened to intrigue the compiler. *Concerning Cats* (1892) by Rosamund Watson, under the pseudonym Graham R. Tomson, was a pioneering work in poetry; Agnes Repplier's *The Cat* (1912) is a classic in the potpourri field. N. A. Crawford's *Cats in Prose and Verse* is another outstanding collection, its contents divided by subject matter. No matter what their arrangement, however, the anthologies make good reading. Even repetitions in content are bearable, since they tend to represent the better selections in their field.

General books cover the cat in many aspects, depending on the author's objective. Here, too, there are of necessity many repetitions, but these are overshadowed by numerous fascinating additions. Champfleury's *Les Chats* (1870), a French cat classic, was translated into English as *The Cat Past and Present* by Mrs. Cashel Hoey in 1885, predating Weir's *Our Cats* by four years. Agnes Repplier's *The Fireside Sphinx* came

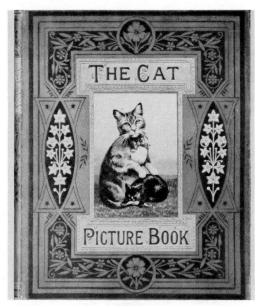

Mrs. H. B. Paull's 1880 cat book was a big success in London.

out in 1901. All three books are superior in their own special way, as is C. H. Ross' *The Book of Cats* (1868), which is not so well-known but is filled with feline facts not found elsewhere.

Present-day publications reflect a preference by cat fanciers for picture books with a minimum of text. Although almost too many of these are now being ground out, the collector can select from such works as Méry's *The Life, History and Magic of The Cat* (1968, in print, a translation of his *Le Chat*), which has magnificent illustrations.

Collections of cat artists' works, or books illustrated by them, should be in every cat library regardless of its other limitations. The cats of Steinlen, Lambert, Mind, Ronner, Foujita, Nam, Bacon, Wain and others should be familiar to every cat enthusiast. Recent general books are making this more feasible with their vast array of art illustrations.

Cartoon books should also be included in the cat library to provide a light touch. Cats lend themselves so well to this art that the range of such books is wide. There are collections of single artists, like George Herriman's famous *Krazy Kat* (1975, in print) and B. Kliban's *Cat* (1975, in print), as well as general collections.

Then there are the photographic books — those that tell you how to photograph cats and those that present you with the results by both master and amateur photographers. The photographic collections are often humorously captioned; they might also tell a story. A good proportion of these books are excellent, and the choice among them will depend on the collector's preference of treatment.

Discussions of the cat in the world of art can be found in several of the general books, particularly Van Vechten's *The Tiger in The House*, acclaimed by many as *the* cat book. The history of the cat can also be gleaned from these books, including its folklore and religious aspects; however books devoted to folklore and religion are generally mediocre.

Among the other types of cat books being consistently published are the numerous anatomy, physiology and veterinary works which discuss what makes a cat a cat, including its psychology. The classic in this area is Mivart's *The Cat* (1881), now quite rare, which despite its partly outdated text is highly readable. Only two titles are slanted for popular consumption: Ida May Mellen's *The Science and The Mystery of The Cat* and Necker's *The Natural History of Cats*. Some cat care books touch briefly on biology; one example is Leon Whitney's *The Complete Book of Cat Care* (1953, in print); another is Terri McGinnis' *The Well Cat Book* (1975, in print).

And not to be overlooked is the humorous segment of cat literature. Cats being what they are, you can find humor of every form. The satire, cartoons and captioned photographs have already been mentioned. Anne Spencer's *The Cat Who Tasted Cinnamon Toast* and Baron Ireland's (Nate Salsbury's) *Our Cat* can be relished by all cat owners, but most humor is a very individual thing and other so-called humorous cat books like Anthony Cox's *The Professor on Paws* and Harry Allen Smith's *Rhubarb* may or may not appeal.

With space but not material running out, here's a list of books still in print which can form the nucleus of your library. For others, both in print and out, check with dealers and public librarians. And don't forget to sample the foreign offerings.

Good hunting!

Claire Necker, an avid cat enthusiast, has written frequently on her favorite subject.

THE CAT'S BOOKSHELF

Gertrude Zeehandelaar

CAREY HUTTNER

HERE IS A comprehensive sampling of the best of the currently available cat books. Except where otherwise noted, all books on this list are hardbound.

General

Grilhe, Gillette, *The Cat and Man* (G. P. Putnam's Sons). The role of the cat in history, myth, legend, literature; care, feeding, diseases, breeds, varieties. Lavishly illustrated with many art reproductions, photos.

Méry, Fernand, *The Life, History & Magic of the Cat* (Grosset & Dunlap, Inc.). Comprehensive study of the cat in civilization, culture, the arts; derivation, anatomy, physiology, psychology, behavior of the domestic cat. Many color plates, photos.

Pond, Grace, (ed.), *The Complete Cat Encyclopedia* (Crown Publishers, Inc.). Detailed discussion of every recognized breed; genetics, evolution, anatomy, nutrition, breeding, diseases. Over 650 black-and-white and color illustrations.

Cat Care and Health

Amberson, Rosanne, *Raising Your Cat* (Crown Publishers, Inc.). Informative text, illustrated with step-by-step photos, on all phases of cat care; nutrition, breeding, grooming, common ailments.

Fox, Dr. M. W., *Understanding Your Cat* (Coward, McCann & Geoghegan, Inc.). What makes Tabby tick; an animal behaviorist's analysis of each aspect of feline experience. Many photos, charts, diagrams.

McGinnis, Terri, *The Well Cat Book* (Random House, Inc.). A veterinarian's guide to understanding and recognizing the common signs of illness and injury; care in health and illness, breeding, reproduction. Many illustrations.

Whitney, Leon F., *The Complete Book of Cat Care* (Doubleday & Co., Inc.). Practical advice from a veterinarian on care, feeding, first aid, treatment of diseases and injuries. Drawings, tables.

Cat Breeding

Ashford, Allison, and Pond, Grace, *Rex, Abyssinian & Turkish Cats* (Arco Publishing Co., Inc.). Detailed discussion of these three breeds; history, characteristics, care, breeding, grooming, common ailments, etc. Many photos.

Dunnill, Mary, *The Siamese Cat Owner's Encyclopedia* (Howell Book House, Inc.). Alphabetical information on all aspects of care, health and breeding, genetics, varieties. Many photos.

Jude, A. C., *Cat Genetics* (TFH Publications). Standard work, in simple language, on cat genetics. Many illustrations.

Lauder, Phyllis, *The Batsford Book of the Siamese Cat* (J. B. Lippincott Co.). History of the breed, varieties, health, care, kittens, showing; comparison of English and U.S. standards. Many photos.

———, *The Rex Cat* (David & Charles, Inc.). Complete discussion of all aspects of health, care, breeding and showing of this breed. Many photos.

Pond, Grace, and Calder, Muriel, *The Longhaired Cats* (Arco Publishing Co., Inc.). Detailed description by well-known breeder and veterinarian of American and British longhairs; their characteristics, varieties, care, showing, etc. Photos, tables.

Ramsdale, Jeanne, *Persian Cats and Other Longhairs* (TFH Publications). Information on all aspects of care, health, breeding, feeding, showing, pedigrees. Many photos.

Wilson, Meredith, *Showing Your Cat* (A. S. Barnes & Co., Inc.). All aspects of The Cat Fancy: associations, record keeping, the ins and outs of showing; discussion of breeds. Many photos.

Fiction

Brown, Philip, *Uncle Whiskers* (Little, Brown & Co.). Story of a courageous cat who enjoys a happy life despite a crippling accident. Illustrated.

Brundage, Burr C., *Gian Carlo* (Valkyrie Press, Inc.). Paperbound. Unforgettable tale of a unique Siamese cat. Illustrated.

Daniels, Mary, *Morris: An Intimate Biography* (William Morrow & Co., Inc.). The life, adventures and loves of the TV superstar. Many photos.

Gallico, Paul, *The Abandoned* (Random House, Inc.). Delightful novel, undoubtedly written by a cat, about the ways of catdom.

————, *The Silent Miaow* (Crown Publishers, Inc.). A manual for homeless cats on how to handle humans. Many photos.

Gordons, The, *That Darn Cat* (Doubleday & Co., Inc.). New edition (originally titled *Undercover Cat*) of the light-hearted story of the Siamese cat who became an FBI informant.

Greenfield, Josh, and Mazursky, Paul, *Harry & Tonto* (E. P. Dutton & Co., Inc.). Warm and witty novel of a man's odyssey across America with his remarkable cat.

Mannin, Ethel, *My Cat Sammy* (Transatlantic Arts, Inc.). Story of the rehabilitation of Sammy, the cat who came in from the cold. Many photos.

Shaw, Richard, *The Cat Book* (Frederick Warne & Co., Inc.). Small but excellent collection of cat literature, with outstanding black-and-white and color illustrations.

Tangye, Derek, *Somewhere a Cat Is Waiting* (Delacorte Press). Life in the English countryside with four cats.

Poetry

Burden, Jean, *A Celebration of Cats* (Paul S. Eriksson, Inc.). Superior collection of more than 300 poems — serious, light, frolicsome, mystical — by immortal, merely famous and some little-known poets.

Carr, Samuel, *The Poetry of Cats* (Viking Press, Inc.). Selection of poems on cats both past and present, with outstanding black-and-white and color illustrations by famous artists.

Photography

Gallico, Paul, *Honorable Cat* (Crown Publishers, Inc.). Thirty-two page introduction explaining the cat's behavior and habits. "Odes to Honorable Cats": free-verse presentation of

the cat's view of humans and the world around it, each poem illustrated with an excellent full-page color photo by the well-known Japanese artist Osamu Nishikawa.

Cartoons

Kliban, B., *Cat* (Workman Publishing, Inc.). Paperbound. Zany interpretations of the cat.

Reed, Marbeth, *Silly About Cats* (Doubleday & Co., Inc.). Paperbound. The best cat cartoons from English and U.S. magazines.

Juveniles

Averill, Esther, *Jenny and the Cat Club* (Harper & Row Publishers, Inc.). Five stories about Jenny Linsky, a little black cat, and her friends. Ages 4–8.

Cleary, Beverly, *Socks* (William Morrow & Co., Inc.). A cat's reactions to the arrival of a first baby. Excellent drawings by B. Darwin. Ages 8–12.

Finlayson, Ann, *House Cat* (Frederick Warne & Co., Inc.). Touching story of a cat's determined efforts to get inside the house. Exceptional black-and-white drawings. Ages 8–12.

Knotts, Howard, *The Winter Cat* (Harper & Row Publishers, Inc.). A homeless cat's domestication. Superior illustrations. Ages 4–8.

Selsam, Millicent E., *How Kittens Grow* (Four Winds Press). Photo-description, in simple language and big print, of the first eight weeks of life of four kittens. Ages 5–9.

Reference Books

Necker, Claire, *The Cat's Got Our Tongue* (Scarecrow Press, Inc.). A thorough and impressive cat dictionary, with cat proverbs and cat quotations in alphabetical order.

Necker, Claire, *Four Centuries of Cat Books 1570–1970* (Scarecrow Press, Inc.). Comprehensive annotated bibliography of cat titles published in English. Includes translations. Subject index; title index.

Gertrude Zeehandelaar, a serious reader, has lived with cats for many years.

EDITOR'S CHOICE:
THE BEST ALL-TIME EVER
STORIES STARRING CATS

The Abandoned **by Paul Gallico.** A touching reworking of a favorite theme: a cat and a boy. Very good fiction by one of the most prolific and qualified of cat authors.

archy & mehitabel **by don marquis.** The crazy and popular free verse of a cockroach named archy who has a lot to say about and do with a cat named mehitabel. She used to be Cleopatra and he used to be a poet. wotthehell.

The Black Cat **by Edgar Allan Poe.** Another frightful, chilling story from the master of horror, this time about the cat as moral agent. Definitely not for children, cat haters or the easily spooked.

Broomsticks **by Walter de la Mare.** A refined English spinster lives alone with her cat in the ancestral home on a deserted moor. Strange events connected with the cat prompt Miss Chauncey to sit up all night by the light of the full moon. A typically understated British chiller.

The Cat **by Colette.** A stylish young marriage on the rocks in the jazzy glitter of 1920s Paris. Saha, the husband's beloved blue cat, is one cause of the trouble. Ultimately, the husband must choose between his childhood pet and his elegant young wife. An ironic, subtle tale of human and feline psychology.

Cat in the Rain **by Ernest Hemingway.** Striking portrait drawn with clean, simple lines of a passionless marriage and a discontented wife who wants to love or be loved. One of the short stories which reveal why this writer became Ernest Hemingway in his own time.

The Cat That Walked by Himself **by Rudyard Kipling.** An amusing rendition of the cat's initial domestication. The cat strikes a bargain with a cave woman: she will feed him milk; he will kill her mice. The rest of the time, he walks alone.

The Cyprian Cat **by Dorothy L. Sayers.** An English summer holiday with bizarre goings-on: a beautiful and mysterious lady, her docile engineer husband and his ailurophobic best friend. The mystery is not "who done it" but "whom did he do it to." Sayers takes an old theme and makes it fun and puzzling all over again.

The King of Cats **by Stephen Vincent Benét.** An extraordinary French conductor conquers New York society. That he conducts with his tail is no small part of his charm. Intrigue with a visiting Siamese princess and a legendary ending finish off this satiric look at the career of a social lion.

The Malediction **by Tennessee Williams.** The sensitive and poignant story of a young man from the country alone in the city. Befriended by a loving cat, he struggles, and finally fails, to succeed in the bitter world. A moving and painful story by one of our foremost dramatists.

Particularly Cats **by Doris Lessing.** Reminiscences from an interesting life spent with lots of cats — in South Africa and in England. Beautifully written and full of understanding about the cat's many lives.

Tobermory **by Saki (H. H. Munro).** A witty little piece of social satire about a talking cat who scandalizes upper-crust society at an English country house weekend. Saki knows a lot about cats and their habits; as usual, he is superb at exposing people at their silliest.

CATS AND WRITERS

WRITERS FIND INSPIRATION in cats. Grace, power, mysticism, blunder carried off with aplomb, greed managed with fastidiousness — these are concerns of the novelist, poet, comic — and qualities of the cat.

Writing is reported to be solitary, lonely, quiet. For a little companionship without a lot of barking, a cat seems to be the answer to the writer's confinement. It is, in fact, the perfect answer, because the cat's demands are so few. He can be there without intruding. Just at the point when neither ideas nor graceful phrasing will come, the writer can turn to the cat for distraction, a silent accomplice in the writer's block. And just at the point when the writer discovers how to finish the last chapter, his animal does not demand attention or need to be taken for a long walk. It is for good reasons that more cats are found in corners of writing rooms than in the offices of stockbrokers.

Mark Twain

Mark Twain's favorite cats: Beelzebub, Blatherskit, Apollinaris and Buffalo Bill.

Lord Byron

Sir Walter Scott

The Bronte Sisters

*Charles
Dickens*

THE FAMOUS CAT
WRITERS SCHOOL

A random sampling of famous writers
who owned cats, and in some cases wrote
about them.

Victor Hugo	*Charles Dickens*
Charles Baudelaire	*Jeremy Bentham*
Anatole France	*Horace Walpole*
Montaigne	*Samuel Butler*
Samuel Johnson	*Henry James*
Sir Walter Scott	*Mark Twain*
Lord Byron	*Ernest Hemingway*
The Brontes	*William Wordsworth*

CAT POEMS

DRAWINGS BY EDWARD LEAR

THE OWL AND THE PUSSY-CAT
EDWARD LEAR

I.

The Owl and the Pussy-Cat went to sea
   In a beautiful pea-green boat,
     They took some honey, and plenty of
      money,
   Wrapped up in a five-pound note.
The Owl looked up to the stars above,
   And sang to a small guitar,
"O lovely Pussy! O Pussy, my love,
   "What a beautiful Pussy you are,
     "You are,
     "You are!
   "What a beautiful Pussy you are!"

Foss, Passant

Foss, regardant

II.

Pussy said to the Owl, "You elegant fowl!
   "How charmingly sweet you sing!
"O let us be married! too long we have tarried
   "But what shall we do for a ring?"
They sailed away for a year and a day,
   To the land where the Bong-tree grows,
And there in a wood a Piggy-wig stood,
   With a ring at the end of his nose,
     His nose,
     His nose,
   With a ring at the end of his nose.

III.

"Dear Pig, are you willing to sell for one shilling
   Your ring?" Said the Piggy, "I will."
So they took it away, and were married next day
   By the Turkey who lives on the hill.
They dined on mince, and slices of quince,
   Which they ate with a runcible spoon;
And hand in hand, on the edge of the sand,
   They danced by the light of the moon,
     The moon,
     The moon,
   They danced by the light of the moon.

Foss dansant

THE KITTEN AND FALLING LEAVES
WILLIAM WORDSWORTH

See the kitten on the wall
Sporting with the leaves that fall,
Withered leaves-one-two-and three —
From the lofty elder tree!

— But the kitten, how she starts,
Crouches, stretches, paws, and darts!
First at one, and then its fellow
Just as light and just as yellow;
There are many now — now one —
Now they stop and there are none.
What intenseness of desire
In her upward eye of fire!
With a tiger-leap half way
Now she meets the coming prey,
Lets it go as fast, and then
Has it in her power again:
Now she works with three or four,
Like an Indian conjurer,
Quick as he in feats of art,
Far beyond in joy of heart. . . .

Foss Couchant

THE CAT OF THE HOUSE
FORD MADOX FORD

Over the hearth with my 'minishing eyes I muse
Until after
The last coal dies.
Every tunnel of the mouse,
Every channel of the cricket,
I have smelt.
I have felt
The secret shifting of the mouldered rafter,
And heard
Every bird in the thicket.
I see
You
Nightingale up in your tree!
I, born of a race of strange things,
Of deserts, great temples, great kings,
In the hot sands where the nightingale never
    sings!

MICE BEFORE MILK
FROM: THE MANCIPLE'S TALE.
BY GEOFFREY CHAUCER

Lat take a cat and fostre hym wel with milk
And tendre flessch and make his couche of silk,
And lat hym seen a mouse go by the wal,
Anon he weyvith milk and flessch and al,
And every deyntee that is in that hous,
Suich appetit he hath to ete a mous.

Foss, a untin.

THE CAT AND THE MOON
W. B. YEATS

The cat went here and there
And the moon spun round like a top
And the nearest kin of the moon,
The creeping cat, looked up.
Black Minnaloushe stared at the moon,
For, wander and wail as he would,
The pure cold light in the sky
Troubled his animal blood.
Minnaloushe runs in the grass
Lifting his delicate feet.
Do you dance, Minnaloushe, do you dance?
When two close kindred meet,
What better than call a dance?
Maybe the moon may learn,
Tired of that courtly fashion
A new dance turn.
Minnaloushe creeps through the grass
From moonlit place to place,
The sacred moon overhead
Has taken a new phase.
Does Minnaloushe know that his pupils
Will pass from change to change,
And that from round to crescent,
From crescent to round they range?
Minnaloushe creeps through the grass
Alone, important and wise,
And lifts to the changing moon
His changing eyes.

TRIPPING OVER THE CAT

Keith Gunderson

The cat's coat
is a map
of a world,
so the world
it is a map of
is cat-shaped.

The cat-map
is a map of
the cat itself,
hence the cat
is a map of itself,
and, hence,
a self of a map.

Anything cat-shaped
is inscrutable.

The cat's coat
is mostly grey
with a tint of
olive-drab
like a dill pickle,
and a faint splash of orange
across her stomach,
and here and there
black stripes
and little dots.

The pickle-colored parts
depict lush forests,
the stripes, rivers and
road winding
through
them;
the orange is desert
and the dots oases.

Here she comes
self-contained
as a globe.

Tripping over her
is no small thing.

It is to collide with
a whole world's
representation.

———————————

I resolve to get
the day
off to a fast start,
tripping
over the cat.

———————————

Not tripping
over the cat
and tripping
over my own feet
I hear my toes
meow.

———————————

It's raining cats
and dogs.

Afterward I go out
and try to walk
from dog to dog.

———————————

We go on vacation
and board the cat at the vet's.

I miss
tripping over
the cat,

tripping over
a tacklebox.

———————————

Tripping over
a friend's dog
I say

"I'm sorry,
there must be
some mistake."

———————————

My small son
tripping
over a kitten

illustrates
the rest
of his life.

Keith Gunderson, poet,
scholar and composer,
teaches philosophy of
science at the
University of Minnesota.

A MONK'S LAMENT FOR HIS CAT

Anne Howland Schotter

Penfield Weir discovered and edited this medieval poem in the early part of this century. Mr. Weir, a learned but eccentric scholar, preferred that none of his discoveries ever be revealed to the world. In his waning years he befriended a young American scholar, Anne Howland Schotter, and bequeathed this manuscript to her as a personal gift. The poem and Weir's editorial notes are published here for the first time with the permission of Anne Howland Schotter, who feels this text is an important contribution to the field of medieval studies and therefore ought to be shared.

T HE MIDDLE ENGLISH poem edited here for the first time is preserved on a small manuscript recently discovered in a Cheshire abbey. Although the text is quite corrupt, having passed through the hands of several scribes, the original dialect appears to have been Northwest Midland. The metrical form of unrhymed, four-stress accentual lines with ornamental alliteration places the poem in the fourteenth-century Alliterative Revival.

Nothing is known of the author beyond what can be inferred from the internal evidence of the poem. The line "Since I forsoke the fikil world" (1.21) suggests that he was a monk. Although cats were common pets in monasteries, it is unlikely that this dream vision is to be taken literally as an elegy on the death of a cat: such intense emotion as this could hardly have been lavished on a dumb beast. Most probably, the poem is an allegorical satire on the late medieval doctrine of the redemption which, by stressing Christ's humanity — His passive suffering — rather than His divinity, inspired a sentimental treatment of the Crucifixion in art and literature. The poet parodies the image of the Lamb of God as sacrificial victim (Apocalypse 5:6, 8–9; 7:14) by portraying him as a mouse.

The erotic overtones of the poem are clearly inappropriate for a cat. Such words as "luflongyng" (1.23) suggest the world of courtly love as seen in dream visions like the *Romance of the Rose*. The traditional *effictio* (11.5–16) — catalogue of physical features usually applied to the heroine of romance — compounds such an impression. The author's purpose in including such details eludes us.

In the month of May,
   when mirthes are many,
I slipped into a slumber, under
   soft leaves,
And dreamed a selcouthe swe-
   ven.
Methought I saw a courteous
   cat
With gleaming eyes of jasper
   green;
Of fine gold was her fetise furr;
An "M" marked the middle
   forhede.

Her precious eres were pointed
   sharp,
Her nose of coral, her nosth-
   irles black.
A collar of comly calsedony
Umbeclypped her throat of
   ivory clene.

Her limmes and haunches lithe
   and smooth,
Her fete the fairest that ever
   freke knew,
With pawes as white as whales
   bone,
And nimble nailes to claw at
   any man.
Her proud tail was tall and de-
   bonair.

"Malkin,"[1] quoth I, "Art thou
   the kitoun
That I haf mourned so many
   night?
Though thou was wont to warm
   my couch,
I haf laid they corse in clotty
   clay.
Since I forsoke the fikil world,
I loved man ne beast as thee!

For thou I suffer luf-longyng,
Fount of my felicité[2]
For when on night I sleped not,
But at my deske did write and
   scrape,
Then did thou look and lepe at
   me,
To nip me sharp, and whurl
   into my ear.

Thou purred[3] softe on my
   parchment,
Under the warme lampe light;
Thou twicched oft thy tikil tail
To mar the ink across the leaf;
Then blenked thine eyen in
   cattes bliss:
I burn, God wot, to stroke thy
   belly soft!"

Then mery Malkin myrtled
   low,
"Almighty Mous made me his
   mate,

In heven to be his hende bride.
O   Goddes Mous, that does
   way,
The sinnes of this wrecched
   world,
That cruelly caught for cattes
   sake,
Was boldly buffeted and slain,
My leman and my leefe Mous,[4]
Guiltless, grant us thy grith."

"Malkin," I axed, "May thou
   alone,
Have honour over other cats?"
"The Mous," quod she, "Has
   many brides,
But none does envy any other.
When we rub his comly corse,
He makes us mirth and gives us
   meat;
His bounty bold knows of no
   stint."

"But mery Malkin," mourned I
   in tene,
"Why left thou me, that loved
   thee long,
The Mous thee loves not more
   than I,
Who couched with thee on cold
   nightes."

In exaumple she answered
   soon,
"A cat fostered with milk and
   meat,

And flattered with a cushion
fine,
May only see a mous run by,
To leave her soft and lufly life.[5]

The Mous my mirth and all my
bliss
Against my wille withholds me
not,
He welcomes me to New
Ailurasylum[6]

To serve him well with freedom
faire.
Thou loved me fain, and locked
me fast;
The Mous would that I chase
him still."

I looked, but she had left me
lorn,
With dreary heart in doel-
dongoun;
But on a hill, then I aspied,
Kitounes quaint an hundred
thowsand,
And four and forty thowsand
more.
On all their forhedes fettled
was
The Mouses name in letter
"M."

Then radly, all in a rush,
Thise kitouns caught the
Mous milde,

To buffet and bat from paw to
paw,
And rend his hide with teeth
full tene.

They wrought a wound both
wide and wet;
From soft sides the blood out-
sprent;
That dainty did they all devour.

Then heard I purring woun-
drous proud,
A roaring rurd like to thunder,
The noise of kitounes nourished
new —
Mikil praise unto the Mous.

That hende hymn did me
awake,
From derfly dream to dayes
light.
I shall fede my fairest never,
But she shall maunge with
Mous forever.

_____

[1]Proverbial name for a loose woman.
Why the poet would use it is an
enigma; "Grimalkin" as a name for
a cat is not cited in the O.E.D. until
1605, in Shakespeare.

[2]Probably a pun on L. felis, "cat." Isi-
dore of Seville writes in his
Etymologiae that "felis dicitur quod

facit monachos felices" (Patrologia
Latina, LXXXI, col. 440).

[3]Since purr is not listed in the O.E.D.
until 1601, this may be an example
of the poet's "good ear," his ability to
coin onomatopoetic expressions of
feline sounds. Cf. "myrtle," 1.34.

[4]The poet is indulging in word-play on
the etymology of leman, OE lief man,
"dear person."

[5]This exemplum is proverbial.
Chaucer uses it in the Manciple's
Tale to illustrate carnal desire for
those of a lower order, and concludes, "Lo, heere hath lust his
dominacioun,/And appetit fleemeth
discrecioun" (Canterbury Tales, IX
[H], 183–84).

[6]This neologism, a twist on the "New
Jerusalem," is puzzling since au-
reate language did not become
popular till the next century. Because I can find no English reference to Gr. aílouros, "cat," before
the sixteenth century, nor does
asylum, < Gr. asylos, "place of refuge," appear till 1430, in Lydgate,
the poet appears to have had rare
philological interests for his day.

*Anne Howland Schotter is a
medievalist who has a cat named
Edgeworth.*

Illuminations by Roni Schotter.

BEDTIME STORIES

To Help Your Cat Nap

MARY RUTT

THE CAT AND THE FOX
Aesop

As THE CAT and the Fox were talking politics together, on a time, in the middle of the forest, Reynard said, Let things turn out ever so bad, he did not care, for he had a thousand tricks for them yet before they should hurt him. But pray, says he, Mrs. Puss, suppose there should be an invasion, what course do you design to take? Nay, says the Cat, I have but one shift for it; and if that won't do, I am undone. I am sorry for you, replies Reynard, with all my heart, and would gladly furnish you with one or two of mine, but indeed, neighbor, as times go, it is not good to trust; we must even be every one for himself, as the saying is, and so your humble servant. These words were scarce out of his mouth, when they were alarmed with a pack of hounds that came upon them full cry. The Cat, by the help of her single shift, ran up a tree, and sat securely among the top branches; from whence she beheld Reynard, who had not been able to get out of sight, overtaken with his thousand tricks, and torn in as many pieces by the dogs which had surrounded him.

Moral: Successful cunning often makes an ostentatious pretension to wisdom.

Reprinted from Fables of Aesop and Others *translated by Samuel Croxall. London, 1797.*

Aesop, a Greek fabulist, wrote often about animals.

CATAMORPHOSIS
Roni Schotter

A S GERTRUDE STEVENS awoke one morning from uneasy dreams, she found herself transformed in her bed into a plump orange cat. When she lifted her head, she could see a long striped tail gracefully arched at the top. Her skin had become soft and furlike, and, beneath her eyes, whiskers protruded.

What has happened to me? She wondered. It had to be a dream. But her small room lay quiet as it did every morning except for the hum of early traffic. On her desk lay the manuscripts she had slaved over the previous night. Gertrude was a book editor who specialized in cats. Her walls were covered with illustrations of felines in various poses — dressed, undressed, capricious, reserved.

As she stretched and let out a soft purr, Gertrude saw that everything was as before. But when she crawled out of bed and tried unsuccessfully to put on her slippers, she realized that something was dreadfully wrong. The day was the kind that Gertrude loved — sunny and bright. A shame to rush off to work, thrash about on the subway, race through the crowds and smile a tired hello to all the grim faces in the publishing house. Instead, she decided, just this once, to curl up on the window sill in the warm yellow sun and take a short nap.

A dreadful knocking sound awakened her, and she arched her back.

"You are late. Don't you want any breakfast?" her roommate yelled loudly through the door.

"Just some milk," Gertrude screeched back at her.

She glanced at her clock radio, from which an even-voiced announcer was explaining that the railroads were running fifteen minutes behind schedule and there was rubbernecking on the Brooklyn-Queens Expressway. It was already 9:00. Gertrude knew she was finished unless she could think up a good one for the editor-in-chief, who was due to pick her up at 9:30 for a meeting downtown. She toyed with the flu, but that meant she would have to stay out at least three more days. A sick relative? No, too complicated.

Then it dawned on her — catatonia. Perfect.

The door opened, and her roommate screamed and dropped the glass she was holding. Milk spilled onto the linoleum in big white puddles.

"Oh, my God! I'll call someone. A G.P.? A vet? Oh, Gertrude, how *could* you? I told you those cat books would get to you. Now see what's happened! Oh dear, dear!"

She slammed the door and scurried away.

Gertrude jumped daintily down to the floor and lapped at the milk until the floor was as clean as before. She cleaned herself, musing happily on a morning minus dental floss. Then she nudged the milk glass that lay abandoned on the linoleum.

She was still rolling it about when she heard a sharp sound and noticed a familiar pair of shoes beside her. They were low-heeled, expensive and somewhat clumsy-looking. She stiffened, glanced upward and let out a piercing shriek. It was the editor-in-chief. Gertrude shivered. Her fur stood on end.

The editor cleared her throat. "You've worked with us quite a while, Gertrude. Nine years to be exact. Your work has been . . . adequate."

For someone who knows so much about words, Gertrude thought, it is amazing how limited her vocabulary is when it comes to compliments.

"Your insight and understanding of the subject matter with which you deal . . . is also adequate."

Gertrude repressed an intense desire to rub up against the editor-in-chief's support hose.

"But I must say that your behavior is out of order. It is not seemly for editors to identify so completely with their subjects. You know what I always say: 'When one loses distance, one loses all.' And you, Gertrude Stevens, have lost both your distance and your job. Your check will be forthcoming. There is no need to come into the office."

Gertrude backed up on her haunches, hissed

and spat with anger. It was just what she had always wanted to do to the editor-in-chief. She was only sorry she was no longer at eye level with her.

The editor-in-chief clicked her tongue and quickly exited from the room. Gertrude glanced at the clock: 10:00 a.m. and absolutely nothing to do. Delicious! She leaped up on her desk, onto the pile of manuscripts, smiled smugly to herself, yawned, curled up and went back to sleep.

Roni Schotter is a writer and a children's book editor.

A MORAL TALE

AUBREY BEARDSLEY

ONCE UPON A TIME, in a village very far away, there lived an honest and earnest young man. He was a happy person, for he loved his work, which was caring for all the sick animals in the surrounding countryside, and he loved his wife, who was good and sweet and kind. Their life seemed perfect — he cared for the animals, she cared for him, and they were destined to live happily ever after.

Their trouble began in the seventh year of their marriage. The young man had befriended a beautiful black cat, a stray who had wandered into the village one stormy night. The cat refused to come and live with him; instead she accompanied him on his rounds every day and then disappeared for the night to some secret hideaway. Knowing the habits of cats, the young man was not particularly curious about this pattern, although he loved the cat and would have been happy to give her a home. At about this same time, the young man awoke one night to discover that his wife was not beside him. Concerned but exhausted from his day's labor, he dozed again and awoke early in the dawn to notice his wife slipping quietly back into bed beside him.

This strange occurrence repeated itself several nights running. The young's man curiosity turned to anger. He began to suspect his wife. Of what he did not know, but he did find this very suspicious. Finally, he laid a trap. He placed a chain latch on their bedroom door, locked it from within, and went to sleep. Awakened suddenly by his sense that his wife was missing, he rushed to the bolted door, confused and angry with frustration. "How is this possible in the ordinary course of things?" he asked himself. Suddenly he saw something black slipping through the door at his feet. In his consternation, he grabbed a fire poker and slashed at what now looked like a cat's paw. A piercing cry of pain was heard and the paw disappeared.

The young man was bereft. His wife did not return. Many animals were sick, for it was winter and cold, and he worked hard, trying to forget his wife and his grief at her mysterious disappearance. Then, as suddenly as she had disappeared, she reappeared. The young man was overjoyed; he wept with delight. Eventually he realized that his beloved wife was also weeping, but not for joy alone. He embraced her and assured her that nothing anymore in the world was worth crying over now that they were reunited. She tried to smile and sniffle away her tears, but as she reached to touch her husband he gasped in horror. Her hand had been chopped off at the wrist.

CAT WATCHING
Robley Wilson, Jr.

CATS, WHEN THEY sleep, habitually go slack-jawed, so that when they are turned on their backs you can see — just at the corners of the mouth — the small glisters of white which are their fangs, and the mouths themselves seem always to be smiling as if upon some inner dream, warm and delicious as blood. It is remarkable, in cats, that the outer life they reveal to their masters is one of perpetual confident boredom. All they betray of the hidden life is by means of symbol; if it were not for the recurring evidences of murder — the disemboweled rabbits, the headless flickers, the torn squirrels — we should forever imagine our cats to be simple pets whose highest ambition is to sleep in the best soft chair, whose worst crime is to sharpen their claws on the carpeting.

★ ★ ★

He was driving home from a business trip and had gotten into town well after midnight. He had traveled from the other end of the state — some 200 miles in all — so he was tired, a bit glazed from narrow highways and the brilliance of headlights. As he turned off Main Street onto Primrose, something darted in front of the car: a large orange cat, which hesitated at the edge of the road, circled once, then jumped into his path. By the time he reacted, lifted his foot to the brake pedal, it was too late. He heard the bumping under the chassis and felt the faint tremor in the steering. He stopped and looked back; the cat lay at the side of the street, not moving.

He drove on. As he pulled into the driveway at home, his own cat came to meet him. It had been asleep on the front step; when his headlights swept over it, it got up, stretched, and descended to the walk. When he got out of the car, the cat was already sniffing at the bumper and the right fender. It looked up at him inscrutably, and he felt accused and guilty.

His wife had waited up for him. He told her how he had run over the orange cat.

"Oh, dear," she said. "You should phone the Humane Society."

"I'm sure it's dead."

"Never mind," she told him. "Maybe it isn't, and anyway, the Humane Society can get it out of the street."

He dialed the number. The call was taken by a man, to whom he explained his accident. He located the cat as precisely as he could, and agreed to meet the Society truck.

When he hung up, he said to his wife: "I feel terrible."

"It wasn't your fault," she said gently.

Driving back up Primrose, he found himself hoping he had only imagined the accident, but in a short time his headlights picked out the object — the stupid cat — exactly where he had last seen it. He parked and got out, looked at the carcass — only a faint trace of red showing at the corner of the mouth — and returned to his car to wait.

In ten minutes, the Humane Society panel truck arrived on the scene. The driver was an old man — perhaps in his sixties — who took a shovel from the back of the truck, lifted the cat with it, and arranged both inside the van.

"I feel terrible about this," he told the old man.

"It happens. Don't fret about it."

"If you find out who owned it, call me. I'll be glad to get them a new one." *Some child's pet,* he was thinking.

"If somebody calls, I'll let you know." The old man swung back into the cab.

"There wasn't much blood," he said to the driver.

"There doesn't need to be," the old man said. The truck drove away.

When he started for home again, he made a wide circle — down Washington, across Lilac, up Lincoln — to get back to Primrose. His detour took him past the place where the cat had jumped across his path; where the cat had lain was only a dark spot on the cement paving. He had not gone more than a block past this spot when the same thing happened again. This time it was a gray cat — tiger-striped — which flashed swiftly into the field of his lights, and as before his reaction was too slow to avoid the collision and the familiar bump under the car. He pulled over and switched off the ignition and lights; sat cold and sweating, trying to dare to go home for more forgiveness.

★ ★ ★

When we were ready to leave on our vacation trip to Canada, we couldn't find the cat anywhere. I scoured the house for her, and sent the children whistling and calling through the neighborhood, but in the end we had to give up. I was disappointed not to find her. It wasn't that we had planned to take her on the trip with us — she was on the verge, again, of having kittens, and we certainly couldn't drive north with that kind of suspense riding in the back of the station wagon with us — but we were very attached to her. We wanted — I wanted, especially, as if motherhood were a bond even between human and non-human — to say our goodbyes; for that, my husband made fun of us.

We had made arrangements with the people next-door to feed her, and now I explained that she had gone off somewhere, asking them to keep an eye out for her and — soon — her kittens. I gave them a key to the house. Before we locked up, I put down food in the kitchen and left the door to the cellar open — just in case, so she could eat and use her box.

It was a lovely long vacation. The weather was crisp but sunny almost every day, and we did a lot of fishing and some swimming on the best afternoons. There was only one "incident," and that came late one day when the baby — she's three — lost her balance while she was wading near the dock and fell into the water. I was on the porch of the cottage, writing letters, and the first I knew of anything was when I looked out to see my baby thrashing madly, face down in the lake. I didn't have time to think; I just went racing down the steps and into the water — slacks, shoes, and all — and pulled her out. She'd swallowed a lot of the lake, but she was all right, thank heaven.

We exchanged postcards a couple of times with the people next-door. They said they hadn't seen our cat, but they were convinced she was outdoors somewhere. They heard meowing in our back yard the night after we left; ever since, they had been putting milk and dry cat food on the back step, and they told us it was being eaten. We decided she must have found a cozy place behind the playhouse to have her kittens; I hoped it wouldn't rain, wherever she was.

At the end of August we packed up and came home. It wasn't a happy homecoming, though the weather was clear, and the traffic was reasonable and the roads good. On the way through town we stopped at the courthouse to tell the police we were back, and they could stop checking the house for burglars. The people next-door saw us pull into the drive; they came out to greet us, and we stood talking while the children ran the stiffness out of their legs. They began calling and whistling for the cat, and I had that strange feeling — as if we'd never been away. But we had been. I was relieved to be home, sorry the summer was over. You know what that's like. We got started with the unpacking, and it was when I put my suitcases in the bedroom that I solved the mystery. I found the cat.

I cried for hours. She was dead — stiff as a piece of wood in front of the closet. Exhaustion or starvation, or both together; that's why she died. The food I'd left in the kitchen had never been touched, though she could have gotten to it if she'd wanted. But where she wanted to be was inside my closet; the door was torn to pieces where she'd clawed at it — great splinters were gouged out of it, and her forepaws were caked with dry blood and bits of white wood. Most of her claws were broken, caught in the graining of the door. She must have been at it for days. The explanation was inside the closet: kittens — five of them, no bigger than field mice, and all of them dead, too, in an empty Capezio shoebox of mine. The children were desolate. We buried the whole family behind the playhouse; we haven't owned any pets since, and I still have nightmares about that poor cat.

Abridged from Nimrod.

Robley Wilson, Jr., writer and poet, is editor of The North American Review.

SPHINX AND CHEOPS
AND TED AND ALICE
AND PUSS AND BOOTS

JURGEN R. GOTHE

A lot of people are into pyramids; you know, putting razor blades and knives into them so they will stay sharp forever. Or they may have a triangle of mandarin oranges piled under a pyramid, still fresh from way before the war. Some people are given to sleeping in pyramids, claiming it enables them to exist on far less sleeping time, and causing them to wake much more refreshed.

I have recently read that some pyramid-power people have discovered their cats enjoy sleeping in pyramids too, being more alert, able to play the trombone after only two or three lessons, and frequently walking about the house reciting Longfellow.

I decided to try this out for myself. I built a lovely pyramid out of mahogany, carefully checked all the size specifications, and put it in the middle of the living room, sprinkled a little trail of catnip to the entrance as an extra measure of enticement, set up a lot of sequential cameras with little trip wires so I could document the entire experiment for *Scientific American* and waited.

Initially, nothing happened. The cats regarded my pyramid as a funny thing with a point on it; it wasn't edible, it didn't run away when prodded and it was difficult to sit on top of it. After about a week, one of the cats decided to venture inside the pyramid and to sleep. This event took place at 3:15 a.m., and the tiny creature's foot-pressure on the sensitive plate inside the pyramid woke me instantly, I fell down the stairs in my rush to witness the event. The startled cat immediately left the pyramid and went into hiding.

Some weeks later, the cat attempted the pyramid again. This time, I was ready. Soothed by a low song from *Eugene Onegin*, the cat soon fell asleep. A few hours later, I reached in to see how he was doing.

Imagine my surprise when I cut myself on his fur!

I now have the sharpest cat on the block, proof positive that pyramids really do work. I've managed to get twelve shaves off one cat without having to put him back into the pyramid to recharge.

Not only that, but he can now open his own tins of cat food, simply by sitting on them and rotating 360°.

There's a lot to this stuff. Don't dismiss it out of hand.

Jurgen R. Gothe is the best-shaved critic in Vancouver, B.C.

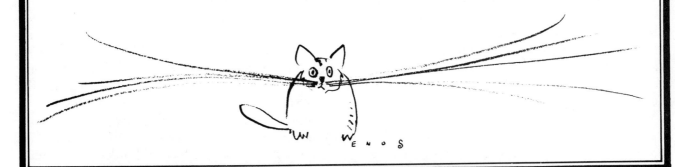

CATS AND CHILDREN'S LITERATURE
A Theoretical Explanation

Roni Schotter

THE MOST RECENT EDITION of the bibliography *Subject Guide to Children's Books in Print* (R. R. Bowker Company) lists close to 400 books on cats for children. It includes books on cat care, poetry about cats and, the largest area of all, stories about cats. A book reviewer at the American Library Association reported that an ever-increasing number of juvenile cat books crossed her desk this year. And juvenile books on cats are rarely "a flash in the pan." Charles Perrault's seventeenth-century *Puss in Boots* is a classic. Wanda Gag's *Millions of Cats*, published in 1928, has sold well over 300,000 copies, and that figure does not include copies sold during the first decade of the book's existence when records were not kept. Writers as diverse as Pearl Buck, Dr. Seuss, T. S. Eliot, Peter De Vries, Beatrix Potter and Rudyard Kipling have written cat books for young readers.

Why are there so many children's books devoted to cats? Since children are rarely in a position to purchase their own books, the mystery cannot be answered by polling the audience for whom these books are written. Even the experts seem dumbfounded. Members of the American Library Association theorize but confess they do not really know. Editors point to puzzling sales statistics: given two books written by the same author, both equally good, one starring a cat, the other a child. The cat book sells; the other barely breaks even. Why? The editors themselves do not know.

But a glance at several juvenile book titles reveals something interesting. *Boss Cat, Bad Cat, Swamp Cat, Puss in Boots, Seri the Conquistador, Pussycat in Business, Space Cat, The Sly Old Cat, A*

Nose for Trouble, etc., are only a few titles that summon up an image of the cat as adventurer, king of the road, tough and clever. Historically, the cat has always been considered an independent creature. What better choice for the protagonist of a children's story? Children, by definition, are beholden to, sometimes prisoners of, adults. When a writer chooses a free, independent character with whom young readers can identify, what better choice than that age-old freebooter, the cat?

Whatever else they may be, cats are prolific creatures. From the street cats of Rome to the farm cats of Kansas, they are ever-present and abundant. Here, then, is fine meat for fiction. Authors can carpet their books with thousands of cats and never be accused of being too fantastical. Only the old woman who lived in the shoe could possibly compete with the numbers of offspring appearing in the following titles: *Twenty-seven Cats Next Door, House of Thirty Cats, A Castle of a Thousand Cats, Millions of Cats.*

One theory that attempts to explain why in recent years there has been one of the greatest influxes of juvenile cat books ever concerns the increasing impact of the Women's Liberation Movement on children's book publishing. Each year, more and more children's books are published showing females, children as well as adults, in more believable, less stereotypical roles. Though there are many exceptions, in the past dogs have been personified as males, cats as females. Many reviewers and librarians theorize that the new and increasing number of cat books on the market portray cats as females more often than males and show them to be as adventurous

IWAO ABE

and liberated as their male dog counterparts. This, they believe, is an indirect result of the women's movement.

In reality, cats are whatever we think they are. Cat haters consider them cold, sneaky and calculating. Cat lovers consider them gentle, sensuous, magical, mysterious and adventurous. Cats are frequently endowed with superhuman characteristics, e.g., nine lives, extreme intelligence, magical abilities, etc. Because of our willingness to accept cats as superhuman creatures, they are the ideal animals with which to work creatively. Writers and illustrators can make them do, say or think almost anything without appearing outrageous or absurd. Cats have no specific or limiting characteristics. Mice are cute, pigs are messy, lions are strong. But cats are what we make them. Since we expect every form of behavior from them, we accept every exploit or attribute an author can concoct for them. Thus a children's writer wishing free reign on his or her imagination can do no better than to choose a cat as protagonist. And so it follows that as long as writers continue to be inspired by the infinite variety of the cat personality they will continue to write more and more books about them and children will have more and better cat books from which to choose.

Caldecott Medal Winners and Honor Books

The Caldecott Award is given annually by the American Library Association to the most distinguished contribution to children's picture books by an illustrator. The following books about cats have been awarded the Caldecott:

1967 WINNER. *Sam, Bangs & Moonshine.* Evaline Ness. Illus. by Evaline Ness. Holt, Rinehart & Winston.

1958 HONOR BOOK. *Anatole & The Cat.* Eve Titus. Illus. by Paul Galdone. McGraw-Hill.

1951 HONOR BOOK. *Dick Whittington & His Cat.* Marcia Brown. Illus. by Marcia Brown. Scribners.

Newbery Award Winners and Honor Books

The Newbery Award is given annually by the American Library Association to the most distinguished contribution to literature for children by an author. The following books about cats have been awarded the Newbery:

1962 HONOR BOOK. *Belling the Tiger.* Mary Stolz. Illus. by Beni Montresor. Harper & Row.

1961 HONOR BOOK. *Cricket in Times Square.* George Selden. Illus. by Garth Williams. Farrar, Straus & Giroux.

1950 HONOR BOOK. *Blue Cat of Castletown.* Catherine Kate Coblentz. Illus. by Janice Holland. Longman. (Out of print. Available in some libraries.)

1931 WINNER. *Cat Who Went to Heaven.* Elizabeth Coatsworth. Illus. by Lynd Ward. Macmillan.

1929 HONOR BOOK. *Millions of Cats.* Wanda Gag. Illus. by Wanda Gag. Coward-McCann.

Roni Schotter is a writer and a children's book editor.

CAT WORDS

Lawrence Paros

GATHER ROUND, all you sharp cats, hepcats, and you cool cats, too, for I want to offer a learned disquisition on the English language. And I don't want any of you 'fraidy cats turning the page just 'cause you never heard of the word "disquisition" before. I'm not one of those folks who can talk a cat and nine kittens to death, so unless you're cat-witted you'll read on and be a pussy cat about it. I'm here to tell you the common house cat stands revealed as a literary lion.

Did you ever wonder why English has two good words — "cat" and "puss" — for one fine animal? It's because all our ancestors knew and valued the cat. The old Romans (who tended to be either fat cats or real tigers) had the word *cattus,* which, thanks to the conquests of Caesar, eventually got to England. The Romans finally left Britain, but the word stayed in shortened form. The newcomers to England were the Germanic barbarians, who had their own word: *puus.* From these two simple words have come more slang terms and phrases than a cat has kittens.

The word "cat" alone has had many slang meanings over the centuries. Besides naming the feline animal, it has also referred to a landlady, a whip, a quart-size pot of beer, a harlot, a hobo and a jazz musician. And there's no need for any of you to grin like Cheshire cats, because I'm not even going to talk about cathouses or catting around. There's more than one way to skin a cat, and I'm not about to talk off-color. My pen is a cat of a different breed, preferring scholarship to pussyfooting around with naughty references. There are plenty of other sorts of astounding examples I can mention — enough, in fact, to make a cat speak and a wise man dumb.

I could, if I were of a mind to, write this entire article about clichés and the cat's anatomy. There are cat's-eyes (children's marbles), cat's hind paws (trivial matters), cat's faces ("help wanted" posters) and cat's hair (cirrus clouds). On the other hand, I have nothing to say about sourpuss, picklepuss drizzlepuss or glamour puss because they are derived from the Irish word for face *(pus)* and not the English word "puss."

There are so many cat clichés that I could probably fill ten pages with them, but it's late and I'm tired. You can look over the list below while I prepare for bed. It's time for me to wind the cat and put out the clock.

Proverbial Cats

raining cats and dogs
fight like Kilkenny cats
let the cat out of the bag

Cat Behavior

catwalk — a narrow pathway
cat nap — forty winks
catcall — a derisive shout

Kitty Litter

kitty-cornered — on the diagonal
have kittens — be extremely upset and agitated
purr like a kitten — behave well
kitty-bar-the-door — a strategy used in hockey
kittens in a blanket — a state of warm intimacy

Breeds of Cats

copycat — an unimaginative imitator
hellcat — a quick-tempered brawler
cat burglar — a thief who scales walls

Maltreated Cats

whipping the cat — briefly lodging with one's employer
cat hunting — stealing beer
turn the cat — betray a cause
hauling the cat — subjecting a person to prolonged questioning

Lawrence Paros is the author of The Great American Cliché.

FRACTURED LEXICON

BARBARA ODABASHIAN

catastrophe: cat show award for *la belle derrière*

catacomb: beauty salon for felines

catalogue: diary of a seafaring cat

catalyst: cat's inclination after too much catnip

cataract: functional furniture of Italian design for kitty's sweater and mittens

catatonic: party fare for cats substituting milk for gin

catechism: manual for turning your doubting tomcat into a true believer

category: Edgar Allan Poe for scaredy-cats or a horror tale

catsup: dinner party for fat cats (catered, of course)

cattle: Yiddish term of endearment for a kitten

catty-cornered or kitty-cornered: Sartre's hell for cats: *No Exit*

Barbara Odabashian teaches English literature in the City University of New York.

Even in Europe the cat's cry is "meow."

CEYLONESE PROVERB

"MEOW IS LIKE ALOHA... IT CAN MEAN **ANYTHING**."

KIT AND CABOODLE

MARY ANN MADDEN

CATS AND COURTSHIP

The Spanish word for a cat door is *gatera*. The *gatera* was cut into the door of old Spanish homes to provide the cat with easy passage in and out of the house. It also provided many a young man with a door to his lady's heart. Young Spanish suitors sometimes conducted courtships by talking through the cat door. When the girl's balcony was too high up for courting conversations, the boy and girl would lie on the floor on either side of the door and flirt through the hole.

TEST YOUR CATS-IN-LITERATURE ACUMEN

ANSWERS AT THE BOTTOM OF THE PAGE.

Score ten percentage points for each correct answer.

100% means you either know a good deal about cats or are
a devoted reader.
90% means the same thing.
80% is only fair — this is an easy test.
70% and below means hit the books.

1. The English novel that has lots of somewhat-important-to-the-story cats in it is:
a. Tom Jones
b. Vanity Fair
c. Bleak House
d. Middlemarch

2. Charmian, a cat who liked to follow her mistress around hour upon hour, belonged to:
a. Mary, Queen of Scots
b. Cleopatra
c. Mrs. Whipple
d. Helen of Troy

3. Who said to some cats that had happened to leap upon a knight's nose, "Avaunt, malignant enchanters! Avaunt, ye witchcraft working rabble!"?
a. Eleanor Roosevelt
b. Alice in Wonderland
c. King Lear
d. Don Quixote

4. Which talking cat in literature killed an ogre who was not very nice anyway, and then won an entire fortune for his owner? (Hint: He also got himself a princess, which he wanted too.)
a. The Cheshire Cat in *Through the Looking Glass*
b. The cat with no name in *Dick Whittington*
c. Puss in Perrault's *Puss in Boots*
d. Morris in *Morris: An Intimate Biography*

5. Who were the dogged (sorry) threesome who invoked the name of the cat Graymalkin?
a. The witches in *Macbeth*
b. The Three Musketeers
c. Chekhov's Three Sisters
d. The Three Stooges

6. A cat named Mistigris in *Père Goriot* is connected to which character?
a. Madame, the Keeper of the Pension
b. Père Goriot
c. Madame, the Keeper of the Pension
d. Madame, the Keeper of the Pension

7. You think *your* cat drives you crazy. Christopher Smart was in London's Bedlam when he wrote a poem to his cat. That cat was named:
a. Jeoffrey
b. Gary
c. David
d. Chet

8. Selima was a real cat belonging to:
a. Horace Walpole
b. Edward Lear
c. Lewis Carroll
d. all of the above

9. Edward Lear, who wrote "The Owl and the Pussycat," himself owned one cat for more than a decade. He was very fond of this cat. Its name was:
a. Boss

b. Foss
c. Hoss
d. Dross

10. Dick Whittington owed a lot to a cat. Due to this cat, he became the mayor of:
a. London
b. Los Angeles
c. Bruges
d. Newark

Answers

1. *Bleak House.* There's Lady Jane, the cat belonging to Krook. Also Mr. Jellyby's cat and Mr. Vohles' cat.

2. Cleopatra. We are not certain where we got this information. Can you disprove it?

3. Don Quixote. He was always talking like that.

4. Puss in Perrault's *Puss in Boots.* That is the point.

5. The witches in *Macbeth.*

6. Madame, the Keeper of the Pension

7. Jeoffrey

8. Horace Walpole. Thomas Gray wrote him a beautiful poem about Selima upon her death in a tub of goldfishes.

9. Foss.

10. London. (Ed. note: English politics have always been curious.)

THE CAT IN MEDIEVAL ART

Louise Caldi

AS ANY CAT LOVER soon realizes, *felis domestica* has independent ways. This fact did not escape the ancient Romans who were responsible for introducing the cat into many areas of Europe during their conquests. A cat was represented at the feet of the great statue of the Goddess of Liberty in Rome, and cats were emblazoned upon the shields and flags of Roman soldiers as symbols of independence. Throughout history the cat has reappeared as a symbol of freedom. It was used on the coat of arms of the early Dukes of Burgundy and by the Burgundian wife of Clovis, the fifth-century Frankish king. The sixteenth-century Sessa printing firm of Venice used a cat as its sign since, like printing, the cat symbolized freedom and therefore enlightenment. In their struggle for liberation during the sixteenth century, the Dutch used the cat as a sign of independence, as did the French two centuries later during their own revolution.

The cat continued to be valued after the fall of the Roman Empire and the coming of Christianity to Europe. In the sixth century Pope St. Gregory the Great was said to have had a pet cat. During medieval times many new associations and beliefs about cats developed. In the later part of the Middle Ages, the cat was symbolic of evil, perhaps because of its independent spirit which was so admired by the Romans, but for many centuries the cat was a medieval symbol on the side of good.

Because of their ability to kill snakes, cats were often associated with St. Patrick, and cats sometimes appear in Irish-Saxon manuscripts. On the monogram page of the *Book of Kells*, for example, two rats are shown eating the bread of the Holy Eucharist while two cats watch them. The rats appear to be symbols of evil assailing virtue, while cats represent the all-seeing Almighty getting ready to pounce.

The cat's role as destroyer of vermin was

F.C. MORGAN

This misericord, or choir stool, in the Hereford Cathedral, shows a cat and fiddle and a goat with a lute.

valued also in a non-religious practical way, and laws were often passed for its protection. In 936 Hyel the Good, Prince of Wales, organized a uniform code of laws which included a section on cats. An original manuscript of this code contains a drawing of a cat at the beginning of the cat codes. Some of the laws dealing with the protection of cat state:

> "The worth of a kitten after it shall kill mice is four legal pence; and so it always remains."
> "There are three animals whose tails, eyes and lives are of the same worth: a calf, a filly, and a cat."

Cats were occasionally used as sculptural decoration on medieval churches. At Moissac in France, a cat and her litter are carved on a Romanesque capital. Cats were often carved on misericords, the hinged seats used in choir stalls; here, they were sometimes shown performing human tasks, possibly to lampoon certain human practices. For example, there are carvings of cats playing the fiddle or some other musical instrument. The noise produced by the instrument was probably regarded as little better than the caterwauling of cats.

Demon-type cats are not usually found among the other fantastic creatures in the architectural decoration of early Gothic churches perhaps because the cat had not yet come to be regarded with distrust. Moreover, in the popular medieval bestiaries allegorical treatises on animals and their habits were portrayed with keen observation, wit and sympathy.

During the thirteenth century, the spirit of St. Francis of Assisi helped give rise to a positive and more compassionate feeling for animals. The beloved Italian saint proclaimed that men

> During the Middle Ages many saints were associated with cats.
> St. Gertrude of Nivelles was known as the patroness of cats.
> St. Agatha was also called St. Gato (cat).
> St. Yves, the patron saint of lawyers, was accompanied by or even represented as a cat, said to symbolize all of the evil qualities associated with lawyers.

St. Jerome, who translated the Bible into Latin, is shown here by Antonello da Messino as a Renaissance scholar in the company of cat.

were the "brothers of all living creatures." In one legend, a cat saved the saint from a plague of mice by miraculously springing from his sleeve. It is not surprising, therefore, that cats became one of the favorite animals represented by Italian artists.

In fact, several great artists had pet cats of their own. Petrarch, the Italian poet, scholar, and patron of learning loved his pet cat and was sometimes painted sitting before a fireplace with his pet. The poet and his "mews" were so attached to each other that during the last years of his life, Petrarch's chief companion was his cat. When the poet died, the cat was put to death and embalmed. Today, the mummified body of the cat lies in a niche decorated with a marble cat and bearing a Latin inscription said to have been written by the poet himself. It declares the cat to have been "second only to Laura," his human love.

The cat was also considered to be a companion of philosophers. St. Jerome was sometimes shown with a cat, as in the painting by Antonello da Messino (c. 1450). There is an old children's poem that refers to St. Jerome and cats:

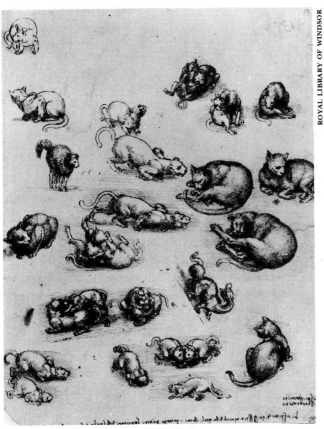

Leonardo's studies of the cat emphasize its alert, hunting nature.

At the end of the Medieval period the cat was regularly associated with evil as in Albrecht Durer's Adam and Eve *(1504).*

If I lost my little cat, I should be sad without it,
I should ask St. Jerome what to do about it,
I should ask St. Jerome, just because of that
He's the only Saint I know that kept a pussy-cat.

The cat could also represent evil. Such artists as Ghirlandaio, Luini and Cellini painted the cat at the feet of Judas (betrayer of Jesus). The use of the cat as a symbol for treachery seems to be an extension of its use as a symbol for independence, and thus for free thinking.

Evil associations with the cat are prominent in a famous engraving by Albrecht Dürer called *Adam and Eve* (1504). The noted art historian Erwin Panofsky says Dürer's cat is a symbol of "choleric cruelty." According to medieval thought, the four "humors" or "fluids" which determine man's temperament fell out of balance with the fall of man. In his engraving Dürer used animals to symbolize these humors.

The rabbit represented the sanguine, or hopeful; the elk, the melancholic; the ox, the phlegmatic; and the cat, the choleric, or easily angered, humor or temperament.

But the cat was not always portrayed as a symbol. It could also be shown on its own natural terms. The Renaissance concept of this scientific approach is best exemplified in the works of Leonardo da Vinci. Leonardo did a study of cats and a dragon in which he drew the cat in its many activities. The artist seemed intrigued by the suppleness of the cat's form and its ever-changing positions. If so great a genius as Leonardo da Vinci was fascinated by cats, is it any wonder that we continue to be captivated by them?

Louise Caldi, an art historian specializing in the Italian Renaissance, dedicates this article to her five cats.

THE CAT IN MODERN WESTERN ART

Laura Battiferi

THE HISTORY OF CATS as depicted in western art unfolds as a study in contrasting points of view. There is no better way to understand the conflicting attitudes people had toward cats than to study their artistic representations.

During the Renaissance, the birth of modern times, there was still a strong tendency to see the world (cats included) as composed of religious symbols the purpose of which was to tell us about a spiritual reality that underlies the everyday world. Cats, during this period, were frequently used as symbols of evil. In Giulio Romano's *Madonna della Gatta* (c. 1523), a sinister cat stares out from the chamber, threatening the viewer and perhaps serving as a reminder of Christ's death to come. The attitude of the cat contrasts with the concerns of the people. The symbols of good are watching the Christ child. The symbol of evil, the cat, looks elsewhere.

Dosso Dossi's cat in *Holy Family with Donors* (1521) may bear the same message: the cat stalks in front of the figures, seemingly enunciating danger. The severe depiction of the entire scene stresses symbolic rather than realistic qualities; traditional mentality still dominates the painting.

JOHN G. JOHNSON COLLECTION, PHILADELPHIA

A cat foreshadows evil in Dosso Dossi, Holy Family with Cat *(1521).*

But the scientific, modern point of view was slowly replacing the religious, symbolic attitudes of the medieval world. Federico Barocci included cats in several of his paintings and they capture a moment in history when attitudes towards the symbolic meaning of animals were changing. In the *Holy Family with Cat* (1573–74) painted fifty years after the strong symbolism of Romano and Dossi, Barocci depicts John the Baptist as an infant teasing a cat with a goldfinch. The bird, with its ability to fly, traditionally symbolizes the soul. By holding it out of the cat's reach, John the Baptist protects the soul from danger (i.e., damnation) and preserves the tran-

MUSEO NAZIONALE, NAPOLI

The cat as an evil symbol is expressed in the stare of the cat in Guilio Romano, Madonna della Gatta *(c. 1523).*

Christian symbolism and modern realism meet in Federico Barocci, Holy Family with Cat *(1573–74).*

quility of the gathering. It is as symbolic as anything in earlier art. But at the same time the naturalism of the scene is remarkable and new. John the Baptist is a real little boy teasing a cat standing in a strikingly real pose. And the naturalism takes its price in lost symbolism. In this painting, unlike in Romano's, one of the good figures has turned his attention away from the Christ Child toward the cat.

In two of Barocci's later paintings the move away from traditional symbolism is even more clear. His *Annunciation* (1582–84) shows a cat sleeping on a chair in the foreground and it is not an ominous figure. The cat now is simply a detail, a tool used to humanize the setting and make the greater event of the Annunciation itself more approachable for the faithful. And in an even later painting of the *Holy Family* (c. 1590) Barocci stays with his natural, domestic and humanized view of the cat. He does not return to the symbolism of his earlier work. In this late painting, a cat with kittens lies on the Virgin's train, perhaps referring to an Italian legend that the Virgin's cat gave birth to kittens at the moment of Christ's birth. The theological symbol of the cat as evil has apparently been forgotten.

By the end of the sixteenth century the cat was being represented as man's companion and was divorced from any moralistic judgments. Jan Breughel the Elder's beautiful painting of *Paradise* (first quarter of the seventeenth cen-

tury) has a supposedly religious theme — Adam and Eve in the Garden of Eden — but is completely naturalistic. Adam and Even are almost invisible in the far landscape. Breughel offers an exquisite vision of a luxuriant forest inhabited by various animals. Among these are two cats living peaceably with two of the neighborhood rats. In a Christian context, the theme speaks of the time before the first sin when loving coexistence was the order of the day. This splendid painting reveals the triumph of naturalism over symbolism in portraying even the most important Biblical stories.

Rich detail dominates this naturalistic setting of Eden in Jan Breughel the Elder, Paradise *(early 1600's).*

A few decades later came Jan Steen's *The Cat's Reading Lesson* (c. 1650) which shows three children attempting to teach a cat how to read. The scene has nothing to do with a religious theme; in fact, its humor depends on a rejection of symbolism. The idea of showing a cat a book is amusing because, of course, a cat is only a cat and cannot read. The painting is one of the several light views of the cat presented in this era. David Teniers the Younger's *The Cat Concert* (c. 1650) shows a groups of cats singing from a libretto, accompanied by a monkey playing the horn. Watteau's *The Sick Cat* (c. 1712) portrays a doctor treating a sick cat protected by its concerned mistress. In this painting, especially, the

The pleasures of the domestic cat are portrayed with a light attitude by Jan Steen, The Cat's Reading Lesson *(c. 1650).*

natural qualities of the cat are stressed.

A little over one hundred years passed between the painting of the cat as a sinister symbol in Romano's *Madonna della Gatta* and the natural portrayal of Steen's *The Cat's Reading Lesson*. Much changed during that era. The modern world was just being born when Romano painted. The scientific revolution was already

Jean Baptiste Greuze, The Wool Winder *(1759), is reminiscent of Barocci, but is natural and domestic rather than symbolic and religious.*

underway when Steen turned to his subject. Now the cat would be represented as a natural creature in a natural setting. The world no longer thought about itself as it once did, not even about cats. The role of symbols was much reduced.

The domesticity of the cat began to be stressed. Jean Baptiste Greuze's *The Wool Winder* (1759) shows a cat playfully trying to distract its mistress as she winds wool. The relation connecting cat, woman, and wool is similar to the relation between cat, John the Baptist, and bird in Barocci's painting two centuries earlier, but in Greuze's painting the relationship is purely natural and represents nothing about another spiritual world.

Auguste Renoir's *Woman with a Cat* (1880) is a mood piece capturing the closeness and intimacy shared by the mistress and her cat. The depiction of the cat had come a long way since the time when it had been presented as a symbol of evil. The sentiment in Renoir's painting is similar to the one in Breughel's picture of Paradise. Cat and mistress share a loving coexistence.

The cat as intimate domestic companion was portrayed by Auguste Renoir, Woman With A Cat *(1880).*

Perhaps the finest representation of cat as pure cat without being good or bad, as in Paul **Gauguin's** *Still-life with Cats* (1899). This deliberately primitive representation of two cats, one asleep, the other staring out at us, creates a sense

Modern portraits of cats can be so peaceful and without moral judgment that they well express the cat's silent mystery. Paul Gauguin, Still-life with Cats *(1899).*

of harmony and serenity. Here the cat's image is purified and contains nothing of the sinister represented in the stare of Romano's cat.

The cat's privacy is disturbed in Mary Cassatt's tender *Children Playing with a Cat* (1908). A baby sitting on his mother's lap reaches out for the cat napping on its young mistress's lap. Like Barocci's painting of the *Holy Family with a Cat*, Cassatt's picture is clearly in the earlier tradition. The setting in Cassatt's painting is as natural and domestic as that of Renoir or of Greuze, but here something else is also happening. In Barocci's painting, the traditionally religious scene was being drained of its symbolism. In Cassatt's painting, a natural scene is gaining symbolism. Now the relationships of the family are again being depicted, this time in a natural hierarchy: the mother is to the child as the child is to the cat. It is a secular view of the earlier Holy Family scene.

Laura Battiferi is an art historian working in New York.

In Mary Cassatt, Children Playing with a Cat *(1908), symbolic relations appear in a secular scene.*

THE STORY OF GOTTFRIED MIND

Liselotte Erlanger

HE WAS KNOWN as the Cat Raphael, and crowned heads of Europe bid for his paintings. But his life — the quiet life of a crippled, slow-witted recluse — did not stir the imagination of biographers, and thus the man who knew how to paint cats as hardly anyone before or after him is now almost forgotten.

His name was Gottfried Mind. His father, a cabinetmaker and mold carver from Hungary, had settled in Bern, Switzerland, where he married a stable servant. Gottfried was born in 1768, a weakly child, physically handicapped and probably mentally retarded.

When he was almost nine years old and still had received no schooling, he attached himself to a landscape painter named Lengel, who visited the paper mill where Gottfried's father had found employment. Lengel was moved by the child's interest in his work and showed him portfolios of drawings and etchings. Attracted by the pictures of animals, the boy showed remarkable aptitude in copying them. Lengel told Gottfried's father about the child's talent, but the father thought wood carving a higher skill than drawing and withheld all paper from the boy. Gottfried reached considerable skill in carving, and later, shortly before his death, returned to

this art, shaping miniatures of animals and children's heads from wild chestnuts. Because of the perishable nature of his medium, we can no longer judge his skill in this field.

A year after meeting Lengel, the boy was sent to a school kept by the famous Swiss educational reformer Pestalozzi. One of the two entries in Pestalozzi's notes about Gottfried describes him as "incapable of any demanding work, but full of talent for drawing, especially God's creatures, which he renders full of artistic caprices and with some wit. . ."

Perhaps such a school was not the place to foster Gottfried's talents, or Pestalozzi thought him incapable of further development; whatever the reasons, Gottfried left after a year and a half. In later years, he never spoke of his stay there, and not even his one personal long-term friend, an amateur art historian named Wagner who wrote Gottfried's necrologue, knew of this interlude.

Upon his return to Bern, Gottfried was apprenticed to a painter and engraver named Freudenberg. He was to outlive his master and remain a member of the Freudenberg household until his death in 1814.

Freudenberg enjoyed a moderate fame as the engraver of Swiss village scenes and costume plates. At the time, color printing was not economically feasible, and plates were printed in black-and-white and hand-colored by apprentices. This became the task assigned to Gottfried in exchange for room and board and some pocket money. Whether Freudenberg knew his helper was capable of creating original work, we do not know; certainly, the master saw no reason to encourage Gottfried's talent when it was in his interest to keep the young man at his task.

By 1802, the year of Freudenberg's death, the market for his decorative village scenes was

KUNSTHAUS ZURICH

drying up as the unsettled conditions in Europe (the outbreak of the Napoleonic Wars) cut into the Swiss tourist trade. Freudenberg's widow was hard-pressed for sources of income. She encouraged Gottfried's output of original drawings and water-colors, and within a few years after his master's death Gottfried rose from the unknown, unnoticed status of a secondary artist to that of an artist of European renown.

In the beginning of Gottfried's activities as an independent artist, he sold his output for small coin, charging according to the number of animals depicted. However, the widow Freudenberg, aware of the enormous demand for Gottfried's work, had no difficulties in realizing gold pieces where the artist had collected coppers. So great was the demand for Gottfried's work that at one time, according to a contemporary, "some Dutchman just purchased all that remained of it and took it with him."

It was during this period that the title "Cat Raphael" was bestowed on him by no less a personage than Madame Vigée-Lebrun, the former court painter of Marie Antoinette. A number of etchers and engravers worked after drawings of Gottfried's, publishing portfolios of them and thus partaking cheaply of his fame.

The question of Gottfried's retardation, his "slow-wittedness," need not make us question his ability as an artist. He was unable to write his name, but what need had he to identify himself in writing when he left some remarkable self-portraits? One shows the small hunchbacked man sketching at his drawing board, a glass jar of frogs near him; another shows him lying down as if asleep, in stocking cap and kerchief. Both testify to his skill, even if we can see some probably genetic defects in his features.

A contemporary described him as "resembling a lion, or a bear, rather than a man, the color of his face a startling purple cast, his features arousing almost fear in the beholder." The human beholder only; animals felt no terror of him. He was surrounded by them. He rarely sat without a cat on his shoulder or lap, remaining in the most uncomfortable positions so as not to disturb his feline friends. His room was alive with cats, and in his sketches and water-colors we become aware of the sensitivity he showed toward them.

Even if the artist is known mostly for his depiction of cats, he tried his hand equally with bears. The city of Bern (in honor of its name, which means "bear") has always kept a bear pit, and Gottfried spent much time watching and sketching the bears, who were so well-acquainted with him that they came out when he approached.

Although generally a quiet, unobtrusive man, he had a fierce pride in his accomplishments. He studied the works of fellow artists, even those far superior to him in skill and fame, and judged them mercilessly for their ability — or inability — to depict animals.

Gottfried Mind died in 1814, aged forty-six. His life was uneventful to the outside world, and no one will ever know what he thought, what he felt, in those hours when he sat watching, observing and then reproducing what he saw with almost photographic fidelity. The kitten at her mother's side, the cautious paw raised, the rough tongue licking, cats at play or repose, their fur drawn softly so that they almost invite a caress, their faces with individual expressions, they remain a testimony to the name he had earned: the Cat Raphael.

Reprinted from Cats *magazine (January, 1976).*
Liselotte Erlanger is a professional researcher and free-lance writer in Mendocino, California.

THE STORY OF LOUIS WAIN

The Cat Artist Who Went Mad

Judy Fireman

DURING THE SIXTY-YEAR span that ran from the 1880s until the outbreak of World War II the children of England were raised on pictures of cats drawn by Louis Wain. A Wain cat is instantly recognizable for its delightful combination of anthropomorphism and accurate feline representation. His cats are charming, mischievous and busy — they ride bicycles, sweep out kitchens, attend tea parties and nap in the best chair. They are domestic and domesticated, common alley cats and rarefied breeds. Wain illustrated at least one hundred books and his work appeared in countless magazines, newspapers and public exhibitions. In 1907, he was brought to America by William Randolph Hearst to draw a newspaper comic strip which ran for two years to the delight of his American fans. Wain's fascination with cats did much to popularize them as lap pets with the English middle class, but tragically this same obsession ultimately destroyed Louis Wain.

At first, Wain's fondness for cats appeared to be only a personal and professional blessing. When he was a young man just beginning to make his way as an illustrator, he and his wife, Emily, enjoyed the companionship of a sweet little kitten named Peter. Soon after Louis' marriage, Emily became fatally ill with cancer and was confined to her bed for over two years until her tragic death in 1887. It was Peter who brought her the little comfort she had during this period. After spending the day teaching art in a London art school, Louis would sit with Emily and, since she was so fond of her cat, Louis began to sketch Peter for Emily's amusement. Emily's dependence on her cat and Louis Wain's skill as an artist combined to produce an unexpected direction for his career. Shortly before her death Emily convinced Louis to submit some of his drawings of Peter to newspapers and magazines, and suddenly his career was defined; Louis Wain became *the* cat artist of England.

By the late 1880s, cats in England were already gaining some respectability, although the majority of Englishmen still thought of them only as skillful ratters and therefore only as functional pets. Public attitudes towards the cat had begun to change at about the time a cat show was held at the Crystal Palace Exhibition of 1871 in London. What was still needed, however, was someone who could focus attention on and express the new appreciation of cats The drawings of Louis Wain were exactly what the changing attitude toward cats demanded.

By 1890, Louis Wain's reputation was established in England. His work appeared in books and magazines; everywhere he went, he was recognized as the eminent artist of cats. One *Punch* editor called him the "Hogarth of Cat Life." In 1890, he succeeded Harrison Weir to the presidency of the National Cat Club. Along with his justifiable fame as an artist he acquired a less-deserved reputation as an authority on cats. Wain's recorded remarks on the nature of cats lack scientific truth, but whatever he drew and said was regarded as authoritative.

The long success of Wain's drawings assured a continuing popular interest in cats, but did not bring him much personal financial stability. Wain was naive about negotiations with publishers; he repeatedly sold his work too cheaply and failed to secure any re-publication rights or

Louis Wain's Performing Cats.

*Louis Wain
(1860–1939)*

benefits. For long periods in his life he was penniless. Because he was such a skillful illustrator, he often paid his bills with quick sketches done to appease his creditors. There are countless anecdotes in London about his appearances at public events, such as plays or art exhibitions. When he was unable to afford the price of admission, his practice was to introduce himself to the ticket-taker, execute a quick drawing on the back of a program or envelope, and thereby gain entrance to the event. These scraps of drawings are now worth much more than the bills they were meant to pay, but they did little to enrich Wain. He simply had no skill in making financial arrangements. He spent two years in America, found popularity and acclaim, and then returned to England as penniless and disorganized as he had been upon his departure.

At about this time, Wain's interest in cats began to turn into an obsession. He drew them exclusively, and even made public statements in which he prescribed the cat as a cure for all ills. Ironically, he believed that owners of cats were safeguarded from nervous ailments. He advised talking daily with a cat to alleviate tendencies toward illness and trouble. Over the years his comments became increasingly peculiar. As his output of cat drawings increased, so did his beliefs in the magical powers of a cat. Meanwhile, his personal problems were growing more difficult. He began to be bothered by "spirits" which visited him; he developed a theory about his powers of healing by electricity — first signs of an oncoming mental aberration.

By his own admission, Wain had been a strange child who often saw visions and was unable to concentrate on the subject at hand. He was born with a harelip, a handicap which apparently bothered him greatly until in early manhood, when he grew a mustache to disguise it. When he was twenty years old his father died

and he became the sole support of his mother and five sisters, one of whom was insane and eventually had to be committed to a public asylum. The early, lingering death of his wife was an additional shock. His quest for fame and fortune brought no fortune and only the loneliest sort of fame. He had few close friends and associates; people who met Wain thought him quiet, kind, and a little odd — an eccentric loner.

It is easy to speculate on how Wain became obsessed with cats. At the time of perhaps his greatest unhappiness, the cat Peter had been his one source of consolation. As financial security and friendships continued to elude him, the pleasure and fame that came from drawing cats was again one of his few sources of happiness. His interest in cats grew first to an obsession and then he went completely mad. He became hostile, incoherent, and visibly paranoid. Business dealings with publishers became impossible. His sisters, who until this time had been under his care, were unable to help him. In 1924, he was declared insane and was committed to the pauper's ward of the Middlesex County Mental Asylum. In one of life's callous twists, Wain's removal to a state hospital was the beginning of an even-greater fame.

A bookseller touring the asylum discovered Wain and publicized his case. A fund was started to help him and his sisters. H.G. Wells wrote an appeal for him, which was broadcast on British radio. Prime Minister Ramsay MacDonald intervened and had him transferred to a better hospital, where he received special care. Suddenly, both the cat artist and his works were enjoying a renewed popularity and marketability. Exhibitions were held to sell his work and aid his cause. He continued to draw and the price for his pictures increased.

During this period, he began to draw in a new style which showed a much greater absorption with pattern. His doctors described these pictures as wallpaper designs rather than as cat portraits. They have become famous as excellent examples of schizophrenic art.

When Wain died in 1939, the entire British nation mourned him. He is famous still in psychiatric circles for the growing illness expressed in his pictures. He is also still famous in cat circles for the loving popularity he helped the cat achieve. And he remains beloved in the hearts of the Englishmen who grew up with his cats in their nurseries and picture books.

THE ART OF HENRIETTE RONNER

Cats were confined in an elegant case while they sat for the famous artist.

Ronner's Brussels studio — cats amid fashionable nineteenth century clutter.

1821–1909

THE CAT IN AMERICAN FOLK ART

Bruce Johnson

THE CAT IS a very personal pet, and folk art is a very personal art. Together, cats and folk art have a special charm that is appealing to everyone. Sensing this double appeal, the Museum of American Folk Art in New York City mounted an exhibition in the spring of 1976 called "America Cat-alogue: The Cat in American Folk Art." The show was enormously successful, drawing more visitors than any other two shows in the Museum's past.

In order to understand the great appeal of cats in folk art it is important to understand what makes folk art itself so unique. Like all the other arts, folk art comes from man's universal urge to be creative. Since the cave drawings of prehistoric times, people have been making pictures that record their lives and surroundings. This urge developed in many forms as man became civilized. While professional artists developed stylized formal and academic art traditions, nonprofessional or folk artists continued to respond to their personal muses.

One of folk art's greatest strengths lies in the honesty of its practitioners. These very human artists depicted what was important to them — their farms, the people and things they loved, their lives. One member of the household that was often fondly portrayed was the family cat. Folk artists, despite their lack of academic technique, managed to paint strong and vital portraits of cats. In many nineteenth-century portraits, especially of children, a cat is a regular feature. Usually the child is rather stiff-looking, almost doll-like, yet the cat is very alive. In many paintings, the viewer can sense the cat's desperate desire to squirm away and be free of the child's clutches.

There are also many portraits of cats alone. The viewer can easily feel the character of individual cats in folk paintings and the appreciation of the artist for these animals. One painting in the museum's exhibition is inscribed on the back, "My cat won first prize at the Genesee County Fair." What a proud cat and a what a proud artist he had!

Folk artists also successfully used the cat as an abstract form. The simplest outline of a cat shape decorated a quilt, a hooked rug or even a cookie mold. It is amazing how these unsophisticated artists understood and utilized abstract and suggestive forms long before the professional academic artists adopted them.

The cat exhibition was fun to do. When word got out that the museum was doing a show on cats, people from all over the country began sending photographs of their cat art. Both public and private collections were contacted. Many collectors and curators claimed they had no cats; yet when we looked at their collections, we found many pieces with felines. True, the cats were not always the primary subject, but they were still there in plain view and usually important to the story of the picture. Looking for cats became a lesson in looking at art — for us and for the collectors.

The cat is tremendously popular and appears in almost every conceivable folk art form. For the exhibition, we wanted as many different art forms with cats as we could find. Besides conventional paintings, drawings and wood carvings, we found cat weather vanes, a cat engraved on a whale's tooth, a cat-shaped cookie cutter, a bean bag with an embroidered cat, many quilts (one with appliquéd furry cats with button eyes), a child's chair with cat-shaped sides, a boot scraper, a painted serving tray, a nutcracker, a gravestone, numerous dolls and toys, a cane with a cat carved in relief on the shaft, a carrousel

A cat corner at the Museum of American Folk Art.

Chalkware Cat with Pipe, Nineteenth Century.

figure of a cat, dolls used at carnivals as targets for baseballs, pillows, pottery and many hooked rugs.

What we found only touched the surface. After the exhibition opened, many people who heard about it or saw the catalogue came forth with great pieces. Because of the incredible popularity of folk cats and the quantity of new material, "The Cat Came Back," a second folk art exhibition devoted to cats, may be a possibility for us in the future.

The late Bruce Johnson was the curator of the Museum of American Folk Art.

THE CAT IN ORIENTAL ART

Jung May Lee

IDEAS ON CATS vary from country to country in the Far East. In some instances, cats suffer from the same prejudices and superstitions found in the West; in other locations, they are as cherished as the modern pedigreed show cat. The cat is found very early in the art of India, but did not become popular in Chinese art until the Sung Dynasty (A.D. 960–1279), more than two thousand years later. Cats are not common in Chinese mythology or folklore. This late appearance of the cat in Chinese as well as Japanese art apparently coincides with the importation of the domestic cat from India. Perhaps another reason for their lack of early popularity was the story that the cat was the only creature in the world which did not mourn the death of Buddha.

During the Sung Dynasty cats and children were often portrayed together. Both the chil-

Aristocratic garden settings as in Li Ti, Hibiscus and Rock *(1114–1137), are typical in Chinese paintings of cats.*

NATIONAL PALACE MUSEUM, TAIWAN

dren and the cats in such paintings are aristocratic and are often represented playing in a corner of a garden. In a painting by the artist Li Ti (1114–1137) called *Hibiscus and Rock* the cat has climbed atop a tall rock in a garden to avoid the barking dog. Tall and fantastically shaped rocks are essential to Chinese gardens and, like the tree in the West, are favorite perches for cats. There is a mood of playfulness in all these paintings; one never sees a cat in the violent act of mousing. This gentle theme became standard in Chinese art and works from modern China continue to depict cats in this way. Such traditional paintings, executed on silk with many colors, were characteristic products of the Chinese Imperial Academy, which aimed for both realism in detail and at pleasing the aristocracy.

The more admired artists among the Chinese, however, were the scholar-painters — learned, skilled amateurs painting for their own enjoyment who espoused high aesthetic, philosophical and moral ideals. Cats began to appear in these amateur ink paintings sometime in the eighteenth century, in the art of the "eccentrics." One such eccentric was Chu Ta (1625–c.1705). His painting of a cat on a rock is as bold and mysterious as the artist himself. Chu Ta was a descendant of the royal house of the Ming Dynasty (1368–1644), and after the fall of that dynasty, he became a Buddhist monk and behaved like a madman; he even abandoned speech.

The Koreans never quite liberated their art from Chinese influence. Paintings by artists in the Office of Arts — the government bureau employing professional artists — resemble Chinese Academic paintings in material, technique and subject. During the early eighteenth century Pyŏn Sang-byŏk, a member of the Office of Arts, was nicknamed "Koyang' i," meaning "cat," because he was a skilled painter of animals, especially cats.

The Japanese were able to create unique and beautiful works of art under Chinese influence. Birds or butterflies in garden settings come from the Sung Dynasty in China. But one technique — multicolor wood-block printing — was a unique achievement of the Japanese.

Unlike China, Japanese society of the seventeenth and eighteenth centuries produced a sophisticated art for consumption by the ordinary populace. This art, which the upper classes scorned, was called Ukiyo-e or "art of the floating world," and its chief contribution was the multicolor wood-block print. Among the favorite subjects of the "floating world" were beautiful women, especially courtesans, and it is with women that cats are most often portrayed. A print by Harunobu (c. 1768–69) shows a girl teasing a cat with a ball tied to the end of a piece of string. The combination of women and cats is as commonplace in the Japanese mind as the combination of children and cats in the Chinese. *Maneki neko* in Japanese folklore is a witch who takes the form of a kitten to entice passers by. The same term is used to describe a beautiful woman with the winning ways of a kitten.

The artist best known for his love and understanding of cats and the humor with which he portrayed them is Kuniyoshi (1798–1861). His cats occur in heroic narrative paintings, in scenes of everyday life, theater scenes, and by themselves. In the print *The Cat Family at Home* (c. 1840) cats are dressed and behave as humans. The setting is probably in a restaurant or one of the pleasure houses so often depicted by Ukiyo-e

artists. The print is in the shape of a fan, an idea originated by the Chinese and favored by the Japanese. Actors and the theater were a popular subject for the Ukiyo-e print maker and Kuniyoshi executed prints of scenes from productions of the play, *The Fifty-three Stations.* One of the play's scenes tells of the cat witch of Okabe and was illustrated by Kuniyoshi in a triptych (1835). Three actors are shown: the one in the central panel portrays the cat witch. In each of the two side panels, a cat is dancing gleefully. Looming behind the entire scene is the huge form of a snarling and menacing cat.

The realistic depiction of the cat in Kuniyoshi, Cats for the Fifty-Three Stations of Tokaido Road *(1848), contrasts with the human cats of some of the artist's earlier work.*

Kuniyoshi's The Cat Family at Home *(c. 1840) is completely at ease with its anthropomorphic style.*

Kuniyoshi also used cats to produce witty "cat alphabets." Around 1842 he executed a series of prints in which cats were joined to form the Japanese names for various kinds of fish. In one such print, cats and catfish are joined to form the word *namadzu,* meaning "catfish."

Kuniyoshi's understanding of cats, however, is best seen in his realistic studies of the animal. In a later triptych called *Cats for the Fifty-three Stations of Tokaido Road* (1848) he depicted groups of cats found in the post stations along this road. Some he whimsically portrayed behaving like humans, but most are doing things cats all over the world do: sleeping, mousing and feeding kittens.

In China, the cat was a playful kitten, a lap pet of the aristocracy. In Japan, this Chinese attitude was at first simply popularized until Kuniyoshi finally added depth to the personality of cats. For this achievement he must stand as the greatest individual ailurophile in Oriental art.

Jung May Lee is an artist and art historian.

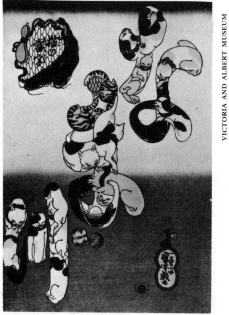

"Catfish" in Japanese is spelled out in this print (c. 1842) by Kuniyoshi.

Aristocratic children and cats were often associated in Chinese paintings. In Children Playing Games on A Winter Day *(Sung Dynasty), we see that even a thousand years ago peacock feathers were used to tease cats.*

Cats dominate the three panels of Kuniyoshi, The Cat-witch of Okabe

THE CAT IN MUSIC

Claire Necker

The atom bomb fell just the other day.
The H-bomb fell in the very same way.
Russia went, England went, and then the U.S.A.
The human race was finished without a chance to pray.

IF YOU KNOW THE SONG "The Cat Came Back," you won't be wondering why the above is the introduction to this summary of the cat's role in music. It's one of the last verses to be added to this famous song that was first published in 1893. Over the years, the tune has continued to gather extra stanzas, giving it far more lives than the cat itself. But always there's the same rousing refrain:

But the cat came back, couldn't stay no longer,
Yes, the cat came back the very next day.
The cat came back, thought he was a goner,
But the cat came back for it wouldn't stay away.

Cat songs are known to have been published since the seventeenth century, but none ever reached the popularity of "The Cat Came Back," probably because of its adaptability to almost any situation — even nuclear warfare. The other cat songs don't have as great a range, but the subjects are as varied as cats themselves. As could be expected, those about love — both feline love and human love with catty connotations — are the most numerous. One of the earliest, *A Catch on the Midnight Cats* (c. 1690) contrasts tomcats with human males in the matter of love-making.

Also sung around that time was "an account of a miserable old woman" who left all her money to her pet cat. Even in those days, people resented such an action. And, naturally, there were the bawdy songs including cats, far more risqué than their modern counterparts.

Many famous poems like Wordsworth's *The Kitten* and Thomas Gray's *The Cat and the Goldfish* have been set to music, as have cat nursery rhymes. Children's songs about cats have always been popular, and a listing of them would cover many pages. Then there are the special songs of famous cartoon cats like Felix and Sylvester.

Instrumental music with a cat theme is as plentiful as are songs about cats. Probably the best-known pieces are Zez Confrey's jazz classic, *Kitten on the Keys* (1921), and Domenico Scarlatti's (1685–1757) *The Cat's Fugue,* both of which imitate a cat running over the keys of a piano. Other instrumental cat pieces include polkas, fox trots, marches, scherzos and schottisches. To appeal to the young piano player there are many simple but effective compositions, some with words.

Mankind has always delighted in imitating animal sounds, and a good portion of instrumental cat music mimics cat vocalization. Composers have been giving us the equivalent of cat meows, spits, caterwauls — the works — since the seventeenth century, and they are so realistic in many cases that cats themselves are frequently fooled by them. A few ballets combine cat music with cat dancing. Tschaikovsky's *The Sleeping Beauty* is the most famous example: two dancers, portraying Puss in Boots and the White Cat, imitate feline movement while the orchestra meows and spits. Ballet itself honors the litheness of cats by naming one of its most difficult steps after them: the *pas de chat*, which emulates cat movement.

But cats have contributed more to music than lyrics and imitations of their vocalization and locomotion. They were furnishing music themselves from the sixteenth to the eighteenth centuries, when so-called cat organs were a popular form of entertainment. These consisted of narrow boxes in which cats were confined so they could not move. Their tails, which protruded from the boxes, were tied to cords attached to the organs' keys so that whenever a key was pressed, a tail was pulled causing the tail's owner to yowl. These yowls were the music which so amused the audiences.

Not quite so barbaric were the showmen in the seventeenth and eighteenth centuries who

Strangely enough, many of them like it, at least some of it. They may prefer certain types, certain instruments, certain voices. Others dislike all people-music, and still others ignore it completely. Most musicians or dilettantes of music seem to have been lucky in having cats who enjoy music, or perhaps it became an acquired taste. Those with a passion for cats performed or composed best when their furry critics were with them. Jenny Lind, so the story goes, used to sit at the window and sing to her pet cat, seated beside her. And so it was that she was discovered and her voice given to the world to enjoy.

Yes, the cat always does come back — wouldn't stay away from music no matter what.

trained their cats to be vocalists. At a given signal, which in one case at least was given by a monkey conductor, the cats meowed in concert. It makes you wonder how long it took the trainer to produce such a phenomenon.

The jazz world chose to incorporate the cat figuratively into its music. Early jazz enthusiasts began to call themselves *cats*. Negro *cats* became *black cats* and other types of cats appeared when needed, such as the *hep cat* and *scat cat*.

To many people, however, jazz merely signifies caterwauling. Those who dislike jazz go a step further and compare it to the feline phenomenon — the yowls, shrieks and other eerie sounds that wake you from a sound sleep in the dead of night. Music critics have also delighted in making a similar comparison, but with the voices of operatic sopranos. Nobody, it seems, enjoys listening to caterwauling.

What, then, do cats think of human music?

IT'S THE CAT'S MEOW

Yes, cats have inspired musical instruments, for centuries, catlike sounds have pervaded the air from the following:

Javanese saron. A type of chime made from a bronze slab, this instrument emits strange meowing sounds.

Samisen. Indigenous to Japan, this three-string guitarlike instrument is used by street singers and geisha.

Musical Saw. This handsaw is played by bending the blade with varrying tension and sounding it with a hammer or violin bow. What a mournful catlike sound it produces!

Sistrum. Used in the temple of Isis, this is an ancient Egyptian percussion instrument consisting of a thin metal frame with numerous metal rods or loops that jingle when shaken. Many depictions of the Egyptian cat gooddess show her holding a Sistrum.

Cat Organ. This sixteenth-century instrument was a box with holes in the bottom, in which cats were placed, their tails extended. To play the instrument, one pulled the cats' tails.

PET BLUES

Nancy Dolensek & Bill Rogers

When the sun goes down, I split from home, take my cat-nip, and I get stoned!

Now that's why — I get high — to for-get I'm a pet.

Moan-in', groan-in', com-plain-in', too — that's what I hear the whole day through.

Hey, big cat, keep the mice from the door, keep your litter off the floor —

You had your din-ner, can't have no more, get your-self lost while I mop off the floor —

Now that's why, I get high, to for-get I'm a pet.

Nancy Dolensek's cats swear this song is not biographical.
Bill Rogers has no cats but plays a mean piano.

CATERWAULING

How much do you know about the cat's contribution to the music world?
See if you can find the answers to the following hidden in the square.

1. Aaron Copland wrote this piece.
2. Appears in Edgar Stillman Kelley's *Alice in Wonderland* suite.
3. First published in 1893, this kitty did not stay away long.
4. Chopin's contribution to the cat world.
5. This cat is a musician in his own right.
6. By Stravinsky, it might put you to sleep.
7. A tom that's not hanging around Park Avenue!
8. *Morning Has Broken* for this Cat.
9. A feline who is on *terra firma*.
10. A cat who loves jazz.
11. Italian composer who wrote *The Cat's Fugue*.
12. Hungarian composer who performed *The Cat's Fugue*.
13. You might catch Ella Fitzgerald doing this kind of singing.
14. This Pretty Kitty of several decades ago batted her big _____.
15. *The Lady and the Tramp* crowd.
16. French composer and great cat lover.
17. Clergyman, philosopher, physician and music scholar, he always had a cat around.
18. Woodwinds denoted the cat's role in this composition by Prokofiev.
19. Thanks to her cat, this lady became famous.
20. Mortimer Wilson wrote about the funeral of this cat.

```
T T E B S S C H W E I T Z E R I S
T H E C A T C A M E B A C K C A B
U P E T E R A N D T H E W O L F T
T H O C H E S H I R E C A T S M N
L U L L A B I E S O F T H E C A T
K J A R E T O T O L A T E S A T E
S J A R E N A P O L I T A N T W O
S E V E R C Q N W Z T I S I P S F
C N C X Y L P F D C N D K H N B C
A N A E S T E R P T F A L E D L O
R Y L H I L T O S S H Q V P Z U S
L L I S Z T P A N T L E N S E E I
A I C F I R E M R N T O M T L E A
T N O L O N E A S S B O B O P Y M
T D S A S L E O N E L Y P L U E E
I K I T T E N O N T H E K E Y S S
L E A F D D O N U C A T V A L S E
```

Answers

1. *The Cat and the Mouse.*
2. Cheshire Cat.
3. *The Cat Came Back.*
4. *Cat Valse.*
5. *Kitten on the Keys.*
6. *Lullabies of the Cat.*
7. *Alley Cat.*
8. Stevens.
9. Eartha Kitt.
10. Hep.
11. Scarlatti.
12. Liszt.
13. Scat.
14. Blue Eyes.
15. Siamese.
16. Saint-Saens.
17. Schweitzer.
18. *Peter and the Wolf.*
19. Jenny Lind.
20. Calico.

IV. THE WELL BRED CAT

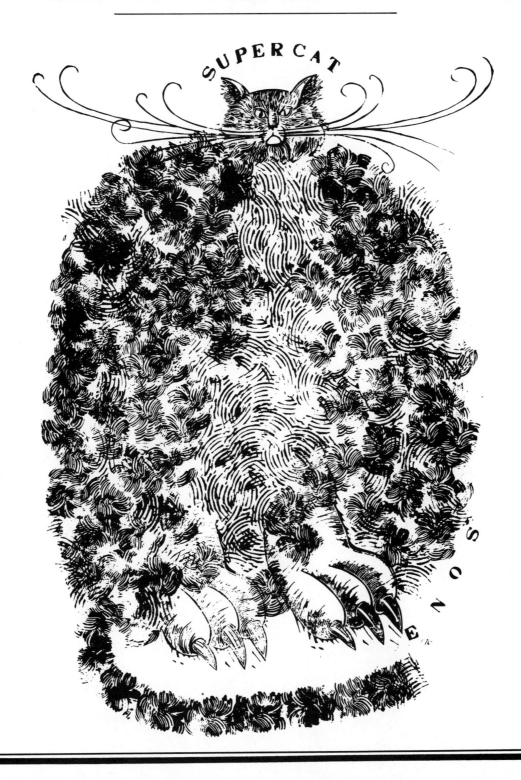

SUPER CAT

ENOS

THE BREDS

Will Thompson

CATS DIVIDE INTO two major groups: domestic and feral (wild). Both groups share many traits and mannerisms — purring, washing, playing, napping, intelligence, independence and characteristic body movements. We can appreciate the beauty and grace of all cats, but we are, quite naturally, most concerned with the cats with whom we share our home — the domestic cat.

Millions of cat owners love and prize their pets whether or not they are beautiful to look at or come from a long line of fancy forefathers. However, domestic cats do divide into two groups: non-pedigreed and pedigreed cats. As you might suspect, the non-pedigreed cat accounts for the bulk of domestic pets. More than 38 million cats in the United States alone are not registered. Non-pedigreed cats, for the most part, cannot be registered (there are limited exceptions), and their lineage cannot be traced.

The pedigreed cats are those whose ancestry or lineage is recorded and registered with a body such as the Cat Fanciers' Association, Incorporated. The C.F.A. is the largest registering organization for cats in the world; last year it registered approximately 36,000 cats. The enormous variety of pedigreed cats is unfamiliar to most cat owners. In this chapter we present pictures and descriptions of different breeds recognized by the C.F.A.

Breed Categories

For the most part, we will confine ourselves to those breeds of pedigreed cats eligible for competition under the rules of the Cat Fanciers' Association. (Some smaller registering bodies, as well as foreign registering bodies, do recognize other cats for competition in championship cat shows; additionally, cats are grouped differently by other cat associations.)

Show cats fall into four major categories which, in the C.F.A., are defined according to breeding and registration rules. The four categories are:

1. Natural Breed — Those cats reproduced by mating like-to-like, e.g., Persian-to-Persian or Siamese-to-Siamese. These include: Abyssinian, American Shorthair, Egyptian Mau, Japanese Bobtail, Main Coon, Manx, Persian, Russian Blue, Turkish Angora and Siamese.

2. Established Breed — Those cats who were originally produced by mating two or more Natural Breeds, but can now *only* be reproduced by mating like-to-like. The need for hybridization is no longer necessary or allowed; the breed is *established*. These include: Balinese, Birman, Burmese, Havana Brown and Korat.

3. Hybrid Breed — Those cats who are produced by mating two or more Natural Breeds. These include: Bombay, Colorpoint Shorthair, Exotic Shorthair, Himalayan and Oriental Shorthair.

4. Mutations — Those cats who were produced by mutation, thereby producing a new kind of cat such as the Rex.

All recognized breeds of domestic cats fall into one of these four categories.

Color and Pattern

Nature has provided the cat lover with an exciting spectrum of color and pattern to choose from. The non-pedigreed household companion cats wear coats defined only by nature's whimsy. For these delightful cats, both longhair and shorthair, no rules exist when it comes to color and pattern. Within genetic limits (that is, no green cats, basic-blue cats, purple, lemon-yellow), all colors and color combinations along with complete or partial patterns are produced in the household companion cat.

There are very stringent requirements relating to color and pattern of most show cats. These colors and patterns are rigidly defined. The following descriptions are adapted from the standards of the C.F.A.

Spectrum A

I. Solid Colors

A. White — Pure, glistening white. Nose leather and paw pads are pink. Eye color can be deep blue, brilliant copper or "odd-eyes" (one blue eye and one copper eye of equal color depth).

B. Black — Dense coal-black; sound from the roots to the tip of the fur and free from any tinge of rust on tips and no "smoky" undercoat. Nose leather is black, and paw pads may be black or brown. Eye color is brilliant copper.

C. Blue — Blue (a shade of gray), lighter shade (often called lavender-blue) preferred; one-level tone from nose to tip of tail; coat color must be sound to the roots; a sound darker shade is more acceptable than an unsound lighter shade. Nose leather and paw pads are blue. Eye color is brilliant copper.

D. Red — Deep, rich, clear, brilliant red and *without* shading, markings or ticking. Lips and chin are the same color as the coat. Nose leather and paw pads are brick-red. Eye color is brilliant copper.

E. Cream — One-level shade of buff cream, without markings; sound to the root; lighter shades preferred. Nose leather and paw pads are pink. Eye color is brilliant copper.

II. Shaded

A. Chinchilla Silver — Pure white undercoat; coat on the back, flanks, head and tail is lightly tipped with black, giving it a characteristic sparkling, silver appearance. Legs may be slightly shaded with tipping. Chin, ear tufts, stomach and chest are pure white. Rims of the eyes, lips and nose are outlined with black. Nose leather is brick-red; paw pads are black. Eye color is green or blue-green.

B. Shaded Silver — White undercoat, with a mantle of black tipping shading down from the sides, face and tail from dark on the ridge to white on the chin, chest, stomach and under the tail. Legs are the same tone as the face. (The general effect is much darker than the Chinchilla Silver; the perfect Shaded Silver gives a pewter appearance.) Rims of the eyes, lips and nose are outlined with black. Nose leather is brick-red; paw pads are black. Eye color is green or blue-green.

C. Shell Cameo (Red Chinchilla) — White undercoat; coat on the back, flanks, head and tail is sufficiently tipped with red to give a characteristic, sparkling appearance. Face and legs may be very slightly shaded with tipping. Chin, ear tufts, stomach and chest are white. Nose leather, rims of eyes and paw pads are rose. Eye color is brilliant copper.

D. Shaded Cameo (Red Shaded) — White undercoat with a mantle of red tipping shading down the sides, face and tail from dark on the ridge to white on the chin, chest, stomach and under the tail. Legs are the same tone as the face. (General efffect is to appear much redder than the Shell Cameo.) Nose leather, rims of eyes and paw pads are rose. Eye color is brilliant copper.

III. Smoke

A. Black Smoke — White undercoat, deeply tipped with black. (In repose, the cat appears to be solid black; in motion, its white undercoat is clearly apparent.) Points and mask are black, with a narrow band of white at the base of the hairs next to the skin which may be seen only when the fur is parted. Ruff (frill) and ear tufts are light silver in color. Nose leather and paw pads are black. Eye color is brilliant copper.

B. Blue Smoke — Same as Black Smoke *except* substitute *blue* for black in description of coat. Frill and ear tufts are white. Nose leather and paw pads are blue. Eye color is brilliant copper.

C. Red Smoke — White undercoat, deeply tipped with red. (In repose, the cat appears red; when in motion, its white undercoat is clearly apparent.) Points and mask are red, with a narrow band of white at the base of the hairs next to the skin which may be seen only when the fur is parted. Nose leather, paw pads and rims of eyes are rose. Eye color is brilliant gold.

IV. Tabbies

Tabbies are patterned cats. There are two recognized tabby patterns, Classic Tabby and Mackerel Tabby.

Classic Tabby Pattern. The markings of the pattern are dense, clearly defined and broad. The legs are evenly barred with bracelets coming up to meet the body markings. The tail is evenly ringed. There are several unbroken necklaces on the neck and upper chest (the more, the better). There are frown marks on the forehead which form the pattern of an intricate M. An unbroken line runs back from the outer corner of the eye, and there are swirls on the cheeks. Vertical lines run over the back of the head and extend to the shoulder markings, which are in the shape of a butterfly with both upper and lower wings distinctly outlined and marked with dots inside the outlines of butterfly wings. Back markings consist of a vertical line down the spine from butterfly to tail with a vertical stripe paralleling it on each side; the three stripes are well-separated by stripes of the ground color; these lines are referred to as "spinals." There is a large, solid blotch on each side encircled by one or more unbroken rings; these are referred to as "bull's-eyes." The side markings (bull's-eyes) should be the same on both sides. There is a double, vertical row of "buttons" on the chest and stomach. The Classic Tabby Pattern consists of all of these elements (the M, butterflies, spinals, bull's-eyes, necklaces, bracelets and buttons), which are of a dense, clearly defined color on a contrasting ground color.

Mackerel Tabby Pattern. The markings are dense, clearly defined and consist of all narrow pencilings. The legs are evenly barred with narrow bracelets, coming up to meet the body markings. The tail is barred, and there are distinct necklaces on the neck and chest which are like so many chains. The head is barred with an M on the forehead, and unbroken lines run back from the eyes. There are lines running down the head to meet the shoulders; the spine lines run together to form a narrow saddle. Narrow pencilings run around the body. The body pattern may be likened to the cloud patterns in a buttermilk sky.

All colors of tabbies occur in both the Classic Tabby Pattern and the Mackerel Tabby Pattern.

A. Silver Tabby — Ground color (including lips and chin) is pale, clear silver; markings are dense black. Nose leather is brick-red; paw pads are black. Eye color is green or hazel.

B. Red Tabby — Ground color (including lips and chin) is red; markings are deep, rich red. Nose leather is brick-red; paw pads are pink. Eye color is brilliant copper.

C. Brown Tabby — Ground color is brilliant coppery brown; markings are dense black. Lips and chin are the same shade as the rings around the eyes; back of the leg is black from the paw to the heel. Nose leather is brick-red; paw pads are black or brown. Eye color is brilliant copper.

D. Cream Tabby — Ground color (including lips and chin) is very pale cream; markings are buff or cream, sufficiently darker than the ground color to afford a good contrast but remaining a tone and shade of cream. Nose leather and paw pads are pink. Eye color is brilliant copper.

E. Blue Tabby — Ground color (including lips and chin) is pale bluish ivory; markings are a very deep blue, thereby affording a good contrast with the ground color; warm, fawn overtones (or patina) cover the entire coat. Nose leather is old rose; paw pads are rose. Eye color is brilliant copper.

F. Cameo Tabby — Ground color is off-white; markings are red. Nose leather and paw pads are rose. Eye color is brilliant copper.

V. Parti-Colors

A. Tortoise-Shell — Basically, a black cat with clearly defined, unbrindled and well-broken patches of red and cream on both the body and the extremities; a blaze of red or cream is desirable. Eye color is brilliant copper.

B. Calico — White with unbrindled patches of black and red; the white is predomi-

nant on the underparts. (The Calico looks as if a black-and-red spotted cat had stepped in a pail of milk, turning the under half of the cat white. Small red and black spots on a predominantly white coat do *not* mean the cat is a Calico; this unrecognized color is called Harlequin!) Eye color is brilliant copper.

C. Dilute Calico — White with unbrindled patches of blue and cream; white predominant on underparts. Eye color is brilliant copper.

D. Blue-Cream — Blue with clearly defined, well-broken patches of solid cream on both the body and the extremities; the paler shades of blue and cream are preferred. Eye color is brilliant copper.

E. Bi-Color — Black-and-white, blue-and-white, red-and-white, *or* cream-and-white with the white being the feet, legs, undersides, chest and muzzle; an inverted V-blaze on the face is desirable; white under the tail and a white collar are allowable. Eye color is brilliant copper.

Spectrum B

This spectrum describes the color point pattern and the four classic colors: Seal Point, Chocolate Point, Blue Point and Lilac Point.

The color point pattern consists of two basic parts: the body color and the contrasting point color. There must be a definite contrast between the body color and the point color; however, the body color usually darkens with age. This pattern has also been referred to as "temperature points," as the point color appears on the cooler extremities of the cat.

The points are the mask, ears, legs, feet, tail and sex organs; they are all of the same color density and are well-defined. The mask covers the entire face (including the whisker pads) and is connected to the ears by tracings; it should not extend over the top of the head (producing an undesirable "hood"). There should not be any ticking or white hairs in the points. The eye color is deep, vivid blue in all cases.

A. Seal Point — Body color is even, pale fawn to cream, warm in tone, and shades to a lighter color on the stomach and chest. Points are deep seal-brown. Nose leather and paw pads are the same color as the points.

B. Chocolate Point — body color is ivory with no shading. Points are milk-chocolate in color and warm in tone. Nose leather and paw pads are cinnamon-pink.

C. Blue Point — Body color is bluish-white, cold in tone, and shades gradually to white on the stomach and chest. Points are deep blue. Nose leather and paw pads are slate-blue.

D. Lilac Point — Body color is glacial white with no shading. Points are frosty gray with a pinkish tone. Nose leather and paw pads are lavender-pink.

THE BREEDS

ABYSSINIAN

In general, the Abyssinian is a colorful cat of medium size, well-muscled, alert, active; of all domestic cats, the Aby is the most feral in appearance.

With large, alert and moderately pointed ears, the Aby is an appealing cat who always appears to be ready to go! The head is a slightly rounded wedge completely without flat planes. The eyes are large, brilliant, very expressive and almond-shaped.

The Abyssinian's body is medium in length, and is lithe and graceful. A happy, busy cat, the Aby exhibits characteristic careful but eager movement and shows a lively interest in all surroundings.

The voice is small and is often referred to as "bell-like."

The coat is soft, silky, fine-textured, very dense and resilient to the touch.

There are two colors of Abys: Ruddy and Red.

Ruddy. Reddish brown coat ticked with various shades of darker brown and black; the extreme outer tip of the hair is the darkest, with an orange-brown undercoat ruddy to the skin; undersides and inside of the forelegs are of a tint to harmonize with the overall color; preference is given to the unmarked burnt sienna. Nose leather is tile-red; paw pads are black or brown. Eye color is gold or green (the more richness and

depth of color, the better).

Red. Warm, glowing red, distinctly ticked with chocolate-brown; the deeper shades of red are preferred. Ears and tail are tipped with chocolate brown. Eye color is gold or green (the richer, the better).

The Aby has long been called the cat from the Blue Nile; fanciers identify this cat with the cats of ancient Egypt.

THE BREEDS

AMERICAN SHORTHAIR

This is the All-American Cat and is indigenous to the United States. He adapts himself to the needs of man and is thought of as a working cat.

Also called the domestic shorthair at one time, this cat has shared the American fireside since pre-Revolutionary times. There is a tale of a domestic shorthair sharing the *Mayflower* in the 1600s with the Pilgrims.

The protector of the farm and home, he easily adapts to all life styles — from the poet's library, the prelate's palace, to the simple sod hut of the pioneer settlers. The American Shorthair has maintained a check on the rodent population and has provided the feelings of warmth associated with the home and fireside.

The ASH is recognized in all colors and patterns of Spectrum A.

In appearance, this cat can be likened to a trained athlete with great latent power in reserve and well-developed, rippling musculature.

The head is large, giving the impression of an oblong slightly longer than wide. The neck is medium in length, muscular and strong. He has a square muzzle, firm and well-developed chin, medium, wide-set ears which are slightly rounded, and round wide eyes which are set well apart and are bright, clear and alert.

The body is medium to large in size, well-knit, powerful and hard, with a well-developed chest and heavy shoulders.

The legs are medium in length, as is the tail.

Overall, the American Shorthair is a solid citizen, good companion, powerful ally and protector of the home and hearth.

THE BREEDS

BALINESE

The Balinese is a svelte, dainty cat with long, tapering lines; it is lithe and elegant in appearance. It falls into Spectrum B in color and pattern.

This cat is the longhaired version of the short tight-coated Siamese. Beneath the long, fine and silky coat is the tight-muscled, slim and streamlined body.

Having appeared naturally in litters of pure-bred Siamese, the Balinese are believed by many fanciers to be a coat-length mutation of the Siamese. They are classified as an Established Breed and can only be produced by Balinese being mated to Balinese.

The head is a long, tapering wedge; the wedge starts at the nose and flares out to the tips of the ears in *straight* lines forming a triangle. In profile, a long, straight line is seen from the top of the head to the tip of the nose.

The muzzle is fine and wedge-shaped. The ears are strikingly large, pointed, wide at the base, and continue the lines of the wedge. The eyes are almond-shaped and must never be crossed.

The Balinese body is medium in size and is a balanced combination of fine bones and firm muscles. The body is tubular in shape and is the same width at the shoulders and hips.

The legs are long, slim and elegant. The tail bone structure is long, thin, and tapers to a fine point. The tail hair spreads out and presents a plumelike appearance.

The Balinese is a study in slim elegance but must never be emaciated or weak. A strong and healthy cat when well cared for, the Balinese appeals to those who love both the Siamese refined, streamlined conformation and the beauty of a long, silky coat.

THE BREEDS

THE BREEDS

BIRMAN

The Birman, or Sacred Cat of Burma, is believed by fanciers to have originated as a breed in the temples of Burma. This lovely, white-gloved longhair falls under Color Spectrum B (except for the four white feet).

Having appeared in France in the early 1920s, the Birman nearly disappeared during World War II. Fortunately, enough cats were conserved to provide for their resurgence in the postwar years.

The most important single physical feature of this cat is his white gloves. On the front paws, the gloves end in an *even* line across the paw at the third joint; on the back paws, the white gloves cover the entire paw and must end in a point (called "the laces") which goes up the back of the hock.

In their native Burma, the Birmans are accorded special treatment since many believe them to be reincarnations of Burmese priests. A charming legend holds that the Birman descends from a loyal white cat who placed his paws on his priest-master at the moment the priest was struck down by temple raiders. With paws on his priest companion's lifeless face, the white cat faced the sapphire-eyed golden statue of the goddess who watches over the transmutation of souls. She rewarded the faithful cat by changing his color to gold (except for the four white feet) and his eyes to blue. Upon death, these cats carry to paradise the priestly souls with which they are imbued.

The head is broad and rounded. The ears are medium in length; the eyes are almost round. The body is long; the legs are medium in length and heavy; the paws are large, round and firm; the tail is medium in length. The coat is long and silken-textured, with a heavy ruff around the neck, and the hair is slightly curly on the stomach; the fur, because of its texture, does not mat. There must be no visible kink in the tail; crossed eyes are not permitted.

THE BREEDS

BOMBAY

An interesting and very recent addition to the American Show Bench is this shiny black hybrid cat produced by crossing the tight-coated sable brown Burmese with the American Shorthair. One of the Bombays' leading proponents refers to them as the cats with the patent leather coat and copper penny eyes. Of all cats on today's show bench, the Bombay is evaluated more on coat and color (55 percent) than any other.

The coat is described as being fine, short and satin-like in texture; it is very close-lying, producing a patent leather sheen no other black-colored cat possesses. The jet-black patent leather coat color is black to its roots. The nose leather and paw pads are black. The eye color ranges from yellow to deep copper — the greater the depth and brilliance, the better. As stated, in judging evaluation 55 percent of the Bombay standard is concerned with body color, eye color and the shortness, texture and close-lying of the coat.

In conformation, the Bombay is nearly a duplicate of the Burmese. The head is rounded and has no flat planes whether viewed from the front or the side. The face is full, with considerable breadth between the eyes, tapering slightly to a short, well-developed muzzle. When viewed in profile, there is a visible nose break.

The ears are medium in size and are set well apart on a rounded skull; they are alert, tilted slightly forward and are broad at the base with slightly rounded tips. The eyes are set far apart and have a *rounded* aperture.

The body is medium in size, muscular and neither compact nor rangy. The legs are in proportion to the body and the straight medium-length tail.

The Bombay must *not* have a kinked or abnormal tail, white spots (lockets or buttons), incorrect nose leather or paw pad color, or green eyes.

THE BREEDS

BURMESE

The overall impression of the perfect Burmese would be of a medium-sized cat whose short, close-lying, satin-textured coat of deep sable brown covers a substantial bone structure, good muscular development and surprising weight for his size. Add to this impression the expressive yellow-to-gold eyes, round in aperture, and a sweet-faced expression, and you have the Burmese.

Burmese were developed in the United States by the hard work and knowledgeable, selective breeding by dedicated cat lovers. All Burmese can be traced back to a single brown female (herself most likely a Siamese hybrid) named Wong Mau. Wong Mau, it is believed, was brought to the United States in 1930 by a sailor whose ship reached port in New Orleans. She eventually was given to Dr. Joseph C. Thompson of San Francisco, California. Dr. Thompson fortunately realized that Wong Mau was an unusual treasure; he subsequently set himself the task of perpetuating this sable brown breed. With the assistance of geneticists and responsible breeders, an experimental breeding program was devised. The complexities of the program were increased by the lack of a sable brown male and Wong Mau's own hybrid ancestry. Fortunately for lovers of these little brown cats, the many problems were solved and today's sable Burmese are the pleasing result. Interestingly, Wong Mau's daughter, Topaz Mau, closely resembles many of today's show Burmese.

The Burmese head can be described as a ball with a tiny strawberry-box-shaped muzzle. The head is pleasingly rounded, *without* flat planes whether viewed from the front or the side. The face is full, with considerable breadth between the eyes, tapering slightly to a short, well-developed muzzle (the strawberry box). In profile, there is a visible nose break.

The ears are medium in

(Continued on page 126)

THE BREEDS

COLORPOINT SHORTHAIR

The colorpoint pattern of the four classic colors of Siamese (Seal Point, Chocolate Point, Blue Point and Lilac Point) is admired and appreciated by cat lovers the world over. Responsible breeders found the colorpoint pattern not only beautiful but also challenging. The pattern (defined in Color Spectrum B) consists of two parts: the clearly defined points and the contrasting body color. Breeders were challenged by the limitation of the four classic Siamese colors and set themselves the problem of extending the colorpoint range to include both additional colors *and* patterns to be contained within the points. They wished to retain the body

style and conformation of the Siamese but were inspired to extend the color and pattern range beyond the four classic colors.

To meet this challenge, the breeders turned to hybridization between the Siamese and the American Shorthair. From the Siamese, they extracted Siamese type and colorpoint factor; from the American Shorthair, they extracted only color and pattern. That they succeeded in solving this genetic problem is demonstrated by the presence of Grand Champion Colorpoint Shorthairs on the show bench.

The Colorpoint Shorthair is a svelte, dainty cat with long,

tapering lines, very lithe and muscular. He is identical in appearance to the Siamese in all respects *except* color. (A detailed description of the Siamese conformation appears in the Siamese Breed Section of this book.) It is particularly interesting to note that the hybridization between the Siamese and American Shorthair has produced Colorpoint shorthairs with amazing eye color. Many Colorpoint Shorthairs have intense deep-blue eyes which sometimes have an electric quality that produces a cat of astonishing beauty.

Colorpoint Shorthairs can

(Continued on page 126)

THE BREEDS
EGYPTIAN MAU

The Egyptian Mau is the only domesticated natural breed of spotted cat. Having been bred from cats imported from Egypt, the Egyptian Mau's spotted coat brings to mind the fresco from a tomb at Thebes which is dated 1500 B.C. The fresco depicts a hunting scene, most probably on the River Nile, in which a spotted cat is demonstrating his training in hunting ducks for the Egyptian hunter. Similarly marked cats are depicted in a papyrus of the Twentieth Dynasty.

The Mau's conformation is a balance between the compactness of the Burmese and the svelte elegance of the Siamese. The general appearance is that of an active, colorful, spotted cat of medium size and well-developed musculature. Three colors of Egyptian Mau are recognized; all three require light or gooseberry green eye color (amber cast is, however, acceptable).

The Mau head is described as a modified, slightly rounded wedge without flat planes; the brow, cheek and profile all show a gentle contour. There is a slight rise from the bridge of the nose to the forehead, which then flows into the arched neck without a break. The muzzle is not pointed. Allowance is made for broad heads and stud jowls in males.

The ears are alert, large and moderately pointed; they are broad at the base and upstanding, with ample width between the ears. The hair on the ears is short and close-lying; the inner ear is a delicate, almost transparent shell pink. The ears may be tufted.

The eyes are large and alert, almond-shaped with a slight upward slant (toward the ears). The eye aperture is neither round nor "Oriental."

The body is medium in length and graceful, showing well-developed muscular strength. The hind legs are longer than the front legs.

(Continued on page 127)

THE BREEDS

EXOTIC SHORTHAIR

Occurring in all colors and patterns of Color Spectrum A, the Exotic Shorthair first gained the attention of cat fanciers in the colors of chinchilla and shaded silver. This beautiful "man-made" breed was produced by serious breeders through matings between the Persian and any shorthair. The resulting kittens were carefully mated in order to produce the desired medium-coated Persian-style cat of today. Currently, only the hybrid cross of Persian to American Shorthair is permitted; no other hybridizing is allowed.

In appearance, the Exotic Shorthair is identical to the Persian, except for one very important feature: length of coat. Unlike the Persian's long, flowing coat, immense ruff and full tail, the Exotic's coat is *medium* in length, dense, soft in texture, glossy and full of life. As stated, the conformation of the Exotic Shorthair is identical with that of the Persian. (Refer to the Persian Section for a detailed description of the conformation.)

The Exotic Shorthair is an exquisite addition to the rolls of pedigreed cats. A gap was filled by the Exotic for those who admire the beauty of the Persian but who are not willing or prepared to cope with the problems inherent in the Persian's long, flowing coat. The pleasing expression of the Persian has been retained, as have the large, round eyes, short, snubbed nose, cobby body, short, thick legs and small ears. For today's busy urbanite, the medium-coated Exotic Shorthair provides both beauty and companionship.

THE BREEDS

HAVANA BROWN

The Havana Brown, a solid-colored, rich, warm, mahogany brown shorthaired cat, was first produced by nature. A search of cat records in England reveals that a solid-brown shorthair cat was exhibited in 1894 under the category "Swiss Mountain Cat." Another such cat was shown in 1930 under the category "Brown Cat." From time to time, additional shorthaired brown cats appeared at English shows.

Even though the solid-brown shorthair was not recognized for championship competition, English breeders decided to work on the genetic problem of producing a solid-brown shorthair which would breed true, that is, produce similar solid-brown kittens when mated. Working with Siamese, Russian Blues and shorthair cats of unknown ancestry, the breeders were successful and the solid-brown shorthair was established. The breed was named Havana Brown, not because of any relationship to Havana, Cuba, but rather because of the color, which is close to that of the rich, tobacco brown color of both the cat and Havana cigars. In England, the Havana Brown has been renamed the Chestnut Brown.

Nonetheless, a Havana by any other name remains a sweet and beautiful cat.

The Havana's head is slightly longer than it is wide. There is a *distinct* profile stop at the eyes. The head narrows to a rounded muzzle, with a slight break behind the whiskers.

The neck is in proportion to the body.

The whiskers are *brown!*

The ears are large, round-tipped and wide-set on the head, but not flaring. There is very little hair inside or outside the ear. Similarly, often there is

(Continued on page 128)

THE BREEDS

HIMALAYAN

If a book were to be written titled *The Gentle Art of Breeding,* or perhaps (à la Izaak Walton) *The Compleat Breeder,* the high point of the book would be a section devoted to the Himalayan. In this cat, breeders triumphed in producing a Persian-style cat with Siamese coloration and pattern. The Himalayan has gained immense popularity and public acceptance. Within the past twenty-five years or so, this magnificent hybrid has surpassed all other breeds in popularity except those two from whom it was predominantly developed — the Siamese (number one) and the Persian (number two). In producing the Himalayan, breeders had to work with the problems of dominant and recessive genes. Without belaboring the point, suffice it to say that every desired genetic trait is recessive — longhair and colorpoint pattern!

Himalayan-style cats appeared from time to time prior to serious efforts to develop this breed. A book on cats published in Paris in 1932, *Nos Compagnons . . . Les Chats* by M. Boilève de la Gombaudière, President of the Cat Club of Paris, pictures a Himalayan-type cat identified as "*Métis persan et siamois.*" These early cats were also called Khmers.

In England and the United Kingdom, breeders worked not only with the Siamese and Persians, but also with other shorthair colors including the Chestnut Brown. American breeders confined their hybridizing efforts to the use of Siamese and Persians only. A great deal of genetic research, time and effort were expended to produce the Himalayan. One early breeder pointed out that nineteen cats were used to produce her first successful

(Continued on page 128)

JAPANESE BOBTAIL

Classified as a Natural Breed, the Japanese Bobtail was first imported into the United States in 1969. Considered by most fanciers as the indigenous cat of Japan, it is possible that this cat originated in China or Korea.

The Japanese Bobtail has been present for centuries in Japan. In its most popular and traditional coat color and pattern, the cat is believed to bring good luck to the household in which it resides. The traditional good-luck color is the MI-KE (pronounced *mee'-kay*), which is jet-black, brilliant red-orange, and white, the black and red-orange forming well-defined spots or irregular shapes on a pristine white ground color.

In general, the Japanese Bobtail gives the impression of a well-muscled, clean-lined, slender cat of medium size. With uniquely set eyes, high cheekbones and a long nose defined by parallel lines, the face is that of Japanese cast. The distinctive short bobtail is usually strong and rigid (except at the base) rather than jointed — and may be either straight or composed of one or several curves and angles. The tail is usually carried upright when the cat is relaxed and is covered by hair which is longer and thicker than the medium-lengthed, soft and silky body coat. The tail hair grows outward in all directions creating a pom-pom or bunny-like shape which disguises the underlying bone structure.

The head forms an almost perfect equilateral triangle. The ears are large, set wide apart and at right angles to the head; they do not flare outward. The muzzle is fairly broad and rounds into a noticeable whisker break. The eyes are large and oval, wide, alert and set into the skull at a pronounced slant (when viewed in profile). The body is medium in size, long and lean. The legs are long, slender and high but are not dainty or fragile in

(Continued on page 129)

THE BREEDS

KORAT

In the Bangkok National Museum of Bangkok, Thailand, hangs a papyrus book, the *Smud Khoi*, on which are painted pictures of Thai cats, each of which is accompanied by a poem. The work of a Thai monk, the papyrus is dated by some historians as early as 1350 A.D.; other experts place the work c. 1767. Depicted is the beautiful silver-blue, green-gold-eyed Korat. (In trans-literation, the cat's name is KORAJ; however, the Thai pronunciation of "j" is equivalent to a soft "t," hence the name Korat.) Found in the northeastern province of Korat, these cats are also called by their native Thai name, *Si-Sawat*. An Established Breed, the term *Si-Sawat* can be translated as a cat with the color of the *"Look–Sawat*, a wild fruit plant whose seed is the silver blue color identified with the Korat.

The Korat is considered a good luck cat. This Thai native has long been cherished by the Thai people and originally could only be obtained by being given as a gift from one owner to another who was deemed worthy of such a valued gift. The silver tipping signifies silver to the tradesman and merchant, young rice plants (the green-gold eyes) and rain clouds to the farm-dweller, and a happy marriage and home to a bride.

The Korat was exhibited in England at a show in 1896; in 1906, *The Journal of Cat Genetics* refers to silver-blue cats existing on the Korat Plateau of Thailand. Imported into the United States sometime in 1930–1940, the Korats of Thai imported to the United States numbered six in 1965. Anxious to protect the purity of cats of Thai ancestry, only those cats having proof of import via documentation were registered as true Korats. (A few may have been registered without proper import papers; however today's Korats can be, for the most part, traced to Thai beginnings. The Korat Cat Fanciers Association,

(Continued on page 129)

MAINE COON

The Maine Coon Cat, a Natural Breed, is to other breeds of longhaired cats as the American Shorthair is to other short-haired breeds. Each has an ancestry which is obscure but which is identified with the early history of the United States. Each has come to be accepted as an "indigenous" American Cat — one with a semi-long, shaggy coat, the other with a short, thick, even and hard-textured coat.

Some cat experts are of the opinion that the Maine Coon is a by-product of random matings between the already present shorthaired domestic cats who may have been brought from England by the

Pilgrims in 1640 and Angora or Persian Cats brought to this country by the far-ranging, seafaring New Englanders of the 1800s. Whether or not this is actually the origin of the cat, the Maine Coon has been valued by New England cat lovers as being the biggest, smartest, most beautiful cat anywhere. Early legends held that these robust cats with snow-shoe feet were part-raccoon; size and tabby markings on early Maine Coon Cats contributed to the belief in this biological impossibility.

Very proud — and justi-fiably so — of their super-sized cats, cat lovers in Maine have kept registration and pedigree information on the

Maine Coon Cats for many years. Each year, a Maine State Champion Coon Cat is chosen and proudly exhibited.

The size and coat are the most readily recognizable features of the true Maine Coon Cat. The body is muscular, broad-chested, medium to large in size, and long — with all parts in proportion to create a rectangular appearance. The legs are substantial, wide-set, of medium length and in proportion with the body; the paws are large, round and well-tufted. This latter feature produces paws well suited to "snowshoe-ing" it across the

(Continued on page 130)

THE BREEDS
MANX

Set in the Irish Sea off the west coast of England is the 221-square-mile Isle of Man, the home of the unique cat named for it, the Manx.

Various myths attempt to explain the origin of the tailless cat or link it to the short- or bob-tailed cats of the Orient, but modern scientific research by Dr. Neil Todd of Harvard Medical School has determined that the Manx cat has a different phenotype and is genetically a different strain from that of the cats in the Far East. Generally identified by the complete lack of a tail, the Manx cat actually exists in three tail variations:

1. *Rumpy:* total absence of tail; a dimple or hollow is found where the tail normally begins.

2. *Stumpy:* a tail stump of one or more vertebrae is present, but the tail is incomplete. The length is approximately one to five inches.

3. *Full-tail or Longie:* a complete tail is present.

All three tail lengths can be and often are produced in one litter of purebred Manx breeding. Only the tailless Manx is acceptable for show. However, even with a partial or full tail, good Manx cats are recognizable by other characteristics.

Other identifying characteristics of the breed include the arched back which contributes to the Manx's short, round look. The unique Manx coat is also an important identifying characteristic. The distinctive double coat is beautifully plush, a thick, cottony undercoat topped by an overcoat of harder glossier guard hairs.

The overall impression of the Manx should be one of roundness: rounded head, round muzzle, round broad chest, substantial round short front legs, arched back, round about the ribs, *and* round about the rump. This repetition of curves and circular lines

(Continued on page 130)

ORIENTAL SHORTHAIR

Provisionally accepted for show, the Oriental Shorthair is a Hybrid Breed produced by the knowledgeable crossing of Siamese, American Shorthairs, Colorpoint Shorthairs and other Oriental Shorthairs.

The conformation of the Siamese has been combined with most colors of Spectrum A; the colorpoint pattern of Spectrum B has been eliminated.

The Oriental Shorthair Standard differs only in minor points from that of the Siamese. The Oriental Shorthair Standard adds: males may be somewhat larger than females; the tail is thin at the base; the show specimen is penalized for having crossed-eyes.

The major difference between the Siamese and the Oriental Shorthair is in color and pattern. Also, the Oriental Shorthair allows green eye color; amber is permitted except in the white Oriental Shorthair where the eye color may be green or bright blue; odd-eyed white Oriental Shorthairs are not accepted for show.

Colors of the Oriental Shorthair: White, Ebony (Black), Blue, Chestnut (Self-Chocolate), Lavender, Red, Cream, Silver, Cameo, Ebony (Black) Smoke, Blue Smoke, Chestnut (Chocolate) Smoke, Lavender Smoke and Cameo (Red) Smoke. Tabby-patterned Oriental Shorthairs are recognized in Classic Tabby Pattern, Mackerel Tabby Pattern and Spotted Tabby Pattern.

The Oriental Shorthair will appeal greatly to those who admire the elegance of the Siamese appearance, but who are also attracted to more exotic colorations. Many breeders have worked very hard to transfer the colorpoint pattern to the longhaired, Persian-style Himalayan; now many are working to transfer colors and patterns to the Siamese-style cat.

THE BREEDS

PERSIAN

The Persian is the *ne plus ultra* of pedigreed cats. Admired by cat lovers for its beautiful, long, fine-textured, glossy coat, sweet expression, round face, large round eyes, small ears, huge ruff and frill and full-brush tail, the Persian is the aristocrat of the domestic cat world.

The origin of this Natural Breed will probably never be proved. Some authorities place the origin of the ancestors of the Persian in Persia and Turkey. Longhaired cats are known to have existed in the nineteenth century in Afghanistan, Burma, China, Persia, Russia and Turkey. The breed is believed by some naturalists to be descended from an Asiatic wild

cat. Whatever its ancestry, the Persian cat stands supreme in its popularity as the most popular longhaired breed.

The Persian occurs in all colors of Spectrum A.

The head of the Persian is round and massive with great breadth of skull; it is well-set on a short thick neck. The ears are small, tipped, tilted forward and are not unduly open at the base; they are set far apart and low on the head, fitting into, but not distorting, the rounded contour of the head.

The eyes are large, round and full, set far apart and brilliant; they give a sweet expression to the face.

The nose is short, snub and

broad. There is a definite nose break which is clearly apparent when the head is viewed in profile. The cheeks are full; the jaws are broad and powerful; and the chin is full and well-developed.

The body of the Persian is low on the legs, deep in the chest, equally massive across the shoulders and rump, with a short well–rounded middle piece. The cat is large or medium in size, but quality is more important than size. The back is level; the legs are large, round and firm. As with all pedigreed cats, the Persian has five toes on the front paws and

(Continued on page 131)

THE BREEDS

REX

The Rex is a mutation. It is a spontaneous mutation of the domestic cat which accentuates the characteristic features of the domestic by creating a longer, slighter and more agile feline than its ancestors. The Rex's arched back and muscular hind legs insure flexibility for high jumps, quick starts, changes of direction and amazing speed. When handled, the Rex feels warm to the touch because of its short, tightly curled coat of the softest fur imaginable.

The first Rex discovered was in 1950 on a farm in Bodmin Moor, Cornwall, England. Named Kallibunker, his sire was unknown and his dam was a normal-coated shorthair. His owner, Mrs. Nina Ennismore, sought expert advice concerning the future of the kitten and a breeding program was defined which would perpetuate the mutation and begin the Rex breed. The first step was to breed Kallibunker back to his dam; this cross resulted in several curly coated progeny. Continued outcrossing to normal-coated cats with successive inbreeding of resultant progeny further established the Kallibunker bloodline of Rex (Cornish Rex).

The second discovery of the spontaneous Rex mutation was made in Germany by Dr. Scheur-Karpin. This Rex, Lammchen, was a female and her breeding was similarly and carefully planned to assure continued development of the Lammchen bloodlines (German Rex).

The next important mutation was the Devon Rex. This kitten, Kirklee, was discovered in 1960. Further genetic research resulted in the nomenclature of Devon Rex, Cat Gene 2; Gene 1 was assigned to the Kallibunker bloodline.

In San Bernardino, California, a longhair version of the very short-coated Rex was found in an animal shelter. This longhair version of the Rex was named the Marcel. Lack of in-

(Continued on page 131)

THE BREEDS

RUSSIAN BLUE

There are several breeds of shorthairs whose blue color is recognized by cat fanciers. The variance among the many blue shorthairs is apparent to the trained eye if the cats are outstanding examples of their particular breed. However, if the specimen is of poor quality, not even the expert can be completely sure of the actual breed.

The following are recognized breeds of blue shorthairs: Blue American Shorthair, British Blue, Maltese (believed by some to be merely a fancy name for a shorthaired blue cat), Korat, Chartreux, Blue Burmese, Blue Oriental Shorthair, Blue Exotic Shorthair, Blue Japanese Bobtail (not eas-ily confused if a pom-pom tail is in evidence), Blue Manx "Lon-gie" (Normal-tailed Manx) and Russian Blue.

Each of these cats has certain distinct characteristics which identify the particular breed. For example, each blue breed has differently colored eyes. Also, the distinct features tend to become a bit hazy. If the body type, head type and conformation are mediocre, the breeds can easily be confused.

The most easily identifiable characteristic of the Russian Blue is its coat, which is short, dense, fine and plush. The perfect Russian Blue coat can best be likened to that of the short-coated beaver. It is possible in both the coat of the beaver and in the proper Russian Blue to trace designs with your finger, and the designs will remain until you brush them out of the coat by stroking it. This unusual blue-colored coat is seldom seen in shows today because Russian Blues which have outstanding coats seldom have good conformation and type; those with good body type lack outstanding coats. In short, the Russian Blue is a very challenging breed with which to work.

The origin of the Russian Blue breed is confused and unknown. Some experts believe this cat first appeared in Russia

(Continued on page 131)

THE BREEDS
SIAMESE

The most popular of all breeds, the Siamese is generally agreed to have originated in Thailand (Siam). How much truth there is in the story that these elegant colorpoint-patterned cats were the royal property of the King of Siam and were trained to guard the Royal Palace by pacing its walls and leaping upon the backs of unwary intruders is certainly open to question. Nevertheless, the first recorded pair of Siamese in the western world was imported into England by the English Consul General for Bangkok in 1884. These cats were exhibited at the Crystal Palace in London in 1885. Siamese cats first appeared in the United States about 1890 and were first exhibited here in the early 1900s. Purportedly, these cats were the gift of the King of Siam to an American friend.

The early Siamese cats were quite unlike the sleek, fine boned, wedge-shape-headed, elegant cats seen today. They were cats who were round–headed, relatively stocky of body, often cross-eyed and visibly kink-tailed. A tremendous amount of skill, hard work and time has been spent by devoted Siamese breeders to produce the flashy Siamese Show Cat of today.

The value of the Siamese breed is readily apparent to all cat fanciers. This Natural Breed has been utilized in the realization of a surprising number of today's many breeds. Among these breeds are the: Balinese, Bombay (indirectly), Colorpoint Shorthair, Havana Brown, Himalayan, Lilac Foreign Shorthair, Manxamese, Oriental Shorthair and Tonkinese. It is almost certain that other breeds using the Siamese as a contributor have, or will be, produced.

Top winners in shows for many years, these lovable, attention-demanding, winners of the popularity poll retain their individual identities and are highly valued in their own

(Continued on page 132)

THE BREEDS
TURKISH ANGORA

A Natural Breed, the Turkish Angora is one of the oldest recognized breeds of cat. Indigenous to Turkey, the name Angora is probably a corruption of the Turkish city of Ankara.

Most experts agree that the Persian cat of today is a descendant of matings between the Angora and the long-haired cat from the Near East (Afghanistan). In fact, for a long time the terms Persian and Angora were interchangeable.

At one time, the preference on the part of cat fanciers for the luxurious long-coated, heavy-boned, full-bodied Persian all but eliminated the Angora as a breed. However, the officials at the Ankara Zoo res-

cued the breed from extinction. This pride in their cultural heritage inspired them to obtain several pairs of Turkish Angoras and to begin a carefully planned breeding program. They chose to preserve only the pure white Angora with three possible eye colors — blue-eyed, amber-eyed and odd-eyed (one blue and one amber eye). It was through friendship with zoo officials that Colonel Walter Grant of the U.S. Army was able to bring two unrelated pairs of white Turkish Angoras to the United States, the first pair in 1962; the second pair in 1966. Interest was aroused among cat fanciers who saw these original imports, and now many dedi-

cated breeders are working with the Turkish Angora.

Currently, only the pure white Turkish Angoras are eligible for Championship Competition. Other colors from Spectrum A exist and are pedigreed Turkish Angoras. These colored and patterned cats are used in breeding programs to produce better white specimens of the breed. It is possible that other colors of Angora will some day be permitted to compete for Championship and Grand Championship recognition.

The size of the Turkish An-

(Continued on page 132)

THE BREEDS
OTHER BREEDS

Sphinx

Other types of cats, both rare and also relatively common, are recognized as breeds. Currently none are accepted for show competition.

British Shorthair — The British Shorthair (best known as the British Blue) occurs in the colors of Spectrum A. This cat also is recognized in the Spotted Tabby pattern. Most British Shorthairs are outcrossed every three to five generations to a longhair in order that conformation and coat can be retained. This cat carries a short, fine and dense coat.

Chartreux — Indigenous Blue Shorthair of France, the orange or golden-yellow-eyed Chartreux is a solid, stocky, short-legged cat with a round head. The cheeks of the Chartreux are very full.

Copper or Supilak — Another cat from Thailand whose coat is a copper-colored hue of the brown spectrum.

Cymric (Longhaired Manx) — A hybrid produced most probably by crossing shorthaired Manx with Persians in order to improve the Manx coat and type. Believed by some to be a mutation.

Himbur — Hybrid produced by crossing the Himalayan with the Burmese.

Manxamese — Colorpoint patterned cat (Spectrum B) hybridized by crossing Manx with Siamese.

Ocicat — Spotted Hybrid Breed produced by crossing the Abyssinian with the American Shorthair or either of these with the Ocicat itself.

THE BREEDS

Scottish Fold

Scottish Fold — A recent mutation (1961) in the cat world, the Scottish Fold is a very appealing cat. First discovered on a farm in Perthshire, Scotland, this cat is quickly gaining in popularity. Breeders have worked closely with geneticists to preserve the mutation. A round, massive headed cat, with a short, muscular body, large round eyes, thick dense short coat and the distinctive ear with its definite fold line, the Scottish Fold breed will probably prove to be both popular and successful.

Somali — Longhaired Abyssinians. These cats are gaining popularity quickly because of their alert disposition and graceful form.

Sphinx — Another mutation, this is the hairless cat. Except for a slight fuzz on the head and chest, these cats are completely without hair. They closely resemble the sad-eyed, wrinkled-brow Pug dog. They are very warm to the touch and have the feel of hot, smooth skin. Although both European and American breeders have produced this mutation, there appears to be little interest in a hairless cat. Also known as Moon Cats, Mexican Hairless and *Chat Sans Poile* (cat without hair).

Turkish Van Cat — A lovely, Angora-type cat from the Lake Van area of Turkey is a white cat with auburn markings or splotches on the head and auburn rings on the tail. This cat purportedly enjoys water and is happiest when allowed an occasional dip! A few have been imported in England; rare now outside of Turkey.

BURMESE

(Continued from page 108)

size, set well apart on the rounded skull, alert, tilted slightly forward and having slightly rounded tips. The eyes are set far apart and have rounded apertures.

The body of the Burmese is medium in size, muscular and compact. Males are larger in size than females. They have an ample, rounded chest, and the back is *level* from the shoulder to the base of the tail. The legs are well-proportioned to the body; the paws are round. The tail is straight and medium in length.

The color of the mature Burmese is a rich, warm sable brown which shades imperceptibly to a lighter hue on the cat's underparts; otherwise, the cat's color is without shadings or markings of any kind.

The nose leather and paw pads are brown; the eye color ranges from yellow to gold — the greater the depth and brilliance, the better. Green eyes are penalized, and blue eyes are a disqualification on the show bench. Similarly, there must be no kink or abnormality in the tail, nor any lockets or buttons (white spots).

Being an established breed whose hybrid ancestry can be traced to one cat, Wong Mau, matings have produced other colors of Burmese — most notably the champagne, blue and platinum Burmese. In England, continued hybridization has produced many additional colors of Spectrum A. Burmese purists hold the opinion that Dr. Thompson's noble experimental breeding program was one which set out to produce a solid-color, satin-sheen sable brown cat. That he succeeded is evinced by the many Best in Show Sable Burmese during the past 25 years or so. The "other than sable-colored" Burmese represent genetic by-products or throwbacks; they are currently not accepted for Championship Competition by the C.F.A.

Hardy and sociable, the Sable Burmese is an outstanding cat companion who regards the family circle as his — and his alone!

COLORPOINT SHORTHAIR

(Continued from page 109)
be divided into three categories defined by their points: Solid Color Point; Lynx Point (Tabby Point); Parti-Color Point. All colors require deep, vivid blue eye color.

Color Spectrum of the Colorpoint Shorthair

Solid Color Point

Red Point: Body — clear white with any shading in the same tone as the points. Points — deep red. Nose leather and paw pads — flesh or coral pink.

Cream Point: Body — clear white with any shading in the same tone as the points. Points — apricot. Nose leather and paw pads — flesh or coral pink.

Lynx Point

In all colors, the body color may be lightly shaded by ghost striping. The points contain darker shaded bars which are distinct and separated by lighter background color. The ears are marked with a paler shade of the basic color in the form of a thumb print.

Seal Lynx Point: Body — cream or pale fawn. Points — seal brown on lighter ground. Ears — seal brown with paler thumb print in center. Nose leather — seal brown or pink edged in seal brown. Paw pads — seal brown.

Chocolate Lynx Point: Body — ivory. Points — warm milk chocolate on lighter ground. Ears — warm milk chocolate brown with paler thumb print in center. Nose leather — cinnamon or pink edged in cinnamon. Paw pads — cinnamon.

Blue Lynx Point: Body — bluish white to platinum gray, cold in tone, shading to lighter color on stomach and chest. Points — deep blue-gray on lighter ground. Ears — deep blue-gray with lighter thumb print in center. Nose leather — slate-colored or pink edged in slate. Paw pads — slate-colored.

Lilac Lynx Point: Body — glacial white. Points — frosty gray with pinkish tone on lighter ground. Ears — frosty gray with pinkish tone, lighter thumb print in center. Nose leather — lavender pink or pink edged in lavender pink. Paw pads — lavender pink.

Red Lynx Point: Body — white. Points — deep red on lighter ground. Ears — deep red with paler thumb print in center. Nose leather and paw pads — flesh or coral pink.

Parti-Color Point

The points are of a basic solid color mottled with patches of one or more contrasting colors. In all colors, a blaze on the mask is desirable. In the older cat, the body color is also mottled. When blaze is present, the nose leather may be mottled.

Seal Tortie Point: Body — pale fawn to cream, shading to lighter color on stomach and chest. Points — seal brown uniformly mottled with red and cream. Nose leather — seal brown; flesh or coral pink mottling permitted with blaze. Paw pads — seal brown; flesh or coral pink mottling permitted where point color mottling extends into the paw pads.

Chocolate Cream Point: Body —

ivory. Points — warm milk chocolate uniformly mottled with cream. Nose leather — cinnamon; flesh or coral pink mottling permitted with blaze. Paw pads — cinnamon; flesh or coral pink mottling permitted where point color mottling extends into paw pads.

Blue Cream Point: Body — bluish white to platinum gray, cold in tone, shading to lighter color on stomach and chest. Points — deep blue-gray uniformly mottled with cream. Nose leather — slate-colored; flesh or coral pink mottling permitted with blaze. Paw pads — slate-colored; flesh or coral pink mottling permitted where point color mottling extends into the paw pads.

Lilac Cream Point: Body — glacial white. Points — frosty gray with pinkish tone uniformly mottled with pale cream. Nose leather — lavender pink; flesh or coral pink mottling permitted with blaze. Paw pads — lavender pink; flesh or coral pink mottling permitted where point color mottling extends into the paw pads.

A striking example of the color-point pattern and its extension beyond the four classic Siamese colors, the Colorpoint Shorthair is an outstanding illustration of the art of knowledgeable selective breeding. Warm, friendly and people-oriented, the Colorpoint is a welcome addition to the cat lover's home.

EGYPTIAN MAU

(Continued from page 110)

When standing upright, the impression should be one of standing on tiptoe. The paws are small, dainty and slightly oval (almost round) in shape. The tail is medium in length, thick at the base and with a slight taper.

The coat is silky, fine in texture and resilient to the touch, and has a lustrous sheen. The hair is medium-length yet long enough to accommodate two or more bands of ticking which are separated by lighter colored bands.

On the show bench, the Egyptian Mau is penalized for having a short or round head, pointed muzzle, small ears, small, round or "Oriental" eyes, cobby or svelte ("Oriental") body, short or whip tail, body spots that run together and poor condition. The cat is disqualified for lack of spots or wrong eye color.

The Egyptian Mau Pattern

The coat color displays a good contrast between a pale ground color and the deeper colored markings. The forehead is barred with a characteristic M and frown marks which form lines between the ears and continue down the back of the neck, ideally breaking into elongated "spots" along the spine. As these spinal lines reach the rear haunches, they mold together to form a dorsal stripe which continues along the top of the tail to its tip. The tail itself is heavily banded (ringed) and has a dark tip.

The cheeks are barred with "mascara" lines, the first of which starts at the outer corner of the eye and continues along the contour of the cheek; the second "mascara" line starts at the center of the cheek and curves upward, almost meeting the first at a point below the base of the ear.

On the upper chest there are one or more necklaces (preferably broken in the center of each necklace).

The shoulder markings are a transitional form best described as being medial between stripes and spots.

The upper forelegs are heavily barred; the bars do not necessarily match in number or placement on each leg.

Markings on the body are in the form of random spots varying in both size and shape; evenly distributed spots are preferred. The pattern of spots on each side of the body may not match, but spots should *not* run together forming a broken, mackerel pattern.

Markings on the haunches and upper hind legs are transitional spots and stripes breaking into bars on the thighs and back to elongated spots on the lower hind leg.

There are "vest button" spots on the underside of the body which are dark in color against the corresponding pale ground color.

Egyptian Mau Colors

Silver: Pale silver ground color across the head, shoulders, outer legs, back and tail, fading on the underside to a brilliant pale silver. All markings are charcoal color, producing a good contrast against the lighter silver ground colors. The backs of the ears are grayish pink; the ears are tipped in black. The upper throat area, chin and area around the nostrils are pale, clear silver (appearing to be almost white). The nose leather is brick-red and the paw pads are black. The hair between the toes is black; on the hind paws, the black extends slightly beyond the paws.

Bronze: Light bronze ground color across the head, shoulders, outer legs, back and tail, being darkest on the saddle (over the shoulders) and lightening to a tawny buff on the sides. The ground color fades to a creamy ivory on the underside. All markings are dark brown, producing a good contrast against the lighter bronze ground colors. The backs of the ears are tawny pink; the ears are tipped in dark brown. The nose, lips and eyes are outlined in dark brown; the bridge of the nose is ocherous. The upper throat area, chin and area around the nostrils are pale, creamy white. The nose leather is brick-red; the paw pads are black or dark brown, with the same color between the toes and extending beyond the paws of the hind legs.

Smoke: Charcoal gray color with silver undercoat across the head, shoulders, legs, tail and underside. All markings are jet-black, with sufficient contrast against the ground color for the pattern to be plainly visible. The nose, lips and eyes are outlined in jet-black. The upper throat area, chin and area around the nostrils are lightest charcoal gray color. The nose leather and paw pads are black. The black between the toes extends beyond the paws of the hind legs.

It is exciting to view the living counterparts of the Egyptian Mau pictured in tombs and papyrus paintings created centuries ago. While relatively rare and currently only provisionally accepted by the C.F.A to the show bench, the beauty of our one domesticated truly spotted cat assures its place in the homes of today's cat lovers.

HAVANA BROWN

(Continued from page 112)
little hair (sparse furnishings) on the lower lip. The eyes are oval and are chartreuse green in color — the greener shades are preferred.

The body is medium in length, firm and muscular. The legs are in proportion to the body. The tail, medium in length, is also in proportion to the body. Paws are oval-shaped.

The Havana's coat is medium in length and smooth. In color, the coat is best described as being a rich, warm, mahogany brown (as opposed to the darker, sable brown coat of the short and glossy-coated Burmese); the entire coat should be one sound shade of brown to the skin.

The nose leather and paw pads are of a definite rosy-toned shade which harmonizes with the coat color.

The Havana is penalized for having black nose leather or paw pads, Siamese head type (shape and conformation), a weak chin (receding) or the lack of a distinct profile stop at the eyes. They are disqualified on the show bench for having a kinked or abnormal tail, a locket or button (white spots).

Originally hybridized in England and later hybridized by American breeders by crossing Siamese, Burmese and Russian Blues, the Havana Brown is now classed as an Established Breed — only Havana to Havana matings are acceptable.

A pixyish, soft-voiced cat, the Havana usually exhibits the peculiar trait of using his paws to investigate, feel and touch interesting objects, as opposed to other breeds who characteristically use their noses and sense of smell to investigate curious objects.

With startling chartreuse green eyes, rosy-toned nose and rich mahogany-colored coat, the Havana Brown is a living portrait most appreciated by those who are fortunate enough to have a highly developed sense of color and the beaux-arts.

HIMALAYAN

(Continued from page 113)
Himalayan! In the United States, the breed is identified as Himalayan, the Himalayan pattern having already been recognized in other animals; in England, the cat is recognized as the Colourpoint Longhair. Currently, Siamese-Persian crosses can be registered as Himalayans; however, in the near future, only Persians will be permitted for use in continued Himalayan hybridization in the United States.

In conformation, the Himalayan is a Persian-style cat. Round, massive head, short thick neck, small ears, cobby body, large round eyes, deep nose break, short thick legs, large round paws and long thick coat are all Persian traits. (See the section on Persians for a detailed description of conformation.) In addition, the Himalayan is penalized for any resemblance to the Peke-Face and is disqualified for deformity of the skull or mouth.

The coat color and pattern are described in Spectrum B. The classic four colors of Spectrum B are recognized colors of the Himalayan (Seal Point, Chocolate Point, Blue Point and Lilac Point). In addition, the colors Flame Point, Tortie Point and Blue Cream Point are recognized. (All *must* have deep blue eyes.)

Flame Point: Body — creamy white. Point color — delicate orange flame. Nose leather and paw pads — flesh or coral pink.

Tortie Point: Body — creamy white or pale fawn. Point color — seal brown with unbrindled patches of red and cream; a blaze of red or cream on the face is desirable. Nose leather and paw pads — seal brown with flesh and/or coral pink mottling to conform with colors or points.

Blue Cream Point: Body — bluish white or creamy white shading gradually to white on the stomach and chest. Point color — blue with patches of cream. Nose leather and paw pads — slate-blue, pink or a combination of both.

As a result of being able to utilize all Persians and Persian colors (Spectrum A), additional colors of Himalayans are being produced. Most notable are the Lynx Point Himalayans (see color descriptions of Lynx Point Colorpoint Shorthairs), solid Chocolate and solid Lilac.

The latter two colors, while not "pointed" cats, are of particular beauty. Cat lovers have long sought to produce a solid, rich, warm mahogany or chocolate brown longhair. The solid Chocolate Himalayan is that dream's realization. The dilute of this solid chocolate color is the equally striking and beautiful solid Lilac. Both the solid Chocolate and solid Lilac Himalayans have gold to copper eye color. The Lilac can best be described as a shade of pinkish beige.

With the advent of the solid Chocolate and solid Lilac Himalayans, breeders have expanded the color spectrum of cats by producing such exotic-colored longhairs as Lilac Cream Points, Chocolate Cream Points, Chocolate and Lilac Shades, Smokes, Parti-Colors, Tabbies and Bi-Colors. Currently not recognized for competition on the Championship Show Bench, it is not possible to predict whether the Chocolate or Lilac colors will be defined as an extension of the Himalayan breed or as a completely new breed. Most important, however, is the exquisite beauty of the extended color spectrum of these gorgeous and rare colors of long hair.

The fastest-growing breed in the world today, the Himalayan has proved of great value. Several have been named Best in Show many, many times. Thousands of others are valued friends in cat-loving homes around the world.

JAPANESE BOBTAIL

(Continued from page 114)
appearance. The hind legs are noticeably longer than the forelegs, but are deeply angled when the cat is standing so that the torso is nearly level with little if any rise toward the rear. The forelegs of the standing cat form two continuous straight lines and are close together. The Japanese Bobtail *must* have a pom-pom tail, and the pom-pom *must* begin at the base of the spine, as opposed to a "delayed pom-pom," which begins after an inch or two of straight tail.

In color, preference is given to the traditional MI-KE and to those colors which produce the three-colored cat: white, black, red, black-and-white, red-and-white, tortoise shell-and-white and tortoise shell. Other colors and patterns are acceptable. Eye color, nose leather and paw pad color should harmonize with coat color and pattern as described in Color Spectrum A. Colors in Spectrum B are unacceptable. In all colors, preference is given to bold dramatic markings and to vividly contrasting colors.

From ancient times in Japan, the pom-pom or chrysanthemum-tailed Japanese Bobtail still sits by the door with one or sometimes both paws raised in greeting or invitation to play, bringing good luck to his owners and their home.

KORAT

(Continued from page 115)
founded in 1965 by Korat-owners who can prove that their cats are of authentic Thai bloodlines, protects the purity of bloodlines by assuring true Korats.)

The Korat is a relatively rare breed of cat even in his native Thailand. The cat's general appearance is that of a silver blue cat, medium in size, hard and muscular. The cat's lines are made up of all smooth curves. His huge, prominent, luminous green or green-gold eyes are prominent, brilliant, alert and expressive.

The head, when viewed from the front, or when viewed looking down from just back of the head, is heart-shaped; there is breadth between and across the eyes. The "eyebrow" ridges form the top of the heart and the sides of the face curve gently down to the chin, completing the bottom of the heart-shape. In profile, there is a slight stop between the nose and the forehead. The nose has a lion-like downward curve just above the nose leather. The chin is strong and well developed, properly completing the heart-shape by providing a balancing line for the profile. The ears are large, round-tipped and have a large flare at the base. They are set high on the head; the inner ear is sparsely furnished while the outside of the ear is covered with extremely short close-lying hair.

The body is muscular and supple with a feeling of "coiled-spring" power. The male cat is surprisingly heavy in weight; the female is somewhat smaller. The legs are well-proportioned to the body, hind legs being slightly longer than the front legs. The tail is medium in length, heavier at the base and tapering to a rounded tip. A *non-visible* kink in the tail is permitted on the Show Bench.

The eyes are large and luminous and are particularly prominent with extraordinary depth and brilliance. They are wide-open and oversized for the face. The eye aperture which is well-rounded when fully open has an Asian or Oriental slant when partially or fully closed. The eye color is luminous green; however, an amber cast to the eye color is acceptable. As with most green-eyed cats, the eye color in the Korat kitten and young cat may be yellow, amber or amber-green. The true green color usually develops with maturity.

Nose leather and lips are dark blue or lavender. The paw pads are dark blue, ranging to lavender with a pinkish tinge.

The coat color is silver blue tipped with silver and is without shading or tabby markings. The silver tipping should appear all over the coat and is intensified where the coat is shortest. There must not be any white spots, lockets or buttons. The true Korat is always silver blue in color.

MAINE COON

(Continued from page 116)
winter snows of the Maine countryside.

The coat, probably developed in part by the winter climate of Maine, is heavy and shaggy. It is shorter on the shoulders, longer on the stomach and in the britches. The coat's texture is silky, and falls smoothly. The shaggy appearance is evident on the underside of the cat and in the long, wide-based and tapering, long-haired tail. The frontal ruff is best described as being "mutton-chops." (A large frill between the legs is not required as on the Persian and Himalayan.)

The head is medium in width and length and has a characteristic squareness to the muzzle. The cheekbones are high; the chin is firm and in line with the nose and upper lip.

The nose is medium-long. The ears are large, well-tufted, having inner-ear furnishings, and taper so as to appear pointed. They are set high on the head and well apart. "Lynxline tips" — hair tufts on the tips of the ear forming a characteristic lynx type of ear tuft — are very desirable as they add to the apparent pointed-ear shape. The eyes are large and wide-set with a slightly oblique setting (upward tilt toward the ears).

The Maine Coon Cat is penalized for having delicate bone structure, a short or overall-even coat. They are disqualified for having an undershot chin, crossed-eyes, kinked tail, incorrect number of toes (five in front and four on back paws). Polydactylism is very undesirable in this breed.

The Maine Coon Cat is recognized in every color and combination of Spectrum A. However, eye color may be green, gold or copper except in whites where the eye color may also be either blue or odd-eyed (two differently colored eyes). In addition, combinations of tabby with white, shaded with white or *any* color or combination of colors except those in Spectrum B and its by-products are acceptable. Ultimately, the desired colors will doubtlessly fall completely within Spectrum A except for the probable continued acceptance of any eye color already described.

For those who are of "the bigger the better" school of animal lovers, the Maine Coon Cat is the most treasured of all domestic cats. It is easy to picture the sailor from Maine who loved and protected this longhaired American cat saying at sea, "Thar she blows!" and at home, "Thar she goes!" as his big, healthy, shaggy coated cat made good use of her snowshoe, heavily tufted paws to run across the snow to meet those returning home from the sea!

MANX

(Continued from page 117)
produces a cat of great durability, substance and power.

The head is round with prominent, jowly cheeks, medium in length without a definite nose break when viewed in profile. The muzzle tapers, but not to a sharp point. Manx ears are rather wide at the base and taper to a point, relatively long, but in proportion to the head. The body is solid, compact and well-balanced.

The front legs are short and well set apart to show good depth of chest. The back legs are much longer with a heavy, muscular thigh tapering to a substantial lower leg. The lower back leg will often have the hair worn off because of this cat's habit of resting on this part as often as on the paws. In being judged, Manx cats are disqualified for having a definite visible tail joint, wrong number of toes — five in front, four behind, or the inability to stand or walk properly.

The Manx appears in all colors of Spectrum A. Combinations of colors and patterns combined with white are also acceptable. Colors of Spectrum B and their derivatives are unacceptable in this Natural Breed. Color and eye color are of relative unimportance in the Manx since taillessness is the most distinctive characteristic of this breed.

These healthy, intelligent, people-loving cats are very popular with those who know and understand them. However, the breeding of Manx cats is best left to expert Manx breeders because of a possible lethal gene.

PERSIAN

(Continued from page 119)

four on the hind paws. The tail is short but in proportion to body length; it is carried without a curve and at an angle lower than the back.

The Persian coat is long and thick and stands off from the body. It is of fine texture, glossy, full of life, and should be long all over the body including the shoulders. The ruff is immense and continues in a deep frill between the front legs. The ear tufts (furnishings) and toe tufts are long. The brush (hair on the tail) is very full.

The show Persian must *not* have a locket or button (white spots), a kinked or abnormal tail. And, as with all breeds of pedigreed cats, the Persian must have the correct number of toes on each paw; polydactylism is a highly undesirable trait.

Peke-Face Persian. The Peke-Face Persian occurs in only two recognized colors, Red and Red Tabby. Different in appearance from other Persians, the Peke-Face appears to occur spontaneously in litters from standard Red and Red Tabby Persians. The head should resemble as much as possible that of the Pekinese dog, from which it gets its name.

The Persian's coat must be groomed and cared for religiously. If you are willing to cope with a daily grooming routine, the Persian's beauty will more than compensate. Brushing or combing to remove dead hair will pretty much eliminate the hairy furniture problem.

For those who treasure *objets d'art* and *objets de virtue*, the Persian will be a welcome addition to a collection. Persians are sedate for the most part and, because they know they are beautiful, they love to pose against backgrounds which show them off to good advantage.

REX

(Continued from page 120)

terest in this unusual type of Rex resulted in the loss of the longhair Rex. The cat discovered in San Bernardino was, however, successfully used in short-coated Rex breeding programs.

The head of the Rex is comparatively small and narrow. There is a definite whisker break; the muzzle narrows slightly to a rounded end. The ears are large, erect and come to a modified point at the top. The eyes are medium to large in size, oval in shape, slant slightly upward, and are a full eye's width apart. The eye color should be clear, intense and appropriate to the coat color. The nose is Roman; in profile there is a straight line from the end of the nose to the chin. The body of the female Rex is small to medium size; the male is proportionately larger. The torso is long and slender. The back is arched and the lower line of the body follows the upward curve of the arched back — a distinct "tuck-up."

The important Rex coat is short, extremely soft, silky and completely free of guard hairs. It is relatively dense with a tight uniform marcel wave lying close to the body. The fur on the underside of the chin and on the chest and abdomen is short and noticeably wavy. When being shown, the Rex is disqualified for having a kinked or abnormal tail, the incorrect number of toes, or any coarse or guard hairs.

The Rex colors are primarily those of Spectrum A. In addition, Other Rex Colors (O.R.C.) are accepted for show. In all cases, the eye color of the various O.R.C. combinations should be appropriate to the predominant color of the cat.

Because of its exotic appearance, the Rex is the cat for those who have *avant-garde* tastes in general. It may also be the cat for the many people who are allergic to cat hair — often they are not allergic to the Rex because of its very special coat.

RUSSIAN

(Continued from page 121)

and was brought to England by sailors who sailed between England and Archangel, Russia. In fact, the cat was called the Archangel cat for many years. Irrespective of the Russian Blue's origin and its various names, the cat is a beautiful and artistically satisfying creature.

The eyes are vivid green and round in shape. The face is broad across the eyes due to the wide set of the eyes and the thick fur. The ears are large and wide at the base with the tips more pointed than rounded. They are set far apart and are as much on the side as on the top of the head. The skin of the ears is thin and translucent, with very little inside furnishing. The outside of the ear is scantily covered with short, very fine hair.

The neck is long and slender, but appears short due to the thick fur on the neck and the high placement of the shoulder blades. In perfect placement, the shoulder blades nearly touch at a point behind the cat's neck and over the spine.

The body is fine-boned, long, lithe and graceful in outline and carriage. When the cat is seated, there is almost a serpentlike quality to the outline of the cat's sinuous body. The show cat must *not* have a kinked or abnormal tail, a locket or buttons (white spots), and must have the correct number of toes. Lighter or lavender shades of blue are preferred. The guard hairs of the coat are silver-tipped, giving the Russian Blue a silvery sheen or lustrous appearance. The nose leather is slate gray; paw pads are lavender-pink or mauve.

Tradition holds that the Russian Blue was the treasured cat of the Russian czars. Even without a Winter Palace, you should consider this green-eyed, lavender-blue, plush-coated cat if you are looking for a lovely pet.

SIAMESE

(Continued from page 122)
right.

The Siamese color pattern is that of Spectrum B. The ideal Siamese is a svelte, dainty cat with long tapering lines. The cat is very lithe but also very muscular; its tubular body emphasizes its sleek lines.

The Siamese head is a long, tapering wedge, medium in size and in good proportion to the body. There is no break at the whiskers; when the whiskers are smoothed back, the underlying bone structure is apparent. Allowance must be made for jowls, which disguise the smooth lines of the wedge, in the stud cat. The skull is flat; in profile, a long straight line is seen from the top of the head to the tip of the nose.

The ears of this breed are strikingly large, pointed, wide at the base, and continue the lines of the wedge. The eyes are almond-shaped and medium–sized; they neither protrude nor are they recessed. The eyes are slanted toward the nose in harmony with the lines of the wedge and the ears; for show quality, they must be *uncrossed*.

To be shown, the Siamese must be in excellent physical condition. The eyes must be clear, the body muscular and lithe, neither flabby nor bony. Judges will penalize the Siamese for having off-color or spotted paw pads or nose leather. The cat is disqualified for any evidence of illness or poor health, weak hind legs, mouth-breathing due to nasal obstruction or poor occlusion, emaciation, a visible tail kink, other than blue eyes, or for having white toes and/or feet.

Over the years, careful selective breeding has completely changed the physical appearance of the Siamese breed. However, the disqualified, visibly kink-tailed or cross-eyed Siamese may be a perfect companion pet even if it does not meet show standards. If you expect a lot of attention and a demand for closeness and affection from your cat, the Siamese could well be your kind of cat.

TURKISH ANGORA

(Continued from page 123)
gora's head is small to medium. It is wedge-shaped, wide at the top with a definite taper toward the chin. Allowance is made for jowls in the stud cat. The ears are wide at the base, long, pointed, tufted and set high on the head. The eyes are large, almond-shaped-to-round and slant upwards slightly. The nose is medium-long and has a gentle slope with no break. The chin is gently rounded, and the tip of the chin forms a perpendicular line with the nose.

The body is small to medium-sized in the female, slightly larger in the male. The torso is long, graceful and lithe; the rump is slightly higher than the front of the cat.

The Angora's tail, described as a full brush, is long and tapering, wide at the base, narrow at the end. When relaxed and moving, the Angora's tail is carried horizontally over the body, sometimes almost touching the head.

The coat, pure white in color, is medium long on the body, long at the ruff. The hair is wavier on the stomach than it is on other parts of the cat where the hair is very fine and has a silken sheen. There are tufts of hair between the toes. The paw pads, nose leather and lips are pink.

If being shown, this breed is penalized for having a kinked or abnormal tail, paw pads or nose leather mottled or other than pink in color. The cat is also disqualified for having a Persian body type or for being any color other than white.

We are fortunate that the graceful Turkish Angora was protected from extinction by the Turkish Government and the Ankara Zoo. The only breed which has the standard distinction of carrying its tail in a "full-time salute" over the back when moving, the Turkish Angora is a very special cat.

Will Thompson is the editor of All Cats *magazine and a regional director of C.F.A.*

Creszentia Allen is a world-famous cat photographer.

V. THE PUBLIC CAT

A GUIDE TO THE CAT FANCY

Isabel Archer

To the outsider the world of cat shows, cat breeders and cat clubs is bound to seem a curious and difficult place. The prize-winning cat strikes the uneducated eye as looking exactly like most of the other members of the breed in a show. The differences between the various cat associations are also often obscure to non-members. But once you learn a few of the ground rules and, especially, attend a show or two, it all begins to be serious, understandable fun. Questions of breed and breeding become clearer. The novice who once thought the whole thing seemed beyond him (and perhaps slightly mad) discovers a new and enlarged enjoyment of cats.

Cat Fancy is a name that encompasses all of those people who love and show cats and who devote themselves to the welfare and breeding of pedigreed cats. You are a member of the Cat Fancy if you are interested in well-bred cats — whether or not you breed or show them yourself and whether or nor you belong to any formal organization of cat owners. Put simply, the Cat Fancy is interested in fancy cats, or, the Cat Fancy includes in its membership anyone who is a fancier of cats. The term Cat Fancy is a general one, of uncertain etymology, and refers to a large group composed of many parts.

The first formal institution of the Cat Fancy was organized in England in 1887 and came to be known as the National Cat Club. What were at first small groups of cat fanciers eventually grew into a national network of clubs devoted to breeding, registering and showing cats. The first cat show at the Crystal Palace Exhibition in 1871 was a great success and publicized the growing English enthusiasm for cats.

Cat Shows

Today, a century after that first cat show, the Cat Fancy is well organized and world-wide. The easiest route of entry into the Cat Fancy is still by attending a local cat show. There are many shows held each year in every region of the country and it should not take much more than a phone call or two to learn the date of a forthcoming, nearby cat show. At this point in your efforts there is no need to worry about details such as the sponsoring organization's special rules. These sorts of distinctions will only be meaningful after you know a bit more about show cats. At this point your eye has to become more experienced.

Visiting a cat show is in itself a fascinating and delightful experience. There are all those cats, waiting quietly and nonchalantly to be touched, stroked, stretched and examined

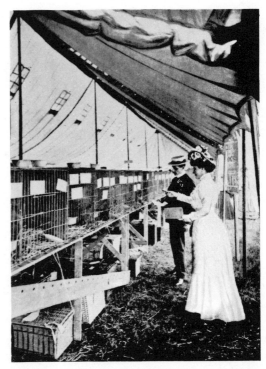

Judging at an early cat show.

Modern cat shows are more crowded than earlier ones.

assiduously by the judges who look at subtle differentiations in form, color, coat condition and size. And the cats are all gorgeous to begin with. So they sit, and their owners hover protectively, and the public saunters by, murmuring appreciatively at a particularly fine specimen of a rare breed. The ribbons are awarded and the crowd passes on to the next judging ring to watch another category of cats go through the same procedure — and then more ribbons.

It is all very businesslike and professional. The standards for judging vary with each organization, but the reverence for the cats is universal. Generally, cats are judged by age, sex, breed, color and past show performance. To the untrained eye, all the cats in any given judging competition will look almost exactly alike. Half the fun for the uninitiated at a cat show is learning the basic differences. And soon it begins to come clear. There are differences, remarkable ones, and the new connoisseur is born.

The first time a novice spots a flaw in coloring is a memorable experience. It means that the eye is being trained, the mind informed. The individuality of cats is becoming more clear, and now the newcomer is beginning to have an experienced understanding of what cat breeding is all about. Each cat is a real, living animal and, therefore, only an approximation of an ideal. Cats are judged on the basis of how closely they approach the ideal and naturally the Cat Fancy is anxious to insure that future generations of cats will also approach the same ideal in color, coat, bone structure, size, etc. The breeding of champions with champions is the best way to preserve and enhance the near perfection of present generations.

Cat Associations

Since people have different visions of an ideal, it should not be surprising to learn that there are a number of different associations organizing cat shows. They differ among themselves on questions of what constitutes a breed, what is the ideal for each particular breed and how many generations back a pedigree should be traced. There are also differences of organization.

Nine different associations comprise the formal, organized North American Cat Fancy. All of these groups can be useful and helpful to a beginner interested in learning about pedigreed cats. As you learn more you will be able to say whether the differences are or are not important to you. In many cases, cats are registered and shown in more than one of the nine associations.

The largest association is the *Cat Fanciers' Association* (C.F.A.). Founded in 1906, this group has no individual members, but many cat clubs are affiliated with the C.F.A. and, therefore, to participate in its programs you must join a C.F.A.-member club. In 1975 the C.F.A. counted 464 club memberships in the United States, Canada and Japan. Approximately 36,000 cats were registered with the C.F.A. in 1975 and it expects to sponsor about 200 shows all over the country this coming year.

The oldest association is the *American Cat Association* (A.C.A.), which was founded in 1904. The *American Cat Fanciers' Association* (A.C.F.A.) is the second largest of the groups. It has registered about 9,000 cats and expects to hold about 75 shows in the coming year.

Other institutions comprising the North American Cat Fancy are the *Canadian Cat Association* (C.C.A.), *Cat Fanciers' Federation* (C.F.F.) *Crown Cat Fanciers' Federation* (CROWN), *Independent Cat Federation* (ICF), *National Cat Fanciers' Association* (N.C.F.A.), and *United Cat Federation* (U.C.F.).

The American tendency to develop large and multiple organizations, with their own jargon and mystique, can frighten anybody not born into membership. But the important fact about the Cat Fancy is that all members, official or not, are devoted to cats and to the perpetuation of lines of pedigree cats. If you are interested in cats and cat breeds, you are already part of the Cat Fancy and with a little effort you can become an informed and active member.

Isabel Archer lives in New York and loves exploring new worlds.

CAT LISTINGS

CAT REGISTRIES

American Cat Association

Ms. Althea A. Frahm, Secretary
302B S. Brand Boulevard
Glendale, California 91204
213/247-1220

American Cat Fanciers Association

Mrs. Cora Swan, Secretary
P. O. Box 203
Point Lookout, Missouri 65726
417/334-5430

Canadian Cat Association

Mrs. Dorothy Lamb, Secretary
14 Nelson Street W., Suite 5
Brampton, Ontario, Canada
416/459-1481

Cat Fanciers' Association, Inc.

Mrs. Jean B. Rose, Executive Director
P. O. Box 430
Red Bank, New Jersey 07701
201/842-2470

Cat Fanciers' Federation

Mrs. Grace Clute, Corresponding
  Secretary
2013 Elizabeth Street
Schenectady, New York 12303
518/355-4091

Crown Cat Fanciers Federation

Mrs. Martha Rose Underwood, Secretary
1379 Tyler Park Drive
Louisville, Kentucky 40204

Independent Cat Federation

Ms. Frances Welch
Box 1203
Southampton, New York 11968
516/283-0922

Ms. Vera M. Cronin
31 Irving Street
Salem, Massachusetts 01970

National Cat Fanciers Association, Inc.

Mrs. Frances Kosierowski, Secretary
1450 North Bukhart Road
Howell, Michigan 48843
517/546-2951

United Cat Federation

Mrs. Jean Ford, Secretary
6616 E. Hereford Drive
Los Angeles, California 90022

BREED CLUBS

Abyssinian Cat Club of America

Mrs. Marjorie Pallady, Secretary
1121 Wilshire Boulevard
Oklahoma City, Oklahoma 73116

Abyssinian Midwest Breeders

Mrs. Ann H. Anderson, Secretary
7650 South Cork
Justice, Illinois 60458

Chocolate & Lilac Longhairs of America

1621 N. Lindendale Avenue
Fullerton, California 92631
714/871-9590

Golden Persian Club

Ms. Wanda Shellner, Secretary
Box 281
Muldraugh, Kentucky 40155

The Himalayan Society

Ms. Lee Coburn, Membership Chairman
101 Brittany Drive
Lansing, Michigan 48906

Korat Cat Fanciers Association

Alan & Sheila Walicke
14642 N. 25th Drive
Phoenix, Arizona 85023
602/942-5723

Leopard Cat Information Center

Virginia English
P. O. Box 3632
Hollywood, California 90028
213/874-9817

Maine Coon Breeders & Fanciers Association

E. L. Eastman, Corresponding Secretary
R.F.D. 2
Brunswick, Maine 04011
207/725-7815

Manx International

Marge S. Wanter (Membership)
1291 N. Michigan Avenue
Pasadena, California 91104

Ragdoll Society

Mrs. Ruby Spagnol, Secretary
6816 Sunbury Road
Westerville, Ohio 43081
614/882-8639

Sacred Cat of Burma Fanciers (CFA)

Pam Pugliano
86 Cortland Drive
McKees Rocks, Pennsylvania 15136

Siamese Society of America

Sam Scheer, Secretary
2588-C South Vaughn Way
Denver, Colorado 80232

Somali Cat Club of America

Mrs. H. E. Mague, President
10 Western Boulevard
Gillette, New Jersey 07933
201/647-2275

Tonkinese Breed Club of U.S.A. Canada, Australia

156 Berkley Street
Waltham, Massachusetts 02154
617/899-8949

United Burmese Cat Fanciers

Mrs. T. H. Griffey, Secretary
14435 Chadbourne
Houston, Texas 77024

CAT MAGAZINES

All Cats

All Cats Magazine, Inc.
Suite 7
15113 Sunset Blvd.
Pacific Palisades, California 90272
Six-Issue Subscription, $10.00

Cat Fancy

Subscription Division, Cat Fancy
   Magazine
P.O. Box 24648
Los Angeles, California 90024
Eight-Issue Subscription, $6.95; 16
   Issues, $12.95

Cat-Tab

Subscription Department
P. O. Box 249
Milford, Ohio 45150
One-Year Subscription, 22 Issues,
   $10.00

Cat World

Subscription Department
5395 South Miller Street
Littleton, Colorado 80123
Six-Issue Subscription, $6.00

Cats

Cats Subscription Department
P. O. Box 83048
Lincoln, Nebraska 68501
One-Year Subscription, 12 Issues, $7.95

Pet News

44 Court Street
Brooklyn, New York 11201
Twelve-Issue Bi-monthly Subscription,
   $7.95

THE FIRST CAT SHOW

Harrison Weir

Harrison Weir, first president of the English National Cat Club, organized the first cat show at the Crystal Palace in London in 1871. The following reminiscences about the first day of the first cat show are excerpted from Weir's 1889 book Our Cats and All About Them.

ON THE DAY for judging, at Ludgate Hill in London, I took a ticket and the train for the Crystal Palace. Sitting alone in the comfortable cushioned compartment of a "first class," I confess I felt somewhat more than anxious as to the issue of the experiment . . . I could in no way picture to myself the scene; it was all so new. Presently, and while I was musing on the subject, the door was opened, and a friend got in. "Ah!" said he, "how are you?" "Tolerably well," said I; "I am on my way to the Cat Show." "What!" said my friend, "that surpasses everything! A show of cats! Why, I hate the things; I drive them off my premises when I see them. You'll have a fine bother with them in their cages! Or are they to be tied up?" . . . "I am sorry, very sorry," said I, "that you do not like cats. For my part, I think they are extremely beautiful, also very graceful in all their actions, and they are quite as domestic in their habits as the dog, if not more so. They are very useful in catching rats and mice; they are not deficient in sense; they will jump up at doors to push up latches with their paws . . . They know Sunday from the weekday, and do not go out to wait for the meat barrow on that day; they —" "Stop," said my friend, "I see you do like cats, and I do not, so let the matter drop." "No," said I, "not so. That is why I instituted this Cat Show; I wish every one to see how beautiful a well-cared-for cat is, and how docile, gentle, and — may I use the term? — cossetty. Why should not the cat that sits purring in front of us before the fire be an object of interest, and be selected for its colour, markings, and form? Now come with me, my dear old friend, and see the first Cat Show."

Inside the Crystal Palace stood my friend and I. Instead of the noise and struggles to escape, there lay the cats in their different pens, reclining on crimson cushions, making no sound save now and then a homely purring, as from time to time they lapped the nice new milk provided for them. Yes, there they were, big cats, very big cats, middling-sized cats, and small cats, cats of all colours and markings, and beautiful pure white Persian cats; and as we passed down the front of the cages I saw that my friend became interested; presently he said: "What a beauty this is! and here's another!" "And no doubt," said I, "many of the cats you have seen before would be quite as beautiful if they were as well cared for, or at least cared for at all; generally they are driven about and ill-fed, and often ill-used, simply for the reason that they are cats, and for no other. Yet I feel a great pleasure in telling you the show would have been much larger were it not for the difficulty of inducing the owners to send their pets from home, though you see the great care that is taken of them." "Well, I had no idea there was such a variety of form, size, and colour," said my friend, and departed. A few months after, I called on him; he was at luncheon, with two cats on a chair beside him — pets I should say, from their appearance.

This is not a solitary instance of the good of the first Cat Show in leading up to the observation of, and kindly feeling for, the domestic cat. Since then, throughout the length and breadth of the land there have been Cat Shows, and much interest is taken in them by all classes of the community, so much so that large prices have been paid for handsome specimens. It is to be hoped that by these shows the too often despised cat will meet with the attention and kind treatment that every dumb animal should have and ought to receive at the hands of humanity. Even the few instances of the shows generating a love for cats that have come before my own notice are a sufficient pleasure to me not to regret having thought out and planned the first Cat Show at the Crystal Palace.

EARLY CAT SHOWS

Cat shows have changed considerably over the decades. A show Siamese in 1905 was much broader than today. At the 1871 Crystal Palace Show, owners accompanied cats into the ring.

The Crystal Palace, London, was the site of the first cat show.

BUNNELL'S CAT SHOW

The first important cat show in America was held in March, 1881, at Bunnell's Museum, New York. The exhibition provoked much comment and saw many visitors. The following are excerpted from the New York Times *reports on the show.*

Preparation

Manager Bunnell stood in the center of his museum on Broadway, his hands in his hair, utterly perplexed, late last night. He was surrounded by cats in cages, cats in wooden boxes, cats in band-boxes, cats in bags, half of them yelling, spitting and scratching, as mad as cats can be in uncomfortable quarters and in a strange place. A deep scratch on his nose and three fingers tied up in oil and rags told how inexperienced he was in the way of cats. As fast as the cages were completed and the cats were placed in little sections, each one alone, they settled down for the night, and silence reigned. *(Sunday, March 6)*

Essay Contest

Mr. G.B. Bunnell . . . offered, before the opening of the show, a prize for the best essay on cats . . . Mr. Bunnell's office is now flooded with poetic, comic, serious and historic effusions from all parts of the country . . . A poor student in the Connecticut Literary Institution . . . sends a short essay and an urgent letter asking the committee to "Please let me know at once concerning the prize." The essay is as follows: "The cat is a domestic animal. She is the smallest of the family of the great cat tribe. This tribe consists of the lion, tiger, panther and other fierce animals, but the household cat is a domestic creature." *(Wednesday, March 16)*

A JUDGE'S STORY

Richard Gebhardt

CRESZENTIA ALLEN

AS IN ALL professions, experts who judge are a hard breed to classify: there are those acclaimed for knowledge of pedigreed cats; those whose interest lies in developing new breeds; and those whose aim is solely to preserve a breed type or color.

But one thing is certain in the profession: cat judges are increasingly in demand, for interest in pedigreed cat show competition is on the rise. Cat Fanciers' Association judges are among the most highly regarded. They travel throughout the United States and overseas, they are well-paid and are in constant demand.

In my work as a judge for twenty-three years, I have seen many changes in the profession. Fewer breeds were recognized when my interest in cats began. Since that time, many new colors in the existing breeds have developed; mutations have occurred, developing into new breeds; and both the size of the shows and the audiences have grown enormously.

Fanciers who wish to become judges today must anticipate a more difficult time than in previous years, for they must know so much more.

Qualifying for Judging

Anyone aspiring to become a cat judge must have acquired certain basic experience. Active participation in a cat club and first-hand knowledge of its attendant activities are both "musts." Acting as a cat show manager or official will also add to one's expertise. Being able to clerk (log cats into competitions) and to understand fully all of the mechanics of the judging procedure are additional plusses. Every qualified judge must, of necessity, know in exacting detail the standards for all breeds being shown. He must also be able to choose a single Best Cat after having evaluated as many as 375 cats — the maximum a judge may handle in a two-day show.

Today, a professional judge must have had at least five years' experience in the breeding and showing of cats. He must also be able to produce a record of champions and grand champions in his own breeding program. I cannot express too strongly the importance of gaining as much actual experience as possible in the breeding of a wide variety of breeds as well as the ability to act as handler and/or agent frequently in order to broaden one's perspective of cats.

Finally, before a would-be judge can qualify as a fully licensed C.F.A. judge, he must undergo a rigid training program.

The Good Judge

One must always remember that exhibitors at a cat show are *paying* for valid opinions and expert evaluation of their selective breeding results. The judge's findings are therefore taken very seriously by the exhibitors; indeed, some owners become highly emotional over the results. The respect of the exhibitors can only be won by a judge who is authoritative, fair, quick and definite in his decisions.

It is essential to his public image that a judge be well-groomed while in the ring. Fastidiousness impresses the exhibitors and makes them feel secure in the fact that the person handling their cats has taken all possible sanitary precautions.

ALICE SU

William Eisenman concentrates fully as he examines a Lynx Point.

Developing a style of handling cats so as to display the exhibit in a way that reveals its finest qualifications can also be very much to the advantage of a judge. Regular handling of cats in the ring builds confidence as well as skill. A capable judge should, in addition, be keenly sensitive to any unexpected movements of a cat and detect immediately any signs that the cat may be about to "act up."

A good cat judge will make certain to examine all parts of the cat to get the general feel of the cat for firm muscle tone, healthy skin and coat. It is also within his province to note the behavior and temperament of the cat. In fact, cats that show well and are a pleasure to handle have a decided advantage over a perhaps better-bred cat that does not show well.

To show the seasonal changes that affect the cat's coat and color, to be aware of the difference in caliber of cats either across the country or in the specific judging area, not to be so critical that one discourages the breeders — these, too, are important criteria for a judge. Part of a judge's responsibility is to help direct breeders in their developmental programs by making them aware of weaknesses of which they have undoubtedly been unaware. (Many exhibitors tend to become extremely authoritative because they live too close to the results of their breeding.)

Judging a cat show is a heavy responsibility, but it is also extremely rewarding. To finish a job knowing one would have judged all the exhibits in exactly the same way, given a second opportunity with the same cats, is a very satisfying experience. Long ago, I realized that I can make happy only those exhibitors who win — therefore, it is most important that I, the judge, am pleased with myself.

Richard H. Gebhardt is president of the Cat Fanciers' Association, Inc.

CAT SHOWS IN THE UNITED STATES AND CANADA

	73–74 Total			74–75 Show Season														
				Midwest		East		West		N. West		South		Total			
	Sh	Ent	Av.	Sh	Ent	Sh	Ent	Sh	Ent	Sh	Ent	Sh	Ent	Sh	Ent	Av.
ACA	20	3,119	156	—	—	4	791	8	1,304	—	—	—	—	12	2,095	175
ACFA	60	12,504	203	13	2,949	2	359	17	3,521	15	2,865	21	4,105	68	13,799	203
CCA	10	1,832	183	—	—	13	2,224	—	—	1	135	—	—	14	2,359	169
CFA	159	38,610	258	38	10,753	39	10,749	39	8,513	14	2,507	48	13,433	178	45,955	258
CFF	23	5,542	241	6	1,076	14	3,258	1	243	—	—	3	624	24	5,201	217
CROWN	6	850	142	1	133	2	278	—	—	—	—	2	277	5	688	138
ICF	1	161	161	—	—	3	439	—	—	—	—	—	—	3	439	146
NCFA	6	639	107	—	—	2	270	—	—	—	—	2	171	4	441	110
UCF	6	940	155	—	—	—	—	4	598	2	333	—	—	6	931	155
Total	291	64,197	221	58	14,911	79	18,368	69	14,179	32	5,840	76	18,610	314	71,908	229

Key: Sh = Shows; Ent = Entries; Av. = Average   Reprinted from *Cats* magazine (October, 1975).

A VISIT TO A CATTERY

Judy Fireman

I HAD NEVER BEEN to a cattery; in fact, I did not know exactly what one was, but as I became involved in the cat world, I kept hearing the term, so I decided to investigate.

Finding a cattery is tricky. You might buy a magazine devoted to cats and read the ads in the back, but such magazines, are usually sold only by subscription. You could also peruse newspaper classified sections in the hope of finding a legitimate cattery, however, I was determined to do this the right way so I called the national office of the Cat Fanciers' Association in Redbank, N. J.

"Do you have a certain breed in mind?" asked an extremely cooperative person on the other end of the line.

"No," I said. "I'm interested in seeing a cattery, not the cats."

He harumphed at my lack of discrimination, then suggested the LeShin-Wieler Cattery just outside New York City in White Plains, New York. "That way you can get a good look at the spring greenery as well."

To a city dweller, that idea sounded fine. I called immediately and made an appointment for the following Saturday.

The lovely spring greenery was almost invisible as I crept along the thruway in a driving rain — so much for a day in the country. I squinted through the torrent for signs — 9A, 287 South-North, 100A. Nowhere, did it say, "This way to Cattery!"

When I finally found the LeShin-Wieler establishment, it was not at all as I had imagined: the "cattery" was a lovely cottage sitting alone on a hillock covered with flowers and lush gardens; standing at the door, waiting to greet me, were William Wieler and Eb LeSchin. (The spelling of Eb's last name has been changed in the cattery name because a cattery name can have only twelve letters.)

Eb and Bill got their first cat eighteen years ago; since then, they have never stopped acquiring. Now there are thirty cats (one pregnant); the numbers are continually fluctuating. Wieler and LeSchin raise three very fancy breeds — Turkish Angoras, Burmese and Siamese.

Eb and Bill explained that their house consists of two levels: the Turkish Angoras, a few pet cats and Eb and Bill share the upper level; the lower, or basement level, is exclusively cat domain. We went for a tour of the lower level right away. It is divided into three parts. The center area is a sitting room and kitchen, the familiar rumpus-room look, but with a difference: from the low rafters are hung hundreds, no thousands, of ribbons — the trophies their cats have brought home throughout the years. The effect is marvelous. It is dark, warm and cozy down there, an exotic tent hung with many-colored ribbons. There is a couch for sitting and reading, or more likely, sitting and playing with cats. The cats' food is prepared in the kitchen.

To the left of the sitting room and kitchen is the area devoted to Siamese studs. The studs are housed by pairs in caged rooms about 10′ x 12′; within each room are two private standard show-size cages (22″ x 52″ x 25″). Each cat is rotated hourly out of its private cage into the larger area. While one Siamese is taking his constitu-

In Victorian catteries the cats had maids as well as visitors.

HOW TO BUY A SHOW CAT

If you are in the market for a show cat, shop around: the prices vary widely even though at first glance cats may look alike. You have to look carefully at a lot of cats before you will be able to recognize those which will not make it in the show world.

If you are serious about buying a show-quality cat, write the Cat Fanciers' Association, P.O. Box 430, Red Bank, New Jersey 07701, for the C.F.A. Breeders' Directory or the C.F.A. Yearbook. Both list registered catteries throughout the country. *Cats* magazine also lists cattery locations. It is also a good idea to attend meetings of a local cat club before committing yourself to the purchase of a cat you are buying for "show."

Prices for cats vary greatly around the country. Pet pure-breds range from $35 to $125. Show-types with papers average between $150–$250. Some catteries get $400 or more for Russian Blues. Persians have been reported to cost as much as $500 in some catteries.

tional, the other is sitting in his private cage taking a snooze or watching his roommate stalk about. (When we entered, however, they all sat up regally and observed the newcomer in their midst.) Eb and Bill said that the rotation schedule is demanding, but absolutely necessary; it insures each cat its own time to exercise, climb, scratch and walk about at ease. Each cat is fed individually; each has his own litter box — very posh surroundings.

To the right of the sitting room is another area — this one housing assorted cats, some Burmese and some Siamese. Unlike the Siamese stud area, there are both males and females in this room, but the arrangement is basically the same; the cats are always separated by the wire of their cages.

We returned upstairs to the living room for a sherry and a long chat about the world of the cattery. Bill explained that cattery owners differ about caging show cats, but he is adamant about the wisdom of keeping theirs in cages. (Show cats have to be cage-trained from an early age so that they can withstand the rigors of the show trail; they must be able to sit forty-eight hours in a cage while awaiting the judge's call.)

"Since they are raised for show and breeding, they must live their lives as what they are — show animals," Bill said.

He insisted that caging is not cruel to the cats, and appearances bear him out: the cats were not nervous, all looked well-cared for, and they seemed to be used to being handled and loved. Yet, they seemed equally happy to return to their cages.

The regimen of running a cattery is frightening to an outsider. In addition to the hourly exercise rotation, the cats are fed three times a day; their cages are washed and cleaned thoroughly once a day. Add up thirty cages and ninety meals per day, and you have an idea of what owning a responsible cattery involves.

The cattery, that is, the house, is immaculate: a harsh critic, I had sniffed as soon as I walked in the door. Aside from the fact that there were eight cats in view, I would not have been able to tell cats lived there. The house was obviously designed for cats: all the furniture is leather or plastic; tables are glass-covered and have few knick-knacks on them; the plants are where the cats cannot eat them — outside the house; even the toilet paper dispenser is cat-proofed with a sliding cover.

With a Grand Champion Siamese curled in a ball in my lap, I asked Eb and Bill what showing cats entails. To achieve Grand

Reception room in a turn-of-the-century Chicago cattery.

This Victorian cattery had an infirmary and more cages inside.

Champion status, they explained, a cat must appear in numerous shows each season. The number of shows varies with the breed, age of the cat and the competition; but a cat being seriously "campaigned" for national status will appear in forty shows a year, minimum. (About twenty shows are held simultaneously every weekend across the country, so the opportunities are there.) That means forty weekends on the road for the cat and his owner; about $150 per weekend for travel expenses, motels, entrance and vetting fees for at least one round in the competition. If more than one cat is being shown, which is common, the expenses mount; also there is the expense of hiring a reliable cat sitter for those left back home. Showing cats is not cheap, nor is it lucrative.

The LeShin-Wieler Cattery does sell cats; the prices range from $85 to $250 for a kitten. (A cat's value increases with the number of competitions won and with the strength of his bloodlines; but even the best-connected cat can turn out too long in the body, or with ill-matched markings.) Eb and Bill have several such cats; but rather than sell them they keep them as pets.

"Selling them would be a way to make a little easy cash, but it would not be fair to the buyers or to the kittens these cats might sire," Eb said.

The LeShin-Wieler cattery sells to three categories of buyers. Kittens are sold as pets to people who agree to alter them; pedigree papers are given to these buyers as soon as the cats have been altered. The second category of buyer wants a cat for breeding; the third, to acquire a show cat. (Show animals are not sold until they have been shown by the breeder. This policy insures the buyer of a qualified show cat.)

I sat and thought for a moment about all that I had heard: the necessity of cat-proofing the house; the expenses of breeding and showing; the all-consuming schedule Eb and Bill must follow to maintain their cats properly.

"Why do you do it?" I asked.

"We love cats!" they said.

Bill, a retired Shakespearian scholar, said, "I believe that cat lovers are this century's religious zealots. They are committed to their cats with an orthodox fervor."

And the cats love their owners. The entire time we sat there chatting, cats came to pay their respects. Gliding through the room with great dignity, each cat would check in with Bill or Eb, stop by for a pet, or a snooze on someone's shoulder, before sailing off for a turn around the house. The ribbons, loving cups and silver bowls do please Eb and Bill, but the cats themselves please them more — they paid close attention to our conversation, but they never lost track of which cat was where.

The rain had not let up, so I resigned myself to another death-defying trip back to the city. I had learned what a cattery is — it's a house where cats are raised for breed and show. It's a house where cats come first — *not people*. And it is a house where cultists live, not because they profit from their cats — they can't with the fees, risks and expenses involved in running a clean, pleasant cattery — but because they love their cats!

Judy Fireman is the editor of the Cat Catalog.

A CAT PEDIGREE

Cat Fanciers' Association, Inc.
PEDIGREE BLANK AND REGISTRATION FORM

PEDIGREE OF
(Give Two Choices of Names)

LeShin-Wieler Saipsboy
First Choice

Second Choice

Siamese _Breed_

Male _Sex_

Sealpoint _Color_

Blue _Eye Color_

11 Jan. 1968 _Date of Birth_

LeSchin-Wieler _Owner_

19 Park Avenue _Street Address_

White Plains, New York 10603
City _State_ _Zip_

I certify that, to the best of my knowledge and belief, the above pedigree is true and correct.

Signed LeSchin-Wieler _Breeder_

Cattery Name LeShin-Wieler _Number_

SIRE

Gr.Ch. LeShin-Wieler Saipan
Name of Sire

CFA Reg. No. _____

Siamese _Breed_ Sealpoint _Color_

LeSchin-Wieler _Owner_

19 Park Avenue _Street Address_

White Plains, N.Y. 10603
City _State_ _Zip_

DAM

MaKhanDa Cricket
Name of Dam

CFA Reg. No. _____

Siamese _Breed_ Sealpoint _Color_

LeSchin-Wieler _Owner_

19 Park Avenue _Street Address_

White Plains, New York 10603
City _State_ _Zip_

Ch. LeShin-Wieler Tuy Han
Color Sealpoint
CFA No. _____

Medicine Lake Singora II
Co.or Sealpoint
CFA No. _____

Gr.Ch. MaKhanDa Marauder
Sealpoint
Color
CFA No. _____

MaKhanDa Taffy
Color Sealpoint
CFA No. _____

Ch.Bridle Trail's Pingsor of Alray
Color Sealpoint
CFA No. _____

Nana of LeShin-Wieler (Imp)
Color Sealpoint
CFA No. _____

Kitti Livin' Doll
Color Sealpoint
CFA No. _____

Gr.Ch. Medicine Lake Texx-ess Rose
Color Sealpoint
CFA No. _____

Medicine Lake Mikado of MaKhanDa
Color Sealpoint
CFA No. _____

Ch. Usaf Shooting Star of MaKhanDa
Color Sealpoint
CFA No. _____

Ch. MaKhnaDa Griffin
Color Chocolatepoint
CFA No. _____

MaKhanDa Susi
Color Seal point
CFA No. _____

Ch. Bridle Trail's Ping No S/P
Ch. Singa Godiva of Bridle Trail S/P

Ch. Killdown Sultan S/P
Zara S/P

Ch. Medicine Lake Devon (Kitti) S/P
Bonee Gal Kitti S/P

Ch.Cuthpa Nu Zano S/P
Ch. Wee Sal of Medicine Lake S/P

Ch. Medicine Lake Wee Zano Kitti S/P
Ch. Wee Sal of Medicine Lake S/P

Gr.Ch. Interceptor of Usaf S/P
Neal Da's Voodoo of Usaf S/P

Gr.Ch. MaKhanDa Gizmo S/P
MaKhanDa Mimbu S/P

Medicine Lake Mikado of MaKhanDa S/P
Blue Orchid of New Moon B/P

The official pedigree form of the Cat Fanciers' Association traces a cat's bloodlines and catteries back for four generations. Because the cattery it came from is important, a listed cat's full name begins with the name of the cattery where it was bred and then the given name. This is the pedigree of LeShin-Wieler Saipsboy, a male Siamese bred at the LeShin-Wieler cattery, whose ancestry for several generations comes from this cattery: Champion Tuy Han sired out of the dam Singora II a grand champion male, Saipan. Then Saipan sired out of dam Cricket the male champion, Saipsboy. Of Saipsboy's twenty-two ancestors shown on the pedigree, five were grand champions and eleven were champions.

HOW TO ADOPT A STRAY

Kathy Roth

MORRIS H. JAFFE

DID YOU KNOW that for every cat with a home there are twelve strays? We have all seen them — huddled in doorways, foraging through garbage, frightened, sick, unwanted. The average street cat has a limited life expectancy; poorly fed, he risks death from untreated ailments, automobiles, and the cold. It is of no help to think someone else will do something about the stray. In most cases no one does. The A.S.P.C.A. can do no more than pick up some of them. What stray cats need are *homes*.

Adopting a stray can be rewarding and fun for you and the cat, but be aware before you bring the cat home of what the costs will be. Every stray will need at least a check-up, shots and neutering as soon as possible after adoption. Many veterinarians (not all, but many) will reduce fees if you tell them that the animal you have adopted was a stray. If your veterinarian cannot help with costs, find one who can — they do exist. Your local A.S.P.C.A. or humane society can probably make recommendations.

The first step in adopting a stray is, of course, getting him home. Approach the cat slowly, talk to him reassuringly. Touch him, pet him. Pick him up by placing your right hand under his rib cage between his two sets of legs, your left hand around his rump supporting his back legs, and lifting gently. If you have a distance to go, wrap him inside your coat or sweater, for a sudden noise on the street might cause him to start and jump from your arms. Hold him close to your body so that he will be comforted by your body heat.

The stray in need of help is often the most docile, the most trusting. The seriously injured stray needs help most, yet because people dislike the problems this situation creates so this is the cat most often ignored. Take the injured cat to a veterinarian immediately. Even if it must be euthanized, it is far worse to walk away and leave the cat to suffer.

Pregnant cats present other problems, particularly if they are strays. You will not help reduce the stray population by taking in the mother and then plan to abandon the newborn kittens. If you assume responsibility for a cat's welfare, you should be prepared to assume total responsibility. Therefore, if you are unable to deal with the difficulties of finding good homes for kittens (as anyone who has tried knows, it is nearly an impossible job), then it is best to have the kittens aborted.

If you are bringing the stray into a household where there is another cat, totally isolate the stray on arrival and until it has been examined by your vet. The most frequent health problems one confronts in strays are parasites — ear mites, worms and fleas. Although these can be treated quickly and effectively, they are easily transmitted to other cats. Strays may also suffer from upper respiratory ailments — symptoms are running eyes, sneezing and nasal discharge. Do not think of this as "just a cold." Upper respiratory ailments can kill cats.

If you already have a cat, you probably know about feline distemper. This is a virus which may be fatal to cats. If your cat has been innoculated, he runs no risk of catching this virus from a stray (nor do you, since it affects only cats). During the past two years, I have rescued fourteen strays. None of these had distemper and only one died from an upper respiratory illness. Do not be overly concerned about the possibilities of the stray being seriously sick. Just follow two simple precautions: keep the stray isolated from other cats for the first few days and have him examined by a doctor as soon as possible.

Once treated for ailments and restored to good health, strays require no more special care than any other cats. Some people think that stray cats, like dogs, should be bathed. It is best to let the cat take care of himself unless he has gotten into some terrible mess that only a scrubbing, and not a self-licking, will clean up. Secure in a new home, even the dingiest stray will soon make himself shine again.

Stray cats, like all cats, do not need much training to be house-broken. Introduce the stray to the litter pan and he will quickly get the idea. If your stray seems slow catching on, put him in the pan and help him make digging motions in the litter with his front paws, as you would a kitten. One or two lessons should be sufficient.

Because of poor diet, strays often suffer from constipation or diarrhea when first picked up. If your cat is suffering from constipation, feed him a half-teaspoon of unmedicated petroleum jelly. If he is suffering from diarrhea, mix a little cooked white rice with his food. If you notice blood in the cat's stool, it may be the result of the stray's having eaten bones or sharp objects or having gotten worms while living outside on the street. Don't panic; take a stool sample to your veterinarian to be analyzed.

The adoption of a stray should be enjoyable, but it is no fun living with a cat who has not been spayed or neutered. Adult males tend to spray the furniture with urine; females cry all night long, particularly when in heat. Do not believe the old stories about how neutering or spaying will change the disposition of a cat. It does not, as your veterinarian will tell you.

Once you have provided the physical comforts and medical necessities of your new pet, you may begin to worry about his adjustment to his new life. The best advice is not to worry. If this is your first cat, relax and enjoy getting to know him. He will be nervous and shy for a few days, but gradually he will begin to come to you for petting and play sessions. You are providing him with food and shelter, and in a short time he will begin to show his appreciation of your care. If you already have a cat, let the new cat adjust gradually. Do not try to force the cats to accept each other — they will want to maintain distance for a time. No matter how much explaining you do, your original cat will feel threatened and jealous. Reassure him by giving him extra attention. There will be growling and hissing, but ignore everything for at least three days. In most cases, by the end of this period the original cat usually tires of hostilities and begins to establish a negotiated peace.

As soon as your new cat begins to feel at home, he will sleep a lot. A little food, a little quiet, and you may not see much of your new pet for a few days. I have known strays to sleep almost uninterruptedly for a week after being rescued from the rigors of street life. If the vet found the cat healthy, do not worry. Let him rest and, in a few days, he will feel more sociable.

People often mistakenly think that cats who have lived on the street must be permitted to go outside. A former street cat will quickly adjust to life in the home and come to depend on the food and comforts he has been deprived of for so long. To let your cat back out on the streets is to expose him once more to the risks of becoming a stray again. You are not breaking natural laws, you are establishing a new, happy life the stray deserves.

Kathy Roth is an artist and cat humanitarian in New York City.

THE POLITICS OF STRAYS

Kitty Smith

THIS YEAR IN the United States alone over fifty million kittens will be born, most of them doomed to short lives. With our pet population conservatively estimated at a current 600 million — thirty-six million American families have at least one dog, not to mention additional dogs, cats, gerbils, hamsters, fish, parakeets, turtles, newts, snakes, and horses — there is little room by the fire for even the most adorable, purring ball of fur. Many who want a little kitten already have one — or two, or three.

America is in the midst of an animal crisis. At a time when we have a shortage of so many things, we have a glut of puppy dogs and pussy cats. Secretary of Agriculture Earl Butz was not far off the mark when he raised such a furor in 1975 by remarking that we should kill half our dogs and cats to offset the food shortage.

The Public Price of Strays

Set aside for a moment the emotional aspect, the humane values involved, and concentrate on the cold cash cost; no matter how it is figured, the expense of excess animals is enormous. Each year more than twenty million strays and un-wanted pets reach the nation's some 2,000 public pounds and private shelters. They each spend an average of 48 to 72 hours in these shelters. In 1973 it was figured that the average per-animal

handling cost for this amount of time was $7; today it is more likely to be $10. At the latter rate the expenditure is $200 million per year, though some estimates put it at $500 million and term that figure low. And of that amount no less than seventy-five per cent goes for killing the un-placeables and unplaced, too few of them old and ill, most of them capable of rehabilitation, and many of them as gentle and healthy as your pets and mine.

Nor is the cost of pounds and shelters the only expense. On the road, traffic accidents caused by unleashed, free-roaming and aban-doned animals are on a sharp increase, while in the country farmers count a minimum of $5 mil-lion yearly in cattle losses caused by wild dogs. In major cities, the public pound is seldom, if ever, the only institution involved with strays. In most cities the police, fire, sanitation, health, and con-sumer affairs departments are to some degree diverted from their primary functions by the animal crisis. Two years ago a National League-of Cities poll showed that 60.7 percent of mayors representing cities with populations exceeding 30,000 listed "dogs and other pet control prob-lems" as their number one complaint, ranking above taxes, crime, housing, health care, and fire protection.

There is not an area in America where con-

A STRAY'S LIFE

Authorities on stray work agree that the life-span of a street-bred stray is at most two years, and this figure is true for only the smartest, fastest, and wiliest of urban animals, usually cats who band together in protective packs. City strays have a better chance for survival than their country cousins because in town there are more places of refuge, more refuse to eat, and more people to pick them up. Street survivors are wise and tough. They are alert to the activities of building maintenance men, garbage collectors and stray workers. Yet, tough and smart as they are, the best they can hope for is two short years of fighting, getting sick, and breeding more of their kind.

cerned individuals who have already paid taxes for pound assistance, bought dog licenses, and donated to humane organizations, are not pouring vast sums into feeding, transporting, medicating, neutering, holding, adopting out or humanely destroying thousands upon thousands of strays and unwanted pets at a base cost of from $5 to $10 per animal.

Even so there are millions of animals who either do not reach shelters or have to be turned away. Many die of cold, hunger, disease, or injuries. Shelters that destroy animals rarely are able to keep them more than seventy-two hours. Those that do not kill must severely limit the number of animals they take in. There is not a shelter or pound in this country that is not frantic for additonal funds — some so frantic they sell strays to laboratories in order to pay for giving haven to others. And there is hardly a facility that does not think that it needs to expand to keep up with the explosive volume of excess animals.

In an age when contraception is the norm and population control imperative, people continue to allow millions of unwanted animals to be born. Too few facilities neuter before placing mature animals for adoption, and those that require adopters to prepay for neutering seldom have an effective followup program. Owners who do not control their pets' breeding solve the problem by handing out kittens to anyone who will take one, by leaving them with already overcrowded shelters or by simply dumping the new litter by the roadside or in a garbage can. Even people involved in human work devote most of their time and money to saving the few, ignoring the fact that vast numbers of animals must die. No one wants to be associated with mass murder; yet mass murder is perpetrated by this refusal to face and solve the crisis.

The Slowly Changing Public Mood

In 1974 the Congress of the National League of Cities adopted a policy urging the establishment of local public education programs and the passage of measures requiring pet owners to restrain their cats and dogs and to control their breeding. Only one city government, Los Angeles, is committed to a broad program of public education, law enforcement, strict licensing, and low-cost neutering; and Los Angeles is the only place in America where the animal death rate is actually being lowered.

The animal crisis is becoming increasingly political. Politicians who used to concentrate on kissing babies are beginning to make a show of backing animal legislation. So far, such legislation is negative: a proposed amendment to the federal Lacy Act, *The Live Domesticated Animal Public Health Protection Bill,* would impose a fine and/or jail for anyone "housing a dog or any other domesticated animal in a private house or apartment." As in Reykjavik, Iceland, where dogs were outlawed in the 1920s, American cities may be moving toward being petless. Normally law-abiding individuals deliberately flaunt social strictures when it comes to their pets. Among the least enforced and adhered-to laws are those concerning licensing, leashing, curbing, and abandoning animals, with the result that in urban areas more and more housing projects are refusing tenants with pets and anti-pet protestors are organizing and becoming, often justifiable, vocal.

America is affluent, peaceful and overrun with unwanted animals. It is a frightening commentary on our society that we value the quality of life less then we do the cost of destroying the quantity. It is we who are causing the problem, and it is because of us that millions of animals must suffer or be destroyed.

Kitty Smith is a writer and cat humanitarian in New York City.

HUMANE ORGANIZATIONS

The cart of The Royal Institution for Lost and Starving Cats, 1903.

The following list is intended as a guide to what services are available and does not necessarily mean that they are recommended. For the location of your local chapter of the A.S.P.C.A. or Humane Society, check the Yellow Pages of your local telephone directory.

American Anti-Vivisection Society
1903 Chestnut Street
Philadelphia, Pennsylvania 19103
Investigates and disseminates information on all forms of animal cruelty. Lobbies for abolition of vivisection. Publication: *The AV Quarterly.*

American Humane Association (A.H.A.)
P. O. Box 1266
Denver, Colorado 80201
Federation of 1500 humane organizations for children and animals. Offers training programs, teaching units and supplies for schools, film rentals, workshops. Publications: *The National Humane Review, The National Humane Junior Review,* approximately 300 pamphlets.

American Society For The Prevention of Cruelty To Animals (A.S.P.C.A.)
441 East 92nd Street
New York, New York 10028

Founded in 1866, the first humane society in the United States. Hospital and Clinic facilities. Low-cost spaying and neutering. Shelter for strays. Adoption service. Licensing. Humane education and activities. Animalport at Kennedy International Airport for care of animals before, after and between flights. Legislative lobbying. Destroys animals not adopted after days. Note: Although many A.S.P.C.A.s are patterned after New York's, they are all independent of one another.

Animal Protection Institute (A.P.I.)
P. O. Box 22505
Sacramento, California 95822
Educational and information programs. Advocates neutering and spaying. Lobbies for pets and wildlife. Publication: *Mainstream.*

Bide-A-Wee Home Association
(Centered in New York State)
410 East 38th Street
New York, New York 10016
Rescue and adoption services. Maintains hospitals, clinics, country shelters and pet cemetery. *Guarantees no animal ever destroyed unless incurably ill.* Publication: Bi-monthly newsletter.

California Humane Council
4432 Canoga Avenue
Woodland Hills, California 91364
Coordinates humane societies throughout the State of California. Lobbies for humane legislation, with special emphasis on control of breeders and pet shops selling animals for research. Sponsors low-cost neuter and spay clinics.

Friends Of Animals (F.O.A.)
11 West 60th Street
New York, New York 10023
Subsidizes cost of neutering and spaying. Lobbies against inhumane practices for pets and wildlife. Animal birth control educational programs. Publication: *FOA Actionline.*

Fund For Animals
140 West 57th Street
New York, New York 10019
Cleveland Amory's "foundation" for funding qualified recipients who work to stop all categories of animal suffering. Aids existing projects and those wishing to initiate humane societies. Subsidizes neutering and spaying programs.

Humane Society Of The United States (H.S.U.S.)
1604 K Street, N. W.
Washington, D. C. 20006
Primarily a lobby "to promote the humane treatment of living things and instill compassion in mankind." Sponsors Education and Nature Center in East Haddam, Connecticut. Humane, Education Development and Evaluation Project with the University of Tulsa, Oklahoma. Publication: *News of the HSUS,* bi-monthly. NOTE: Local humane societies are independent of the national H.S.U.S.

Mercy Crusade, Inc.
(Centered in the State of California)
P. O. Box 3265
Van Nuys, California 91407
Animal breeding control program and funding. California State Humane Officers Unit for investigation and prosecution of cases of cruelty to animals. Humane education program providing literature, speakers, films, booths and exhibits. Rescue and placement operation. Foster home programs. Lobbying on all levels of government.

Morris Animal Foundation
(No relation to the T.V. star)
531 Guaranty Bank Building
Denver, Colorado 80202
Finances scientific health studies for all pets. Research reports delivered at annual meetings. Sponsors seminars and veterinary lectures. Publication: *Companion Animal News.*

National Anti-Vivisection Society
100 East Ohio Street
Chicago, Illinois 60611
Educational and teaching program on methods of combating vivisection. Compiles statistics. Maintains library. Publications: Bi-monthly bulletin, booklets, pamphlets.

Pet Assistance Foundation, Inc.
P. O. Box 69426
Los Angeles, California 90069
Entirely voluntary organization devoted to curtailment of breeding. Runs nine separate answering services in southern California to refer owners to low-cost spaying and neutering clinics and other animal needs.

Pet Pride
15113 Sunset Boulevard
Pacific Palisades, California 90272
Humane society devoted solely to cats. Rescue and adoption service. Shelter. Clinic. Low-cost neutering and spaying. Anti-declawing program. Educational service on inhumane practices toward cats. Cats' rights program.

Society For Animal Rights
900 First Avenue
New York, New York 10022
Educational and lobbying organization to prevent cruelty to and suffering in all animals. Planned parenthood for pets and anti-declawing campaigns. Boycotts. Makes available literature, reprints, brochures, pins, buttons and free educational films.

United Action for Animals
205 East 42nd Street
New York, New York 10017
Exposes and protests cruelty to animals used in research. Promotes alternatives, such as tissue and organ culture studies. Lobbies for modern methods of research.

VI. THE PHYSICAL CAT

THE FAMILY OF CATS

Kenneth Anderson

O N THE AFRICAN plain, a lion slowly oh, so slowly lifts a paw and silently stalks a zebra. In a nearby village, a common domestic cat slowly, slowly lifts a paw and stalks one of the village chickens. Cats of the world — big or little striped or spotted, tan or black — are much alike in their behavioral patterns. They are an ancient family of hunters. The genealogy of most cats is as hazy as it is for most humans, but we do know that ultimately the cats of the world have a common ancestry.

According to fossil evidence, cats evolved over tens of millions of years. Exactly when the first true cat set foot on earth is not known, but apparently there were cats we would recognize as cats some fifty to sixty million years ago. Other mammals, the grouping of larger animals that includes cats, had evolved about one hundred fifty million years earlier. Some scientists believe that this early period was a great era for cats and that their way of life was already perfected.

One of the earliest cats known was the saber-tooth tiger which was dominant throughout much of the world until, for mysterious reasons, they became extinct about forty million years ago. As later species of cats evolved and multiplied, they developed into nearly forty distinct species. But how and why they went their separate ways is something of a puzzle.

The exact relationship between the big cats and the various domestic (or little) cats is not precisely known. At sometime in the past, probably due to adaptive changes, domestic cats appeared. The common American domestic cat of the short-haired variety may be a mixture of an African bush cat and a wild cat that once roamed Europe. But, according to some experts, spotted cats among the domestic varieties may have acquired this trait from the spotted wildcat of India.

Although all cats have much in common, they have, during the years, evolved many different characteristics, and most rules of cat

Big or little, the cats of the world are predators.

NANCY LOU GAHAN

conduct are broken by the characteristics of one or more species. Almost any member of the cat family likes to stalk small animals, but the fishing cat of Asia will sit peacefully by a stream or pond and flip fish onto the land with its paw. Most cats, when compared with other hunting mammals, have only average speed. The cheetah, by comparison, is the fastest land animal in the world, achieving a top speed of seventy miles per hours — faster than most birds can fly. Cats generally avoid the water; yet the Latin American jaguar actually enjoys swimming and may spend hours swimming in forest pools and rivers. Cats live in all sorts of terrains and climates. Their ability to adapt to their particular climate has been the reason for their survival over so many millions of years of changing environmental conditions.

Kenneth Anderson is a science writer specializing in medicine and biology.

THE ANATOMY OF THE CAT

Kenneth Anderson

EVERYBODY KNOWS THAT the cat is a four-legged animal. Not everyone realizes, however, that only two of the cat's legs are jointed with knees. The front legs are like arms; they have elbow joints instead of knees and are joined to the trunk of the body by shoulder joints. Thus, the basic cat frame is much like the basic human frame.

This similarity between cats and people is not too surprising since both are members of the large, warm-blooded group of animals called mammals, but cats and humans are not quite the same kind of mammals. Cats are carnivores, the meat-eating group that also includes dogs, bears and seals. Humans are primates — a category that includes baboons, apes and monkeys.

As mammals, cats and humans have in common a backbone, a four-chambered heart, a muscular diaphragm to aid in breathing,

mammary glands and offspring that are born live rather than being hatched from eggs.

Another important characteristic shared by all mammals is hair. Some scientists believe that the layer of hair on the skin made it possible for cats and other mammals to evolve successfully from their reptile-like ancestors about 200 million years ago. Just when and how cats and other mammals acquired hair cannot be determined because hair is never found in the fossil remains of ancient mammals. But there is little doubt that hair, which traps a layer of air next to the body, provided a valuable insulation that helped to maintain an even body temperature during changes in climate.

Another significant factor in the survival of mammals through the ages has been the dependence of the young on the mother for food and protection during infancy. As a result of this relationship, young mammals have an opportunity to learn from the older generation. This learning fostered development of intelligent behavior and training for survival in an otherwise hostile world. Over the years, cats evolved a rather advanced type of brain for their size and, as a result, were quick to display their intelligence.

The Skeletal System.

The skeleton was one of the great developments of animal evolution since it supports the body, protects the soft tissues, and serves as levers for moving jointed body parts. A young adult cat has about two-hundred eighty-seven bones in its body, including twenty-one or twenty-two tail bones (if he has a full tail) and forty sesamoid bones, or bones like the patella of the knee joint which are actually part of a tendon. As in the human body, the skeleton of a young animal may have more separate bones than an older

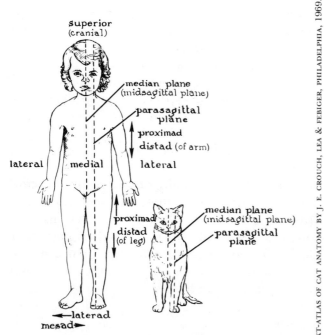

Cats and humans are alike in many structural ways.

TEXT-ATLAS OF CAT ANATOMY BY J. E. CROUCH, LEA & FEBIGER, PHILADELPHIA, 1969.

Falling cats use their tails to help right themselves.

member of the species because some of the individual bones fuse together as the animal ages.

The arrangement of bones in a cat's body and their connecting joints permit a wide variety of activities important for the survival of the animal. Some joints provide a kind of gliding movement. The cat, like the giraffe and the camel, walks by moving both left feet and then both right feet. This pattern accounts for the smooth, gliding gait of the animal. Another type of joint is the ball-and-socket, or universal joint, that permits a wide range of movement around a common center. For example, the hip socket accounts for much of the cat's agility in climbing and jumping. The elbow (front leg) is an example of a hinge joint, and similar joints can be found in the knee (back leg) and the jaw bones. Still another kind of bone-to-bone arrangement that permits a unique kind of action is the pivot joint, as seen in the neck which can allow the head to turn from side to side. The pivot joints in the neck are extremely useful to the cat in its everyday life. Because of these joints the cat is able to reach almost any part of its body for licking and cleaning — the only absolutely impossible place for a cat to reach is directly behind its head, between its shoulder blades.

The tail of the cat, which is an extension of the spinal column, enables the cat to communicate pleasure or anger to humans or to other cats. In addition, the tail is important in helping the cat to balance itself in climbing, leaping and probably in the still-mysterious trick of righting itself should it fall from a height. In a long fall, the agile cat whips its tail about to help turn the body into a position that will make for a soft landing on all four legs. Cats can fall clumsily though; their ability to land right side up is not totally infallible.

The Sensory System

The sense organs of the cat include the eyes, ears, nose, tongue and skin and are similar to our own organs. Most of the functions of the body, be it cat or human, are coordinated by a brain which depends on signals sent to it by the various sense organs.

When a sensory organ is stimulated by, for example, a flash of light on the retina of the eye or the beating of sound waves on the eardrum, a nerve impulse is triggered and sent to the brain. Biologists believe that all nerve impulses are alike and that the brain translates a signal's meaning on the basis of where the message is received.

The Eye of the Cat. Perhaps the most remarkable sense organ of the cat is its eye. Certainly it is the cat's eye which has long fascinated people because it sees well in the dark and, with its special color and slant, seems to detect mysteries we can only guess at. Yet to a biologist the eye of the cat is similar in most details to the human eye. Protected by a bony socket in the skull, the eye is controlled by six different muscles that can move it up and down and from side to side while the head remains motionless. Tiny muscles and ligaments can change the size of the pupil opening (making it smaller in bright light and larger in dim light). Changes in light can also change the shape of the eye lens for near or distant vision. Yet cats are apparently unable to distinguish color and see images only in shades of gray, such as on a black-and-white television set.

Cats do have a special layer of cells in the retina that make it possible for them to see with no more light than is available on a starlit, moonless night. These special cells, called *tepetum,* act as a mirror in collecting and

The cat's mouth cuts like pinking shears.

much like the human ear; however, because of some specialized nerve endings the cat is more sensitive to high-pitched sounds than we are, and cats can hear noises made by prey which humans cannot hear at all.

The Cat's Whiskers. Although the cat's whiskers are coarse hairs, they serve as sense organs which represent a power lacking in people. These whiskers grow on the upper lip, the cheeks and the upper eyelids. Sensitive nerve endings at the base of the hairs are stimulated when the tips brush an object. Thus, they can help to guide a cat through tall grass or shrubs when it is stalking a rodent. Also, because the whiskers extend to about the width of the cat's shoulders, they are thought by some to provide the cat with information about the amount of room it has available for moving through a darkened hole or tunnel.

The Cat's Nose. The nose of the cat is composed of several tough layers of skin. The appearance of a cat's nose may be any color from pale pink, through gray to black, including a mottled coloration. Internally, or course, the nose is a sense organ and in cats it is an organ of great sensitivity. Because of the structure of their noses cats can detect an odor that would be imperceptible to a human.

Cat Skin and Hair. The skin of a cat is a tough but flexible membrane that keeps the moisture content of the inner body at the proper level. It

reflecting back into the eye any available light. This effect, known as eyeshine, is what causes a cat's eyes to glow or shine in the dark. It is also what allows a cat to roam about and hunt successfully at night.

The cat's eye has, in addition, a third eyelid called a nictating membrane, which acts as a protection for the eye. This may be either pale pink or dark in color. The third eyelid closes over the eye during sleep, and may become visible when a cat is frightened or ill.

The Ear of the Cat. As in humans, ears of a cat serve a double function. In addition to hearing, a cat's ears contain a tiny organ which helps the animal maintain its balance. The canals of the ear are lined with sensory nerve cells; a fluid circulates through the canals, and when the head is moved in any direction the fluid flows over the nerve-cell endings. The pressure of the fluid, which is controlled by simple gravity, is always triggering messages to the brain no matter how the head is positioned. By translating the nerve messages, the brain can tell whether the head is right-side up, upside down, or whatever. Other nerve receptors in the limbs of the body also aid the brain in determining the position of the body with respect to the ground, or the pull of gravity.

The hearing portion of the ear begins with the external ear itself. Anyone who has watched a cat's ears while the animal is listening to a strange sound must have observed how the cat aims its ears so as to lock onto the source of the sound waves. The interior of the cat's ear works

THE PURR

One of the long-standing mysteries of the cat is its ability to make purring noises. Cats of all species purr when they are contented, although the purring sound can also occur when they are in pain. Biologists have determined that purring does not originate in the larynx (voice box). One prevalent theory is that it is generated by vibrations in the chest of the cat which are brought on by increased activity in major blood vessels there. But ultimately, the origin and function of the purr remain unexplained.

also protects the body from disease organisms in the environment. The cat's coat of hair, which is a specialized modification of the skin cells, as mentioned before, traps a layer of air and thus insulates the body temperature changes in the environment. By shedding hair in warm weather and growing a thicker coat in cold weather, the cat can partially control the amount of insulation. Cats living indoors all year adapt to their more stable environment by continuously shedding a little hair.

Pads and Claws in the Cat. The hairless footpads found on the front and hind feet of the cat are a specialized part of its skin. There is one pad for each digit (toe) plus a large pad under the bones of the hind foot and forefoot. On the forefoot, there is an additional pad under the "wrist" or carpus bone. Each pad is made up of thick tough pigmented skin which can withstand a lot of wear and tear. Although the cat does not have sweat glands elsewhere in his body, his footpads contain sweat glands with tiny ducts that weave through the layers of skin to discharge any fluids at the outside.

The cat's horny claws, like fingernails and toenails in humans, are also a specialized part of the skin. When not in use for climbing, hunting or self-defense, the claw is retracted into skin folds above the digital pad.

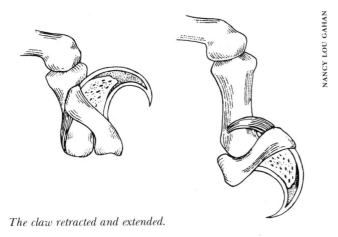

The claw retracted and extended.

The Heart of the Cat

The heart is located almost in the center of the lung activity. Like humans, cats have a four-chambered heart which forms a twin set of pumps, working side by side. One of the pumps circulates blood through the lungs; the other

pump keeps the blood circulating through the rest of the body. The teamwork of the lungs and heart therefore demands that they be as close together as is feasible.

The Reproductive System

A major difference between the reproductive organs of the female cat and the human female is that the female cat has a combined opening for the vagina and urethra, called the urogenital sinus. The sinus, or vestibule, also contains a clitoris. The female reproductive organs otherwise are essentially the same as in a human. A cervix at the end of the vagina opens into the uterus and two horns of the uterus, comparable to the human Fallopian tubes, extend into the ovaries.

The cat's anatomy is therefore surprisingly similar to the human's. It is specialized, of course, and yet we can recognize much that is our own. In biology different creatures, even if they are as different as cats and people, represent variations upon related themes.

Serious birth defects are rare. Buffon's Natural History, *1767, showed this monster cat.*

NANCY LOU GAHAN

THE BEHAVIOR OF THE CAT

Jani Anderson

THE DOMESTIC CAT is a solitary animal. Scientists believe the modern domestic cat descended from the African wild cat *Felis Libyca,* an animal which lives and hunts alone. The cat's solitary behavior is considered part of his specialization as a lone carnivirous hunter. With his truncated shearing jaw, long retractile claws, long canines, good eyesight and skeletal adaptation for leaping, the cat is a master of stealth and the sudden ambush. He does not need company when he hunts his prey. In fact, because the cat generally hunts prey smaller than himself, he must do so several times a day to satisfy his own dietary needs. Group hunting or the close contact of other cats who might compete for his meal would be a hindrance to his survival. The lion, considered the only social feline, is an exception to this. Lions will stalk prey together, although the actual killing is normally done by only one individual.

Almost the only social group which exists among cats is the mother and her litter. Males and females almost never form pair-bonds. They may have partner preferences which they express during periods of sexual heat, but these partnerships are rarely carried into areas outside the actual process of mating. The male for example, does not usually help in rearing the young.

Mother-Family

The mother cat lies on her side and encloses the kittens by moving her forelegs down and her hind legs up around them. The kittens nuzzle and tap their noses against the mother's abdomen until they locate a nipple. When the kitten finds one, he mouths, grasps the nipple and suckles. Actual feeding does not take place until one or two hours after birth, but suckling is almost continuous for the first twenty-four hours. On the second day, the mother cat will periodically leave the nest.

By the third day, most kittens establish a preference for a particular nipple on the mother's body, which they identify by odor and texture. A kitten may occasionally grasp another nipple but will allow himself to be pushed aside when the true owner arrives. After the kitten has established a nipple preference, he develops paths through the nest and along the mother's body to reach that nipple.

For about the first three weeks, the mother initiates all suckling. She lies by the kittens in the nursing position and rouses them to suckle by licking their bodies. The kittens are nursed several times a day. At first, each kitten spends about 25 percent of his time nursing. The mother may spend as much as 70 percent of her time nursing, as the kittens will not all nurse at the same time. "Purring" appears in the kitten during nursing and is, according to one theory, produced when the kitten is taking breaths between swallows.

During the first weeks of the kittens' lives, almost all social interaction is related to nursing and grooming. The mother nuzzles, licks and vocalizes to the kittens. She facilitates elimination by licking the kittens in the anal region.

Before the kittens' visual ability is well-developed, they display a strong attachment to the nesting region. If for any reason a kitten becomes separated from the nest, he vocalizes in a sharp cry. The vocalization increases in intensity the farther the kitten is from the nest. The mother cat will respond to the kitten's cries by carrying the kitten back to the nest, gripped by the neck. This attachment to the nest allows the mother to leave the kittens by themselves while she goes out on her own. In spite of this, the mother generally stays in or close to the nest for the first three weeks of the kittens' lives.

The kittens are able to identify the nest by the odor of the mother's birth fluids and fur deposits. A kitten placed near the nest is able to crawl back to it by following a trail of the mother's scent, which becomes stronger nearer the nest as the mother has spent greater time in direct contact with the area.

Between the fourteenth and thirtieth day, the kittens' visual ability improves markedly. Soon, they are able to focus without difficulty on the mother as she moves around outside the nest. The kittens, apparently gaining a sense of confidence in their ability to locate their mother and litter mates, begin to leave the nest. When this stage is reached, nursing is initiated by the kittens as well as the mother. The kittens will approach the mother and nuzzle her to lie down in the nursing position.

Kittens enjoy playing with each other.

Play-behavior is seen from about the third week and increases in intensity to the point where, in or around the fifth week, the mother cat begins to spend longer and longer periods away from the kittens. A change in the nursing relationship takes place. The kittens now have to initiate all nursing. They follow the mother around, nuzzle her, meow, and eventually force her to lie down so they can attach to a nipple. Some mother cats will respond to this treatment by hissing or batting at the kitten.

Kittens will eat solid food starting around the fifth week. Farm kittens will eat dead prey brought by their mother and will also follow the mother on hunting trips.

For at least another month, until he is weaned, much of the kitten's social life revolves around his litter mates. Together, the kittens stalk, bite, paw, leap and climb, displaying in irregular and exaggerated form all the basic movements the adult cat uses to hunt or fight. The kitten will play not only with inanimate objects but with hallucinatory spots in the air. His

play involves elements of hunting (stalking, leaping), environmental exploration (hiding, climbing) and social interaction (fighting, affection). A kitten inviting a litter mate to play will show his "play face": wide eyes and ears pressed forward. He may also roll seductively onto his side. Kittens during play usually hold their tails in a hooked down position. If the kittens are highly aroused, their tails will be looped up.

In addition to the socialization of play, both the kittens and mother will devote time to mutual grooming. Grooming is a basis for social interaction throughout the cat's entire life.

Predatory Behavior

The cat creeps across a field. She holds her body close to the ground. If the mouse she is stalking shows any signs of fear or recognition, the cat stops and waits. If the mouse does not dart away and the cat reaches a spot close enough to attack, she leaps atop her prey. Holding on to it with extended claws, she administers a swift killing bite to the dorsal (back) side of the neck.

This cat is an experienced hunter. Not all domestic cats kill. All cats have the innate potential to kill, but the act of killing requires learning and experience.

The silent stalk is typical of cats.

The sensitive period during which the mother cat can most easily teach her kittens to kill is between the sixth and twentieth weeks of life. The sight of the live prey is not thought to be enough stimulus in and of itself to incite kittens to kill. The kitten requires the added stimulation of the mother's and litter mates' competition. Kittens who do not learn to kill at this point in life may learn later, but with much greater difficulty.

Initially, kittens are frightened by prey animals and may be put off entirely by any attempted escapes. Most mother cats will bring their young kittens already injured prey to kill. Then, as the kittens experience success as hunters, they gain confidence and will boldly dash after the prey.

Position in the litter can sometimes affect the ease with which kittens learn to kill. Higher-ranking kittens learn faster than lower-ranking kittens. A short-term loss of status may cause a kitten to temporarily lose whatever hunting ability he had.

Aiming the bite at the general area of the neck is an innate response. The dorsal bite is learned. The kitten has to attack prey many times before he learns, sometimes through unhappy experience, how to bite in the most effective manner.

Even a farm cat who has been fed dead prey by his mother does not at first understand the connection between food and the animal he has killed. He may kill with enthusiasm, but it is only after he makes a connection between the act of killing and obtaining food that hunger will trigger the hunting response.

The subroutines of hunting, i.e., stalking, pawing, leaping, biting, are never fixed in one set pattern. The mature hunter uses these

A hissing threat display.

There is, indeed, no single quality of the cat that man could not emulate to his advantage.

CARL VAN VECHTEN

routines and others of his own creation, in combinations of his own design. P. Leyhausen, an authority on animal behavior, suggests that these subroutines may be in and of themselves satisfying to the cat, and that the cat has in fact an internal drive to express them. Because the cat's prey is small and he may have to hunt several times a day, it could be of adaptive value that the cat derives satisfaction from stalking or leaping, as he may have to perform these activities many times before he finally obtains food.

If a cat is frequently hungry, it is more likely that his hunting behavior will be turned to the serious business of killing prey. However, if he is well-fed, chances are these same behaviors will be displayed as play. Cats have been known to ignore prey entirely in favor of wads of paper. In the same manner, cats may play with a prey animal rather than deliberately kill it.

Communication

Cats communicate by using visual, auditory, olfactory and tactile clues. Most of their expressive behavior is structured for close-range communication. Aside from mating and territorial marking, there does not seem to be a great need for long-distance communication in the social structure of cats. They are particularly rich in visual signals. This type of communication undoubtedly puts to good advantage cats' form vision, which is as well developed as man's.

Included among the physical signals used by the cat are the following:

Visual signals — ear position, eye position, degree of eye-opening, tail movement, hair bristling, mouth-opening, bearing and walk, body patterns (tufts of hair on cheeks, color).

Vocalization—There are sixteen different vocal patterns used by the cat. These can be catagorized as murmur patterns, vowel patterns and strained intensity. The murmur pattern ("purr") indicates a friendly, relaxed state. The vowel pattern ("meow") is used to solicit care or express frustration. Strained intensity ("hiss,

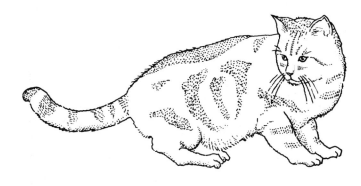

NANCY LOU GAHAN

A cat taking a submissive posture.

on stiff erect legs, arching his back. His fur bristles, especially that on his tail. The tail is held to one side. In this posture the cat looks larger than usual. The cat may expose his teeth, hiss and growl. His eyes normally dilate. Defensive threat is used when the cat is afraid and may in fact be willing to run away.

Offensive threat is used when the cat is more self-confident or more willing to engage in battle. Two cats confronting each other in this attitude face each other head-on, staring directly into each other's face. Their pupils contract. They may flick their tails from side to side. They hiss and scream excitedly, retaining this posture until fighting breaks out, or intimidation is achieved and one cat defers.

A female cat defending her young stands with her side to the intruder. She holds her tail against her side and gallops toward the intruder in this posture, hissing, growling and exposing her teeth.

A cat angered by human teasing crouches down with his body extended and flicks his tail. If pushed beyond this point, he folds his ears back, growls and exposes his teeth.

Male cats sometimes communicate attitudes of dominance and submission by mating postures. The dominant male mounts the submissive male, grasps him by the neck and treads. The submissive male crouches in the posture of a receptive female. In certain situations, the posture of crouching while avoiding eye contact communicates a submissive attitude.

Amicable Behavior — The cat encourages social contact and expresses pleasure through play, social grooming and a number of social signals.

A kitten greeting his mother holds his tail vertically, vocalizes in a special greeting call, sniffs the mother's tail and touches the mother's nose with his own. This same cat greeting his

growl — scream") is heard during attacks, defense and mating.

Scratching is sometimes used as a sound signal.

Olfactory signals — The cat marks by urinating, and with scent glands located in the tail (caudal gland), forehead (temporal gland), lips (perioral gland), chin and anal area.

Tactile signals — licking, nuzzling, rubbing, pawing.

Threat Display — The cat uses threat displays to avoid actual combat. These are particularly expressive and varied. Slight changes in the degree of fear or rage will bring about corresponding changes in the display.

A cat approached by a menacing dog reacts with a defensive threat display. With his side facing the dog, his ears pushed back, the cat stands

FEAR AND ANGER IN A CAT

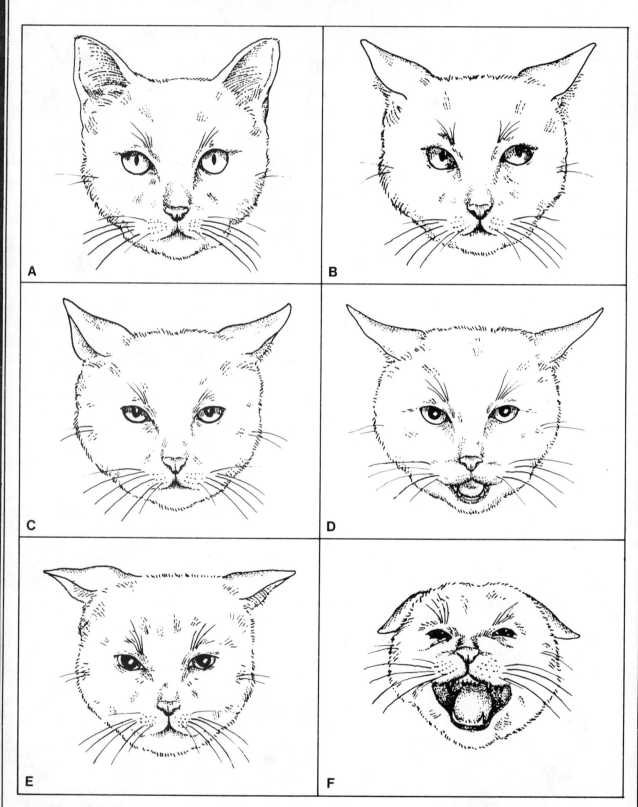

As a cat is challenged its facial expression changes from alertness (a), through offensive threat (b), to increasing fear (c). Indecision between flight and attack (d) then appears and the cat makes a defensive threat (e) that ends in a snarl (f). Note: the ears sink, pupils dilate and mouth opens.

owner holds his ears erect, rubs against the owner's legs with his back arched and marks the owner by rubbing his lips and forehead against the owner's hand.

Group Ecology and Social Structure

The domestic cat, putting himself at the mercy of human choice, has no control over the location of his home. In consequence, domestic cats as a group cannot control how many of their number live in a particular region or how they are dispersed. For this reason, it is difficult to draw conclusions about how cats might arrange themselves in space if they were left totally to their own devices and, in addition, prevented from sharing a home with man.

Cats do seem tolerant toward sharing a home, not only with humans and dogs, but with other cats as well. Most solitary mammals are lenient about sharing the home area with animals of other species but are not tolerant toward animals of their own species, particularly when like-sexed. In the field, cats will shun each other's company.

Although cats do have home ranges, these frequently overlap, and more than one cat will have a particular field or path as part of his territory. The mother cat will strenuously defend her nesting area, but cats generally control space in terms of limiting personal encounters rather than in defending a particular territory.

Cats try to avoid using the same area at the same time. Encounters can be controlled through visual contact. Marking is thought to be another means by which cats can warn each other that a particular spot is or has been recently occupied. Cats will urinate on objects or mark them with any of the numerous glands on their bodies.

A cat coming upon a tree marked by a previous cat will respond with the Flehman reaction: he will sniff the marking with his eyes closed and mouth held slightly open. This may facilitate the cat's recognition or interpretation of the scent. Cats will not mark over a spot where another cat has urinated but will mark over those where another cat has marked with his chin or lips. Cats also mark by scratching environmental objects.

If a cat on his travels sees another cat further along the path, he will most likely stop, sit, sniff the ground and wait until the other cat is out of visual range. If both cats see each other at a crosspath, they may both stop and sniff the ground until one or the other decides to move

An offensive-threat display.

on. They rarely go out of their way to attack each other on these occasions but may do so if they have never fought before.

An adult cat usually has only one serious fight with each strange cat he encounters. After the better fighter has proven himself, other hostile encounters will be worked out in threat displays rather than in combat. Male cats are generally more aggressive and concerned with relative ranking than females, yet at the same time males are more tolerant of casual social contact.

The social ranking established through combat following chance encounters is in most situations relative. While in certain situations the dominant cat will have his way, at other times he will defer to the lower-ranking cat. Higher-ranking cats will often give way to the lower-ranking cat if the latter is farther ahead on a path or is first to reach a favorite spot.

Man would seem to have for the cat the advantages of social contact without the innate repulsiveness cats might have for each other. And on the part of man there has always been the social inclination to care for animals.

Jani Anderson, a member of the Interscience Publishing Group of John Wiley & Sons, Inc., is interested in animal behavior and psychology.

CAT GENETICS

Casey Rice

SUPPOSE YOU BRED two cats, a black and a tabby, hoping to get at least one or two black kittens from the resulting litter. After all, it seems logical, does it not, that about half the kittens would turn out black? But six weeks later, the tabby mother is smugly nursing six squirming kittens that all look exactly like her.

Genetics, the study of how certain characteristics are passed from one generation to another, gives us the answer. Which characteristic an offspring inherits from each parent is determined by certain fixed genetic principles. In the case of the tabby mother and black father, it is possible to predict fairly accurately what the kittens will look like if you know something about the inherited characteristics of each parent.

Heredity in cats and all other living things operates according to the same basic genetic principles. An Austrian monk, Gregor Mendel, first discovered these principles nearly one hundred years ago by breeding short and tall garden pea plants. His results were comparable to the results you would obtain from mating black and tabby cats: when Mendel crossed tall pea plants with dwarf pea plants, instead of getting medium-sized plants or even a mix, all the new plants were tall. Then, when he crossed those plants, he came up with a mixture of three tall plants for every short one. Like Mendel's pea plants, if you bred two of the tabby kittens you would probably get at least three tabbies, and finally, one black kitten.

Since Mendel's simple experiments with peas, genetics has grown into a complex science that forms the basis of a modern breeding industry. Basically, genetics works like this. Each cell in an individual's body contains the genes which control all inherited characteristics. The genes are linked together like beads on strands. The strands are called chromosomes and almost always occur in identical pairs. Cats have nineteen pairs of chromosomes in every cell.

Determination of the characteristics of kittens begins even before two cats mate. During the joining of the egg and sperm cells (both called germ cells), the paired chromosomes separate and the germ cell itself splits in half to form two new cells, each of these containing nineteen *individual* chromosomes. During mating a germ cell from each parent combines to form a complete cell containing nineteen pairs of chromosomes. Each pair consists of one chromosome from the father and one from the mother. In the cross of our tabby mother and black father, the fertilized cell contains a tabby gene and a black gene.

The appearance of each kitten depends on how the genes from each parent are combined. Some genes, like tabby coloring, are dominant, meaning they always determine the appearance of the individual. Other genes, like black, are recessive and are never expressed if they are combined with a dominant gene. A black kitten receives a black gene from each parent.

Using the symbole *TT* (two dominant tabby genes) to describe the genetic color make-up of the pure tabby mother, and *bb* (two recessive black genes) to describe the pure black father, here is how their cross produces only tabby-appearing kittens: The mother can only pass on one tabby gene *(T)* to each kitten and the father can only pass one black gene *(b)*. As a result, each kitten's color genes will be *Tb*. Since tabby is dominant over black, the kittens will be tabby.

We can work out the genetic possibilities that could result from a particular cross by making a chart called a "Mendelian checkerboard." The mating of a pure tabby *(TT)* and a pure black *(bb)* would look like this:

		Tabby mother	
TT x bb		T	T
	b	Tb	Tb
Black father	b	Tb	Tb

All the kittens will appear tabby, but will have one recessive black gene.

If the mother instead carried one tabby gene and one black gene *(Tb)*, she would still have tabby coloring, but the results of breeding her to a black cat *(bb)* would be different. While the black father would still pass only black genes to each offspring, the mother could pass on either a tabby gene or a black gene. With this cross, their kittens are as likely to be tabby with a recessive black gene *(Tb)*, as black *(bb)*. In that case the chart would be as follows:

Tb x bb   Tabby mother
                    T   b

	T	b
b	Tb	bb
b	Tb	bb

Black father

In the case of our example all kittens were tabby so we know that the mother was a pure tabby *(TT)*. We also know that even though all the kittens look like the mother their genetic makeup is different. They are all *Tb* and if you breed two of the new kittens you will get the following litter:

Tb x Tb   Tabby mother
                    T   b

	T	b
T	TT	Tb
b	Tb	bb

Tabby father

The result is one pure tabby *(TT)*, two kittens with a tabby appearance and a recessive black gene *(Tb)*, and one black *(bb)*.

If you are interested in breeding black cats, you can be confident that mating two black offspring will produce a black litter:

bb x bb   Black mother
                    b   b

	b	b
b	bb	bb
b	bb	bb

Black father

Using the same technique, you can work out the possibilities for short and long hair. In cats, short hair *(S)* is dominant over long hair *(l)*. If you mate short-and long-haired cats, the offspring *may* all have short hair but then the next generation will include a few long-haired cats.

By now, you should really feel like a geneticist. Try combining the genes for color and hair length, then work out the possibilities that could result from different crosses. For example, suppose you mate a pure-bred, short-haired tabby (TT, SS) with a long-haired black cat (bb,ll):

TTSS x bbll Short-haired tabby mother
                     TS   TS

	TS	TS
bl	TbSl	TbSl
bl	TbSl	TbSl

Long-haired
black father

The result will be a litter of tabby kittens with short hair that all carry recessive genes for black color and long hair. Now try crossing two of these kittens to see what you will get.

These crossings demonstrate basic genetics. Heredity is often much more complicated because not all genes react to other genes on the basis of simple dominant-versus-recessive traits. Some hereditary characteristics are linked to the sex of the cat. For example, a male cat can carry only one gene for red coloring. As a result, in order to produce a red female kitten, both parents must have a red appearance. Because of sex-linked genes, only females normally appear tortoise shell. The rare tortoise shell male is usually sterile. Some characteristics are linked to other traits. For example, white blue-eyed cats often turn out to be deaf. Breeders have been trying for years to selectively breed away the deafness but their efforts have not been successful.

To complicate matters further, some genes modify, rather than dominate, the genes they are linked with, or the dominant effect may be incomplete. Some genes mimic the effect of other genes, while others complement certain genes. Some colors are produced when another color is genetically diluted. Gray, for example, is diluted black, and cream is diluted red.

Occasionally, an unexpected change in genes during formation of the germ cell (called a mutation) will produce an unusual new characteristic. An accident like that is thought to account for the tailless Manx cat. The seemingly endless possibilities for genetic combinations have resulted in the enormous variety of breeds, colors, stripes and spots that cats come in.

Casey Rice, a science writer, is senior editor of Hospital Physician *magazine.*

BOSTON IS FOOTHOLD
OF CATS WITH EXTRA TOES

ROBERT COOKE

Call it "The Case of the Polydactyl Pussycats," or more simply, "Where'd Boston's Cats Get All Them Extra Toes?"

The extra-toes syndrome occurs in almost 12 percent of the cats in Greater Boston, and a Boston University biologist now says he can roughly trace where our early New England settlers migrated by finding out where such oddball cats live today.

Many extra-toed cats, for example, are found in Canadian cities where colonial Loyalists fled during the American Revolution. Very few such cats are found in cities like Philadelphia, which received few Boston-area émigrés.

"It seems to me we can now suggest that this mutant (the extra-toed cat) arose in, or reached, Boston in the very early history of the settlement," Neil Todd, adjunct professor of biology at Boston University, says. "Only in this way could it have gained the foothold it now has." Todd, explains that a single gene mutation is believed responsible for giving some cats extra toes, and that this mutation can be expressed in several ways. He goes on to say, "Some cats may have only five toes, but one will be enlarged. Others will have six toes, and still others will have seven toes, on either the front or back feet."

Among biologists and geneticists, it is a deformation known as polydactyly, and resembles a birth defect of the same name that occurs sometimes in humans. "Often," Todd says, "people don't spot the extra-toes condition of a nest kitten until they get it home. It's not always noticeable," he added, "until you get to the seven-toe condition, when it begins to look like the cat is wearing baseball gloves."

Todd reports that he and colleagues inspected 311 cats in Greater Boston and found 39 with polydactyly. Similar occurrence rates for the mutant were found in New Bedford and Salem, Massachusetts, in Peterborough, New Hampshire, and Barre, Vermont. "In Ithaca, New York, legend traces it to a particular tomcat in 1917, and reports indicate the polydactyly is not unusual now among cats in Ithaca. We don't know the frequency, but it is probably pretty high."

The important point, Todd says, is that most of today's centers of extra-toed cats are linked directly to Boston either by past immigration patterns or by commercial contacts through old ocean shipping routes.

Areas that haven't seen large migrations from Boston or extensive old shipping contacts with the city do not show higher frequencies of these odd cats today. "In New York City, the frequency of polydactyl cats is two-tenths of one percent or less; in Philadelphia, it's half of one percent." In Columbus Ohio, according to Todd, only one cat out of 231 cats inspected had extra toes, while in Chicago there was one in 250. Most sailing ships, had cats aboard both as pets and for control of rats, and the cats with extra toes might have been novel enough to lead seamen to select them instead of normal cats.

Even today, Todd suspects that the novelty factor is one thing that promotes the spread of this genetic change. "There's no evidence it (polydactyly) confers any disadvantage," he concludes.

Reprinted with permission from The Boston Globe, *February 7, 1976.*

VII. THE PASSIONATE CAT

THE REPRODUCTIVE LIFE OF THE CAT

David Zimmerman

CATS — UNLESS NEUTERED — live for sex. They need it with an intensity that surprises and often frightens humans. In the middle of the night, veterinarians regularly receive urgent phone calls from people whose cats are rubbing them, the furniture and floor, all the while caterwauling in a most distressing manner. More than likely, the veterinarian will simply explain that the cat is seeking to relieve its immediate sexual need.

For long-term emotional and physical health, unaltered cats need periodic bouts of sex. In addition, breeding females also need pregnancy and parenthood. British feline practitioner, Dr. Joan Joshua, believes unspayed females *need* to reproduce three or four times yearly, attributing infertility in purebred show females to the deprivation of mating until their "show years" are over.

How to Tell the Sex of Your Cat

Almost the first thing an owner wants to know about a cat is its sex (many people will not buy one until they know whether it is male or female). Toms are widely preferred since there is no risk of kittens. There are, however, some troublesome problems in owning a tom.

To ascertain a cat's sex gently lift its tail to gain an unobstructed view of its rear end. The uppermost opening — the one closest to the base of the tail — is the anus. The anus is round. In a female, below the anus, the vulva is visible as a vertical slit: two openings appear together as a small *i* (the shaft is the vulva, the dot, the anus). In males, both openings are round. The bottom "dot" is the tip of the penis. On older, unaltered males the testicles can be seen and felt below the anus in their scrotal sacs; however, the testicles are not obvious in kittens.

Cats become sexually mature at a tender age. There is at least one record of a female becoming pregnant when four months old. In most cases, however, females attain sexual maturity somewhere between six and twelve months, while males mature a bit later — usually at 11 months. It should also be noted that male cats may need to mature socially and emotionally before they show any willingness to breed. Breedable females, despite their fertility, share this timidity in their first breeding.

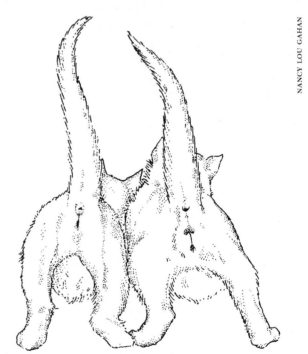

NANCY LOU GAHAN

The female is on the left; the male is on the right.

The Female Reproductive Cycle

Female cats are often called queens, especially when they are fertile or breeding cats.

Like other mammals, female cats experience an *estrous cycle* and are only fertile periodically. Unlike humans — but like dogs and many

Let the female cat run; the tomcat will catch her.

GERMAN PROVERB

other mammals — queens are sexually active only when in season; toms can mate at any time.

When a queen is sexually inactive, she is in the *anestrous* stage. This inactive period varies according to the individual cat and environmental factors such as climate. (See Jani Anderson's "The Behavior of the Cat.")

When sexually active, the queen is in the *estrus* period. Most queens have more than two heats each year. If the cat is not allowed to breed, the number of heats per year will increase, recurring at intervals of about two or three weeks, and continuing until she copulates. Cats are unusual in that they require copulation to stimulate ovulation, and that they can become pregnant at the same time by more than one male. A queen serviced in succession by two or more toms may carry kittens sired by each tom.

Before *estrus* begins, the ovaries secrete hormones that prepare the cat to become pregnant: the inner walls of the queen's uterus engorge with blood and several *ova*, or eggs, begin to grow in each ovary. While a few weeks before she may have snapped at or ignored an adventuresome tom now, as she passes into *estrus*, she literally goes through contortions to attract one or many.

The Sex Life of Toms

A healthy tomcat is virtually always ready for sex; however, before mating, the male, unlike the female, needs to feel on "home ground."

A tomcat with ready access to the outdoors will establish his mating territory in one of two ways: he will spray a "free zone," thereby marking it as his to defend or he will invade other toms' territories in the search for *estrus* females. In either case, wherever there is a female in heat a fight will generally ensue between competing males; and the toms, as part of the mating ritual, will spray. The great disadvantage to an unaltered, free-roaming male is not the sex he engages in, but the scratches, tears and bites he brings home after competing for neighborhood queens. The other disadvantage is spraying —

toms recognize no law which says they may spray the neighborhood all day but not the living room couch.

Spraying

Spraying, the squirting of urine, usually against any vertical objects, is a problem most often associated with the tomcat (although old females and neuters will sometimes spray in response to environmental changes, or if suffering from a urinary disease). The association of spraying with toms is apt, for tomcat urine has a particularly pungent odor which is almost impossible to remove. It is widely thought that tom spray contains musk; indeed, the word "musk" in English derives from the Sanskrit "mushka," meaning "testicle."

NANCY LOU GAHAN

Spraying can be a nuisance.

Confined Toms and Queens

Unaltered males deprived of females suffer greatly, as do similarly deprived queens in *estrus*. The tom, however, has no *estrous* cycle to relieve him of frustration. As long as he remains without queens, the tom will continue to howl, cry,

THE BARBED PENIS

Tomcats have an interesting anatomic trait that may influence feline breeding behavior, especially that of the female: the tip of the tom's penis is covered with barbs.

When climax occurs, the queen gives a high-pitched scream, pulls away and slaps her mate. Some say that the queen is enraged that she is being ripped internally by the barbs. Others disagree and believe the cry and cuffing to be the reaction of intense pleasure.

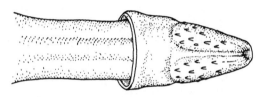

Perhaps the barbs play no part at all in the mating behavior. Many years ago the scientist William Greulich found that by inserting a smooth glass rod into a queen's vagina he could induce her both to ovulate and to utter the piercing mating cry.

pace. He will urinate repeatedly throughout the house, masturbate, and mount objects. This behavior will continue until he is altered, or brought a queen in *estrus*.

When the queen is in *estrus*, she, too, dramatically displays her frustration. She vocalizes non-stop, treads in the mating stance day after day until *estrus* is over. Although deprivation of sex through several seasons does no harm, a queen will often if continually deprived, suffer psychologically and perhaps physiologically in later years.

Courtship and Copulation

The tom courts the queen by circling carefully around her. If there is more than one tom, fights will break out. The victor of the fights may be first to mate with the queen; but sometimes a less aggressive, or older, more experienced tom may mount the queen while the other males are fighting. It is the female who makes the ultimate choice.

The scene is less violent when a tom is alone with a queen. As he circles, the queen will crouch, rub against the ground or against the male's body, and tread with her feet. When the tom senses the queen is ready to mate, he bounds in from his circle, utters a low-pitched sound and seizes the back of her neck with his teeth. By this time, she has raised her back end so that her sexual orifice is pointed upward and her front end lowered to the ground enabling her to use forepaws, claws and chest to clutch the ground for balance.

NANCY LOU GAHAN

In copulation the female cries out.

Still grasping the queen by the back of the neck, the tom mounts her. She shifts her tail to one side, and his penis emerges from its sheath. He thrusts at her, while she shifts her body for correct positioning. The male inserts his penis into the queen's vagina, ejaculates, and springs away quickly. The whole sequence takes only a few seconds, at most a quarter of a minute.

The male's copulatory sound is a deep grunt, the female's a high cry and, as she voices it, she often lurches forward and takes a strong swipe at the male. The male leaps away from this brief, vicious threat. Owners who offer toms for stud sometimes nail a small shelf on a wall several feet off the floor, to which the tom can leap to safety.

The two cats quickly relax. They will lick their sexual organs, pause and groom their fur. They may then repeat part of the courtship ritual, copulating many more times before their ardor cools.

RECOGNIZING HEAT

Females in heat call, cry, caterwaul and yowl. Animated by their hormones, they roll on the floor, wriggle their backs on the carpet, rub against everything they can find; and spray, their spray containing hormonal products that attract males from afar.

The queen's behavior is so out of her usual character that it is little wonder that some cat owners, on first seeing it, worry that their pets have contracted a dire illness. However, there is a simple technique for differentiating mating behavior: grasp the animal firmly by the scruff of the neck — as the tom will with his teeth during mating — and rub her back affectionately or stroke her gently under the tail. If in *estrus,* she will assume the mating stance, raising her hindquarters and moving her tail aside, she will tread up and down with her hind feet.

Ovulation and Fertilization

Stimulated by copulation, ovulation usually begins within twenty-seven hours. When ovulation begins, the queen will no longer be receptive to mating. As the ova leave her ovaries and pass into the Fallopian tubes, or oviducts, the spermatozoa swim up to meet them, and fertilization occurs. Then the fertilized eggs pass through the uterus into two long horns of the uterus where they attach themselves to the nutrient-rich lining and begin to grow.

Pregnancy and Delivery

The gestation period for cats is roughly nine weeks. At first, there is little in the queen's behavior to indicate that she is pregnant. The kittens become clearly visible on X-rays after about the fortieth day, and about ten days later the queen's abdomen is swollen perceptibly.

Cats' needs change very little during pregnancy. While there may be as many pregnancy diets for cats as there are owners of pregnant cats, veterinarians point out that as felines are creatures of habit, it may be well *not* to make major changes in diet — or in any other area of daily life. The pregnant queen will need *more* food: after the fifth week a breakfast is recommended. Daily consumption in ounces of food per pound of body weight will remain remarkably steady. A daily multi-vitamin will provide a margin of safety, but the most important aspect of the pregnancy diet is that it be well-balanced. (For further information on diet see Dava Sobel's "The Nutritional Cat.")

As the time for birth approaches, some cats become quiet and sedentary, lying for long periods in a comfortable spot — by a window in the sun, alongside a radiator, or on a favorite bed or cushion. Very often these are the spots where their kittens will be born. However, as the actual moment of birth approaches, the queen will sometimes find a new spot such as a shirt drawer that has been left open in a bureau or the laundry bin in the basement in which to deliver her young.

Veterinarians who treat a wide variety of animals remark that cats are better able to attend themselves at birth than other domestic animals. For this reason, the only step that many owners of pregnant cats have to take is to provide a maternity box — a container made of an ordinary cardboard box with lid and lined with newspaper or cloth. An entranceway for the mother is cut in the side a few inches up from the bottom of the box; the high lip remaining will keep the kittens inside. The box should then be placed in a quiet corner or closet. Most cats prefer isolation and privacy when delivering their kittens. They may ignore the prepared nest, however familiar, and find their own spot.

"I have always encouraged people not to make a spectacle out of kittening," says Richard Green of the Animal Medical Center, New York City. "The mother cat gets nervous when she realizes the people are nervous — and that is what you do not want her to be."

The exception to this admonition may be high-strung cats who will not do anything without master or mistress close by, although these

No workman can build a door which shall be proof against a cat or a lover.

FRENCH PROVERB

varieties, the Siamese, for example, may also become agitated and slip through a half-opened door to have the kittens under a parked car or in some similarly unsuitable place. First-time mothers, too, are likely to be nervous. When labor begins, if the queen becomes hysterical, she may be given a tranquilizer upon advice from a veterinarian.

Recognizing the onset of labor. One of the first signs of labor is a sudden restlessness. The queen may appear as though pushed here and there by unfamiliar forces in her mid-section. She may salivate and lick a lot, or try to relieve herself of the unaccustomed pressure by squatting in her litter box. She may chew or claw up some favorite item. When labor begins, it is important that the cat be confined indoors, near her maternity box, so that she will not try to escape. There are cases in which a queen may have to be assisted in her delivery.

The First Kitten Emerges

When it is time for the first kitten to be born, the queen's body begins to stretch and strain. It may take a few minutes, or an hour, before the first kitten is pushed free of the mother. This is the worst possible time to disturb the cat, she has urgent things to do. The kitten, surrounded by its birth sac, is not yet breathing.

As soon as the first kitten appears, the mother will begin licking and eating the membrane, or afterbirth, breaking the umbilical cord in the process. As the mother licks the obstructive material from the kitten's nose and mouth, it gasps irregularly for breath. By the time the mother has finished her licking, however, its fur has begun to dry and the kitten is breathing normally.

A few minutes later, a second kitten appears, and sometimes a third. There may be a pause that can last several hours before additional kittens emerge. There is no certain explanation for why the queen pauses in her kittening, although this could be a protective mechanism that insures at least some of the litter surviving in case of a predator's attack. Conceivably, too, first one horn of the uterus empties itself, then the other. The average litter is three to five kittens.

How Much Help Does A Queen Need in Delivering?

In most cases, queens need no help in delivering; however, there are exceptions.

The smallest feline is a masterpiece.

LEONARDO DA VINCI

If the mother fails to break the amniotic membrane following delivery, you must do this without delay so that the kitten can begin breathing. Hold the kitten in your hand in a towel, support its head carefully, and shake it head down. This helps in removing fluids from the kitten's nose and mouth. Always keep in mind that this is the most important part of the process for the kitten cannot breathe until the obstacles are removed from its nose and mouth. The kitten will begin to cry as soon as it is breathing properly. Then towel it dry.

If the mother fails to sever the umbilical cord, you can do it by tying a tight knot around the cord close to the kitten's body with a clean piece of thread. Cut the cord with scissors on the side of the knot *away* from the kitten's body.

If one of the kittens becomes stuck in the mother's vagina, call your veterinarian. He can tell from your description of the case whether you can perform the delivery yourself or need to take the mother in for emergency treatment. Since moving a queen during kittening significantly adds to her tension, the best method is to treat her at home whenever possible. The vet may counsel you to scrub your hands until they are sterile; then, having lubricated your finger with vaseline, attempt to insert it in the vagina and move it around the kitten, trying to nudge it forward. The kitten should be gently grasped by the shoulders, not by the head, and its body tugged carefully in an outward and downward direction.

Kitten Care in the First Weeks

After they have been cleaned and have started to breathe, new kittens need two things: maternal warmth and milk. *Colostrum,* the first day's milk, is particularly important as it contains an enormous amount of *antibodies* to protect the kittens against disease until their own protective mechanisms begin to function.

Kittens that remain with their mothers are likely to need very little special care. They should

A CAT GIVES BIRTH

PHOTO SEQUENCE BY MARTIN IGER

The first of the litter begins to emerge.

Dry, but still blind, the kittens stand together.

The mother eats the amniotic sac.

The mother tends the kittens carefully.

The mother helps with the delivery of the last kitten.

Cats frequently move the litter around.

The newborn kittens huddle together for warmth.

A month after birth the kittens are still dependent.

*A kitten is more amusing than half the people
one is obliged to live with.*

LADY SYDNEY MORGAN

not be handled except when necessary. After one week, each can be taken out of the maternity box and closely inspected, so that any defects or deformities can be called to the vet's attention.

The nursing queen needs nothing so much as peace and quiet, and, as her kittens' demand on her milk increases with growth, she needs more and more food. She may consume three times her pre-breeding intake. Because of this enormous need for food, many cat owners allow their queens to eat as much as they wish during lactation. If a mother cat shows signs of weakness, looks ill, or has conspicuous or unusual vaginal discharges that do not quickly abate, she should immediately be taken to the vet.

Weaning

The mother cat will begin to wean her kittens after three to four weeks. At that point, they must be provided supplemental food — and care must be taken that they, and not the mother, eat it.

If kittens look sick, the vet should be called. One common problem is eye trouble — conjunctivitis — which is a viral condition that reddens the eyes and causes them to run. More dangerous is diarrhea, which can be caused by parasites or any of a number of other factors. Kittens who have the "runs" can lose so much body fluid that they die quickly of dehydration or of a resulting imbalance in body chemicals.

How can you tell if kittens are healthy? "If they eat and sleep a lot, they are probably healthy. If they cry a lot, there is probably something wrong," says Richard Greene.

When kittens are six to eight weeks old, it is time for their first trip to the vet for an examination, shots and worming. They are no longer babies. They are young cats — growing up, and on their way.

The Rejected Kitten

Sometimes, a kitten after being delivered is abandoned, by being left or kept away from the maternity box or from the remainder of the litter. If you try to return it, still wet, to its mother, she may shove it away or eat it. She seems not to recognize it as her own.

Since a rejected kitten is just one among the millions too many born each year, and since it has been "naturally" abandoned by its mother, some vets counsel that the kitten be left to die. Rescue is difficult. If attempted, the kitten should be dried off, and then warmed with a hair dryer or other heat source until it is almost hot to the touch. The rescuer should try to find some of the afterbirth remaining near the mother and smear it on the kitten. Then an attempt can be made to reintroduce it into the litter. The best time to try this is when the other kittens are already suckling. The mother cat should be rubbed and comforted, after or during which two or three of the suckling kittens should be picked up and held in the rescuer's hand. The rejected kitten should then be mixed in with them and all returned at once to the mother.

Meddling with a mother cat in this way — or in any way — can be dangerous; she may turn on her kittens and destroy the entire litter. For this reason, some experts say that the best course of action in rescuing a rejected kitten is to treat it like an orphan, and rear it by hand.

ALICE SU

MYTHS ABOUT NEUTERS

1. *"Neutered cats become fat and lazy."* Actually, the daily calorie intake requirements of cats are lowered by neutering. Therefore, the answer to "what shall I do with my fat, neutered cat?" is simple: give it less food.

2. *"Neutered males are prone to urinary blockage."* Many male cats, whether castrated or left toms, have problems with urinary blockage because of their extremely narrow urethras. Female cats have this problem more rarely.

3. *"It is cruel to deprive cats of their sex."* It certainly is. But one must either give females and males the right to mate and reproduce, or alter them. The unaltered female who is kept inside year after year during *estrus* will suffer by becoming neurotic, easily frightened and, in some cases, will develop an infected uterus. The frustrated male will make your life virtually impossible.

4. *Variations on a theme: "Male cats should be allowed one litter before neutering"* and *"females should be allowed one litter before spaying."* In both cases, neutering should be performed before the full maturity of the animals is attained. Having one litter neither adds to nor subtracts from the cat's personality.

The problem of what and how to feed orphan and rejected kittens recently has been resolved by a commercial supplier, the Borden Company, which now markets *kmr*®, a kitten-milk replacer formulated especially for this problem.

Very young kittens must be shielded from drafts, and need to be kept warm. The easiest resource for warmth is a *reliable* electric heating pad. Put the pad in a box with the kitten, cover the bottom of the box with paper or scraps of rags, and put an accurate thermometer into the box to measure air temperature. For the first week, the temperature should be kept quite warm — between 85° and 90° F. After that, the temperature can be lowered to about 80° F. When a kitten is about three weeks old, it can be acclimated gradually from excessive heat to room temperature.

Birth Control

The most common medical question that arises about cats is that of birth control. The reasons are obvious: a healthy queen easily can deliver three or four litters a year, for many years. Assuming that each litter has only four surviving kittens, that still leaves a dozen kittens a year to be fed, or gotten rid of, and few cat owners, other than breeders, know very many people who are willing to take kittens off their hands. The result is that tens of thousands of kittens are put to sleep each year, or abandoned. Many cat owners feel it is far better to prevent so many unwanted births from happening.

Castration and Vasectomy

Kittens can be castrated after they are six months old. In general, veterinarians believe that it is better to perform the operation before the kitten reaches maturity, before tom behavioral traits have become well established.

The operation is quick and simple: The cat is premedicated with a tranquilizer and atropine, which quickens the heart rate and relaxes the muscles. Then the cat is put to sleep. The hair is trimmed from the scrotal sacs. The doctor slits one sac, pulls out the testicle, ties off the vascular bundle, and cuts away the testicle. After suturing the slit, he repeats the procedure on the other side. He gives the cat local and systemic antibiotics, and allows it to awaken. The cat is ready to go home the same day. Eventually, the empty sacs recede and vanish.

Castration reduces or eliminates spraying and roaming in most cases; if castrated when young, a neutered cat may never display these behavioral traits. Cats castrated after gaining maturity may stop spraying and roaming immediately, or it may happen gradually. The reaction depends on the age, breed and individual temperament of the cat. Similarly, there will be a decline in copulatory behavior. Some neuters never mount a female or, if they do, seem not to know the proper approach and mount backward. Other cats will mount correctly but with less ardor.

Castration, the removal of the testicles, is the most widely used method of male birth con-

PHOTO SEQUENCE BY ALICE SU

THE SPAYING OPERATION

Administration of anethesia.

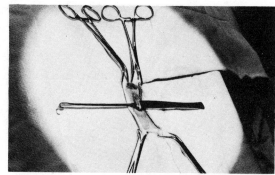

Isolation and delivery of one horn of the uterus.

Pressure applied to bladder to express urine.

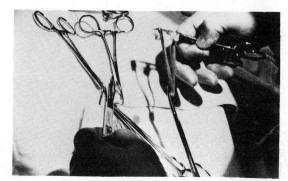

Removal of both ovaries and the uterus.

Hair is clipped from the surgical site.

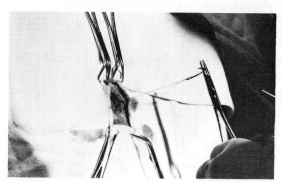

Closure of the surgical incision.

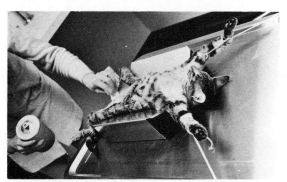

Sterilization of the surgical site.

The cat recuperating in a recovery cage.

A NEW BIRTH CONTROL IDEA

In a recent issue of *Cat Fancy* magazine, Thomas A. Easton suggests constructing a cardboard collar to fit over the female's neck to prevent her from having sexual relations. Because a bite on the female's neck by the male seems to be a necessary part of breeding behavior, Easton suggests that covering the neck may prevent copulation. This imaginative method has not been tested scientifically, however, and cannot be guaranteed to work.

trol in cats. There is, however, another method — the vasectomy. Vasectomy — binding off the sperm-carrying tube the *vas deferens* — renders the tom infertile, but does not interfere with the production of the male sex hormone, testosterone. As this hormone is the stimulus for his masculine behavior, the operation does not eliminate spraying. It is also a more complicated operation than castration, therefore, more expensive and not widely practiced.

Spaying

Spaying, the removal of the female reproductive organs, is a longer, more complicated operation than either castration or vasectomy. During the operation, both ovaries, which produce the female hormones, must be removed as well as the Fallopian tubes and the uterus, in which conception and development occur. The technical name for the operation is *ovariohysterectomy*. Nonetheless, the operation is routinely done, safe, and quick — the entire procedure takes about 15 minutes.

For spaying, a small area of the female cat's belly is shaved and scrubbed with antiseptic preparations. She is anesthetized, then a slit, about an inch long, is made along the midline of her belly, just behind the navel. After cutting through skin, subcutaneous fat and muscle into the peritoneal cavity, a "spay hook," is inserted and the uterus is pulled out. The ovarian end of the uterine horn is tied off, after which the second horn is pulled out and the process repeated. A tight knot is tied around the lower end of the uterus, the cervix, near the point where it attaches to the vagina. The doctor next removes the uterus and ovaries, allowing the cervix to slip back into the body cavity. Finally, he sutures the cat's abdomen and the cat begins to return to consciousness.

The recovery and convalescent period is longer than with males. Usually, after spaying, the cat will remain in the hospital overnight, but within several days, a correctly spayed cat will appear essentially recovered. Unlike the neutered male, the spayed female immediately loses her sexual interests.

Other Birth Control for Females

If the owner of a female cat strongly objects to spaying, there are other forms of birth control: if the queen is in *estrus*, ovulation can be induced by probing her vagina with a smooth glass rod. This induces a "false pregnancy," which extends the *anestrous* period to about a month (instead of the two to three weeks' cycle of the female who has received no stimulation).

It is also possible to bind the cat's Fallopian tubes so that she can no longer become pregnant. But, as with the vasectomy, hormone production continues in the ovaries and all her natural behavioral liabilities continue.

Much work on feline birth control pills has been done on both sides of the Atlantic. Some such products have been on the market and withdrawn. Thus far, there is no widespread marketing of a commercial feline hormonal contraceptive.

David Zimmerman is a medical and science writer whose latest book is To Save a Bird in Peril.

VIII. THE HEALTHY CAT

Eugène Mihaesco.

THE COMPLETE PHYSICAL

Kenneth Anderson

WHEN YOU VISIT a doctor's office for a checkup, the doctor listens to your heart and lungs, looks into your mouth and ears, and gently pokes his fingers into your body areas in search of abnormalities or signs of disease. A sound health-care program for your cat should include a similar weekly examination which you can perform yourself. Preventive medicine is extremely important in protecting your cat: animals are unlikely to complain of symptoms; a serious illness can progress insidiously until the condition becomes life-threatening. You may be able to detect early signs of illness or malfunction in your cat's body. As an added benefit, you will learn about your cat by knowing every part of his body.

Generally, you follow the same procedures as your veterinarian. Place the cat on a table in a well-lighted area. Hold the animal firmly but gently with one hand around the shoulder area. Some cats will not be cooperative, so the first attempt at examination may be brief. As your cat becomes familiar with the routine, you can increase the length and extent of the examination. It is a good idea to try your first examination not long after a vet has examined your cat. Then you will know that you are dealing with a healthy animal.

The basic examination procedure involves the technique of palpation. This means, simply, feeling the anatomy with your hands . . . with practice you will discover that different parts of your hands are more sensitive. The fingertips, for example, may be most sensitive for examining structural differences in the body; the backs of the fingers may be more sensitive than the fingertips in detecting temperature variations; the palm near the base of the fingers may be most sensitive for detecting vibrations of body organs, such as the heart. By careful palpation you can determine something about the texture and flexibility, size and shape, tenderness, and normal or abnormal growth in nearly all tissues accessible through external examination.

Taking Your Cat's Pulse

To check the cat's pulse, locate the femoral artery, the major blood vessel of the hind leg, which is on the inner surface near the hip joint. By placing your fingers over the artery at a place where it is close to the skin, you should be able to feel the pulse and measure the rate of heartbeat. Using the second hand of a watch, count the number of pulse beats for 15 seconds. Then multiply the number of beats by 4 to give you the cat's pulse in beats per minute. The normal rate ranges between 100 and 130; a higher than normal rate indicates either disease or merely nervousness.

Taking Your Cat's Temperature

To take a cat's temperature, always use a rectal thermometer. Coat the bulb end of the thermometer lightly with petroleum jelly or vegetable oil. To insert the thermometer, place the cat on a level surface and hold its body between your elbows or between your body and one arm. Lift the cat's tail with one hand and gently but firmly push the lubricated end of the thermometer into the cat's rectum. It should be inserted a distance of one and a half inches. Rotate the thermometer as you insert it if you feel any resistance. Leave it in the rectum for at least one full minute or as long as three minutes if possible. A reading of 101.5°F. is considered normal, but a variation of one degree higher or lower than that is within the normal range. However, if your cat's temperature is 103°F. or more, you should call your veterinarian. A higher than normal reading can be a sign of disease or other factors. Temperature varies not only with age and physical activity but also sex, since females usually have a slightly higher temperature during heat.

Kenneth Anderson is a science and medical writer.

CHECKLIST FOR WEEKLY HOME EXAMINATIONS

The weekly home exam is the best preventive medicine a cat can have. It is a simple procedure; basically, one feels or palpates the cat from head to foot. If done weekly, the owner will soon know his cat's body, and be able to pinpoint trouble spots before serious complications arise. The following is a list of parts to examine:

Head. Feel the skull; locate the muscles in the cheeks and temple area, which allow the jaws to move, and the bump behind the ears (the occipital protuberance).

Neck. Moving along the back of the neck, palpate the spine and muscles; feel the side of the neck for the esophagus and trachea.

Spine. Feel the vertebrae and connective muscles.

Shoulder and forelegs. Palpate and flex the joints; they should move without grinding sensations.

Pelvic girdle and hind legs. Repeat the above procedure.

Ribs. Feel along the ribs from the spine to the front of the chest.

Feet. Feel each bone; check the pads and between the pads for foreign matter; extend the claws.

Skin and fur. Examine the skin for parasites and rashes; look for bald patches in the fur.

Supracaudal oil gland and anal sacs. Check for excessive secretion from the oil gland at the top of the tail; lift the tail to check the sacs on either side of the anus.

Lymph nodes. Turn the cat on its back and check the lymph nodes along the cat's underside: there are two nodes on each side under the jaws; one on each side of the upper chest where the foreleg joins the chest; one on each side of the rib cage, spaced widely apart; two spaced together in the lower abdominal area; and one on each side where the hindlegs join the body.

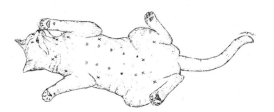

Lymph nodes and nipples should not be swollen.

Eyes, teeth, ears and mouth. Look for discharges from the eyes, discoloration of teeth or gums, and excessive paleness of gums; these are all abnormal conditions.

Pulse and temperature. A cat's normal pulse rate is 110–130 beats per minute; the normal temperature, 101–102.5° F.

Check the pulse at the femoral artery.

BASIC CAT HEALTH

Rebecca B. Marcus

TAKING CARE OF your cat requires only a bit of common sense, a small amount of time, and a cheerful bundle of love. Some problems require a veterinarian's professional attention, but many can be handled right in the home. The personal care given a cat also helps strengthen the bonds between you and your pet. As you come to understand and care for its needs, you will know the animal better and take a justifiable pride in its health.

Grooming

Although they keep themselves reasonably clean, cats depend on their owners for sleek coats. Brushing and combing a cat's coat several times a week, more often for long-haired cats, will give it a glossy look. Use a small comb, small scrub brush or grooming mitt, such as those sold in pet shops and, starting at the head, brush in one direction only. Your cat will learn to enjoy these brushing sessions; you will enjoy both the new-found beauty brushing produces and the absence of hair on furniture and rugs.

A house cat's front claws should be trimmed regularly. Grasp the cat's toe with your thumb and forefinger with the finger on the bottom of the toe, the thumb on top just behind the first joint. Press your finger and thumb together: the claw will extend. Clip the tip where it begins to curve downward; *do not clip into the pink area of the claw* or bleeding will ensue. Specially designed nail clippers from pet stores are easier to use than scissors. (See Paul Rowan's and Richard Greene's articles on the question of declawing.)

Trimmed claws do not prevent cats from scratching furniture. Providing a scratching post may help; any type will do — homemade ones or those sold in pet shops. It may be better to try the homemade variety first. Many a cat owner has come home with a scratching post only to have his animal take one look and never go near it again. Put the post in a corner where the cat can get at it easily. The first time the cat scratches the furniture, reprimand your cat with a sharp "no," and immediately take it to the scratching post. The cat may or may not get the message, depending on the age, adaptability and temperament of the cat.

A cat's teeth should be cleaned weekly to prevent tartar buildup. Tartar not only gives cats bad breath, but leads to gum problems and eventual loss of teeth. Giving animals dry food to chew on will cut tartar buildup. To clean the teeth, use a toothbrush or moist, rough cloth wrapped around your finger; scrub the front of the teeth plus the gums.

Parasites

Fleas can carry disease and they always make cats uncomfortable; many veterinarians recommend a flea collar, fastened loosely around the cat's neck. Avoid wetting the collar and it should be effective for three to four months. If the cat is infested with fleas, bathe it with a medicated cat shampoo especially made to combat the problem. Afterwards, air and vacuum the cat's bed and blankets to prevent re-infestation.

FUR-GONE CONCLUSION
ALAN M. ORMONT

Cats have learned to be proficient
They are always self sufficient.
They clean themselves and lick their
    paws,
They never leave us any flaws.
And 'tho they're sleek and quite well bred
They shed and shed and shed and shed.

ALAN M. ORMONT IS A FINANCIAL PLANNER
IN WEST HARTFORD, CONNECTICUT.

Ticks, which are rarely seen on cats unless they have been venturing through fields and woods, can inflame the skin. To remove a tick, grasp it with your fingernails, as close as possible to where it is imbedded in the cat's skin and yank. Never try to burn ticks off; you are more liable to injure your cat than to destroy the tick.

Mites are seen on cats more often and can usually be identified only by a veterinarian, who will prescribe effective medication. The three most common mites found on cats are ear, head and harvest mites (also known as chiggers or red bugs). Indications of mite infestation are: cats pawing at ears, ears discharging large amounts of wax, holding ears abnormally flattened; incessant scratching on any part of the body; hard layers on skin, or bald spots, especially on the head and ears.

Worms are picked up by eating or from fleas carrying worm eggs. If the cat appears nervous and vomits, lift its tail and look for tiny white or yellowish worms around the anus; also, examine the feces for signs of worms. It is wise to consult the veterinarian before using over-the-counter worming medicines.

Hookworms are a problem in hot, humid climates and can cause death. Some of the symptoms are vomiting, diarrhea, scratching and an anemic appearance. Take the cat to the veterinarian for diagnosis and treatment; hookworms are too small for detection except by an expert.

Ringworm (not actually a worm but a fungus infection), *acne* or *eczema* are skin ailments which should be treated by the veterinarian. Be careful in handling a cat with ringworm; it is infectious to humans. Wash the cat's bed and blankets, and vacuum the house and furniture.

Vaccinations

To insure the best possible start toward a healthy life, kittens must be vaccinated against panleukopenia or cat fever. (This is often called "distemper" but is unrelated to the distemper found in dogs). A viral disease, panleukopenia is fatal to kittens and to older animals if not diagnosed and treated promptly. Kittens should be vaccinated when they are eight to ten weeks old; until then, keep kittens from other cats. If a cat spends his life entirely indoors, no other vaccinations are required. However, if the cat is allowed outdoors, or is exposed to other rabies-receptive animals, it should be given a rabies

HOW TO CHOOSE A VET

Before visiting a veterinarian whom you have not previously met, make a list of things about your cat which have been puzzling you. Armed with the list, make mental notes as soon as you arrive at the veterinarian's office: is the waiting room clean? Is the assistant who takes you into the examining room clean? Is the room, itself, clean? Does the assistant handle your animal gently, appearing firm but not afraid of cats? As the veterinarian enters — where no assistant has been the first contact — ask yourself the same questions. It is important that you and your cat establish rapport with the veterinarian as well as his assistants.

On your first visit, the veterinarian should ask and make notes about the cat's medical history. If he does not; or if he is inattentive as you explain previous treatment difficulties, go to another veterinarian. When you ask your questions, if the veterinarian explains in terms too technical, ask him to clarify. If he cannot articulate in layman's language, or will not, he is not the right veterinarian for you. If he is impatient with you or your cat, go to another vet. Finally, ask his fees before allowing him to examine your cat. If he is unwilling to give them, go elsewhere.

If the doctor, his assistants and office measure up to your standards, ask about his hours: does he handle emergencies on off-hours, holidays and weekends? If not, can he refer you to another veterinarian or clinic which is able to handle emergencies? Keep the name, address and telephone number of the veterinarian, plus the emergency service number and address, in your cat's medicine chest as well as in your personal address book.

vaccination by the time it is three to four months old. The vaccine is effective for one year.

Common Illnesses

A mild redness and tearing in a cat's eye is

usually no cause for alarm; there may be soot or a speck in the eye. Using an eye dropper, wash the eyes with a boric acid solution of one teaspoon of boric to one pint of water, boiled together, then cooled. Hold the eyelids apart; if there is still foreign matter in the eye, very gently remove with a moist cotton swab. If the symptoms persist or a film develops over the eye (prolapsed third eyelid), take the animal to the veterinarian.

HUMANE SOCIETY OF NEW YORK

Any active cat may sooner or later get hurt, break or dislocate limbs. Unless unusually severe sprains, strains and bruises will heal themselves. Fractures are another matter; in this case, tie a temporary splint under the limb (several thicknesses of cardboard will do), and take the cat to the veterinarian. Do not give the cat pain killers or tranquilizers; they may complicate the veterinarian's treatment.

Cats are also subject to respiratory diseases. Sneezing, wheezing and discharges from the eyes and nose may be nothing more than a cold that needs no special care but to keep the cat indoors until the symptoms subside. Fever in addition to the above symptoms may be an indication that the cat has edema of the lungs, bronchitis or asthma, which calls for professional attention.

Vomiting hairballs is normal, as a rule, not a sign of illness. When this occurs, brush your cat more often, especially if it is long-haired.

Digestive Problems

Digestive upsets can frequently be treated at home. Vomiting is not always a sign of illness. If a cat has vomited, do not feed it for twelve hours, then give it small quantities of bland foods, such as baby food or cottage cheese. Recovery should progress steadily until the cat is back to its normal diet. If vomiting persists, is bloody, or if

HOW TO PILL A CAT

First, see if the cat will accept the pill without a struggle. If he spits it out, try trickery: coat the offending pill with his favorite food — whether anchovy paste or peanut butter. If he sees through your maneuver, licks the pill clean and walks away, more forceful tactics are necessary.

First, restrain his legs, particularly the front ones, by wrapping him in a towel. Sit down. Using your knees to hold the cat, proceed to the next step — getting the mouth open. To open, push in on the corners of the mouth with thumb and forefingers; as soon as it opens, tilt the head up and place or drop the pill in the *back* of the mouth. Quickly shut and hold the mouth closed and, with the head still tilted, stroke the throat until the cat swallows. If he is determined not to accept the pill, blow in his face! Startling him will precipitate swallowing.

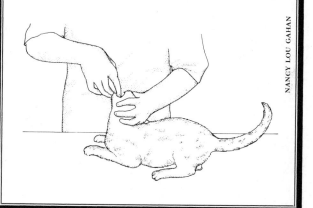

NANCY LOU GAHAN

the cat has fever and seems in discomfort, do not hesitate to have the cat examined by a veterinarian.

Diarrhea — unless persistent, bloody and accompanied by fever — is usually not too serious. Treat it as you would vomiting. After several days of feeding bland food, add starchy products such as cooked rice. (Watch your cat's diet as well; feeding a cat raw beef liver more than twice a week often precipitates diarrhea.)

Constipation is usually the result of faulty diet. Give the cat dry food with more bulk, instead of soft, canned foods. Never attempt to give a cat an enema yourself.

SIGNS OF SERIOUS PROBLEMS

JAY KUHLMAN, D.V.M.

Appetite loss. If your cat shows less than its normal interest in food for more than four or five days, take it to your veterinarian. Also, be on the alert for other signs of illness.

Cloudy eyes. Indicates ulceration, increased pressure in the eye, possibly glaucoma. Professional attention is needed if permanent damage is to be avoided.

Dragging hind quarters. Contrary to popular belief, this does not mean the cat has worms. It indicates irritation: the anal glands may be full and need to be expressed; there may be an infection of the anus; the cat may have swallowed a string or human hair which is trying to pass through; sometimes the irritation is from feces caught in the tail hairs.

Drinking decrease. If the cat stares at the water dish but does not drink, he may have a kidney infection. This behavior means that the cat is thirsty but too sick to drink; it is often done by cats close to dying.

Drinking increase. This may indicate a toxic condition in the body, such as malfunctioning kidneys, or uterine infection. It can also be a sign of diabetes. If your cat continues to drink more than usual, your veterinarian should make clinical tests.

Drooling. This may indicate a foreign object in the mouth which should be removed before infection sets in. Excessive salivation is also a sign of poisoning, or a viral infection.

Enlarged abdomen. Tumors, heart and liver diseases; peritonitis, and infection of the uterus — any of these can cause an enlarged abdomen.

Increased sensitivity. If the back or neck region becomes sensitive to touch, it can indicate that the cat has a slipped disc. Excessive sensivity in the abdominal area, may be caused by an internal infection or injury.

Lumps. Any new lumps should be examined, especially if they increase rapidly in size. The mammary chain in females, especially unspayed cats, should be checked regularly. Too often cats are taken to a veterinarian to have a tumor removed when the tumor has reached such an advanced stage that there is little chance for complete recovery.

Straining to urinate. If the cat is male, this condition is an indication of urinary obstruction. Without treatment, the animal can die within twenty-four hours. Whether male or female, straining to urinate, or the urination of blood-tinged urine, is also an indication of cystitis, or bladder infection.

Straining to defecate. This is a sign that the cat is constipated. Switch its diet to dry foods. If constipation continues, mix one teaspoon of mineral oil in the cat's food. If the condition still does not improve, take the animal to the veterinarian. Never try to give the cat an enema yourself.

Vaginal discharge. This most often indicates infection of the uterus. If the discharge is unusually thick, odorous and blood-tinged, a hysterectomy may be necessary before the toxins can damage other internal organs.

Vomiting. Vomiting can mean a foreign body in the stomach or intestinal tract, or it can mean an infection. Continual vomiting, if not checked, leads to dehydration.

Jay Kuhlman, a veterinarian in New York City, loves cats.

Geriatric Problems

The normal lifespan for a cat is ten to fifteen years. As it gets older, it will develop disabilities and illnesses not often found in young cats. An old cat suffering from arthritis will walk stiffly, especially when it first gets up in the morning. Even if the cat seems uncomfortable, *do not give it aspirin;* aspirin is *toxic* to most cats. While there is no cure for arthritis, the veterinarian will be able to relieve or at least reduce the pain. Deafness may also arrive with old age; nothing can be done. On the other hand, cataracts, which sometimes affect older cats, can safely be removed by surgery.

Another common geriatric problem is constipation caused by loss of muscle tone in the large intestine. Giving the cat bulky foods, under the supervision of your veterinarian, may help relieve this condition. Nephritis is a kidney disease commonly found in older cats. The afflicted cat drinks more than usual, and urinates more. The veterinarian may be able to help clear up the disease; certainly, he can relieve much of the accompanying discomfort.

Difficulty in breathing and a rapid heart beat in an old cat are indicative of congestive heart failure — a condition that eventually proves fatal.

Tumors and cancer are other ailments to which old cats are prone. A simple tumor can be successfully removed. Cancerous growths, even if removed, tend to recur. If the animal has terminal cancer or a serious, irreversible illness, the veterinarian may suggest an easier death. With your consent, he will "put down" the cat painlessly by injecting an overdose of anesthetic.

Emergencies

The first rule is always: *don't panic!*

Cuts and scratches usually heal themselves once proper first-aid treatment has been administered. Cut the hair away from the wound and apply an antiseptic. Bleeding from a deep cut may not be as serious as it looks. Apply pressure by holding a sterile pad firmly against the wound. Only if there is uncontrollable bleeding from a leg or tail should you attempt to use a tourniquet. If you feel it *is* necessary, *remember to loosen the tourniquet* for a moment or two every fifteen minutes, then re-tighten. Otherwise, you will cut off all blood circulation and do more harm than good to your pet. Your veterinarian should look at any wound of this

HOUSEBREAKING PROBLEMS

By its seventh week, a kitten will be housebroken by its mother. If a kitten has been acquired at a younger age, housebreak it by imitating the mother cat's technique: place the kitten in the litter pan and scratch the kitty litter with the kitten's paws. The kitten's digging instincts will soon take over.

Even a housebroken cat may suddenly refuse his litter pan. Perhaps the pan is not clean enough or is too small. Try placing the pan in a different spot, clean it more often, or buy an additional pan. Be aware that cats, as children, will sometimes urinate for attention. If the cat has been left alone too long, he may demonstrate anger by urinating in a forbidden area. Unlike a child, the cat will often return to urinate where he has before; once he has vented his anger on your bathroom mat, he will probably do so again. If this happens, throw the mat away: washing it will not eliminate the odor.

Squatting and straining to urinate outside the litter pan is a sign of cystitis, especially in male cats. Take the cat to the veterinarian immediately.

When a male cat begins to spray urine on the furniture, he has attained sexual maturity. If he is kept away from females, he must be neutered or he will continue to spray.

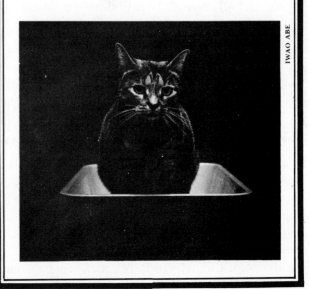

IWAO ABE

GIVING YOUR CAT A BATH

RAY BIALKOWSKI

When it becomes necessary for you to bathe your cat, use the following procedure. Place a rubber mat in the bottom of the kitchen or bathroom sink and fill the sink with warm water, about 80°F., to a depth of three to four inches. Smear petroleum jelly around the cat's eyes to keep the soap and water out. Stand the cat in the sink and hold him by the back of the neck. Talk reassuringly to him throughout the bathing. Begin by pouring water over him; follow with a special cat or baby shampoo. Work slowly and gently. Above all, rinse thoroughly. Dry your cat by rubbing vigorously with a clean bath towel. Wipe the petroleum jelly from around the eyes. Brush and comb the hair until it is thoroughly dry. Some people have success with small hair dryers, but beware of excessive heat. Keep the cat warm and inside the house for several hours after bathing.

type as soon as possible since the cat may need a tetanus shot.

Burns, from whatever source, need immediate treatment. Keep cold water or an ice pack on the burn for about twenty minutes, then apply an antibiotic burn ointment. If none is handy, soak the affected area with a sterile pad which has been dipped in a strong tea solution.

Afterwards, cover the burned area with petroleum jelly and have the cat examined as quickly as possible.

Any severe injury may bring on shock: the cat is prostrate, semi-conscious, its breathing shallow, its pulse rate slow, its temperature low. Treatment must begin *at once*. Keep the cat warm; let it rest for a short period; then take it to a veterinarian.

If your cat is hit by a car, never leave it unattended while you go to get help. Slide it onto a coat or a blanket and pull the injured cat to the side of the road. Look for signs of shock, applying pressure bandages wherever they are needed. If the gums appear gray, there are probably internal injuries. Gently wind strips of material around the body like a corset, put the cat in a box and take it to the veterinarian.

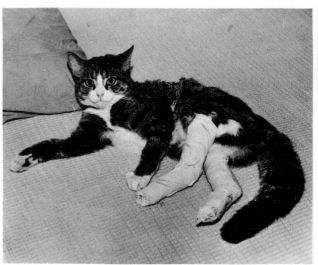

LONG ISLAND PRESS

A cat bitten by an insect and showing signs of an allergic reaction needs medical attention. If you see the stinger of a bee, remove the stinger and apply cold packs or crushed ice to relieve the pain and swelling.

Heat stroke can result when a cat is left for a long period in a hot closed car. Among the symptoms of the heat stroke: heavy labored breathing, prostration, increased pulse rate and a staring expression. When you see these symptoms under likely conditions, put the cat in a cool place and wet it thoroughly with cold water. As soon as the cat stirs, give it a teaspoonful of strong coffee. If you must travel with your cat in a car during really hot weather carry water with you and give the cat *small* amounts frequently. This will keep your pet from becoming dehydrated. Too much water at one time, however, can result in vomiting — and further dehydration.

In cases of extreme emergency, artificial respiration may be necessary. To force air through the cat's nose, the corrective procedure is as follows: open the cat's mouth to look for

NANCY LOU GAHAN

obstructions, clean the area of any residual blood and close the cat's mouth. Inhale air, put your mouth over the cat's muzzle and exhale. Remove your mouth. Allow the cat's chest to deflate. Inhale, again cover the muzzle with your mouth, and exhale. Repeat the process six times per minute until the animal is partially restored to normal breathing. Go to the veterinarian immediately applying artificial respiration on the way to the doctor's office. Artificial respiration serves no purpose unless the animal's heart is still beating when you begin to apply it or if the heart is still beating when you arrive at the veterinarian's office.

Rebecca B. Marcus is a science writer in New York City.

HOW TO GET A CAT OUT OF A TREE

The answer to this problem is simple: don't try. It got up there; eventually it will come down. Creating a hullabaloo under the tree will only frighten you *and* the cat. Cats do not fall out of trees, and they do not starve in trees. Take control of yourself, return to your interrupted activities, and leave the cat to enjoy the view.

CATHERINE N. JONES

YOUR CAT'S MEDICINE CHEST

It is useful for a cat owner to know what supplies are needed to deal with medical emergencies, or, problems that do not require prescription drugs. Here is a list of things to keep in your cat's medicine chest. Add to it your veterinarian's suggestions.

Blunt tweezers
Rectal thermometer
Bandages
Sterile pads
Adhesive tape
Petroleum jelly
Hydrogen peroxide
Absorbent cotton
Small scissors (blunt-pointed)
Eyedropper
Teaspoon
Mineral oil
Antiseptic powder or spray
Small medicine bottle
    (squeeze type or
    baby syringe
    for giving liquid
    medicines)

THE DECLAWING CONTROVERSY

Whether or not to declaw a cat is one of the most controversial issues in the cat care field. Many people fear that declawing, although convenient for owners, is cruel and unnatural to cats. Owners and veterinarians alike disagree about the advantages and disadvantages to cat and owner of having the surgery performed. What follows are two opposing points of view on this issue. We reprint here Paul Rowan's information sheet warning against declawing which he provides to his clients in his exclusively feline practice in New York City. Richard Greene of the Animal Medical Center in New York City presents the argument which supports declawing cats.

YOU CAN'T DECLAW WITH LOVE

Paul Rowan, D.V.M.

DECLAWING MAY PROTECT your furnishings but it does little to protect your cat. If your cat were to be declawed, the operation is generally performed as follows:

1. The cat is given a general anesthetic.
2. The fur around the feet is clipped.
3. A tourniquet is placed around the leg.
4. The nails are rinsed with alcohol.
5. The amputation of the nail is accomplished with a guillotine nail cutter, which cuts across the first joint and may also involve the foot pad.
6. The toes are then bandaged tightly to prevent hemorrhage.
7. The bandage is removed two to three days post-operatively.

There is an alternate procedure in which the nail is removed completely and the skin is sutured over. This procedure is not as common as it is more time-consuming.

Immediate Complications

Physical Complications

1. Because a general anesthetic is necessary, there is the danger of an adverse reaction.
2. If the bandages are put on too tightly, the foot may become gangrenous and necessitate amputation of the leg.
3. When the bandages are removed, many cats will begin to hemorrhage — thus requiring rebandaging.

Emotional Complications

1. Upon recovering from the anesthetic, your healthy cat wonders why his feet are throbbing and bandaged.
2. After the bandages are removed, he wonders what happened to his claws and why it hurts when he walks.

Later Complications

Physical Complications

1. In many instances, the entire nail bed was not removed and one or more claws will begin to regrow. The claws that do regrow are usually misshapen and quite useless.

2. Because a cat's nail is brittle or the trimmer is dull, the bone may shatter and cause what is called a "sequestrum," which serves as a focus for infection and continuous drainage from the toe. This can only be corrected by a second general anesthetic and surgical procedure.

Emotional Complications

1. Frequently, a cat becomes very distrustful of his owner and/or veterinarian. With rare exception, the declawed cat is the most difficult to examine and treat.

2. A declawed cat is more apt to bite if he feels threatened. It doesn't take much for him to feel nervous.

3. The origin of many chronic physical ailments including cystitis and skin disorders can be traced to the period immediately following declawing.

If your cat has been declawed and you've experienced none of these problems, congratulations! Unlike altering, which is substantiated as a major aid in retaining a cat's health, there is no such claim that can be made for declawing.

Fortunately, there is a simple alternative available for you and your cat. It consists of a *good, sturdy* scratching post covered with strong material and lined with catnip. You can make one yourself or it can be purchased. With close attention and lots of encouragement, your cat can be perfectly happy scratching on his own furniture rather than yours. Our cats are.

Dr. Rowan's information sheet is reprinted from Cats Prefer It This Way *by Carole Wilbourn.*

DECLAWING CATS

Richard W. Greene, D.V.M.

THE QUESTION of whether or not to declaw cats is asked of every veterinarian several times a day by cat owners. Most owners have reservations about removing a cat's claws because they have heard it is cruel and inhumane.

As a veterinarian who is a cat lover and owns three (all of which are declawed), I am convinced that this procedure is neither cruel nor inhumane. If your cat is destroying the furnishings in your home and your attempts to train the cat to use a scratching post have met with failure, the only alternative (if you have elected to keep the cat) is to have the claws of the front paws removed. It is important that your pet adapt to your life style rather than you to his.

As already mentioned, an honest attempt should be made to deter the cat from scratching furnishings. In an article in *Feline Practice* (March–April, 1972), Benjamin L. Hart, D.V.M.

makes several points that might be helpful in achieving this goal:

1. Since cats often develop a favorite spot to scratch, it is important to train them to one particular scratching post as soon as they reach the scratching age. It may be necessary to lay the post horizontally when the cat is very young.

2. Scratching posts should be kept near the area where the cat usually sleeps, since cats tend to scratch just after awakening.

3. The fabric of the post should be one the cat will enjoy, not merely a surface utilized because of its low cost. As the fabric shows signs of wear, it should be recovered.

4. The scratching post should be a strong board or large fixed post that allows the cat to rest comfortably on its back feet while scratching.

5. The cat should be praised for scratching the post and punished each time it scratches fur-

The cat in gloves catches no mice.

BENJAMIN FRANKLIN

niture. As Hart points out, "Scratching is a normal, healthy, inherited behavioral requirement with the purpose of removing old, worn claws to expose new sharp claws beneath."

If you fail in your attempts to train your cat in this manner, or if you adopted a mature cat that had already developed the habit of scratching furnishings, your only alternative is to declaw in order to save the expense of recovering furnishings every few years. Approximately three-hundred cats are declawed each year at our hospital in New York, so don't feel you are alone with this problem.

Cats can be declawed at any age, but most veterinarians recommend that surgery be performed at six to eight months of age. This procedure can be done in conjunction with castration or spaying, if you are planning either of these. From my observations, the younger the cat is, the better it adapts to being declawed. Declawing procedures have been performed on very young cats, even newborn kittens. However, this should not deter you from declawing an older animal.

The surgical procedure of onyxectomy (declawing) involves minimal risk and is performed under general anesthesia. The basal germinal cells of the claw, which are responsible for nail growth, are removed. It is recommended that only the front paws be declawed, since these cause the most damage to furnishings or humans. Once the nails are removed, some veterinarians will suture the paws. I prefer to bandage the paws for two to three days, after which the bandages are removed and the cat sent home. Either method is acceptable. Some cats may exhibit slight tenderness on their front feet at first, but the majority will act normal within five to seven days after surgery. Most cats experience no more pain or discomfort from de-

clawing than they do from altering procedures. I recommend that newspaper be substituted for litter in the pan for ten days following the surgery to avoid any postoperative problems.

It is the rare cat that suffers any serious side effects from a declawing operation. Infection and regrowth of the nail, while possible, are rarely encountered. The cat should be returned to the veterinarian if its feet remain tender for a prolonged period after surgery.

From observations of my own cats and the cats of many clients, I can say that I have seen no harmful behavioral, psychological or physical effects related to declawing. It does not change the cat's personality in any way. In fact, my own cats still go through the motions of scratching, apparently unaware of the fact that they have been declawed. I have found cats to be less nervous when declawed because they are no longer being reprimanded for destroying rugs and furniture in the home.

Richard Greene is staff surgeon at the Animal Medical Center in New York City.

DECLAWING

SUZANNE WEAVER

A cat who had a manicure,
That is, its claws removed,
Was brooding on the state of things,
With hopes they would improve.

No longer could it scratch the couch,
The rug remained intact;
The furniture looked good for once,
The glasses all stayed stacked.

Each day dragged by, the cat was bored,
To motivate got tough.
Without my nails I'm half a cat,
I might as well be stuffed.

A thought came to it with the dawn,
While it was still in bed;
A claw is fine but what the hell,
I'll use my teeth instead.

CATS AND PLANTS

How To Keep Your Cat Out of the Plants and the Plants Out of Your Cat

Joan Lee Faust

CATS ARE CURIOUS, no doubt about it. They smell, paw, poke and investigate anything new around them. They even take a few nibbles if everything smells right. This last habit, nibbling, is the one that often gets them into trouble. If the nibbled thing is a toxic plant, the result may be stomach upset, vomiting, convulsions or illness. In some extreme cases, cats have been killed by eating certain highly toxic plants.

The plant-eating cat syndrome is most common with cats who are kept indoors all the time. Those who are allowed to be outside for part of their day do not usually find resident greenery curious and often ignore it. After all, during the day they are free to smell and investigate the whole outdoors. Indoors, cats may become bored and seek amusement, such as having a chew now and then. Some cats become herbivorous gluttons and eat down to the nub every green thing in sight.

One hypothesis about plant-eating cats is that they like to eat greenery as a form of roughage to clear their stomach of hairballs. Quite frequently, when hairballs are vomited up, chunks of grass or green leaves can be found in the mucus — thus, the unproved theory that they are cleansing their system. Whatever the reason, cats will sometimes eat greenery. A few cats are even attracted to specific plants such as crab grass or wild onions; often, the questionably therapeutic result is sneezing.

There are many ways to circumvent the plant-nibbling problem indoors so that greenery and furry friends can share a life together. Try squirting the cat with your plant mister. If a cat insists on nibbling at leaves and stems, hang plants out of their reach. Or utilize high shelves — really high — to keep plants out of the way of particularly good feline athletes, especially Siamese. Or arrange the plants with little or no cat-sitting space near them.

Sometimes cats like to snuggle into soil around large tubbed plants or to push plants over onto the floor or rug and roll in the soil. Worse yet, some find soil a fascinating litter box. There are several cures for this. Pet shops have available strong-scented aerosol spray repellents which can be utilized around the plant tub and over the surface of the soil, but not on the plant. The spray scent — usually nothing more than treated spicy oils — is not offensive to people, but it does repel cats. A few repeated applications for persistent pets should stop the habit. Or if the manufactured sprays are not obtainable, try shaking a bit of cayenne pepper over the plant soil. This surely works.

Kittens are often the most troublesome in using the tubbed plant soil as a litter box. Here, training is important. If the kitten persists in using the plant soil, a layer of heavy pebbles too difficult to paw may solve the problem. Again, for added insurance, a dash of cayenne pepper is effective, to be sure the kitten gets the idea.

There is yet another solution for jungle marauders. Grow the cats some greens of their own. Wheat and oats are two of the best and easiest plants to grow. The cats can nibble them all they like. The seeds, though hard to find, are cheap. And the plants are simple to raise in pots. If seeds cannot be found, perhaps country friends can find some at the local farm supply store. A pound would last a year or two. Many pet stores sell garden kits for "cat grass," but although these are sometimes effective, most cats

prefer the broader, more succulent grain leaves.

Take care in growing catnip for a cat. This strongly scented plant, which is related to garden mints, is equivalent to a mild drug for cats. It can send them off into highs of ecstasy and cause them to roll and meow as if in heat. It can also send a cat into a sleepy dullness.

Some cat fanciers use catnip at breeding time to stimulate the mating pair. But a little catnip goes a long way. The appeal seems to be more to the cat's owners than to the animal itself, as people are often quite amused at what happens when kitty is high on catnip. Many cat fanciers look upon giving catnip as a way of tempting the animal into some unneeded stimulus. There is no scientific proof of catnip's advantages or disadvantages. If you enjoy seeing your cat high, and the cat does not seem unduly distressed during or after a catnip session, continue to use it — but sparingly. As a general rule, consult your veterinarian about its use; he should be aware of recent relevant medical theories.

There is some thought among cat fanciers that cats have an unrecognized craving for vegetables; hence their attraction to greenery. Sometimes cats can be taken off the plant habit by making sure that they have enough green or raw vegetables in their daily diet. Salad greens such as lettuce are good, or celery tops, carrot peelings, potato peelings, peas, beans and other types of vegetables. Experiment with vegetables and the cat may find one or two favorites. A philodendron freak may become a string bean crazy.

If all attempts do not halt the plant-eating syndrome, you will have to choose your plants wisely if you wish to maintain your indoor forest and your cat's well-being, too. For your peace of mind, select plants that are safe, that are known not to have toxic substances in the leaves or harmful berries. Here are some popular house plants to avoid:

Philodendron, Dieffenbachia (or Dumb cane), *Caladium:* contains calcium oxalate crystals, which cause swelling of the tongue and mouth; vomiting and diarrhea may occur; total blockage of windpipe due to swelling may cause death.

Christmas cherry: has poisonous berries; keep away from cats, who often like to paw, chase and eat them.

Mistletoe: has poisonous berries which can cause vomiting, diarrhea or convulsions; watch for berries falling where cats or children can find them.

Bulb foliage: daffodil and hyacinth foliage can cause digestive upsets or trembling and convulsions.

Ivy: can cause difficulty in breathing and stomach upset.

Dried arrangements: often contain foreign

tropical plant material, such as seed pods and beans, that can be poisonous.

Outdoors, there are numerous plants that are toxic if eaten. Though part of many a garden's splendor, such plants as laurel, holly, rhododendron, yew, foxgloves, delphinium and oleander have poisonous parts. The list is quite extensive, and cat lovers could get themselves into a state of paranoia fearing that poison lurks behind every leaf or bush. In fact, cars and neighborhood dogs are really much more hazardous.

Cats are fairly smart, and animals often sense that something is not good to touch. But if a sudden illness should occur in a cat, the possibility of plant poisoning should not be overlooked. And it behooves anyone who has pets — or children — to be familiar with certain plants that are known to be toxic.

Several excellent references are available on poisonous plants. Those known to be toxic to man are always in some degree toxic to animals. Consult *Deadly Harvest: A Guide to Common Poisonous Plants* by John M. Kingsbury or *Poisonous Plants of the United States* by Walter Conrad Muenscher. Two helpful bulletins are "Common Poisonous Plants" by John M. Kingsbury, *Cornell University Extension Bulletin 538*, Ithaca, New York, and the March/April 1974 issue of *Arnoldia*, "Poisonous Plants," a publication of the Arnold Arboretum, Jamaica Plain, Massachusetts.

If it is suspected that a cat has eaten any quantity of a poisonous plant, consult a veterinarian immediately. Do not wait to see if the cat develops signs of illness. Be sure to know the plant's correct identity, as this will help the doctor know what steps to take. If the plant's name is not known, take it along with the cat to the vet's office.

Plants and cats can get along happily to-

HOW TO GROW WHEAT OR OATS FOR YOUR CAT

The best plan is to plant one pot of wheat or oats every three weeks or so to keep a continual supply of leaf spears available. Once the cats become accustomed to their own pots of greens, they will usually leave other plants alone.

To plant wheat or oat seed, select a pot no less than four inches in size. The roots of these grain plants are extensive, and they will need the room to grow. Use ordinary potting soil — it doesn't have to be fancy. Fill the pot three-quarters full with soil, place about ten to fifteen seeds on the surface, cover generously with soil, water and keep in a warm dark place for a few days, and the seeds will start to germinate. Keep the plant pot in bright light from then on, but out of reach of the cat until the grains are about four or five inches high. The pot may then be put where the cat can nibble to his heart's content. Once cats become fond of the grain leaves, they will nibble quite extensively. For this reason, it is a good idea to keep a continual rotating series of pots of wheat or oats available. Start a fresh one every two to three weeks.

gether. With patience, training and caution, both will thrive in the indoor jungle habitat.

Joan Lee Faust, a cat lover, is the garden editor of THE NEW YORK TIMES.

SOME COMMON POISONOUS PLANTS

The plants in the following chart are poisonous to humans as well as cats.

PLANTS	POISONOUS PARTS	SYMPTOMS
Bittersweet — *Celastrus* **spp.**	Bark, leaves and seeds	Vomiting, diarrhea, convulsions, coma
Dumb cane — *Dieffenbachia*	All parts	Swelling in throat, vomiting, diarrhea; death can result.
Poison hemlock — *Conium maculatum*	All parts	Dizziness, all loss of muscular control, disordered vision (within 15–45 minutes)
Ivy, English and Baltic — *Hedera helix*	Berries and leaves	Labored breathing, diarrhea, coma
Jimson weed, thorn apple — *Datura* **spp.**	All parts (extremely poisonous)	Intense thirst, rapid pulse, convulsions, coma, death
Marigold, marsh marigold — *Caltha palustris*	All parts	Mouth irritation, salivation, diarrhea, nervousness
Marijuana, hemp — *Cannabis sativa*	Resinous substance	Blurred vision, loss of coordination, drowsiness and coma
Mistletoe — *Phoradendron serotinum*	White berries	Vomiting, diarrhea, convulsions, coma
Oleander — *Nerium oleander*	All parts (extremely poisonous)	Vomiting, abnormal heartbeat coma, death may occur.
Philodendron — *Philodendron* **spp.**	All parts	Swelling of mouth and throat, vomiting and diarrhea; death may result from blockage of windpipe
Poinsettia — *Euphorbia pulcherrima*	All parts	Rash or blistering of skin, mouth and throat irritation, vomiting and diarrhea
Poison ivy — *Rhus radicans*	All parts	Itching, redness of skin, small blisters; local swelling of flesh may occur
Potato — *Solanum tuberosum*	Unripe tubers, sprouts from tubers	Vomiting, diarrhea, stupification, coma
Rhubarb — *Rheum rhaponticum*	Leaf blades	Vomiting, muscular weakness, slow pulse, coma and death, even from small amounts

The text of this chart is adapted from ARNOLDIA, *a publication of the Arnold Arboretum of Harvard University.*

GROOVY CATNIP

Vicky McMillan

GIVE A TYPICAL cat catnip, and he will show a striking change in behavior — vigorously purring, growling, rolling, leaping into the air. These are all common feline reactions to *Nepeta cataria,* a species of plant strangely attractive to cats. Furthermore, not only domestic types exhibit this behavior; lions and other wild members of the cat family also enjoy catnip, and lynxes have even been trapped using oil of catnip as bait. Individual reactions to catnip vary, of course, some cats showing greater interest than others.

What makes cats behave so strangely around catnip? So far, no one understands the phenomenon in detail. It is known that, while their sense of smell is not as acute as some other senses, cats do react strongly to the odor of catnip; it is this odor, apparently, rather than the eating of catnip leaves, that produces the typical ecstatic response. To some extent, catnip seems to function as a tranquilizer. (We gave our kittens catnip during their first car trip for this season.) Catnip is also regarded as a cat aphrodisiac, and the rolling response performed by so many cats is remarkably similar to the behavior of a female in heat. Some cat experts advise giving catnip to prospective mates to promote successful pairing, particularly if one or both cats are inexperienced.

Eating catnip leaves is generally harmless to cats, but allowing your cat constant access to catnip may not be wise. On this subject, Richard C. Smith, author of *The Complete Cat Book* (Walker and Co., New York), offers some good advice: "Catnip is to the cat's diet what martinis are to the human diet: fun when taken in moderation, bad for the appetite when taken with a meal, and wholly without nutritive value." However, Euell Gibbons, in *Stalking the Healthful Herbs,* reports that nutrition studies revealed catnip to be a good vitamin C source. Possibly, cats do absorb vitamins and minerals from ingested leaves.

So — give your cat catnip, but don't let him overindulge.

Catnip is a member of the mint family and related to such kitchen herbs as sage and thyme. Originally from Europe, it was introduced in America long ago as a common plant in herb gardens. It soon escaped from cultivation and now grows wild around old homesteads and farms. Reaching a height of about three feet, catnip has heart-shaped leaves that are toothed around their edges, and small white or pinkish spotted flowers. It blooms between July and September.

Catnip is rarely planted today, but it is easily grown in average garden soil. Plant some catnip seeds for your cat — it is a sure way to be assured of a fresh supply, and since catnip is a perennial you need to sow seeds only once. Put them in rows about twenty inches apart; later, thin the plants themselves to about twenty inches apart. Your catnip patch can be enlarged by dividing plants in the spring.

Aside from attracting cats, catnip has uses that have been virtually forgotten today. An aromatic (and delicious) tea can be made by steeping the dried leaves in boiling water, using a covered container. This was once a popular beverage in England, and it reputedly has many medicinal uses — to soothe the nerves and induce sleep, to reduce fever, to relieve indigestion. Drinking cold catnip tea supposedly stimulates the appetite. Euell Gibbons provides an intriguing recipe for candied catnip leaves: they are coated with egg white, lemon juice and granulated sugar, and intended for people, not cats.

Despite numerous potentials for human use, however, catnip will always really belong to cats. When it comes to going into ecstasies over the plant, we are not much of a match and can only watch from the sidelines, wondering what it is all about.

Reprinted from Cat Fancy *magazine (March–April, 1974).*

CATS AND HOUSEHOLD POISONS

Jay I. Luger, D.V.M.

THE INCIDENCE OF poisoning in cats is less than in other carnivores, for both instinct and eating behavior protect the domestic feline. In general, cats are creatures of habit and will often refuse food that tastes different or strange. Cats are not usually gluttonous, and should they eat poisoned food they would probably consume only a small amount and experience only a mild case of poisoning. Furthermore, cats chew their food well, and if poisoned bait is hidden in the food the cat may often taste, then reject the food.

Unfortunately, however, there are certain innate characteristics of feline behavior that are responsible for most of the cases of poisoning seen clinically:

1. Cats have meticulous grooming habits, therefore if a cat steps in a toxic substance or if such a substance should accidentally come into contact with its skin, the cat's reaction will be to remove the substance by licking it.

2. The hunting instinct of cats may cause secondary poisoning if the cat eats a rodent or insect that has consumed poison.

3. The old adage *Curiosity killed the cat* is certainly applicable in cases of poisoning. Anything new or different in the cat's environment is first smelled, and if it is a food item it may be tasted by the ever-curious cat.

Well-Meaning Poison

In addition to keeping poisonous substances in "cat-proof" locations, cat owners should be very careful about the drugs and medicines that they administer to their pets. There are many over-the-counter drugs that can be safely used in the home treatment of cats. However, this should be done only on the recommendation of your vet-erinarian because there are also over-the-counter drugs that are dangerous to your cat.

Administering aspirin to a cat is a prime example of how a caring but uninformed cat owner can inadvertently poison his pet. Giving a 10-pound cat 1 aspirin tablet is almost analogous to giving a 150-pound person 15 aspirin tablets. Aspirin produces inflammation of the stomach, toxic hepatitis and depression of bone marrow when given in high dosages to cats. Any of these conditions can be progressive and lead to death. Other commonly used analgesics, acetamino-phen and phenacetin, are even more toxic to cats than aspirin.

Cod liver oil, often administered by solici-tous cat owners, is very high in unsaturated fatty acids. If given to cats in high dosages for long periods of time, a vitamin E deficiency called steatitis (inflammation of fat) may result.

The vitamin D requirement of cats is very low. Vitamin D, a fat-soluble vitamin, is stored by the body. If cats are given vitamins intended for people or dogs, hypervitaminosis D may occur, producing deposits of calcium in abnormal loca-tions in the body.

Hypervitaminosis A is also produced by the well-meaning owner. This results from cats being fed diets composed mainly of fresh liver. Liver contains very high levels of vitamin A, a fat-soluble vitamin stored by the body. The ef-fects produced by hypervitaminosis A are slow and insidious. After a few years, abnormal bony growths appear on the spinal column in the neck region, producing a painful, arthritis-like condi-tion.

Iodoform is commonly used as a topical an-timicrobial agent for superficial wounds. It is highly toxic if ingested by the cat and produces severe depression, lowered body temperature,

COMMON HOUSEHOLD POISONS

Name	Classification of Poison	Route of Poisoning	Signs of Poisoning	Treatment; Comments
Warfarin (DECON) Pindone (PIVAL)	*Rodenticides*	Oral ingestion	Spontaneous bleeding (from mouth, nose, rectum, urinary tract)	Warfarin interferes with the normal clotting mechanism. Special therapy is available and prompt veterinary care should be sought.
Strychnine Thallium, 1080 (sodium fluoroacetate) ANTU (alpha-naphthyl thiourea)	*Rodenticides*	Oral ingestion	Signs vary with poison	All these rodenticides are highly toxic. Their usage has been decreasing because of the development of safer drugs and government regulation and restriction of their use.
Organophosphates: malathion, chlorthion, trichlorofon, parathion, diazinon, diclorovos	*Insecticides*	Oral ingestion, inhalation and in some instances absorption through unbroken skin	Salivation, vomiting, diarrhea, tremors, convulsions	Used in dips, sprays and flea collars. Specific antidotes are available; seek immediate veterinary care.
Chlorinated hydrocarbons: DDT, aldrin, dieldrin, endrin, chlordane, lindane, methoxychlor, heptachlor	*Insecticides*	Oral ingestion and absorption through unbroken skin	Muscle tremors, convulsions	There is much controversy about the use of these compounds because of their ecological side-effects. Therefore, their usage is decreasing. No specific antidote is available.
Lead	*Heavy Metal*	Oral ingestion	Gastrointestinal and neurologic signs	Cases of lead poisoning are very rare in cats.
Arsenic	*Heavy Metal*	Oral ingestion	Salivation, vomiting, abdominal pain, diarrhea, shock, coma	Used for herbicides and insecticides; specific antidote is available but is not safe for cats.
Ethylene glycol (antifreeze)	*Miscellaneous*	Oral ingestion	Vomiting, incoordination, coma	Animals are attracted by its sweet taste. Specific therapy is available from vets.
Coal and wood tar derivatives: cresol, creosol, naphthalene (mothballs), xylene, paraffin, phenol, toluene, hexachlorophene, pine tar, resorcinol	*Miscellaneous*	Oral ingestion; in some instances, absorbed through unbroken skin	Vomiting, violent abdominal pain, incoordination, coma	Used as antiseptics, disinfectants, wood preservatives, fungicides and herbicides, and in photographic developers. Cats are especially sensitive to phenols. No antidote is available.

gastroenteritis and coma.

Iodine and gentian violet, both of which destroy cells, should never be used to disinfect a cat's wounds.

Beware of Turpentine

Great care should be taken to avoid exposure to turpentine because it can be absorbed through unbroken skin and produce fatal poisoning.

What To Do When The Exterminator Comes

If you use the services of a professional exterminator, ask him the names of the insecticides and rodenticides he will use. The chart at the end of this article provides information on such poisons, the signs of poisoning and treatment for each. As a general precaution, isolate cats during the extermination process and consult your veterinarian to find out when it is safe to release them.

Environmental Poisoning

Minamata is the title of a recently published book by W. Eugene and Aileen Smith (New York: Holt, Rinehart & Winston, 1975). It tells the grim tale of how industrial pollution tragically led to methyl mercury poisoning in a Japanese town. Within a five-year period, the entire feline population of Minamata was destroyed as a result of having been fed fish from the polluted bay. Any owner of cats living near the seashore and those feeding their pets fresh fish must be on guard against similar instances of environmental pollution.

Treatment of Poisoning

There are three ways to treat poisoning:
1. Induce vomiting.
2. Administer specific antidotes for the poison. However, for the vast majority of poisons, no antidotes are available.
3. Give supportive therapy to treat the effects of poison already absorbed.

Cases of poisoning usually require prompt veterinary care. Nevertheless, initial home treatment is most important and can be life-saving. If your cat has just ingested a poison and is not vomiting or showing any signs of illness, vomiting should be induced immediately. Give your cat a teaspoon of hydrogen peroxide, which usually produces vomiting within five-minutes; if a teaspoonful is not effective, the dosage can be repeated twice.

●If your cat has ingested strong acids, strong bases or petroleum distillates, vomiting should *not* be induced. Call a veterinarian immediately.

●If a poison has been applied or inadvertently spilled on the skin, the cat should immediately be thoroughly bathed with mild soap and water to remove the poison as quickly as possible.

●If your cat has consumed a household substance and you are not sure whether it is poisonous, call your local Poison Control Center (consult local phone directory) immediately. Samples of the substance (as well as the vomitus) should be saved. Your veterinarian or a commercial laboratory cannot test a sample for all poisons because there are literally thousands of possibilities. However, if you or the veterinarian have reason to suspect a specific poison, laboratory analysis can be performed for the substance in question.

●Under extreme circumstances when no veterinary care is available, activated charcoal can be administered. Activated charcoal (an over-the-counter item in most pharmacies) *adsorbs* the poison and thereby prevents further *absorption* of the poison by the cat's intestinal tract.

Jay I. Luger is associated with the Forest Hills Cat Hospital, Forest Hills, New York.

HELPFUL HINTS FOR HEALTHY CATS

GERTRUDE ZEEHANDELAAR

Feeding

1. *Meals* should be given twice a day at regularly scheduled hours.
2. *Variety* in diet is essential to the well-being of cats. Provide variety with table scraps, vegetables, canned and dried food, meats, fish and chicken, removing all bones — even fine fish bones.
3. *Canned food.* Always read the ash-content on the label before purchasing: the lower the ash content, the better.
4. *Dry food* is excellent for keeping teeth clean, but should never be considered a complete diet for a cat.
5. *Milk.* If regular milk causes diarrhea, give the cat evaporated milk diluted with warm water, or no milk at all.
6. *Water.* Always keep a bowl of fresh water near the cat's feeding bowl.
7. *Cold food* is unappealing to most cats. Both food and milk should be served at room temperature. Refrigerated canned food should be warmed over hot water before feeding.
8. *Egg whites* are not recommended for cats.

Should Cats Be Allowed Outside?

1. *City Cats* should be kept inside.
2. *Country Cats* may be allowed outside if the area is quiet country or suburb; it is up to the owner to decide. However, country cats kept inside will be healthier, safer, and just as happy.

Why does my cat soil?

Housebroken cats often soil outside the litter pan if:
1. The litter pan is too small.
2. The kitty litter is dirty. Feces should be removed daily; change kitty litter often. A simple test is to pick up the pan: if it feels heavier than when the kitty litter was first put in, change the litter.
3. The pan is dirty. Wash the pan thoroughly with soap and water each time before adding fresh kitty litter. Do not use scented sprays or disinfectants. Cats do not like strange odors, and disinfectants can be harmful.
4. The litter pan has not been placed in a private spot.

Sleeping

If your cat has freedom to choose, his sleeping place will always be your bed. If you do not want him there:
1. Close the bedroom door.
2. Provide him with a dry, warm place of his own with easy access to the litter pan, water bowl and dry food.
3. Do *not* put the cat outdoors to sleep.

New Baby in the House

To protect the infant, a simple solution is to put a screen door with spring hinges on the inside of the baby's room and leave the regular door open. When the baby is in your arms, let the cat come up and sniff. By the time the baby is old enough for a playpen, the cat will most likely have accepted the new arrival.

I Cannot Keep The Cat Any Longer

1. Try to find the cat another home. The older the cat is, the more difficult it will be for him to adjust to new surroundings.
2. Do not put the cat in a shelter; there are too many cats for too few shelters.
3. When all other possibilities are exhausted, the only humane solution is to have the cat put to sleep by your veterinarian. Though harsh-sounding, it is in reality much kinder to the cat than to just put him outside to find a new home for himself — he will probably die instead.

Gertrude Zeehandelaar has owned and cared for cats all her life.

HEALTH AND MEDICAL RECORD

Keep a health and medical record in
the cat's medicine chest.
Record all visits to the veterinarian;
knowing your cat's medical history
will help it in the next illness or
emergency.

Date Vet Visited	Reason for Visit	Diagnosis	Medication Given	Home Treatment	Follow-up Visit Date

VACCINATION RECORD

Vaccine given	Date	Date of next shot in series	Date for booster shots

IX. THE WELL FED CAT

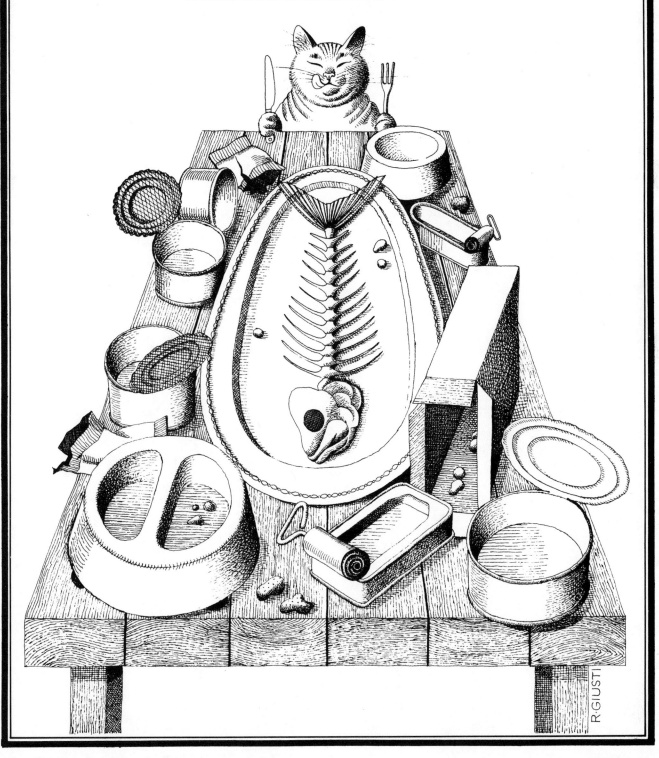

R. GIUSTI

THE NUTRITIONAL CAT

Dava Sobel

NUTRITIONALLY, A CAT is just an undersized lion. She is a meat-eater equipped with teeth and claws to kill and devour other animals. Like her larger wild relatives, she usually prefers to gorge herself at one sitting a day rather than eat several small meals at frequent intervals. And, as far as anyone can tell, domestic cats have the same nutritional requirements as lions and tigers: they all need large quantities of fat and protein, and minimal amounts of carbohydrates. The only significant difference between them is the *quantity* of food required.

The cat's body evolved as a hunter of meat. Her digestive enzymes can metabolize large quantities of protein and fat with ease. Her mouth is a miniature replica of the lion's, with thirty teeth adapted to flesh-eating: the front fangs ensure a firm bite on struggling food, and the sharp scissors of the side teeth can strip meat from bones most efficiently.

Fending for herself, the cat will eat the fresh, raw meat of mice, rats, birds, fish, and even insects and lizards. Although she is a complete carnivore, her hunting life gives her a balanced diet that includes the semidigested cereal and vegetable matter in the stomachs of her prey.

Experts agree that protein is the most important element in the cat's diet.

Everybody Talks About Cat Food, But Nobody Knows Anything About It

Beyond the sweeping generality about high protein demand, very little is known about the exact nutritional requirements of cats because investigators have not had the funding nor the inclination to conduct research on the subject. In fact, according to Dr. Sanford Miller, professor in the Department of Nutrition and Food Science at Massachusetts Institute of Technology, "You could count on your fingers all the people who have ever studied cat nutrition." As one of the rare breed of cat nutritionists, Dr. Miller has

IWAO ABE

several pet theories to explain the small number of feline food studies.

"From a metabolic point of view," he said, "the cat is truly unique." This means that information gleaned from any studies performed on cats will not have application to humans or other animals, so the studies stand a relatively poor chance of receiving support from federal funding agencies. Although industrial research is carried on by pet food companies, the results are not ordinarily made public. The little money that has been available to study cats has gone to support research in feline diseases rather than nutrition.

The cost of keeping a colony of cats for research is high, Dr. Miller added, and the effort may not pay off because the cat's metabolic

The cat that has its mouth burned by drinking hot milk will not drink even buttermilk without blowing upon it.

INDIAN SAYING

peculiarities can make a mockery of nutritional data.

"You have to remember that cats evolved as desert-living carnivores," he explained. "Domestic cats are not too different from those primitive animals, and they can endure starvation very well. In the wild, cats may go for long periods of time without food and suffer no ill effects. It is extremely difficult to interpret responses to food from animals with that ability. They have a positively incredible capacity to adapt themselves to survival on even a poor diet."

Nature Red in Tooth and Claw

Despite all her built-in hunting paraphernalia, a cat who is a companion animal may do little or no hunting, and rely completely on food provided by her owner. An understandable mistake among well-meaning owners is to mimic the hunt by feeding cats a diet of raw meats alone, only to see their pets develop severe deficiencies of calcium and iodine, making them susceptible to pathological bone fractures, loss of hair, and goiter. Commercial food should resemble caught food in its nutritional value and variety — not necessarily in appearance. For life support, a processed chow containing recommended allowances of basic nutrients is much better for a cat than an unvaried regimen of the finest tuna fillets.

Even a well-fed house cat may hunt if she gets the chance, but she may not eat what she catches. Some observers of cat behavior claim that a cat has to learn the hunt-kill-eat pattern from her mother. If she is not taught the procedure in kittenhood, she may never make the connection as an adult. Instead, she is likely to hunt for sport and bring the prey home to her owner.

Historical Perspective

Aside from the fact that cats have maintained themselves over the centuries with or without help from humans, cat owners have been raising healthy pets since long before the days of commercial cat food. Clearly, they must have been doing something right.

Dr. Miller thinks that most pet owners assure their cats a balanced diet by feeding them a wide variety of foods. A varied diet is the next best thing to the menu a feral cat feeds herself in the wild — the protein-rich muscle meats, the vitamin-supplying organ meats, the body fats, the minerals from bones, and carbohydrates from the vegetable matter in the digestive tract

HODGE

FROM: LIFE OF JOHNSON
BY JAMES BOSWELL

I never shall forget the indulgence with which he treated Hodge, his cat; for whom he himself used to go out and buy oysters, lest the servants having that trouble should take a dislike to the poor creature. I am, unluckily, one of those who have an antipathy to a cat, so that I am uneasy when in the room with one; and I own, I frequently suffered a good deal from the presence of the same Hodge. I recollect him one day scrambling up Dr. Johnson's breast, apparently with much satisfaction, while my friend, smiling and half-whistling, rubbed down his back, and pulled him by the tail; and when I observed he was a fine cat, saying, 'Why, yes, Sir, but I have had cats whom I liked better than this;' and then, as if perceiving Hodge to be out of countenance, adding, 'but he is a very fine cat, a very fine cat indeed.'

NOTTINGHAM ART GALLERY

of the prey.

The canned fish products that were once sold as "cat food" by tuna-packing houses were really just by-products of the "human food" industry. They were not balanced diets, nor were they scientifically tested or government-regulated until relatively recently.

About twenty years ago, many cats who were fed wholly or in part on this dark-meat (red) tuna developed steatitis, or yellow fat disease, characterized by serious painful inflammation of the body fat. The reason was that the fat content of the fish made the food so appealing in scent and taste that the animals tended to become exclusively addicted to it. Tuna-hooked cats consumed so much highly unsaturated fat that they depleted their own body stores of vitamin E in digesting it. Vitamin E deficiency is the real cause of steatitis. The issue spurred pet food manufacturers to add supplemental vitamin E (also called alpha-tocopherol) directly to the products to avoid the toxic effects of an all-fish diet. For the past ten years, nearly every fish-type pet food has contained this additive. But even with this built-in safeguard, the pet's best protection is a varied diet.

The profusion of the many varieties of cat and dog food — and some supermarkets devote an entire aisle to these products — is new and indicative of changing attitudes toward animals as well as modern standards of convenience.

"Until the 1960s," Dr. Miller said, "there was no worthwhile commercial cat food." Laboratory chows and prescription diets had been used by veterinarians and other scientists, but were not easily available.

The Pet Food Jungle

Labels on packages of cat food are often boastful and deceptive, but the careful shopper can protect his pet by understanding the code. The 1969 Guides for the Dog and Cat Food Industry, set by the Federal Trade Commission, require that any food labeled "complete," "scientific" or "balanced" must be capable of supporting a normal animal at any stage of the life cycle, including pregnancy and lactation, as the sole source of nourishment. These foods meet the basic requirements for laboratory animals established by the National Academy of Sciences–National Research Council in 1962. Any food that does not meet the requirements is considered a supplement, or snack, and should be so labeled. But, as the September 1972 *Consumer Reports* investi-

A cat with little ones has never a good mouthful.

FRENCH PROVERB

gation of cat food showed, the language on the label can be a study in obfuscation. Moreover, the members of the N.A.S.–N.R.C. research group who set the standards admitted that they had little to say about the *precise* nutritional requirements for cats.

Owners can take heart, however, that continued testing has proved the grades of commercial food to be reliable. Words like "complete" and "balanced" are status symbols for a pet food, and will appear, most likely, in a prominent place on the label. The rest of the information on the package — the fine print and detailed chemical analyses — may baffle even the most nutritionwise shopper.

Bag, Box or Can

A cat's preference for one texture of food over another may, like her tastes, be the result of early experience. Dr. Sanford Miller of M.I.T. recommends the semi-moist types because he was once part of a research group at Rutgers University that first experimented with them. However, Dr. Miller adds that cats in one experimental colony learned very early to enjoy their basic nutrients in a gel-like medium, and were indifferent to other foods. If the cat is agreeable to dry, semi-moist or moist food, the choice may be simply a question of which is most convenient or aesthetically appealing to the owner.

The *Consumer Reports* evaluation mentioned above tested all three types. The investigators were specifically concerned with adequate diets for kittens after weaning (about eight weeks old), which is a period of continued rapid growth. The study tested twenty-two foods of which seventeen were moist (canned), three were dry chows, and two were the semi-moist type. Of the five rated "acceptable" as the sole food for kittens, two were dry and three were moist. Both the semi-moist types got "inconclusive" ratings (as did eleven other tested products) because some kittens thrived on them and some did not. Four foods, according to the study, were clearly "not acceptable for kittens," although their labels

did not always say as much. The report concluded by advising owners to accustom kittens to a varied diet.

A word about the *Consumer Reports* test: Some researchers have criticized the experiment as being poorly designed. Dr. Stanley Gershoff of the Harvard University School of Public Health pointed out that the test did not account for "finickiness" in cats. Dr. Gershoff, who became interested in feline nutrition more than twenty years ago and helped establish guidelines for the pet food industry, said that two foods may be exactly alike in nutritional value, but any given cat may gobble up one variety and turn tail on the other.

Pet food companies spend considerable time, energy and money in experimenting with "palatability factors," or food additives that titillate feline senses. These factors are jealously guarded trade secrets, and some of them are effectively addicting.

In most cases, an owner who wants to change his pet's diet after feeding her only one favorite brand may have to watch his cat refuse to eat for several days. At some frustrating point he may ask himself, "Why am I making us both miserable? She's eating a balanced diet already. The label says the food is complete. Why can't I leave her be with the flavor she likes?"

The answer, according to the veterinary staff at Angell Memorial Animal Hospital, is that a cat may need a special diet at some time in her life when she is ill or old. Unless she is used to a variety of foods, any transition will be just so much harder for her. The varied diet makes her more adaptable. In the wild she would not pick and choose, but pounce on whatever edible morsel crossed her path.

Finickiness should not be confused with true anorexia (loss of appetite), which is a sure sign of disease. A cat may die as a result of anorexia rather than from the illness that brought it on. Dr. Gershoff says he has seen a simple ringworm infection kill a cat's appetite to the point where it killed the cat.

A few nutrition specialists maintain that the significant difference between wet food and dry chow is the content of ash, or mineral residues. Dry chows may contain more of it, on a dry weight basis, than moist canned foods. (Owners who compare labels should remember that wet foods are about 75 percent water by weight, and dry foods only 12 percent moisture. A real comparison of ash or protein content involves some

Little White Kitties Into Mischief, *Currier & Ives, 1871.*

serious mathematic calculations to arrive at the dry weight content of both foods.)

Some researchers, including Dr. Sanford Miller of M.I.T., believe that the ash content in dry chow contributes to the formation of stones in the feline urinary tract. The condition is called cystitis. Some veterinarians prescribe a low-mineral diet for cats who have suffered from cystitis. Other factors seem to be involved, however: virus, injury, hormonal imbalance, or generally poor diet could be causes. Since the frequency of the problem is highest among castrated males, veterinarian Dr. Michael Fox is often asked about the advisability of feeding dry food. His answer appears in his book, *Understanding Your Cat:* "It is not really the diet that causes cystitis and calculi (stones) in castrated cats but, more probably, a metabolic anomaly that follows castration. In addition, the penis can be smaller so that small calculi cannot be voided. Cats also are prone to develop bladder infections, so don't blame the food. I have a castrated male Abyssinian — I give him Purina chow and every other day a moist canned food, table scraps (he loves corn on the cob and bananas), and grass (lawn, that is). Diversity of diet, but a balanced diet, is a safe rule."

Nutrients

The pet food standards — the labels "complete" and "balanced" — are a measure of the nutritional value of the food. A balanced or complete diet contains all five major groups of nutrients (protein, fat, carbohydrate, vitamin and mineral) in the proper amount. "Proper amounts" are debatable, of course, but complete foods contain the proportions of nutrients advised by the National Academy of Sciences–National Research Council in 1962. Water, although it doesn't seem

very nourishing, is vital and is counted by some nutritionists as a sixth category of nutrient.

A discussion of the various nutrients follows:

Protein is the structural material comprising animal skin, hair, nails, cartilage, muscles, tendons and parts of the bones. It is needed to build and renew body tissues, to metabolize food, maintain the body's self-regulation and fight infection.

Dr. Patricia P. Scott of the Royal Free Hospital School of Medicine in London has stated that the large quantity of protein consumed by adult cats (nearly double the dog's required intake) is used not only for basic body-building, but for energy production as well. Other animals rely heavily on carbohydrates as sources of energy, but cats require less sugar and starch.

"It is possible," Dr. Scott wrote in a 1971 report, "that the obligatory diversion of proteins for energy was originally developed as a means of dealing with the high protein intake forced upon the cat by its predatory habits . . . Experimentally, we have shown that the diet of growing kittens should contain about 33 percent protein of high biological value in a mixed diet, and adults more than 21 percent, both calculated on a dry food basis. We found that as the percentage protein was reduced in the diet of the adult cat, the animal increased its food intake in an apparent attempt to maintain its total protein intake. It became impossible for the animals to compensate by eating more on diets containing less than 19 percent protein on a dry food basis and below this level appetite failed."

The term "high biological value" refers to the quality of protein eaten — whether it comes from muscle or organ meats or from non-meat sources, and how well it supports growth. Muscle meat is generally considered the best source for

The cat would eat fish, and would not wet her feet.

OLD ENGLISH PROVERB

ANOTHER VOICE

Dick Gregory, whose philosophical convictions have made him a fruitarian, wrote a book entitled, *Natural Diet for Folks Who Eat.* Chapter Twelve, "Dick Gregory's Natural Diet for Pets and Plants Who Eat," encourages owners to teach their cats to enjoy the pulp of peaches, pears, plums, apples, avocados, bananas, watermelons, tomatoes and grapes.

Gregory agrees that raw meat belongs in the cat's diet, but adds this caveat:

"If I were a pet owner, my own personal conviction would demand that my pet get its source of protein from non-flesh sources. Once a pet is taken into the home, it is not living in its ancestral natural environment anyway, and my reading and conversation have convinced me that a pet could live quite healthily on a balanced non-flesh diet."

(Incidentally, observers note that cats raised on a vegetarian diet will still hunt and kill prey if they get the chance, although they are less likely to eat what they catch.)

To "streamline a feline," Dick Gregory recommends a seven-day menu as follows (to be repeated for as many weeks as necessary and accompanied by exercise):

Day 1: Turnip greens, string beans and celery steamed together. Add one ounce raw beef and one-half cup grated raw celery.

Day 2: Fresh corn, chard and broccoli steamed together. Add a raw egg yolk.

Day 3: Spinach, peas, okra and peppers, steamed. An ounce of cottage cheese with chopped raw lettuce. Or nut butter (made by grinding raw nuts in a grinder or using a blender) in place of cottage cheese.

Day 4: Two bowls of raw milk, goat's milk or soy milk mixed with one-half cup prune juice.

Day 5: Two bowls of vegetable broth, with one raw egg yolk.

Day 6: Steamed cabbage, peas and string beans. A very small amount of raw meat is optional.

Day 7: Water, raw milk, soy milk *or* fruit juice with honey added.

cats, but other protein foods can be "beefed up" with supplements to augment their nutritional value. Dr. Scott concluded:

"Economically the domestic cat is at a grave disadvantage compared to other pets, even the dog, since it requires relatively large amounts of protein of high biological value for its size. In a world where animal proteins are both scarce and expensive, attempts must obviously be made to substitute these by protein of vegetable or other origin."

Milk, although it contains high-quality protein, is not tolerated by all adult cats. Most of them lose the ability to digest milk as they grow up, and drinking it may give them diarrhea. (Cat's milk, incidentally, differs from cow's milk in that it contains about 9.5 percent protein by weight. Cow's milk has 3.5 percent, and human's milk only 1.6 percent.) If an owner raises his cat from the time she is a kitten, he may be able to keep her in the habit of drinking milk. As a rule, however, kittens *do* outgrow their need for milk almost as soon as they are weaned.

Eggs and cheese may also supplement a pet cat's protein intake, if the cat will eat them. Some owners feel that a raw egg mixed into the food once a week or so will improve the quality of the cat's coat. Raw egg white has actually contributed to skin problems in some pets, however, and the cat may better appreciate cooked eggs or just the raw yolk with her meal.

Fats serve as a concentrated source of energy and as body padding. Since flavors and aromas are fat-soluble substances, the fat content may determine whether or not a cat will eat a certain food, and pet food companies rely on fats and oils as palatability factors. The vitamins A, D, E and K are frequently carried in fat. Dr. Patricia Scott's studies indicate that, under natural conditions, cats obtain 60 percent of their calories from fat.

In a booklet called *Cat Care* published by the American Humane Education Society, feeding instructions say that "cats have a high re-

*Joseph, a tabby of 48 pounds,
was left a bequest by his owner,
Miss Agatha Isabel Frazer Higgins,
upon her death in 1969.
He is famous in England
for both his size and his wealth.
Whatever became of him
after he got rich is unknown.*

quirement for fats, which they often enjoy in the form of meat scraps, butter, bacon, and bacon grease." The booklet recommends cheese as an excellent source of both protein and fat.

Carbohydrates are not essential in a cat's diet, and some of them — like the sugar in milk (lactose) — may make her quite uncomfortable. Carbohydrates can be a useful source of calories for a kitten or cat, however, provided she is getting adequate amounts of protein and fat.

Most processed foods contain cereal, which is carbohydrate, that adds variety to the meat or fish. As mentioned earlier, a wild cat will eat the stomach contents of her prey. This material, already broken down by the smaller animal's digestive juices, is a lot like cooked cereal. Both add bulk to the diet for needed calories, but cannot take the place of protein.

According to guidelines prepared by the veterinary staff at Angell Memorial Animal Hospital, "Carbohydrates such as potatoes, bread, noodles, and the like may constitute part

of the diet of cats. In fact, an owner should foster a cat's taste for such foods, as many cats in old age develop kidney disease, a condition which calls for less protein in the diet and increased carbohydrates. Such a modification in an elderly cat's diet is usually accepted only if the cat is already conditioned to enjoy a certain amount of starchy food."

Vitamins needed for disease prevention and the regulation of body processes occur naturally in foods. Normal kittens and cats who are fed properly and get out of doors do not need vitamin supplements. However, a veterinarian may prescribe vitamins for old, ill cats, or for housebound pets with limited tastes in food.

Cats require minuscule amounts of most vitamins, as shown by the accompanying chart prepared by Dr. Patricia P. Scott to summarize existing knowledge. It is very easy to give a cat an overdose of vitamins that can harm her, so most owners wisely avoid administering vitamins without veterinary supervision. Since many of

There are more ways of killing a cat than choking her with cream.

CHARLES KINGSLEY

the vitamins that go into commercially prepared pet food can be lost through heat processing or long periods of time on the supermarket shelf, variety is the best policy. A cat who eats a balanced diet of many different foods is unlikely to suffer any vitamin deficiencies.

There is some evidence, according to Dr. Scott, that cats have "a highly efficient mechanism for forming vitamin D in the skin or fur, under the influence of light." She notes that healthy cats spend considerable time licking their fur, and that "the few clinical cases of classical rickets reported seem to have been in kittens kept in the dark."

Minerals are used to build the cat's skeletal structure and soft body tissues. Her requirements for calcium are understandably highest when she is a kitten and during lactation. Estimated requirements are summarized in the chart below, from Dr. Scott's research.

Some owners feed bones to their cats as a "natural source" of minerals. Most pets, however, are prone to choking and gagging on splintering bones, and get ample minerals from their regular food. In some cases, a veterinarian may prescribe a powdered mineral supplement for a pregnant or nursing cat.

Water accounts for 70 percent of the cat's weight and figures importantly in her body's every function. Yet, in the wild state, a cat may drink as infrequently as once every twenty-four hours. After all, the cat evolved as a desert animal.

A hunting cat gets ample fluids from the carcasses of prey (which are also about 70 percent water), but a housecat needs water mixed into the diet or served as a side dish. Most canned cat foods are about 70 percent moisture by weight. Dry chows are only 12 percent moisture at most, and should be fed with a bowl of fresh water handy.

Green Needs

Cats bite and swallow their food so quickly that they do not seem to allow themselves time to taste what they are eating. Their teeth are most adept at tearing and cutting. Grinding motions are impossible because of the way cats' jaws are hinged together.

A cat eating a carcass will shear meat from bone with the knife-edges of her teeth. Then she will use the rough, hook-shaped papillae of her tongue to scrape the bones clean. The last step is to tidy herself by using the small incisor teeth at the front of her mouth to pick debris out of her coat, and lick her fur with the cleaning fluid in her saliva.

While grooming, the cat may swallow so much of her own fur that the hairs clump together in her stomach and make her vomit. Some cats will deliberately eat grass to help them vomit up these wads of fur.

Dr. Michael W. Fox, the veterinarian who wrote *Understanding Your Cat*, recommends occasionally feeding a little fresh grass to confined apartment cats as a tonic. (He also advises grooming the animal daily with a good brush so she does not have to lick away all her loose hairs and accumulated dust.) Dr. Fox thinks that cats who eat houseplants are expressing a need for green in their diets. Many people, he says, grow an indoor box of greens specifically for cat consumption. (See Joan Lee Faust's article "Cats and Plants" for instructions on how to grow greens for your cat.)

Animal or Vegetable?

While a cat may enjoy a little grass from time to time, she does not derive much nutritional value from plant foods. For example, cats lack the enzyme necessary to make vitamin A from carotene. They could consume massive quantities of carrots and still develop vitamin A deficiencies. A cat must get her vitamin A from organ meats like liver or from a vitamin supplement.

It seems clear that cats were not meant to be vegetarians.

Raw vs. Cooked

Laboratory studies performed in 1939 and 1947 compared the value of cooked and uncooked foods for cats. According to these studies, test animals experienced better growth, development, reproduction and lactation when they were fed raw meat and milk.

Today, all processed cat foods are cooked. However, modern understanding of nutritional requirements, coupled with continued testing,

CALORIE COUNTING FOR CATS

For those who wish to compute the calories in any food formula, this is how it is done. Consider only the protein, carbohydrate (which may be expressed as nitrogen-free extract), and fat. Disregard the rest. Multiply the protein and carbohydrate by four, because a gram of either, when burned, yields four calories. Multiply the fat by nine; a gram of fat burns to yield nine calories. This will give you the number of calories in one hundred grams of food. Since there are 454 grams in a pound, you can convert the answer to pounds by multiplying by 4.5.

How many calories in a one-pound can of a certain canned food? The guarantee says:

Protein	9%
Carbohydrate	11%
Fat	2%
Fiber	2%
Water	74%
Ash	1%

Protein	9 × 4 =	36
Carbohydrate	11 × 4 =	44
Fat	2 × 9 =	18

$$98 \times 4.5 = 441 \text{ calories per lb.}$$

How many calories in a pound of top round? It contains about 21 percent protein, 10.5 percent fat, and the rest is mostly water.

Protein	21 × 4 =	84
Fat	10.5 × 9 =	94.5

$$178.5 \times 4.5 = 803.25 \text{ calories per lb.}$$

How many calories in a pound of a certain dehydrated cat food? It has 25 percent protein, 57 percent carbohydrate, 4.5 percent fat.

Protein	25 × 4 =	100
Carbohydrate	57 × 4 =	228
Fat	4.5 × 9 =	40.5

$$368.5 \times 4.5 = 1658.25 \text{ calories per lb.}$$

It is also necessary, however, to consider what part of the total caloric volume is actually usable, because sometimes the protein and carbohydrates may not be so completely available as those in other foods. Even so, a dehydrated ration which furnishes sixteen hundred calories certainly should recommend itself for our consideration, especially since some fat could readily be added to it.

have made these products the nutritional equivalent of the hunt-and-pounce diet. In fact, hunting may be unsafe for cats, since the prey may contain tapeworms or other parasites.

Meal Plan

Most cats are "occasional" as opposed to "continuous" feeders, which means they like to eat once or, at most, twice a day. Growing kittens and pregnant or lactating females, however, need to eat more frequently. Although the proper daily amount of food differs from one animal to another, most cats can regulate themselves and do not naturally overeat. If they have water and chow available at all times, they will most likely eat only what they need.

One bizarre predilection of cats is their taste for ethylene glycol. Dr. Jean Holzworth of the Angell Memorial Animal Hospital reports that most cats share an uncanny attraction to the sweet taste of ordinary antifreeze. "They love it and will go out of their way to get at it," she says, "although it's a deadly poison. The antidote for it is a good, stiff drink. When I catch my cats licking at a puddle of it under a car, I give them a bowl of vodka and milk."

Fat Cats

Dr. Francis A. Kallfelz of the New York State College of Veterinary Medicine at Cornell University has a simple technique for diagnosing obesity in cats. "We do not have height and weight charts," he says. "But if we can see the animal's ribs, it is too skinny. On an animal with good flesh, we can feel the ribs. If we can not feel them, however, it is too fat."

Dr. Kallfelz says that overweight is among the biggest health problems seen in the outpatient veterinary clinics at Cornell; it decreases the animal's life span by increasing the likelihood of heart or joint disease. As with humans, the only remedy for overweight is to undereat.

The cat's calorie requirements decrease as she grows older, and owners should reduce portions given to aging pets. It is generally agreed that neutering an animal does not cause overweight, but overfeeding does.

Pregnant and Nursing Mothers

A pregnant cat may eat as many as three meals a day by the time her kittens are due, and keep up her increased appetite until they are weaned. Her vitamin and mineral intake should be doubled or trebled during this period. After she gives birth, her first meal will be the afterbirth (placenta) expelled with each newborn. In his picture-rich book *The Compleat Cat,* Joseph R. Spies offers three reasons for this act: "(1) in the wild state, the mother would be unable to obtain food elsewhere for a considerable time; (2) in the wild state, the scent of the afterbirth might attract enemies; and (3) the afterbirth may provide hormones needed for body functions or immunities." It may also stimulate the flow of milk.

Dr. Patricia Scott has found that, during lactation, a cat who normally eats 150 grams of wet food per day may increase her intake to between 300 and 500 grams per day, depending on the number of kittens she is supporting.

"During lactation," Dr. Scott wrote in 1964, "the skeleton acts as a reserve for calcium which is secreted into the milk. On a low-calcium diet, the mother may lose more than one-third of her total skeletal store during lactation when there are five to six kittens." Dr. Scott recommended supplements of bone meal as a source of additional calcium for nursing mothers.

Kitten Fare

Few mammals grow as fast as young kittens, who double their birth weight in about one week. Their high demand for calcium — and all other nutrients, for that matter — is met entirely by their mother's milk until they are several weeks old, at which point the wild mother would begin to bring her young the freshly killed small prey she had hunted for them.

The composition of cat milk was studied by Dr. J. P. Greaves at the Royal Free Hospital School of Medicine, London, and found to contain the following nutrient amounts per 100 grams of milk:

Protein: 9.5 grams
Fat: 6.8 grams
Lactose: 10.0 grams
Calories: 142
Calcium: 34 milligrams
Phosphorus: 70 milligrams

Since cat milk contains about three times the protein of ordinary cow's milk, orphaned kittens fare best with a foster mother — preferably feline, but canine will do if the dog agrees (dog's milk is 7.1 percent protein) — or hand-reared on evaporated milk (twice the protein of ordinary cow's milk) fed with an eyedropper or a doll bottle by a conscientious owner. The kitten's stomach is no bigger than an acorn, but she needs frequent small meals to ensure and ease her rapid growth.

Joseph Spies offers the following kitten-weaning menu, stipulating that all meals should be served close to the cat's body temperature of 101.5° F. (the kitten is still receiving regular helpings of mother's milk throughout this regimen):

4th–5th weeks: cow or goat milk; add yolk of egg after third day, serve once a day.

5th–6th weeks: baby meats, finely cut fresh kidney and infant cereal (50-50) with egg yolk and sufficient whole milk to create mush, serve three times a day.

7th–8th weeks: baby meats, finely cut meats and baby vegetables or soft-cooked cereals (50-50) with egg yolk and milk; serve four times a day.

Of course, many owners are just too busy to care for kittens in this way. They rely on one of the "complete" or "balanced" foods as a supplement to mother's milk. As for the new specialty foods for kittens, Dr. Francis Kallfelz at Cornell University says they are no better than the ordinary chow. He feels such products are a direct result of consumer — *human,* not animal — demand.

"Many balanced foods on the market have been demonstrated to be satisfactory for growing kittens," Dr. Kallfelz says, "yet so-called 'baby chows' are introduced and will sell because of the public's belief in the necessity for specialty items for infants."

The kitten's permanent teeth replace the milk teeth at about six or seven months. The

CALORIC REQUIREMENTS OF
CATS BY WEIGHT

Approximate caloric requirements of cats by weight. Find the weight of your cat on the left-hand side and follow the line toward the right to its point of intersection with the heavy black line. Then drop downward to the bottom *line, where you will find the daily calorie requirement.*

From The Complete Book of Cat Care, *copyright © 1953 by Leon F. Whitney. Reprinted by permission of Doubleday & Co., Inc.*

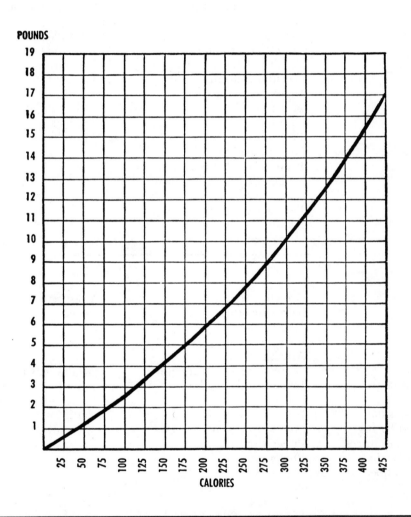

rapid growth of the first nine months of life tapers off until the cat reaches full size at about sixteen months.

A Final Word

A varied diet of complete foods, along with periodic visits to a veterinarian, should keep a cat healthy. Owners need to feed their pets "complete" or "balanced" foods, avoid limiting them to only one flavor or variety, and not administer supplements without the advice of a veterinarian. Even though a pet cat has a lot in common with the lion, she lives in a human environment and has come to depend on tender loving care.

Dava Sobel lives in Maine and is a member of the National Association of Science Writers.

VITAMINS: THEIR PROPERTIES, FUNCTIONS AND SOURCES

VITAMINS	CONCERNED WITH	SOURCES
A (and carotene)		
Stable at boiling temperatures Spoils with age if exposed to air Body stores it Fat soluble	General metabolism Growth Skin health Muscle coordination Fertility Calcium utilization Digestion Hearing Vision Prevention of infection Nerve health Prevention of one type of bladder-stone formation Pituitary-gland function Prevention of one form of diarrhea	Alfalfa-leaf meal Butter Carrots Egg yolks Fish livers Glandular organs Leaves of plants Milk, whole Spinach Many dark green vegetables
B Complex		

Biotin
Pantothenic acid
Riboflavin, thiamin
Folic acid
Niacin
Pyridoxin
   Animal protein factor
   Water soluble
   Body storage — small
   Some destroyed by high cooking temperatures, but not riboflavin
   Biotin effects robbed by raw egg white
	Growth promotion
	Nerve health
	Heart health
	Liver function
	Appetite
	Gastro-intestinal function
	Intestinal absorption
	Lactation
	Fertility
	Muscle function
	Prevention of anemia
	Prevention of black tongue
	Prevention of Vincent's disease
	Kidney and bladder function
	Blood health
	Prevention of one type of paralysis
		Yeast
		Cereals
		Milk
		Eggs
		Liver
		Alfalfa-leaf meal
		Rapidly growing plants
		Bacterial growth
		Cattle paunch and intestinal contents

C		

Ascorbic acid
   Water soluble
   Unstable at cooking temperatures
	Prevention of scurvy in some pets
	Not necessary in cats
		Fruit juices and vegetables
		Alfalfa-leaf meal

D

Irradiated ergosterol
  Well stored by body
  Stands considerable heat
  Resists decomposition
  Fat soluble
	Regulation of calcium and
	  phosphorus in blood
	Calcium and phosphorus
	  metabolism
	Prevention of rickets
	Normal skeletal development
	Muscular co-ordination
	Lactation
		Fish livers and oils extracted
		Some animal fats

E

Tocopherol
  Fat soluble
  Body stores it
  Perishes when exposed
    to air
  Stands ordinary cooking
    temperatures
	Muscular co-ordination
	Fertility in some species
	Muscular development in
	  kittens
	Sound hearts
	Survival of young animals
	Growth
	Pituitary gland health
		Seed germs

K

Fat soluble	Blood-clotting Young kitten health	Alfalfa-leaf meal

Unsaturated Fatty Acids (sometimes called vitamin F)

Linoleic acid Linolenic acid Arachnidic acid	Coat and skin health	Wheat-germ oil Linseed oil Rapeseed oil Many seed oils

ALICE SU

DEBUNKING MYTHS ABOUT CAT NUTRITION

Michael Milts, D.V.M.

EVERYONE KNOWS CATS are carnivores. What could be better for your pet — and more natural — than a juicy steak, lovingly chopped, served raw? Practically nothing except liver. Cats love liver, so why not feed it to them every day? They would not eat it if it were not good for them.

If you think these statements are true, your cat is in trouble. A greater amount of misinformation persists about feeding the cat than about any other species domesticated by man. The dietary requirements differ even from our other popular pet, the dog. Some pet food manufacturers add to the confusion by advertisements urging you to buy unsupplemented all-meat products. If you want your cat to live a long life in good health, you had better get the facts and use them.

It is true that cats are carnivores, but carnivorous animals in the wild eat entire animals, including the bones, not just the flesh. When cats live outdoors and are free to forage for themselves, they kill rats, mice, birds and other small animals, which enable them to balance their diet. However, most pet cats depend on us to feed them. (How well grandmother's country cats got along does not pertain to house pets.) In my practice I see the following nutritional problems that well-meaning owners inflict on their pets.

Muscle meat, liver, chicken or boned fish result in a diet that is very high in phosphorus. Calcium and phosphorus exist in the bloodstream in a carefully balanced ratio that the body will attempt to maintain at all costs. Increasing the phosphorus content of the diet has the effect of drawing calcium out of the skeletal system and excreting it in the urine along with the extra phosphorus. The skeletal system becomes weakened. This disease, nutritional secondary hyperparathyroidism, has varied symptoms. Young animals can have their growth stunted. Multiple fractures can occur, including paralysis of the hind legs from the pelvis being crushed due to the strength of the muscles pressing on the weakened bone structure. Adult cats will be less affected than kittens, but fractures will heal slowly and will happen more frequently. Resultant periodontal disease from calcium deficiency can affect both young and adult animals.

Many people feed their cats a diet very high in or exclusively of liver. *Liver is a poor choice for anything other than an occasional diet supplement,* preferably not more than once a week. Besides being too high in phosphorus, liver is a poor quality protein and unreliable as the main source of that nutrient. The main problem resulting from a diet high in liver comes from its high content of vitamin A, a fat-soluble vitamin. Excess vitamin A is stored in the body rather than eliminated, as are vitamins of the B complex family and vitamin C. If the cat has too much vitamin A, vitamin A toxicity will occur. The degree and speed at which symptoms will appear depend on how much liver your cat is eating and whether or not your are feeding sup-

---

HEALTHY HINTS

SUZANNE WEAVER

There once was a cat named Knishes,
Who ate lots of fattening dishes.
When put on a diet,
He caused such a riot —
His owner, he meowed, was delicious.

plements very high in vitamin A, such as cod liver oil. Excess vitamin A will cause damage to the articular surfaces of bones, which will in turn cause pain and difficulty in moving the neck and limbs.

A diet of red tuna, which is cheaper than white because it is less aesthetically pleasing to humans, and other fish foods containing a high percentage of unsaturated fatty acids can result in a disease called steatitis. Steatitis, or yellow fat disease, is caused by a vitamin E deficiency. Unsaturated fatty acids destroy vitamin E. Most manufacturers of these products today add large supplements of vitamin E to prevent the problem; therefore, the disease is much less frequently encountered today than in the past. But cats fed diets of fresh red tuna do not have this protection, and if such a diet is to be used to any degree, vitamin E must be supplemented. I would recommend caution even with the supplemented canned product; restrict it to one or two times weekly. Food that is merely tuna-flavored is not subject to this problem.

A diet of raw fish can result in deficiency of thiamine due to the presence of thiaminase, a thiamine-destroying enzyme. The disease can cause vomiting and nervous disorders, even convulsions and death. So many species of fish caught have this enzyme in varying concentrations that it is easier merely to avoid raw fish in your cat's diet.

Feeding Your Cat

How should you feed your cat? Much research has gone into cat nutrition, and although there is still a lot to be learned, today we have a pretty good idea of what it takes to keep your cat healthy. The best single thing you can do for your cat is to feed it one of the balanced, properly supplemented commercial rations. These come in three general forms: moist canned, semi-moist in cellophane or foil packages, and dry.

Canned cat foods have been around for a long time, but not too many years ago the main concern of the manufacturers was palatability — would cats eat it? Obviously, palatability is still important, but it is no longer the only sufficient consideration. Strict federal labeling standards are enforced. If a can of food has the words "complete cat food," "complete diet" or a similar phrase on the label, it should be considered safe for your cat's complete diet. Be careful of words such as "wonderful taste treat for your cat." If the label doesn't say that the food is a *complete* or *balanced* ration, it probably isn't. Such a food should be fed only occasionally, but, in general, why even bother? Cats are not finicky and spoiled by nature; they are taught to be so by well-meaning, anthropomorphizing humans. Remember, even if officially balanced, tuna and other one hundred percent fish foods have special problems, so I recommend feeding these foods only once or twice a week. The palatability of these foods is very high, and often so is the cost. On a canned food diet, some cats may not drink any additional water, but fresh water should always be available.

Semi-moist foods are a relatively new invention. They are all balanced rations, and most — but not all — cats like and do well on them. No cans to carry around or open and a less noticeable odor are the main advantages of these foods. It is especially important to give your cat free choice of water to drink when using this type, since the food itself contains less water than moist foods do.

Dry cat foods have been in use for over fifteen years. They come in a variety of flavors and

ECONOMY CAT FOOD

This recipe was suggested to us by Jeanne Adlon, owner of the Cat Cottage, a specialty store for cats in New York City. The recipe provides a nutritious, tasty way to feed your cats on a limited budget. The food provides all the nutrients your cat needs, and helps insure that the cat is accustomed to different kinds of food. Experiment with it and vary the spices to suit your cat's taste.

1 6½-ounce can Friskies® or Puss n' Boots®
1 12½-ounce can Lovin' Spoonful® (these two same flavor)
1 small can French-style string beans, drained
Salt to taste
Garlic powder
Tomato juice (enough to moisten mixture)

Combine all ingredients and mix thoroughly. Your cat should love this dish. The tomato juice is a good acidifier, particularly helpful to cats with a tendency to contract cystitis. The garlic powder adds to the taste and is thought by many to help cleanse the system. String beans are rich in vitamins and will help make your cat grow big and strong.

are completely balanced rations. Most cats do very well on them, and such foods have the advantage of being relatively inexpensive. Another advantage is that you can leave out a large bowl of the food and several dishes of water when you go away for the weekend — no need to board the cat. It is extremely important, however, to always leave your cat water to drink since on this diet the cat has no other source of liquid.

It is impossible to discuss dry cat food without talking briefly about a syndrome called urolithiasis. Feline urolithiasis is a disease characterized by partial or complete obstruction of the urinary tract by mineral deposits, causing pain and difficulty in urinating and frequently resulting in death. Although the disease can occur in the male and female cat, it is much more common and deadly in the male due to the relatively long narrow urethra. The ash content of dry food has been singled out as a possible major cause of urolithiasis. Unfortunately, the disease cannot be cured or prevented by eliminating dry cat food. Many studies have been run over the past few years, and there does not seem to be any direct connection between feeding dry food and urolithiasis. Since many cats eat dry food and since urolithiasis is a common problem, it is reasonable to assume that some cats eating dry food will get the disease, and some will not. But incidence of urolithiasis in cats eating dry food is no higher than with other foods.

A problem I have encountered in my practice is the cat that has been switched from moist to dry food often becomes affected. The cat may have needed to drink very little water while on the moist food diet. Cats are creatures of habit, however, and after switching to the dry food they might not have drunk any water for a day or so, resulting in a very concentrated urine. A cat prone to the urolithiasis condition would possibly be more likely to get it at this time. To be on the safe side, make any change from moist to dry rations gradually over several days.

A word about dog food and cats. Many people feed their cats dog food. In general, this is not a good idea. Cats require a higher protein and fat content than dogs and a higher density of calories. If you use dog food, supplement it with a good protein and fat source such as a small amount of cheese. *Do not supplement with milk.* Many adult cats get diarrhea from milk because they do not have an enzyme called lactase, which digests a milk sugar called lactose. If your cat eats dog food, a low-potency general vitamin supplement is important. It is a good idea for all cats, as well.

As a general rule, I advise against table scraps for cats. What is good for humans may not be good for cats, and there is little advantage in accustoming your cat to a diet of food which may not be nutritionally balanced.

Michael H. Milts, a practicing veterinarian in New York City, is actively involved in a low-cost neutering program and other humane groups. He is the veterinarian for all the New York City zoos.

THE CAT PRODUCT MARKET

THE FOLLOWING STATISTICS on the pet population and what owners buy for their pets were compiled by the Radio Advertising Bureau, an organization which prepares profiles on leading business categories for radio advertisers.

Size of the Business

Pets/Supplies/Marketing, a trade journal, estimated the 1974 household pet population at 41 million dogs, 28 million cats, 23 million birds, 340 million fish and 125 million assorted other pets. This total of 557 million pets is 110 percent greater than the 1968 pet population of 264 million. The total retail sales of the major goods and services (other than medical services) in millions of dollars, for 1974 were:

	Foods	Accessories	Grooming
1974	$2,050	$1,090	$280
1972	1,730	860	200
1970	1,370	680	180

Specific Products (1975 figures)

Food Type	Total Sales ($ millions)	Dry	Canned	Moist
Dog Food	$1,733	52%	31%	17%
Cat Food	738	29%	59%	12%
Bird Food	137			
Fish Food	24			

Non-Food Products

Dogs	Cats	Fish	Birds
$233	$50	$154	$62

Leading Pet Food Companies

The following figures are a percentage tabulation of which pet food companies control the pet food market. (Figures from *Ad/Age Maxwell Report*, May, 1976.)

Ralston Purina	30.8%	General Foods	10.5%
Quaker Oats	10.4%	Liggett & Myers	7.4%
Carnation	11.1%		

Supermarket Sales

Two and one-tenth percent of the average supermarket's total volume comes from the pet department, where the typical store offers 334 different brands and sizes of products. *Chain Store Age* breaks down pet food department sales into the following percentages:

Canned dog food	29.1%	Canned cat food	20.7%
Dry dog food	15.6%	Dry cat food	7.7%
Semi-moist dog food	11.6%	Semi-moist cat food	2.6%
Bird food	2.7%	All other items	5.4%

Pet Shop Sales

Sales for the typical pet shop break down in the following percentages: (Figures from *Pets/Supplies/Marketing*, 1975.)

Fish and fish supplies	36%
Dogs and dog supplies	30%
Birds and bird supplies	7%
Other pets and supplies	13%
Cats and cat supplies	6%
Grooming services	8%

Christmas accounts for 13.2% of the average pet shop's sales. (*Pets/Supplies/Marketing* 1975).

RESEARCH REVEALS

Cat owners prefer *Time;* non-owners prefer *Newsweek.*

The more cats you own, the more likely you are to enjoy Sonny and Cher.

If you live on the Pacific Coast, you are more likely to own a cat than if living elsewhere.

The television soap opera, *The Young and the Restless,* especially attracts cat lovers.

People with two cats often call themselves ecology-minded; people with three or more rarely do.

Single people are least likely to be cat owners.

Acid rock radio broadcasts are especially appealing to cat owners.

Cat owners are less likely to be unemployed than non-owners.

Cat owners especially like *Better Homes & Gardens* magazine.

One-third of the readers of *Guns & Ammo* magazine own cats, while only one-fifth of *Cosmopolitan* readers do.

The household most likely to have a cat is one with five or more people.

Source: Axiom Market Research Bureau, Inc., Target Group Index, 1975.

X. THE MEDICAL CAT

CAT RESEARCH

Rosemonde Peltz, M.D.

WHEN OUR CATS get sick, each of us wants an accurate diagnosis and a cure. But what happens when we are told there is no cure? It is then that "research" becomes an important word in our vocabulary. Unfortunately, very few cat owners understand what research really means — what it involves and how it affects both them and their cats.

What is it? Basic research involves the study of a problem or a facet of a problem. The knowledge acquired may shed new light on the solution of a question related to the diagnosis, prevention and cure of a specific disease.

Where does it happen? Many investigators do research work in the major schools of veterinary medicine. Research is also conducted in the laboratories of major pharmaceutical manufacturers. On a smaller but no less important scale, your own veterinarian may study a series of cases and present his findings at a symposium of his colleagues. Research is conducted in many places, with many different people making contributions to the work.

What problems need solutions? In order to understand the directions that research may take, consider the cat as a whole and think about what can happen to the cat from the time of conception to death. Cats, like people, can suffer from a wide variety of diseases, organic defects and physical injuries.

Stillbirth is the major cause of death in kittens. The kitten may die before birth because of injury or illness in the mother cat, the use of antibiotics to treat the pregnant cat or unknown causes. The kitten may also suffer from genetic defects serious enough to be fatal.

None of these threats to cat health are fully understood, and all pose questions that need study. Research may be directed toward the development of tests for accurate diagnoses, medicines for treatment, vaccines for prevention of disease, and even mechanical instruments and devices to make examination and treatment easier.

THE ANIMAL MEDICAL CENTER

The Animal Medical Center, in New York City, is the world's largest clinical veterinary hospital. Because of the large number of animals it sees (over 80,000 per year) , the center is able to investigate the nature and association of symptoms in a wide variety of cases. The Center's computer system makes the medical histories of its many animal patients available for ongoing research. Much of its study is concerned with the relation between diseases in animals and people. The Center's cancer research is conducted in conjunction with the Memorial Sloan-Kettering Cancer Center.

How much and how good? The quality of research is high because there are so many requests for funds that foundations supporting research can be highly selective in awarding grants. Most money is directed toward animal research that will directly benefit man. Diseases in cattle, poultry and swine receive much more attention than those in cats. Diseases among pets that might affect humans are studied extensively; however, if it is proved that there is no danger to humans from a particular cat disease, funds are harder to locate. Thus much of the research done on cat diseases depends on contributions made to universities and private foundations that have a special interest in animals.

Cat associations are an important source of research funds. The Cat Fanciers' Association established the Robert H. Winn Foundation for Cat Research, which awards grants to schools of veterinary medicine in the United States for the sole purpose of research in cats. In addition,

ANGELL MEMORIAL ANIMAL HOSPITAL

Boston's Angell Memorial Animal Hospital is sometimes called the Mayo Clinic of animal medical centers because of its extensive files. Like the Mayo Clinic, the animal hospital is able to refer to meticulously detailed clinical records. These case files — which include lengthy operation descriptions, autopsy reports and slides of actual animal tissue — constitute what is probably the world's best collection on small animal pathology. The hospital conducts no experimental research, but its files are a major source of clinical information and it has become a center for the study of feline leukemia.

CFA has a research committee to keep members aware of current research developments in cats and has established the Jane Martinke Feline Reference Center to provide closer communication between breeders and the veterinary research community. In England, the Feline Advisory Bureau supplies breeders with information and answers problems about cats. In Canada, a similar organization has been established.

What about recent research? The two most serious respiratory diseases are rhinotracheitis, which can be fatal, and calcivirus infection. Research has led to the development of a vaccine to protect against both of these ailments.

Feline infectious peritonitis is a uniformly fatal viral infection. Once a cat becomes infected, death usually occurs within six weeks. Considerable research is being done now to grow the virus in the laboratory with the hope of ultimately producing a protective vaccine.

Much research has been conducted in the United States and Scotland on leukemia in cats. A screening test for the presence of the virus has been developed, and it has been established that cats exposed to feline leukemia virus react in different ways. In Scotland, a vaccine has been developed and is currently being tested in field trials. This work is one of the great examples of what can be achieved through research.

Cats very commonly develop kidney and bladder stones and crystals that obstruct the outflow of urine. Various diets, mineral content of diet and viruses have been implicated as causes of this debilitating problem. No single specific cause has been named, and only temporary, symptomatic treatment is available, but research continues to seek out better solutions.

What next? Answers to old problems often inspire new questions. Recent developments in the study of genetics suggest that in the future inherited diseases of the cat's central nervous system will receive much attention, and hereditary defects of the immunity system will probably receive increased study as well.

Rosemonde Peltz, who lives in Decatur, Georgia, is on the Board of Directors of the Cat Fanciers' Association.

THE MORRIS ANIMAL FOUNDATION

The Morris Animal Foundation, located in Denver, Colorado, sponsors much of the important research into cat diseases being conducted at major universities around the country. Some of the problems under investigation are:

Urinary obstruction, a major source of difficulties in cats, is being studied in several universities. A team at the New York State Veterinary College, Cornell University, has associated viruses with urinary obstruction and is investigating the possibility of developing a vaccine. Doctors at Colorado State University are experimenting with additives for cat food which might stop the formation of body stones that block the urinary track.

Distemper in cats, which is unlike distemper in dogs, has been linked to eye diseases. A program at the University of California, Davis, has determined the proper vaccinating schedule to control and prevent the eye damage associated with feline distemper.

The Morris Animal Foundation, which sponsors seminars to help cat owners become familiar with the results of recent research, is dependent on contributions from individuals and clubs for its continued operation.

FELINE LEUKEMIA

W. D. Hardy, D.V.M. and A. J. McClelland, D. Phil.

THE FELINE LEUKEMIA virus (FeLV) belongs to a group of viruses which cause cancer in a number of animal species. Like the other viruses of this group, it consists of a circular outer shell (or envelope) made up of a few protein molecules, enclosing a core containing the ribonucleic acid (RNA) or genetic (hereditary) material of the virus.

Until recently, it was thought that viruses of this type could be transmitted only from the parents to the offspring of their host species, via the genes. However, it is now known that FeLV, and thus the diseases it causes, can be transmitted from cat to cat by infection or contagion. There are two classes of infectious transmission: (a) epigenetic and (b) contact transmission. In epigenetic (epi=outside; genetic=genes) transmission, FeLV is passed from the mother to the fetus across the placenta (in the uterus) or from the mother to the kittens via the milk. Infectious FeLV has, in fact, been found in milk from infected queens. For contact transmission the virus must be shed by routes other than via the milk. FeLV has been found in the urine, saliva and blood of infected cats. It is likely, therefore, that the virus is spread from cat to cat via the feeding bowls and litter pans. Biting, scratching and licking may also be methods of infectious spread of the virus. Cat fleas may be carriers of the virus, although this has not yet been proved. At the present time, there is no evidence that FeLV is spread by genetic means.

When FeLV infects a cell, it directs the cell to produce more virus. As a result of FeLV infection the cell may be altered, and cancer, or other diseases, may develop.

The Consequences of FeLV Infection

All animals, including cats, have a natural defense mechanism (the immune system) which protects them from invading foreign organisms such as bacteria and viruses. The fate of a healthy cat exposed to FeLV depends on how its immune system responds to the virus.

If a cat is able to react against the virus and form antibodies against the outer shell of the virus, it can become resistant to FeLV infection. If the cat reacts to the virally caused cancerous changes in the infected cell surface, it can become resistant to the development of leukemia. In this respect, there are four main categories of cats:

1. Cats can be uninfected but susceptible to both FeLV infection and leukemia development. Most cats in the general population are non-immune and are in this category.
2. Cats can be uninfected and resistant to both FeLV infection and leukemia development. These cats are immune to FeLV and leukemia due to a previous temporary infection with FeLV.
3. Cats can be FeLV-infected but resistant (immune) to leukemia development. These cats are "carrier" cats and are a potential source of FeLV infection for susceptible cats.
4. Cats can be healthy and FeLV-infected but susceptible to leukemia development. Most infected cats will develop leukemia, or the other FeLV-caused diseases, from three months to three years after the initial infection.

Diseases Caused by FeLV

FeLV can infect many different types of cells. Many factors (most of them unknown) determine the type of disease that subsequently develops. The time of disease development, after infection, varies from a few weeks to years. The following diseases are known to be caused by FeLV:

1. *Lymphosarcoma (leukemia).* Lymphosarcoma is a fatal cancerous disease of the white blood cells (the lymphocytes). It has no particular breed or sex bias, and it occurs in cats of all ages, although it is more common in young cats. Lymphosarcoma is the most common form of cancer in the cat, occurring annually in approximately 150 cats per 100,000 cats in the population at risk. The signs of lymphosarcoma are unfortunately not specific for this one disease and are also not consistent from cat to cat. However, the following signs are commonly seen: pale gums (indicating anemia), enlarged lymph nodes, listlessness, lack of appetite, difficulty in breathing and a poor coat condition.
2. *Anemia (nonresponsive).* In some cats, FeLV infection results in the destruction of those cells which produce red blood cells and this results in a severe anemia. The FeLV-caused anemia should be distinguished from the other (responsive) anemias caused by agents such as a haemobartonella (parasites of red blood cells). Nonresponsive anemia is a progressive and fatal disease characterized by pale gums, weakness and weight loss.
3. *Panleukopenia-like syndrome (distemper [enteritis]-like disease).* In some cats FeLV infection results in the destruction of white blood cells, which causes a fatal disease. This disease often occurs after the FeLV-infected healthy cat has been subjected to stresses such as hospitalization, cat fights and abscesses. The signs of the disease include bloody diarrhea (dysentery), loss of weight and mimic classical "distemper." However, the disease occurs in FeLV-infected healthy cats who are immune to the distemper (panleukopenia) virus.
4. *Thymic atrophy (fading kitten syndrome).* This disease occurs in kittens born from FeLV-infected queens or in kittens infected shortly after birth. As a result of FeLV infection, the thymus, an important gland controlling the immune defense system of the body, degenerates and thus renders the kitten more susceptible to other infections. The kittens progress poorly and die from various infections (usually bacterial) within one or two weeks of birth.

In addition to these diseases, several others are thought, but have not yet been proven, to be caused by FeLV. These include cancerous diseases of the red blood cells (myeloproliferative diseases) and fetal abortions or resorptions. The abortions or resorptions associated with FeLV usually occur late in the pregnancy of FeLV-infected queens.

These is no cure available for any of the FeLV-caused diseases. Although some drugs may produce temporary remissions, there is no known way to eliminate the virus once a cat has been infected. All efforts should therefore be taken to prevent the FeLV infection of healthy cats.

The Occurrence of FeLV in Pet Cats

FeLV in healthy cats. Only a few healthy cats in the general cat population are persistently infected with FeLV despite the fact that most cats are susceptible to infection. Since most cats are susceptible but, in fact, are not infected, it must be concluded that FeLV is *not widespread in the*

JERRY DARVIN

general cat population. Only 0.14 percent of healthy cats are persistently infected with FeLV. However, once an FeLV-infected cat (whether healthy or sick) lives with other cats (e.g., in catteries), a large proportion (35 percent) of the uninfected cats will become infected. After infection, they have a greatly increased chance of developing one of the FeLV-caused diseases.

FeLV in diseased cats. A high percentage of cats with FeLV diseases are infected with the virus. Approximately 90 percent of the cats with lymphosarcoma and 40–70 percent of the cats with nonresponsive anemia are infected with FeLV. It is not yet known what the percent occurrence of FeLV is in cats with the panleukopenia-like and fading kitten syndromes or why some cats with FeLV diseases are not infected with the virus.

Detection of FeLV in Cats Living in Their Natural Environment

A simple test for the detection of FeLV infection, requiring only a few drops of blood, has been developed. When done properly by a responsible laboratory, this test is specific for FeLV, but, since the virus causes a number of diseases and can also be present in healthy cats, it is not a diagnostic test for any one disease (i.e., it is *not* a test for leukemia). Moreover, a negative test result does not mean that the cat will never develop an FeLV-related disease. However, the test can be used by the veterinarian as an *aid* in diagnosis and by the cat owner to help prevent the spread of the virus, and its related diseases, to other cats.

When and How Often to Test for FeLV

To help in making a diagnosis, cats suspected of having an FeLV-caused disease should be tested for FeLV, as should all cats exposed to either leukemic or FeLV-infected cats. In addition, breeding cats (both queens and studs) and cats about to be brought into a cattery or multiple-cat household should be tested for the virus. If possible, cats should be bought from catteries which have been certified free of FeLV by one of the reputable testing laboratories.

Sick cats and healthy cats with no known FeLV exposure need only be tested once. Cats who have been exposed to FeLV should be tested twice in accordance with the FeLV test and removal program for controlling the spread of FeLV in the natural environment.

The Control of FeLV

Although no cure is available for the diseases caused by FeLV, the spread of the virus (and thus disease) to uninfected cats can be prevented by using the FeLV Test and Removal Program outlined below:

1. Remove all FeLV-infected sick cats from the household. Euthanasia is recommended since the outlook for infected sick cats is poor.
2. If there are no other cats in the household, wait thirty days before acquiring a new cat. By that time all remaining FeLV in the household will have died.
3. If there are other cats in the household, immediately FeLV-test *all* of them.
4. Remove or isolate all FeLV-infected cats. Euthanasia is recommended (even if the cat is healthy) because of the danger to other cats.
5. Discard the feeding bowls and litter pans. Clean and disinfect the household with ordinary household cleaners to inactivate the virus.
6. Do not introduce new cats into the household.

WINK BLAIR

7. Do not sell, trade or give away the remaining uninfected cats until after a second FeLV test.

8. Three months after the first test, retest all the remaining cats to check whether any were infected just prior to the first test (if they were infected just before the first test, they may not have tested positive because of the long incubation period needed for the virus).

9. If *all* the remaining cats are negative (uninfected) in the second FeLV test, the household may be considered FeLV-free and cats may be bought, sold or given away.

10. All cats should be tested for FeLV before being allowed into an FeLV-free household.

When used under veterinary supervision, the FeLV Test and Removal Program has been successful in eliminating FeLV, and in preventing the development of diseases caused by FeLV, in numerous households. If a cat owner suspects that one of his cats has developed an FeLV disease, or has been exposed to an FeLV-infected cat, he should consult his veterinarian immediately.

The Possibilities of an Effective FeLV Vaccine

The most effective method of controlling an infectious agent such as FeLV is by vaccination. The prospects for an efficient vaccine appear to be good. There is already experimental evidence that vaccines against FeLV are feasible; however, much work needs to be done before a safe and effective FeLV vacine will be available for routine veterinary use.

Public Health Aspects of FeLV

FeLV can infect the cells of other species, such as those of dogs and humans, when these cells are grown in the laboratory. It is also known that FeLV can cause lymphosarcoma in newborn puppies. There is thus some uncertainty about whether or not FeLV is a health hazard to humans, although, there is *no* evidence that FeLV infects human beings. Many people who have lived with FeLV-infected cats have been tested for the virus and so far no one has been found to be infected. It must be remembered also that the occurrence of FeLV in the general cat population is low and that therefore there is no need for concern among cat owners in general. Because of the uncertainties about the public health risks of FeLV and also because of the known contagious nature of FeLV for cats, we recommend that all FeLV-infected cats be euthanized.

W. D. Hardy and A. J. McClelland are on the staff of the Laboratory of Veterinary Oncology, Memorial Sloan-Kettering Cancer Center, New York City.

EUTHANASIA: A DEADLY VITAL SUBJECT

Louis J. Camuti, D.V.S.

Cats' tombstones in a dog cemetery, Hyde Park, London.

THIS SUBJECT IS as old as medicine. All through the ages euthanasia has been discussed as to its use or application in humans as well as animals. Unfortunately, this use was often for nefarious reasons, giving the word a sinister meaning in spite of its definition.

The dictionaries define it as "an easy death or the act or practice of killing individuals, either persons or animals, that are hopelessly sick or injured, for reasons of mercy." This definition has long lost its meaning because the reasons for performing euthanasia have been greatly expanded. Destroying for mercy's sake is only a small part of the whole subject. A recent article titled "The Problem of Euthanasia," in the May-June 1975 issue of *DVM*, written by Dr. H.R. Ferguson of Colorado State University, gives a most complete and thorough dissertation on the subject. It proves that what was once only of

peripheral importance has now become a major facet of our profession. This article certainly gives an up-to-date outline of the various methods, with all the pros and cons of each. I think it goes a long way toward evoking a greater awareness of this subject on our part.

The general problem needs no further discussion. However, for some of us who have a very specialized practice, the euthanasia of a household pet (and here I have special reference to the cat) presents problems and procedures peculiar to that type of work. In my case, I am obliged to perform this act in the house of the owner, creating a more personal and intimate involvement. I have had to develop a method which takes into consideration such factors as the emotional attitude of the owner, how the animal may react to my presence and many other conditions not normally encountered in an office or

AN ETERNAL COMPANION

LOUIS J. CAMUTI, D.V.S.

The depth of attachment people have for their cats is best exemplified by a case I have in mind. This cat belonged to a lonely, elderly widow who had made the provision in her will that the cat was to be buried with her. It happened that the cat died before she did, so she had the body placed in a casket and sent to the receiving vault of a pet cemetery. I advised that she check with her state health authorities to see if it was permissible to have her cat placed in the coffin with her. Of course, the answer was no, in a vein that would indicate the lady to be — at the very least — a bit peculiar. For two years, her mind worked on a way to beat the authorities. When she was convinced she had solved the problem, she called me to have the cat cremated — with the provison that the ashes be returned to her. I did as she asked, then requested the favor of being let in on her plans for them. I got the answer, all right: she had sewn the ashes inside the hem of her wedding dress in which she was to be buried. She died happily, knowing that her final request had been granted.

hospital. The method of approach must be based on the emotional state that the owner is in. When owners are hesitant or only partly convinced that they are doing the right thing, and if the pet is not suffering unduly, I usually advise them to wait one more day on their decision to make sure their minds are thoroughly made up, and, more importantly, that they will remain that way. On many occasions I am called up on the next day with the following expression: "If we had waited, the pet might have gotten better." Waiting another day very often obviates that possibility.

My method has had to be simple, humane, relatively fast and not too frightening to the cat. It also has had to be done in away which would not activate, in the mind of the owner, the thought that it was an execution. Since the owners are to be present, I have to minimize the trauma on their part upon seeing the pet's life snuffed out. To do that I have them hold the cat in their arms, explaining that the first injection of pentobarbital sodium, which I administer intraperitoneally, is an anesthetic dose and that, being hypnotic, it will sever completely the thinking ability of the animal. The cat relaxes in the arms of the owner, simulating normal sleep. When owners realize that their pet is unaware of anything, they gladly place it on a table. This ends the owner's participation. After seeing that the animal is completely anesthetized, I ask them to leave the room. When I am alone, I inject a lethal amount of the same material directly into the heart. When it is certain that the animal is dead, I ask the owners to come back in the room to see that the pet is exactly in the same position as when they left it. The owner has lived through this terrible ordeal with the least amount of emotional disturbance and is reassured that the cat was never aware of what was going on. This procedure makes euthanasia of a cat in the home practical in most cases, regardless of individual situations. People may forget the number of times you have saved their pet, but they will always remember your dignified effort in putting their pet to sleep.

Louis J. Camuti, a veterinarian in New York, cares for all his patients in their homes. This article is reprinted from Feline Practice *(November-December, 1975), a professional journal for veterinarians in which Dr. Camuti writes a regular column.*

THE ITINERANT VETERINARIAN

Cats love Dr. Louis J. Camuti: he treats them with all the respect and love they deserve, and he takes care of them in their own homes — whether they need surgery or just a quick examination. Dr. Camuti, who is eighty-two, has been a practicing veterinarian in and around New York City for fifty-six years. As a young man, Camuti, a 1916 Cornell graduate, served as the city poultry inspector, but he quickly changed allegiance and has devoted most of his long and active life to the care of cats.

Cat owners know the value of having a trustworthy veterinarian, but a dedicated veterinarian who visits all cats at home, and at any hour of the day or night, is a rare phenomenon. In fact, Dr. Camuti makes most of his calls at night, late, when he is feeling energetic and the owners are at home to consult with him.

Dr. Camuti averages thirty house calls a week, and it is not unusual for him to cover hundreds of miles in one day checking up on various patients. Long known for his skill and concern, he has taken care of many famous people's cats — including those of James Mason and Tallulah Bankhead — but he does not confine himself to celebrity cats. Dr. Camuti is on stand-by duty all the time to help people with strays they have rescued; he insists that most of his clients are just regular people with especially wonderful cats.

Dr. Camuti is a spry, generous and joyful man, long respected in his profession and adored by all his patients and clients. He writes a regular column in *Feline Practice*, a professional journal for veterinarians, and is the author of a forthcoming book about his life.

LEARNING ABILITY IN CATS

Benjamin L. Hart, D.V.M., Ph.D.

WHEN IT COMES to a consideration of learning ability in cats, people often take one of two extreme positions. The first is that cats are not nearly as intelligent as other carnivores, such as dogs, as evidenced by the almost universal lack of responsiveness in cats to human vocal commands such as "sit," "heel" or "stay." The other extreme is that cats are smarter because they can more easily fend for themselves if necessary.

The truth of the matter is that cats are probably not appreciably more or less intelligent than other domesticated mammals. The comparison of one species with another in regard to learning ability must take into account differences in sensory and motor capacity. Most important, however, is an animal's inherited behavioral predispositions. Because they do not relate socially to human owners in the same way as dogs, cats do not respond as well to the incentives of attention, affection and petting. Furthermore, in handling animals such as dogs, horses and cattle, physical or verbal punishment, or the threat of punishment, is often an effective training procedure, as well as a reinforcement of the dominance-subordination relationship between man and animal. With cats, such punishment is almost always ineffective in training because it innately evokes a tendency to fight back or escape rather than to conform. By capitalizing on a cat's natural response tendencies and using positive reward, cats can be taught some useful behavioral tasks that would probably be impossible to teach a dog.

Toilet Training

The procedure used to toilet-train the cat in the accompanying photograph was rather simple and took advantage of the cat's natural tendency

to urinate and defecate in a sandy area. This cat was conditioned to use the toilet by a procedure called "successive approximation." To start with, the normal litter box was kept in the bathroom, and after the cat was regularly using it in this location it was removed and a different "litter box" was fashioned. A cardboard rim was cut in the shape of the toilet seat and covered with a sheet of clear plastic material. This was then fastened by wires to the underside of the toilet seat so that when the litter material was placed in the toilet seat the rim of the seat formed the edge of the litter box and the plastic sheet formed the bottom. With plenty of litter material in the toilet seat, the cat readily used the new litter box, which was, of course, temporarily removed from human use.

In a few days, after the cat became accustomed to using the toilet seat with litter, the amount of litter was reduced by about half. The cat had learned by this time to stand with its feet on the toilet seat (probably because of the insecurity of the plastic bottom of the litter box). Subsequently, over the next few days, more litter was removed, and holes were made in the plastic to allow urine to drip through. Finally, all the litter and the plastic sheet were removed.

With this type of toilet training, it must be kept in mind that there is a good deal of variation in the degree to which cats will adapt to the new arrangement and therefore to the rate at which litter is removed from the toilet seat. If the cat stops using the toilet seat because litter has been removed too rapidly, the owner will have to go back to an earlier stage in the training procedure.

A cat is likely to slip off the toilet seat at least once and fall into the toilet bowl. This would have made a great illustration for another photo, but unfortunately the camera was not handy when this happened to the cat shown. At any rate, such an accident may require the cat's being retrained to the toilet seat by again placing litter on top of a sheet of plastic.

Learning to Use a Cat Door

Many people find a small "cat door" useful to allow their pets to enter and leave the house as they wish. To teach a cat to use a door usually requires that the door be tied or propped open and the cat induced to walk through the small opening in order to obtain food or get into the house. After the habit is established, the door can be suspended halfway open with a piece of string so that the opening is still visible but the cat has to partially push the door while entering or leaving. In two or three phases, over the next few days, the door is propped open less until the cat is pushing the door open from the completely closed position.

A door that swings freely in both directions can be a problem if other cats in the neighborhood watch the resident animal enter the house through the opening and decide to follow. One of the cat doors commercially available allows the owner to greatly reduce the likelihood of this possibility by requiring its animal to learn an additional procedure that is difficult for strange cats to readily pick up. This type of cat door swings only in the outward direction. To open the door from the outside the cat has to reach and pull the door out and slide underneath it.

Training the cat to use this door from the outside also involves the principle of successive approximation. The door is propped open with string or a small block, and the cat learns that it has to push the door open the rest of the way with its head. At a later stage, when the door is lowered still further, the cat learns to use its paw to pull the door out in order to slide its head in underneath.

Learning More Complex Tasks

Psychologists interested in comparative animal learning have studied the ability of cats to learn conceptual problems. In one procedure, referred to as "oddity learning," the animal's task is to choose the odd stimulus from three that are presented to it. For example, when the three objects are two balls and a square block, selecting the square block represents the correct response; when two blocks and one ball are presented, the correct response is the ball. Some cats do well with this type of conceptual learning and, in fact, compare quite favorably with monkeys in this respect.

In laboratory testing, cats are the only species aside from primates in which learning by observation has been demonstrated. Cats allowed to watch others learn such tasks as pulling on a string or pressing a lever to release a latch on a door learned the same tasks themselves much more rapidly than the naïve learners. Learning by observation is apparently not easy for animals but can occur if the observer watches repeated demonstrations, has some degree of familiarity with the movements involved and is able to watch the elimination of errors by the demonstrator during the learning process.

Benjamin L. Hart is associated with the School of Veterinary Medicine at the University of California, Davis. This article is adapted from Feline Practice *(September-October 1975), a veterinarian's journal in which Dr. Hart writes a regular column.*

ACUPUNCTURE FOR CATS

John Ottaviano

IN 1970, I accepted the opportunity to study with a master Chinese acupuncturist and his wife, an American veterinarian. This fascinating man's teaching concerned primarily human study, but his wife continually encouraged me to apply my understanding of acupuncture to animals.

Not long afterwards, I adopted a small black kitten. When she was severely injured in a freak accident, and immediately went into shock, I was frantic. Although I had learned how to treat shock in humans by using acupuncture, adapting this knowledge to the kitten prompted some risk-taking decisions. I tried various needling techniques to revive her, and to my surprise and delight I was successful.

The following day, I took the kitten to my Chinese teacher. By this time, she was out of shock but was completely paralyzed from the head down. The acupuncturist handled the cat for a few moments and explained what I must do. The special technique he recommended is called moxabustion. Small cone-shaped lumps of an herb, *Artemisa vulgaris,* are ignited over certain acupuncture points. The herb is allowed to burn down, but is removed before the skin—or, in this case, the fur—is singed.

Within a week, amazingly, the kitten could move with full reflexes. One problem remained: she could not swallow her food without almost choking to death. Further moxabustion therapy corrected this, and two weeks after the accident the kitten was perfectly normal.

Now, six years later, she is full-grown, has had a litter of kittens and is quite healthy. Needless to say, all this left quite an impression on me.

In the next year, 1971, I continued testing acupuncture on cats and dogs. I was encouraged because the animals responded quickly to this therapy—more quickly than humans. Using harmless medicinal herbs and acupuncture, my results were consistent and positive.

In 1973, a friend at a local university asked me to head a project dealing solely with veterinary acupuncture. Assisted by veterinarians and backed by the California Veterinary Medical Association, the project grew and created a growing interest in veterinary acupuncture across the country and abroad.

Because of the increasing involvement of veterinarians, the National Association for Veterinary Acupuncture (N.A.V.A.) was created in January, 1975. A nonprofit corporation, N.A.V.A. conducts investigations into medical treatment of animals by use of the Chinese art of acupuncture and moxabustion, as well as imparting knowledge to qualified persons through publications, seminars and short courses.

At present, N.A.V.A. offers veterinary professionals a facility where medical cases can be referred for treatment. An average treatment is 10–20 minutes long; the patient remains calm and experiences a minimum of pain. The price per treatment varies, but you can expect to pay from $15 to $20.

N.A.V.A. provides treatment by referral for cats, dogs, horses and unusual animals such as rhinoceroses, zebras, snakes and birds. Generally, our patients come to us after all western medical treatments have failed. Most of our work on cats has been with "HBC" (hit by a car) patients who suffer subsequent posterior paralysis due to spinal injury. We have also successfully treated feline dermatitis (skin problems).

Currently, we are attempting to set up a separate project devoted to clinical research of leukemic cats. We have a formula of acu-

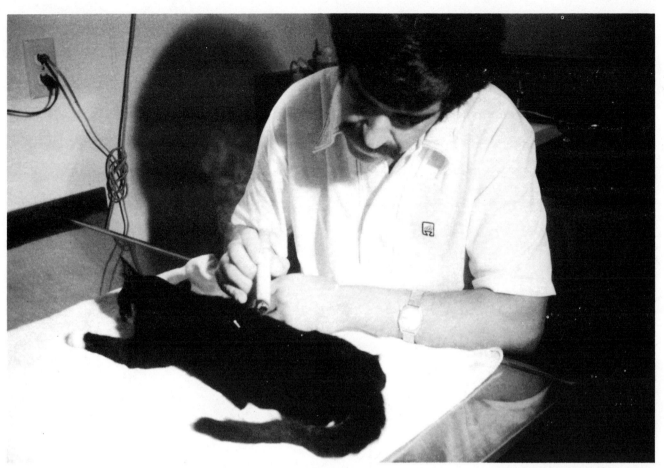

Dr. Michael Gerry heats acupuncture needles with a moxa herb stick before administering acupuncture treatment to a cat.

puncture points which we theorize will reap successful results in the treatment of feline leukemia. Research in this area could provide information that would extend beyond the cat population to combating this disease in man.

Many people assume that acupuncture is successful because of hypnotic suggestion rather than actual healing. My continued interest in veterinary acupuncture is stimulated by this controversy. Because it is impossible to convince an animal that acupuncture will make it feel better, our experiments with cats attest to its actual therapeutic effects.

As noted above, interest in acupuncture among veterinarians is increasing rapidly. If your local veterinarian is unable to provide you with a referral to a veterinary acupuncturist in your area, we at N.A.V.A. are willing to assist you as best we can. Please write to us at the following address:

National Association for Veterinary Acupuncture
P.O. Box 5181
Fullerton, California 92635

John Ottaviano, a human and veterinary acupuncturist, does research in Oriental medical sciences and is director of the Veterinary Project for the National Acupuncture Association.

HOME ACUPUNCTURE TREATMENT

To use this chart, locate the general area which corresponds to your cat's problem. When a point is in need of pressure, the cat will respond by showing slight pain during palpation of the acupressure point. Massage gently for 1–10 minutes. This technique can be used as often as desired to provide relief to the cat. Use massage; only a trained acupuncturist can use needles. Home acupressure treatment cannot replace the advice of a veterinarian.

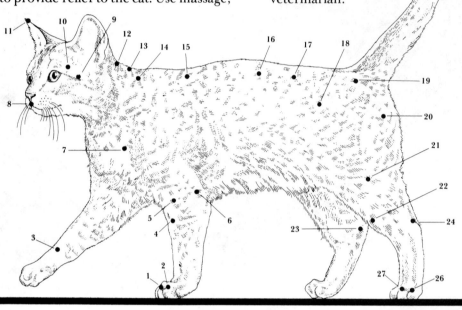

NANCY LOU GAHAN

Acupressure Points

1. Located between front paw webbing. Used for front leg paralysis.
2. Same as No. 1. Used for front leg paralysis and deafness.
3. Local joint pain.
4. One inch below No. 5 in the crease formed by the muscle. Used for local joint pain, constipation.
5. Located in the crease formed by the elbow. Local pain, paralysis of front limb, constipation, dermatitis, itching, cough.
6. For local pain.
7. Located in the shoulder joint. used for shoulder pain.
8. Located in the middle of upper lip. Used for emergency and shock. Apply acupuncture by pinching with thumb and index finger.
9. Used for difficulty in mastication and local pain.
10. Used for eye problems.
11. Tip of ear. Used for eye problems.

12. One inch behind the ear. Used for cervical problems, and deafness.
13. Located on center line one inch inward and below No. 12. Uses are the same as for No. 12.
14. Located in front of scapula one inch from center line (spinal column). Used for cervical pain, arthritis in any joint, bone problems in general.
15. Behind scapula one inch out from spinal column. Thoracic pain, infections, cleansing of the blood.
16. Located opposite the navel on the spinal area and one inch out from that midline. Used for thoracic-lumbar pain, urinary problems, kidney and sexual disorders.
17. In front of the ilium one inch out from spinal midline. Used for lumbar-sacral pain, pain at the hips, and constipation.
18. Located at the crease formed by the head of the femur and hip joint. Used for hip pain.
19. Located one inch up and 45 degrees out from crease of tail. Used for hip, sacral pain and constipation.
20. Located below the head of the femur. Used for lumbar pain, sacral pain and stifle (knee) pain.
21. Located behind the crease formed by flexing of the knee. Used for hind leg paralysis, local knee pain, and any other weakness of lower limbs.
22. Located one inch below the patella (kneecap). Used to increase appetite, for paralysis of hind limbs, tonic to entire systems.
23. Used for urinary problems, and as an aid in the delivery of kittens.
24. Used for local pain and lumbar pain.
25. Located at the tip of the tail. Used for all back problems, constipation and hind leg paralysis.
26. Located in hind paw webbing. Used for hind leg paralysis, urinary problems, and as a tonic to give strength to lower limbs.

TOXOPLASMOSIS: THE CAT DISEASE PEOPLE CAN CATCH

J. K. Frenkel, M. D.

CATS AND PEOPLE are biologically close enough for them to be able to suffer from some of the same diseases and parasites. Some of these ailments are well-known — rabies, because it is so dramatical and terrible, and fleas, because they are so common, are two familiar examples. Less familiar is toxoplasmosis, an animal disease that can be transmitted to man. It is common to all domestic animals, including barnyard species, and, when present, travels through cat feces and through meat.

Any direct contact with cat feces increases the likelihood of contagion. Cattle and sheep can become infected by ingesting contaminated soil while grazing. Their meat then must be cooked. Birds may become infected when eating seeds on the ground or from eating contaminated earthworms. Similarly, your cat, after stalking a mouse or bird, may become a carrier of the disease. Although infected animals may be the means of transmitting the disease, more often than not there is no sign of illness.

Toxoplasmosis is a parasitic disease. Research conducted by my colleagues and myself indicates that the parasite has a complicated life cycle which spreads the disease through many animals. Oocysts (egg spores) are shed in the feces of domestic cats and certain types of wild cats. The spores are spread by contact with the feces. Flies and cockroaches, which eat feces, can serve as transport agents, contaminating animals which do not directly encounter the cat feces. Mice and birds can be infected either from transport agents or through direct contact and can then spread the infection to animals which prey on them. Humans can be infected by eating raw or rare meats. Cats can be infected when they hunt infected mice or birds. At this point, the cycle is complete. A newly infected cat will have oocysts in its feces and the cycle begins again.

Toxoplasmosis deserves special attention because of the serious danger it raises for the unborn human baby. A pregnant woman may have the infection and unknowingly infect the fetus. If not diagnosed and treated in time, her child may be born with permanent brain and eye damage. For this reason, efforts to prevent infection during pregnancy are most important.

CAT FLEAS AND PEOPLE

The bite of the cat flea is more irritating to people than it is to cats. Humans are not the actual host of the cat flea (or any other type of flea, for that matter) and for this reason we are not at all adapted to the bite. Cat-flea bites result in ugly red swellings. Usually the bites are on the lower parts of the leg. Fortunately, cat fleas do not carry any serious diseases, but if your cat has a tape worm the flea can transmit that parasite to you.

POSTULATED TRANSMISSION OF TOXOPLASMOSIS

FINAL HOST: CATS

SPOROGENY
IN FECES
1-5 DAYS

OOCYSTS

"Hamburger,
rare."

CARNIVORISM

FECAL
CONTAMINATION

INTERMEDIATE
HOSTS
INFECTED
BY

DOMESTIC CAT
+ OCELOT
+ JAGUARUNDI
+ BOBCAT
+ PUMA

PLACENTA

DURING
CHRONIC
INFECTION:
MOUSE

DURING
ACUTE
INFECTION:
HUMAN

Treatment is effective against most of the disease manifestations if started early; however, because of the infrequent occurrence of toxoplasmosis, the infection is not often thought of and tests for its diagnosis are not carried out. Further, it has been found that most mothers are symptom-free, even though they infected their babies *in utero*. Therefore, all mothers would have to be tested and those who are negative, tested repeatedly, to find those pregnant mothers who got infected. This procedure is an expensive nuisance, requiring a great deal of organization. Instead, preventive measures are easier, and more effective.

Common sense and good personal hygiene are generally sufficient precautions against contamination by toxoplasmosis, but for their own peace of mind as well as their baby's health, pregnant women should be aware of the procedures that can make infection unlikely.

If a woman is pregnant, there is no need for her to panic. She should keep in mind that she can prevent her cat from shedding the parasites by feeding it dry, canned or cooked food and not allowing it to eat wild birds, mice and fresh meat. Since the most immediate danger is through fecal contamination, care for the litter box should, if possible, be assumed by somebody

PRECAUTIONS FOR PREGNANT WOMEN

The risk of harm to unborn infants from toxoplasmosis can be reduced to practically nil if these simple rules are followed:

1. Keep your cat from hunting. Feed it only dry, canned or cooked food.

2. Delegate maintenance of litter box to someone other than pregnant member of household. If that precaution is impossible, plastic gloves should be worn when handling box.

3. Use work gloves when gardening or working with soil.

4. Cover children's sandbox when not in use.

5. After handling cat, litter box or soil, wash hands before working with food, before eating and before touching face.

6. Avoid eating raw or rare meat.

7. Control flies and cockroaches.

RABIES IN CATS

Due to widespread immunization, the chances of domestic cats contracting rabies in this country are much lower today than in the past. Latest statistics issued by the U. S. Department of Health, Education and Welfare show that reported cases of rabies in both domestic and wild animals have progressively and steadily declined from a total of 8,837 in 1953 to 3,200 in 1974. Of this figure, the incidence of rabies in cats has declined from 538 to 124 in the same period. Despite the reassuring statistics, the American Veterinary Medical Association recommends that all cats be vaccinated regularly on an annual basis starting from the age of five months.

If you are bitten by a cat which you have any reason to suspect might be rabid, report the bite to your doctor and your veterinarian at once. They will advise you about what to do. In most cases doctors are instructed by the local health board to watch the animal for two weeks for signs of rabies; official observation of the animal must begin immediately.

CAT ALLERGY

Quick, define *dander*. It is the one thing some people cannot stand about their cats. Dander brings on allergic symptoms in many people — symptoms that range from runny nose, itchy eyes, and scratchy throat to headache or full-blown asthmatic attack.

Dander is a mixture of the cat's hair, his saliva, and the tiny particles of skin he sheds (much like dandruff in humans). Those who react to cat *dander* usually have multiple allergies. House dust and pollen from ragweed, grasses, and trees may all bring on allergic symptoms.

Allergy to cats affects young children more often than adults. Children frequently grow out of their allergies, however, so some allergists suggest "fostering" the cat for a period of three months. While a friend, neighbor, or relative cares for the pet, there is the chance that a child's symptoms will subside. Meanwhile, the house can be cleaned of *dander*. If the symptoms recur when the cat returns, at least the doctor and patient can be certain it was *dander* causing the trouble in the first place.

other than the pregnant woman. The litter box should be emptied daily, before the spores can become infectious. If it is absolutely necessary for the box to be cleaned by a pregnant woman, she should wear plastic gloves during the work. She should also wear heavy gloves when working in the soil of her yard. Washing hands and cleaning fingernails (but not by biting) after contact with soil, litter box or cats is a good extra common sense precaution.

If your yard is visited by strays and you like to plant flowers, there is no reason to cower in the living room. Avoid contact with the areas where the cats habitually defecate; wear gloves when working in the soil; wash hands after planting or doing other work in the yard. These easy procedures can make the chance of infection most unlikely.

The biggest difficulty is with cats that have easy access to the outdoors and that love to hunt. Some women might feel safer if, during their pregnancy, they boarded the cat out. It is also possible for people to have the toxoplasma antibody. If a pregnant woman is tested and found to have the antibody, the chance of infecting her baby is practically nil. If a cat has antibody, it is likely to be immune; and if it eats a toxoplasma-infected mouse, bird or scrap of meat, it will not often shed oocysts again, or if it does, they will usually be small in number. It is the cat without antibody which, when infected, disseminates large numbers of toxoplasma oocysts. Kittens are the cats least likely to have toxoplasma antibody.

It is possible to give a cat a drug treatment to combat toxoplasmosis. The drugs need to be given two to four times daily for a prolonged period of time. Therefore, prevention with drugs is impractical for outdoor cats and indoor cats whose food is controlled do not need it. Although prevention with drugs might be used after an occasional night foray by your cat, it may promote a false sense of security which can lead to carelessness. Toxoplasmosis is better avoided by remembering that pregnant women should be careful and that we should all follow the common sense rules of personal cleanliness.

J. K. Frenkel, M.D., Ph.D., teaches at the University of Kansas Medical Center and has published many scientific papers on toxoplasmosis. Further reading on toxoplasmosis can be found in J. K. Frenkel's "Toxoplasma in and around us," BioScience *23:343–52, 1973; "Toxoplasmosis" in R. W. Kirk (ed.)* Current Veterinary Therapy *V, pp. 775–80 (Philadelphia: W. B. Saunders Co., 1974); "Toxoplasmosis in Cats and Man" in* Feline Practice *V, pp. 28–41, 1975.*

BITES AND SCRATCHES

If you are bitten or badly scratched by a cat, wash the wound thoroughly with soap and water, then isolate the cat. If there are signs of infection, call your doctor.

The best prevention against bites and scratches is to approach strange cats cautiously. It is interesting to note that even when defending themselves cats must be severely provoked to bite. They would rather flee, crawling or climbing to a place out of reach. Many people who have been bitten by cats admit to having cornered them for one reason or another — teasing them, or, in the case of strays, trying to catch them. (About half of all reported cat bites are by strays.)

Illness is the most reasonable explanation for a cat's biting without apparent provocation. In such a case isolation is imperative because a biting cat may be sick with rabies, distemper, a tumor, or a virus. All of these ailments are potentially dangerous to humans. The cat may also be responding to pain from an undetected ear infection, abscess, or toothache.

A cat bites only as a last resort.

XI. THE PERFORMING CAT

S. TABACK

THE INTERNATIONAL CAT FILM FESTIVAL

Kitty Smith

SOME PEOPLE STILL ask what a cat film is, as if the answer were not obvious. A cat film is a film about cats, and there have been plenty of them. (*Rhubarb, That Darn Cat, Bell Book and Candle,* and *Harry and Tonto* spring quickly to mind.)

When Pola Chapelle, a filmmaker, began to organize the first INTERCAT (International Cat Film Festival) in 1969, she knew of only a handful of films about cats, but once the word got out, the cat filmmakers came out of their cutting rooms. She was easily able to gather a lot of hours of cat-movie footage and has never had to settle for the dozens of Hollywood cat cartoons, feature-length films, or movies made by cat-food companies.

It turns out that there are lots of people, including children, who have been making movies of cats. The films shown at INTERCAT have ranged from the very simple — silent movies of a loved pet — to professional productions with famous actors. For example, she showed the first ten minutes of *The Long Goodbye*, which features Elliott Gould struggling in the wee hours of the morning to persuade his finicky cat to eat an unfamiliar brand of cat food.

The INTERCAT festival was first held in New York and has gone on to be repeated in Paris, Berlin, Amsterdam, London, Winnipeg and Boston. The festival's purpose, wherever it is held, is always to raise money to assist those nameless women and men who get up before the sun, trudge out in all kinds of weather and feed the stray cats of their neighborhoods.

After many years of viewing cat films, Ms. Chapelle says with certainty that films made by women are totally different from those made by men. Men usually are interested in something other than the cat's own nature.

Typical of the male approach is the cat sequence in *Day for Night*. A cat is used to make the audience laugh at the pitfalls of directing animals in front of the movie camera. A trained cat performer refuses to eat on cue and the filming is saved only when somebody finds a stray that turns out not to be so particular. The point of the scene is about film-making, not cats. Director François Truffaut might have used any animal.

Still photo from a short film shown at INTERCAT.

Mildred and Gordon Gordon and the real That Darn Cat.

Women are different explains Ms. Chapelle. Their films are about cats as cats. A good example of their approach is one by Carolee Schneeman, who created a four-hour domestic epic to celebrate her relationship with a beloved gray Maltese, Kitch. In this film the animal's individuality is crucial. Other species or even other cats will not do.

Cats have been used in films for many purposes — for comedy, as symbols, as tools to advance or complicate a plot, and as creatures to be appreciated in their own right. Every season of films includes a new crop of cat sequences which insure that, along with the special films made by cat lovers, there will be another supply of good material for the next INTERCAT festival.

Kitty Smith is a cat lover and film buff.

SOME OTHER FILMS IN INTERCAT

In 1969 the INTERCAT program lasted four hours, in 1973, twelve hours, and the 1976 festival was eight hours long. In addition, when Intercat appears abroad, locally made cat films are added to the program. It is therefore impossible to list all the cat films that have been shown, but some notable parts of the program were:

Sequences from feature-length films: Roberto Rossellini, *Envy;* François Truffaut, *The Soft Skin;* Saul Bass, *Walk on the Wild Side* (title sequence).

Animated films: Mary Beams, *Tub Film* and *Quilt Film;* Robert Breer, *Cats.*

Short films: Stephanie Beroes, *Light Sleeping;* Pola Chapelle, *How to Draw a Cat;* Edward Gray, *Takyttik;* Stan Lawder, *Cat Film for Ursula* and *Cat Film for Katy and Cynnie;* Carroll Ballard, *The Perils of Priscilla;* Claude Underwood, *Pippin's Island;* Kenneth and Grayce Space, *Fluffy the Kitten;* Paul Martin and Mary Jo Smith, *The Animals are Crying;* Ricky Leacock, *Hickory Hill.*

8 millimeter films: Stephen Mitchell, *Stephen's Cat Film;* Conor McCourt, *Conor's Cat.*

SALLY STRUTHERS

I went to a tuxedo shop in Beverly Hills to buy both of my cats a bow tie. Baba is a twelve-pound, all-black cat who refuses to be photographed and Scooty is a twenty-two pound all-white cat who doesn't.

I asked a man behind the counter for two bow ties, preferably different from each other and it was important that they be small.

"I see," he said, "Are they for your little boy?"

"I don't have any children," I quickly replied.

"I see," he said. "But are they for a child?"

"I'm afraid not," was my only response to this second inquiry.

The man was now more curious than ever. He had to know why I was asking for such small bow-ties.

"Maybe I could help you if I knew why you require this smaller size," he most generously offered.

At that moment I seriously considered telling him that my husband was a jockey, but perhaps he knew I wasn't married to anyone.

Feeling somewhat embarrassed, I was now forced to admit, "I'm buying them for my two cats."

With the look the man gave me, I now know I should have lied.

CARL Y. IRI

CATS IN THE COMICS

—

Herbert Galewitz

French Felix: If I were not so rushed I would have given that jerk a piece of my mind.

WHATEVER HAPPENED TO comic strips about cats? Once cats were the stars of popular and admired cartoon adventures. In fact, the very first newspaper comic featured cats — of sorts. Jimmy Swinnerton was the artist and the strip was called, if it had any name, "Bears & Tigers." Swinnerton's tigers were as frisky and cuddly as any four-week old tabby. They became popular soon after they were launched in the *San Francisco Examiner* during the 1890s.

Eventually, the patter of tiny tiger feet reached across the continent and tickled the fancy of William Randolph Hearst, the newspaper tycoon. Hearst summoned young Jimmy Swinnerton to New York and added him to the staff of his *New York Journal*.

All cat owners know that their pet's independent spirit can get them into amusing predicaments. This tendency naturally led to the creation of cartoon cat comedians and they were not restricted to the newspapers. One of the greatest of all cat comics was initially a movie star. "Felix the Cat" starred in the silent ani-

The Pussycat Princess was drawn by Ruth Carroll

mated films of Pat Sullivan and became so popular that by 1923 his fans could follow his antics into many newspapers. Felix is a forerunner of Mickey Mouse and undoubtedly influenced Walt Disney. By itself, "Felix the Cat" was a delightful, humorous strip that had a charm and a wide-eyed innocence. What was remarkable was not the fact that a cat could walk, talk and act like a human, but rather that the humans in the strip never took this phenomenon as anything out of the ordinary!

In the good old days of comics, cats and humans associated so freely that cats behaved like people and sometimes people acted like cats. The Rudolph Dirks strip "The Katzenjammer Kids" takes its name from the German words *Katzen*, meaning "cats," and *jammer*, "yowl." So the strip's title literally means, "The Cats Yowl Kids."

Hans and Fritz, the Katzenjammer Kids, were the humanification of two fat, frisky alley cats. Never content with their basic lot, they were constantly joking, prying, and upsetting their entire surroundings. Their credo was if its fun let us do it and hang the consequences. The "Katzenjammer Kids" proved to be immortal — after three-quarters of a century the comic strip continues to appear in dozens of newspapers both here and abroad.

And cat comics could attract educated as well as mass audiences. The most unusual of all cat strips was "Krazy Kat." Using a scratchy pen style, George Herriman fashioned a cast that included a star that lisped, a mouse protagonist with the unlikely name of Ignatz, and a bewildering array of backgrounds that would change, for no discernible reason from night to day and from a desert scene to a small town within the space of one panel. Like the Katzenjammer Kids, it had plenty of slapstick. One recurring action

showed Ignatz hurling a brick at Krazy (who loved it!) and then a moment later Offissa Pupp rushed in to arrest Ignatz. The variations on this theme were endless and no one could predict what twist of the pen Herriman had concocted for the day. His clever use of puns and alliterations attracted a sizable literary audience which included e.e. cummings and Gilbert Seldes. Even egghead President Wilson is said to have read "Krazy Kat" while munching his morning toast. But the most important fan that Herriman had was his boss, William Randolph Hearst. When self-effacing Herriman protested to Hearst that his $750 per week salary was not warranted by the income generated by his strip, Hearst — to his eternal credit — pooh-poohed the very suggestion. He continued to run "Krazy Kat" in his papers until Herriman's death in 1944.

Then came a change in audience taste. There was a reaction against wild and brilliant strips. The cat appeared as a new kind of comic, one called "The Pussycat Princess." She was a gentle, sweet monarch who ruled over Tabbyland, a nation whose greatest problem was to find ways to make the Earl of Sourface laugh. The solution never arrived until the final panel, when one of the Tabbyland citizens would slip on a banana peel and send the dour Earl into a paroxysm of laughter. The injured citizen was then given the emolient of knighthood and all was at peace until the next Sunday's comic edition appeared.

Mrs. Grace G. Drayton was the artist responsible for this saccharine strip. When Grace

Ignatz, Krazy, Offissa Pup and brick.

Score 1 for Cicero's Cat.

died in 1936, Ruth Carroll took over the drawing. Ruth's pussycats were just as moon-faced, but the line was firmer. The doings of this never-never world continued for ten more years, when the first spring cleaning of post-World War II sent "The Pussycat Princess" to the dustbin of oblivion.

Cats now ceased to be superstars. New strips with cats, like "Cicero's Cat" and "Spooky," were developed to fill a technical need. Called "top pieces," these strips were brief episodes designed to take up space on large-format Sunday comic pages. Tabloid papers with smaller pages ignored them. "Cicero's Cat," for example, was created to accompany "Mutt and Jeff," the invention of Bud Fisher.

Today there are a few comic strips featuring cats, but none has ever achieved the stature of Felix or Krazy. The ignoble truth that we cat fanciers must acknowledge is that the most popular comic strip today features a dog — must we say the name? "Snoopy." But we can console ourselves, for some day another great cat comic will arrive on the scene. We hope.

Herb Galewitz is a free-lance editor and comics connoisseur.

CONFEDERATE CATS

Political artists struggling in the name of liberty have often represented their causes in cat-form. At the start of the Civil War Southerners believed that they were on the side of freedom, opposing federal tyranny. This Confederate cartoon by Adalbert Volck shows Abraham Lincoln, arriving in Washington for his inauguration, being startled by the demands of the South, symbolized by an alert cat.

MORRIS
ON THE "TODAY" SHOW

Mary Daniels

ALL RIGHT, where are the cat people?" asked Gene Shalit as he poked his head into the greenroom of NBC's "Today" show.

Feeling like a character out of an old Flash Gordon episode, I raised my hand and said, "Here!"

"Here!" echoed Bob Martwick, personal escort to Morris, the world's most finicky cat.

Morris did not say anything.

"All right, we'll just go out there and have fun, okay?" said Shalit.

As he turned to leave the greenroom, Shalit stopped and narrowed his eyes, giving a hard look at the feline superstar of all time, who ignored him completely.

"Looks just like a cat I've got," Shalit said.

At seven a.m. Morris's charisma was already going like the mainworks at Consolidated Edison. Even in the elevator, people had shrieked, "Is that. . .? It couldn't be! It is! MMORRISS!"

Mary, Bob, Morris and Gene.

Now the word had spread. As twenty people from the NBC staff clustered about Morris, I wondered who was getting television onto the home screens. They stroked, with trembling hands, that thick, fluffy, pinky-orange fur striped with cinnabar; others scurried after ink pads and index cards to get his pawtograph.

Every once in a while when some truly adoring fan gushed, Morris would give him or her one of his famous headbumps. (What the public may not know is that the real Morris is most affectionate.)

All this was being observed not only by myself, but by Charlton Heston, the other big guest star waiting to go on. When introduced to Mr. Martwick, Heston said, "I saw you and your cat in *Harry and Tonto.*"

"That wasn't Morris," we said coolly.

A few minutes later we "cat people" were ushered into the studio. It is a huge, dark vault with the brightly lighted "Today" desk at the back, and swirls of rubber coils, props, and cameras all about.

"Where's a mike for Morris? Have you got a mike for Morris?" Shalit demanded, as crew people clipped them on the rest of us.

"We have only twenty seconds," a crew member warned.

"Put a mike on him!" Shalit ordered.

"Ten seconds," someone said. A pretty girl slipped a mike around Morris's neck; he was sitting in a director's chair, his name stenciled across the back.

"Two seconds," said the voice. The girl took her hands away.

Then we were on, with Shalit first telling of Morris's stature and success; then switching to ask Martwick how to choose a cat at a shelter (which is how he discovered Morris). I stole a look at the distinguished subject and almost laughed aloud. Just as Martwick was saying, "Well, don't pick a cat that just lies there and doesn't do anything." Morris was slowly sinking into his resting place in a half-snooze.

It was all over quickly. As we left the building, a wave of people fussed over Morris (who mysteriously became very alert again).

Later, talking to Martwick, I asked after Morris, who lives at Martwick's country kennels near Chicago. "Do you still think. . ." I began, and Martwick finished for me, "that he's the greatest cat who ever lived?"

"Yes," he said, then chuckled and added, "and so does he."

Mary Daniels, a writer for the Chicago Tribune, *wrote a biography of Morris.*

HOW TO TAKE CAT PICTURES

Walter Chandoha

PEOPLE OFTEN ASK: "How do I get my cat to cooperate for pictures?" First, you must take pictures when the cat is in the mood, not when you are. Obviously, knowing a cat's moods depends on knowing the cat; you must study your cat's habits and attitudes.

A cat is usually most cooperative after having eaten. As he sits on a sunny window sill and washes, you have an ideal picture-taking situation. The sun will provide enough light for almost any camera. The cat is happy, so he will not give you problems. If you wish to get him to interrupt his washing, make a few soft sounds — a low growl, or a high-pitched meow, or maybe crinkle cellophane. If he is attracted by the sound, shoot your picture.

If you don't want a static picture, you can induce a cat to play by dangling a string in front of him, or gently drawing his paw in the direction you want his attention to turn. Roll a ball of yarn or marble across the floor; a dangling plant will also get a cat's attention.

After the cat has eaten, played or posed a bit, it will be nap time. To intrude with your camera into this part of a cat's life will produce nothing but failure. So let the cat have his nap. He will be ready when he wakes up, you will get lots of yawns — some of them giving the cat the appearance of talking — and stretches. This lazy, waking-up period is an excellent time for picture-taking of cats.

What your cats do, what my cats do and the sequence in which they do them, may not coincide. So you will have to be a cat watcher — of your own cat — before you start taking pictures. After you think you know his routine, try some pictures. You will be surprised how easy it is to get some really good pictures.

Taking a technically good photograph of a cat is also easy, if you follow one elementary rule: don't attempt pictures beyond the capabilities of the camera. Suppose you want to make a big head close-up of your cat, but your camera cannot focus closer than three feet. Go ahead; move in closer; fill the view-finder with the cat's head; *but* when the photographs come back from the developer, they will not be sharp. Solution #1: don't move in closer than three feet — the image will be smaller, but sharp. Solution #2: buy a close-up lens. This is like an eye-glass that fits over the camera lens; with it, you can get *sharp* head portraits of your cat.

Most low and moderately priced cameras are designed to take pictures in bright sunlight, or indoors with flash at distances of no more than fifteen or twenty feet. If you limit your picture-taking to these situations, you will be all right. But suppose you have been taking pictures of your cat playing with leaves in the bright sun, and suddenly he strikes a fantastic pose on a piece of sculpture in a shady part of the garden. If your camera is really limited, and it is set for bright sunlight, you will get a badly underexposed picture. If it is a camera with some lens adjustments, set it for *shade* on the "lighten" setting; or set it as an indoor shot and use a flash.

The camera is not the only element affecting the exposure; the type of film used is also important. Films — both color and black-and-white — are rated with a speed or an exposure index. Color film for slides will have a speed of 25, while another for prints will have a speed of 100 and a general purpose black-and-white film has a speed of 400. The higher the speed of the film the less light you will need to make a clear picture. With a 400 film you can take pictures just about anywhere without a flash.

Walter Chandoha, author of How to Photograph Cats, Dogs, and Other Animals, *is a specialist in animal and nature photography.*

WALTER CHANDOHA

CATS IN ADVERTISING

Irma Reichert

Cat's Paw ® uses the traditional "sign of the cat" approach to promote sales of its rubber heels for shoes.

CATS HAVE BEEN used as advertising symbols for a long time. In the Middle Ages, taverns were often known by names such as "The Sign Of The Blue Cat," and one famous inn on the left bank of medieval Paris was called "The Fishing Cat." Not surprisingly, cats continue to appear in the advertisements and corporate symbols of the modern world. Some wonderful qualities can be conveyed instantly with a picture of a cat. Cats are decorative, cuddly, soft, sleek and sexy. Until recently these characteristics were considered sufficient to encourage someone to remember to buy a product. When first used to promote products, cats were usually allowed to retain their catness. However, a recent trend in advertising is denying the very essence of cats.

Remember the famous Cat's Paw® ad for rubber heels? It is a splendid example of the traditional use of a stylized cat drawing to represent a product. Even an ailurophobe could look at the cat symbol and see a benefit. Rubber heels would pad *your* paws too and give you the silent walk of a cat. Millions of people asked for Cat's Paw® heels, bringing smiles of satisfaction to the faces of admen and buyers alike.

Another simple symbol in the "sign of the cat" tradition is used by the Goodall Rubber Company. Their Manxline fire hose is branded with a profile of the tailless Manx cat and the advertisements use photographs of a charming Manx cat with its namesake hose.

Kittens too have always been advertising favorites. They are sure "grabbers" that catch a person's attention and are often used to remind people of babies. Since 1933 the Chesapeake

The Manx cat has no tail, but in this advertisement the fire hose appears to provide one.

Railroad's symbol has been a cute little kitten called Chessie, a classic example of the kitten as baby in advertising. The picture of Chessie sleeping in an air-conditioned Pullman car is intended to make you say ooh and ah while it conveys the message of comfort.

These days Amtrak carries all long-distance passengers, but the C & O still uses Chessie the sleeping kitten.

Bastet lives. The association of cats with fertility and sexuality, shown in this detail from a My Sin perfume ad, is as old as history.

Sex is even more popular as an advertising theme than cats, so it is common to see sex and the cat coupled in advertising promotions. An ad for My Sin perfume uses the cat in a classic manner that traces straight back to the ancient Egyptians. A slinky mother cat shows off a lineup of irresistible kittens. A thousands-year-old sculpture of Bastet, Egyptian goddess of fertility, shown in Jean Cantin's article on "The Cat in Egypt," unites the same ideas — cats and sex.

And for advertising at its sexy best, there is a recent perfume ad that does cats and people proud. Charles Revson launched his new perfume Cerissa by showing a picture of Lauren Hutton, one of the world's highest paid models, with a gorgeous white cat. The copy reads, "Very pretty. Very feminine. Very, very exciting." Indeed.

The newest trend in cat advertising is the use of film tricks to make cats appear to do things no cat has ever done. As a result, some very strange cats are on television these days, doing some very strange things. They talk, dance and tell jokes. Some of them barely resemble cats. Knowing that many of us baby our cats and think of them as extensions of our family, the advertisers ignore the cat's nature in promoting their prod-

Cat and model combine to express beauty, elegance and feminity.

The Purina Cat Chow commercial ultimately depends on the real charm of real cats. ("Purina," "Cat Chow," and "Chow" are registered trademarks of the Ralston-Purina Company.)

uct. This approach has generated controversy among people who love cats for their independence and for the way they remain creatures of nature even when house-bound.

Many television commercials do not use the cat *qua* cat. There has been a recent tendency to put some of the sales pitch into the mouths of the pets themselves. In one ad, cats with humanly clear enunciation are shown saying, "Meow," and then the human announcer says that Meow Mix® cat food is, "The one cats ask for by name." Other commercials have cats speaking in English. Morris tells viewers his innermost thoughts about 9-Lives® cat food. Taking the talking idea a step farther, cats sing the Purina Cat Chow® jingle while some fancy film editing makes it look as though cats are dancing a Rockettes routine. Many people are outraged by such cinematic tricks and call for boycotts of products so advertised. They want unnatural cats taken off television, but so far the number of such commercials has kept growing.

And so it has been through the advertising ages. Cats are and will continue to be a medium for messages. Whether you laugh because the cat is a cartoon rascal who reminds you of your house tiger, or sigh because just looking at a cat gives you pleasure, what you are reacting to is a cat you can identify with.

Irma Reichert, who has written for radio, television and advertising, has a cat named Molly.

CATS' PAUSE
ALAN M. ORMONT

Has the media convinced you how
All our cats have lost their meow
They dance and speak and refuse their
   chow
Until we cry and plead and bow.
I'd like to kill the guys who write
All the junk that caused this plight.
Things could once again be right
If Morris disappeared from sight.

Alan M. Ormont is a financial planner in West Hartford, Connecticut.

XII. THE PRIVATE CAT

CATS ARE NOT PEOPLE

Anne Mendelson

A FEW MINUTES after seven a.m. the small serious cat abandons her nightly perch on the radiator and drapes herself over the head of her sleeping owner. It is a ritual that has never failed to produce breakfast, and she is not about to relinquish it.

In a kitchen in the same city, the stately dowager on top of the refrigerator barely opens an amber eye as the first to arise in the household appears and begins fumbling with the coffee pot. In the apartment next door, a husky black kitten quietly extricates himself from the warm tangle of feet under the bedclothes and tucks himself into his young master's chin with a sociable purr. Thirty blocks away, his calico sister is screaming into the ears of two semi-conscious, protesting humans. Far to the west of the city, the battered old family villain — one ear still bloody from last night's brawl — hobbles smartly across the lawn toward the kitchen door and the smell of promise.

Young and old, all are cats with thoroughly trained people. It is hard to say whether the cats or their human companions would be more surprised by any break in the ceremony of morning reunion. In the well-tempered cat household, such ceremonies are a major part of the day. Every day, the scarred old tom retreats to an after-breakfast wash in the same corner of the tool shed. An august matron assumes the same look of injury at being thrown off the bed some exasperated human is trying to make. The serious little alarm-clock cat composes herself for nine hours of unexplained solitude until it is time for evening greeting or studied lack of greeting. The black kitten spends the evening shadow-boxing the television set; at eleven the sleeping calico suddenly wakens for half an hour of frenzied nightly calisthenics.

Whether cat life in the dim pre-domestic past had this scheduled, ritual quality no one can say, but a certain amount of ritual appears to be necessary to modern human-feline alliances — perhaps because the co-existence of the two species is so questionable in itself. Every so often a science-fiction writer knocks off a story to the effect that the family tortoise-shell cat is really a secret invader from Mars or Proxima Centauri. The theory does seem to have plausibility. Certainly, an unbiased observer of man and cat might conclude that the two ought to be living in different galaxies.

The human half of the partnership between human and cat has become amazingly expert at rationalizing the situation. "Mysterious animals, aren't they," murmurs the well-trained owner as his twenty-five-pound animal for reasons perfectly clear to itself, unexpectedly levitates four feet into the air, lands on someone's foot, and takes off for parts unknown with unbelievable velocity. Of necessity, cat lovers are shameless anthropomorphizers and coverers-up of all inconsistencies. "They're so deliberate." "So spontaneous" — or so regal, innocent, lazy, busy, sinister, serene, tigerish, dainty. All perfectly good words, but what do they really have to do with cats?

Ailurophiles can hardly get away from a human-oriented vocabulary, but they are always being caught up in its contradictions. "The thing I like about cats" cat owners like to tell dog owners, "is that they are so *independent*." Such a remark is usually made by people who have just spent twenty minutes waving pieces of turkey breast and chanting "Kitty-kitty-kitty" in a vain attempt to demonstrate the sociability of their cat. Not surprisingly, true believers also tend to a

The cat is never vulgar.

CARL VAN VECHTEN

certain defensiveness for cats are not interested in buttressing their owners' fantasies.

Perhaps the cliché which comes closest to the heart of both myth and reality is "inscrutable." People are always commenting that you never know what cats are thinking. The observation tells us a little about cats and a lot more about people. It implies that people *ought* to know what other beings are thinking, and that cats violate this norm in some strange way. Why? We all know that even human beings are inscrutable to each other much of the time, and would not choose to have it any other way. As for cats, who began marching to a different drummer at least 50 million years ago, why *should* we know what they're thinking? Have they not earned the right to evolve ways of thinking and acting which simply do not need to be translated into human terms?

Cats, you will notice, do not appear to rationalize the actions or thinking of people. Or,

if they do, it is for the sake of cats' concrete and honest goals: food, safety, reassuring attention. Ninety-nine percent of human life must make as little sense to cats as many of a cat's reactions (or lack of them) do to us, but cats have the wit to concentrate on what they do recognize instead of projecting their own egos onto what they do not.

The little seven-o'clock riser spends the night on a window radiator three times as high as it is, and starts the day by awakening a creature eighteen times its weight. Its busy, preoccupied owner and his possessions tower over it like props in a horror movie. With restricted color vision and drastically abridged depth perception, the cat looks up from a height of twelve inches at a world the owner would hardly recognize if he were shown a camera simulation of it. Sometimes he talks to the cat with loving sympathy. Sometimes he ignores it. Most of the time the owner is simply not there. The large (to the cat) surroundings it lives in are not always in the

---

CATS' PET PEEVES

Being petted in the wrong direction
Dogs
Curdled milk
Being told how fat they have grown
Falling into the toilet bowl while trying to
    drink
People who yell "Scat!"
Bells around their necks
Pink and blue satin bows
Things that go bump in the night

---

same place, for the owner may get the urge to move the furniture. The cat is not troubled: the daily rituals sustain it among all unknowns. For all its comparatively short memory and inability to make abstract connections, the little creature has taken the most intelligent possible approach to the business of living with its friend. The cat shares what it can with him and does not dream up fancy explanations for the rest.

The battle-hardened veteran cat has never been grateful for its breakfast — or ungrateful. On occasion a cat has been known to tell people that it takes pleasure in something they have done for it. When human members of the household try to express their own pleasure in its lithe body and silky fur and amiable spirit, they may be greeted with a happy purr — or blank stare and dignified retreat. Why not? Why explain it all away? Cats let us alone when they do not understand us. They will owe just so much and no more to our good opinion.

In the end, the intelligent way for a human being to live with a member of another species is the cat way: recognize that the alien has its own perfectly complete mental and physical world which is just as familiar to it as yours is to you. Figure out what you need to know for daily comfort, create a few common rituals out of it, and do not pretend to understand the rest.

The real importance of understanding a cat's behavior has nothing to do with the cat lover's vocabulary of devotion — "elegant," "sophisticated," "sphinx-like" — or with the rigmarole of buying the animal pretty sleeping baskets and calves' liver. It lies in the day-to-day proof that two species can live in a state of mutual trust and appreciation without either compromising its own essential nature, even though they share only a dim understanding of what makes each other tick.

Anne Mendelson is a free-lance writer; her first word is reported to have been "cat."

OWNERSHIP
DAVID J. IRVINE

Man's pet, the kitten, lives nine lives;
Man, one: three score and ten.
Man claims the ownership of earth,
Of every glebe and glen.
What modest claim do kittens make?
——The ownership of men.

David J. Irvine, an educational psychologist, lives near Albany, New York.

A NEW CAT: WHY, HOW AND WHERE TO GET ONE

Jay Kuhlman, D.V.M.

Cats *are trouble-free, self-maintaining pets. All you have to do is feed them and change their litter pans.*

Not so. Before taking on the care of a cat, find out, in fairness to you and to your cat, exactly what's involved. When you own a cat, you'll find that certain living patterns have to be changed. Once-left-open doors and windows, the storage of needlework and toxic household items now must be considered potential problems for you and potential hazards to your cat. Birds and plants must also be strategically relocated before introducing a cat. A cat may be an inexpensive acquisition, but food, litter, veterinary expenses and boarding or sitter fees can add up, so do be aware that you may have additional expenses which may affect your feelings about your new pet.

The only reason anybody gets a cat is loneliness.

Wrong again. The companionship offered is a valid reason for sharing with a pet, but cats also answer numerous needs for a wide variety of people. Many cats are acquired simply for the pragmatic reason that they catch mice. Often, parents try to teach their children responsibility and the facts of life through care for a young cat. The new cat may be a companion for another pet, or it may mean the pursuit of a fascinating hobby through breeding and showing. The reasons for cat-owning are as many and as personal as the people involved.

It is smarter to raise a kitten than to take on an older cat, and besides, kittens are a lot cuter.

TYPICAL CAT OWNERS

	one cat	three or more cats
Most common age group:	35–44	25–34
Education:	attended college	did not attend college
Live in:	suburbs	country
Describe selves as:	amicable, impulsive, stubborn	creative, not impulsive, persuadable
Sport most likely to enjoy:	auto racing	horse racing
Radio preference:	seldom listen	often listen
Favorite weekend TV:	sports	hate weekend TV

Source: Axiom Market Research Bureau, Inc., Target Group Index, 1975.

There's no argument about the appeal of a kitten, and it is true that an owner can influence the shaping of a cat's personality (for better or worse) if the cat is raised from kittenhood. But a kitten does require more care and is physically more delicate. It is prone to illness and to more frequent injury than an adult cat who has gone through the perils of respiratory and intestinal problems. The adult cat has had good and bad experiences with humans and will be slower in trusting people; similarly, the adult cat will be slower in changing or forgetting bad habits picked up in its earlier days.

It doesn't seem fair to alter or neuter a cat.

This is really more naïve than false. The house with an unaltered male is subject to strong urinary odor, fighting, spraying, straying and crying to get out. Two unaltered males will fight, and unaltered males and females will procreate often. The female cat who is not spayed is liable to uterine infections and mammary growths. Her periods of heat will be heard for miles around, and the owner may be faced with the unwanted litter of kits. Neutered cats face far fewer problems and present far fewer to their owners. Altering a house cat is not only fair — it is kind.

Female cats are more docile than males.

The more we know of cats, the more exceptions we discover to this generally applicable rule. Males tend to be more aggressive but may in fact be more dependent on people, whereas the supposedly docile female often has very definite ideas on her proper life style. Cats have general characteristics, but they are individuals,

affected by things they have learned and experienced. It is safe to generalize about cat behavior up to a point, and that point is usually determined by the interaction between you and your cat.

If you want a really good cat, you have got to go to a breeder.

If *good* is meant to signify show quality, with impeccable bloodlines, the statement is true. But show-quality cats are usually available through

LOLA T. FIUR

HOW TO BUY A HEALTHY KITTEN

JEROME J. BENISATTO

If you buy a kitten from a pet shop, it is your right to insist that the kitten be healthy. Ask about the shop's *health guarantees.* A fourteen-day guarantee with full refund should be the minimum acceptable guarantee. Even better is a thirty-day guarantee and a one-year guarantee against congenital defects, which may be slow to appear.

Examine the kitten closely before buying. The eyes should be clear, not watering excessively, and white skin at corners should not show. Nostrils should be clear, not exuding mucus, a sure sign of incubating health problems. The ears, should be clean without excessive dirt or wax-like substance which indicates the presence of mites. Examine the fur by spreading the fur and looking at the skin for sores or scabs indicating fungus condition. Check fur for fleas or flea eggs which look like small black dots. Check kitten's litter pan for signs of diarrhea.

Ask for a written list of shots, including dates and serum type, that may have already been given the kitten. Once you have acquired a healthy kitten it is your responsibility to see that it receives attentive care that will keep it healthy.

Jerome J. Benisatto owns Felines of Distinction, a cat store in New York City.

NEW CAT QUESTIONS

Here are some questions to ask before acquiring a new cat:

Is it healthy?
Why is it being sold or given away?
Has it been checked for worms? When?
Has it been vaccinated? When?
Has the cat been on medication? Why and for how long?
If a kitten, how long has it been weaned?
What times is it used to eating?
What are the arrangements if the cat is found to be ill or possesses a birth defect?
Is there a health guarantee and what is its duration?

other sources, such as pet shops, and often may be obtained at little or no cost through an animal shelter. There are as many ways of obtaining a cat as there are breeds, and each way, like each breed, has its good and bad facets.

Adopting a cat bred in a home is generally a good idea because it will be accustomed to a home atmosphere. Purebred or mixed, planned or unplanned, cats from a home source have received individual care, and the parents are usually in evidence so that a medical history as well as an idea of future appearance and temperament may be formulated.

Professional breeders are the people to see when you know exactly what you want. These are the experts in genetics, cat care and disease prevention. Some breeders have succeeded in eliminating hereditary feline diseases; others are chiefly profit-motivated, and thus cater to a high-volume turnover. The prospective owner must look at the cat, the breeder's quarters and the breeders themselves to get an idea of the quality of the operation. Try to ascertain the health of the new cat and get a clear understanding of what to do if a problem arises regarding its condition. If possible, this should be done in writing. Don't be afraid to shop breeders before buying. They can be located in your area by checking the directory of cat magazines, attending a cat show, or contacting a cat breeding registry or cat club.

Another good source is the animal shelter, where cats have been brought in by owners or finders unable to give them a home. For a minimal fee, you may become the owner of a fine pedigreed cat or kitten. Often, adopting can mean saving the life of the animal, since shelters, too, face problems of space and disease. Shelters are listed in your phone book, and you'll be surprised at how many there are besides the A.S.P.C.A. and the Humane Society.

Make sure, no matter how you acquire a new cat, that you have the cat checked by a veterinarian within three days so that any problem can be spotted early. If any adjustment needs to be made, it can be taken care of while there is still some objectivity and before the cat has captured your heart.

Jay Kuhlman, a veterinarian in New York City, loves cats.

WILD PETS

The reasons for not living with a lion or other wild species of cat are well known and ought to be obvious. Even if they are raised from birth on tender human care, the big cats when full-grown can kill you. Smaller, mild-tempered wild cats, such as the serval, can also be dangerous when provoked.

There is also a philosophical issue at stake. Wild cats have instincts and needs which cannot be satisfied by the life of a house cat and, because they are potentially dangerous, wild cats cannot be given the freedom available to the normal domestic cat. Even if they seem to adapt well to living in a house or backyard, a wild cat pet is being stunted and twisted into a foreign environment.

Yes, it is exciting to have an unusual pet. And yes, it would be a pleasure to have a big cat lie on your lap and purr. But, no, the simple life of your house is not what a wild cat was born to enjoy. The wish to limit a wild cat to a domestic prison is not love. It is instead an unhealthy urge to shape even the wildest of things into our own domestic image.

BILL PLYMPTON

Bill Plympton

SOME CAT CLERIHEWS
RAYMOND D. SMITH

An Abyssinian
Is never a minion;
And a Siamese
Doesn't try too hard to please.

A Domestic
May well be majestic,
But when they call it an American,
Almost swear, I can.

The top longhair version
Is the baby-faced Persian,
But Never ignore a
Nice Turkish Angora.

The Himalayan
Likes to play on;
But it can't catch its tail in ease,
For it's not as lithe as the Balinese.

The Havana Brown
Has just come to town,
But the Burmese
Has long family trees.

In order to vex us,
God made two kinds of Rexes.
Another of His pranks
Is the Manx.

A Russian Blue
May look gray to you,
But don't call it a Maltese,
Please!

Most folks can be pally
With a show cat or alley,
For except for a few,
They are nice, too.

REPRINTED FROM 'CATS' MAGAZINE
(JANUARY, 1966).

RAYMOND D. SMITH IS THE PUBLISHER OF
'CATS' MAGAZINE.

CAT NAMES

Jacob Antelyes, D.V.M.

"Oh, I beg your pardon," cried Alice hastily, afraid that she had hurt the poor animal's feelings, "I quite forgot you didn't like cats."

"Not like cats!" cried the mouse in a shrill, passionate voice. "Would you like cats if you were me?"

"Well perhaps not," said Alice in a soothing tone. "Don't be angry about it. And yet I wish I could show you our cat Dinah. I think you'd take a fancy to cats if you could only see her. She is such a dear, quiet thing."

Alice's Adventures in Wonderland, Lewis Carroll

IN OUR SOCIETY people are a good deal freer about naming a pet animal than they are in choosing a new child's name. Family obligations, tradition, religious attitudes and other conventions so limit the selection that a baby's name very often turns out to be one that the parents themselves do not particularly like, but feel they must accept in order to please others and keep peace in the family. A pet's name, on the other hand, is likely to tell a lot more about you than it does about the pet. In fact, your pet's name probably says a great many things about your character and personality that you are not even aware of yourself. For instance, your wildest fantasies, deepest wishes and fondest hopes, not usually expressible in your daily life, are quite often unconsciously reflected in the name you choose.

Several years ago, Lloyd Prasuhn, a Chicago veterinarian, advanced the theory that a person who gives his cat a familiar human name, such as Peter or Dinah, or a common human nickname such as Bobby or Sue, feels a much greater emotional attachment to the animal than one who gives it an impersonal name, such as Tuffy or Pebbles. This theory not only seemed reasonable, but worked out rather accurately in surveys he and others carried out. People did seem to reveal a much closer, more personal relationship to a cat upon which they had bestowed a human name than to one they had given a commonplace, unsentimental name.

On the average, the owners were more devoted to the cat, spent more money on it, tended to feed it human food more than cat food, allowed it more freedom in the home, such as letting it sit at or on the table during meals. Often the cat was permitted to sleep with them or their children, its use of any piece of furniture that appealed to it was sanctioned, and sometimes this devotion went so far as to tolerate destructiveness in the cat that they would never have stood for from any human family member. On the other hand, outside cats, backdoor beggars, store cats and other strictly utilitarian felines hardly ever seem to have personal human names. Often the owners simply call these creatures "cat." And they get away with it too. The poor homeless animal, looking for a handout, will respond to practically anything a person willing to feed it decides to call it.

The Prasuhn theory, however, only

THE TEN MOST ABUSED NAMES FOR CATS

Fog
Cat
Cleo
Tiny
Tabby
Morris
Midnight
Samantha
Grimalkin
Mr. Patches

ANNA SEES A BUG

MAY 1975

MILTON GLASER

scratches the surface. When an individual names his cat, he doesn't begin to realize the depth of intimate personal disclosure he has made about himself. Of course, most cat names are decided consciously, even the accidental ones such as Wednesday, because "that's the day we found him." But even these names often have hidden meanings.

In general, the basic idea of selecting a cat as a house pet — its color, texture of coat, sex, and other characteristics — reflects a person's attitude towards cats as a species, towards people, and towards himself as well. Sometimes a facetious or satirical name may be given to a cat, such as Shorty to a long-legged feline or Tiny to a great big fellow, but these are used merely to hide the true feelings of the owner. Some people are extremely reluctant to reveal their inner feelings; often they will use ridicule to mask any "sensitive soul" aspect of their personalities. Ask a few questions and you will find that the owner

refers to his cat as "my son," "my daughter," "my only friend," or "my little baby."

Many cats' names reflect the owner's personal aspirations — military rank, social status, royal affinity, unconscious desire for courage, aggressiveness, dominance, and other sometimes unattainable goals.

Western societies, such as the United States, having become more democratic and more egalitarian, no longer recognize a social aristoc-

I call my kittens Shall and Will because no one can tell them apart.

CHRISTOPHER MORLEY

MY STORY ABOUT STAR

ZOE WEAVER

If I had a cat, I think I would name it Star because I like the name — for a cat, that is. Star would be a beautiful cat, a black cat who would purr a lot. This is the adventure we would have:

One day Star and I are walking in Central Park. All of a sudden we fall into a deep hole. We fall down and down — but then we land on a soft cushion. Now Star looks around. At the same time we both see light ahead of us. Star runs ahead to the light, and I follow after him.

What a surprise! There are hundreds, thousands, millions, billions of cats! Star runs to cats that must be his mother and father. I notice a sign that says Cat Land. I think to myself, "I may stay here a day or two so Star can visit his parents. Besides, I will get to cuddle a lot of kitties!"

Not until the second day do I get homesick. I send a letter to the King of Cats. He sends one back, telling me to come to his palace. And what a beautiful palace it turns out to be! There are two beautiful statues of cats with diamond eyes on the staircase.

Inside there is a big cat about three feet tall. He is the King and he says, "Close your eyes and say 'I want to go home. Come with me, Star.'"

I ask the King one thing. And he says yes, I can come back to Cat Land any time. I close my eyes, say the words.

And immediately I am home with Star.

Zoe Weaver is eight years old. She lives in New York and writes about anything she likes, cats included.

racy or stand in awe of the noble heroic figures so revered in the past. Maybe we still yearn for these heroes, or perhaps we unconsciously have a psychological need to look up to those brave champions of yesteryear. Who knows? Half a century ago, Sigmund Freud declared that when a person "dreams of emperors and empresses, kings and queens (they) stand for the parents whom the child glorifies." It is not at all far-fetched, then, to assume that when a person selects a noble, heroic, aggressive or courageous name for his cat that he feels, his family is actually acquiring a new and important member with just those desirable characteristics. Enhanced social status, higher individual rank among friends and neighbors, and improved self-image will seem to the cat owner to be the result — psychologically anyway.

A friend of mine, for instance, is very proud of his cat which he named Oliver Wendell Holmes, and whom he calls Olly, for short. Another friend called his nondescript foundling Little Lord Fauntleroy and, when that one died, gave the title Tarquin, (a legendary Etruscan king who lived some 500 years before Christ), to the next one.

Today, however, people of the lowest socio-economic level — even the poorest family — can boast of including in their midst a King or a Queen; a Prince or a Princess; a Count or Countess; a Colonel or Major; a Samson or Delilah. But whoever heard though of a cat named Buck Private? Or whoever listened to a neighbor stand at his back fence and cry, "Here Welfare Recipient?

People do tend to try to enhance themselves when they name their cats. More than that, they often confer on the cat a name which suggests a life style or a personality structure they undoubtedly wish they possessed themselves. What other reason would there be for cats to be named Devil, Fang, and Slugger; or Humphrey Bogart, Jesse James, and Dillinger? A client of mine found a kitten with a tiny black mustache under his nose. Did he call it Oliver Hardy? No, he named it Adolph Hitler! The role this man wished to play seems obvious enough. A veterinarian friend told me of a client he had, named Mr. Badman, who called his cat Angel — clearly again character self-enhancement.

Sometimes, people identify with their cats, and name them after traits they feel they possess themselves. Another client of mine, for instance, who thinks of himself as highly intelligent, calls his cat Professor. A journalist I know called his cat Mendel, in honor of his own deceased father. He then proceeded to call Mendel's first kitten Felix Mendelsohn, partly facetiously, but mostly lovingly I am sure.

The following table is a list of some of the more common categories of cat names with some examples of each.

Affectionate: *Lover, Baby*
Liquor: *Brandy, Cognac*
Personal: *Bruce, Sheila*
Royal: *Rex, Empress*
Heroic: *Hercules, Helen of Troy*
Biblical: *Ruth, David*
Military, Naval: *Sergeant, Commodore*
Derogatory (put-downs): *Stinky, Ratso*
Intellectual: *Socrates, Aristotle*
Humorous (cover-ups): *Pee Wee (for a big cat), Snowball (for a black cat)*
Aggressive: *Mugger, Killer*
Descriptive: *Blackie, Whitey*

It is difficult to explain why anyone would take the trouble to give a good home to a cat, to love and care for it, and then to give it a disparaging name. Such people may have feelings of inferiority, an ego deficiency, as the psychologists say. Such a person may feel subordinate to the others in his family, inadequate among his friends, have a "low-man-on-the-totem-pole" complex. He desperately needs to feel superior in some aspect of his life, in at least one of his relationships. For him, the cat's name turns out to be the most convenient place. Here he can be unopposed by his choice of a name for his cat.

Jacob Antelyes, a veterinarian for 35 years, has a special interest in relationships between humans and animals.

ELISE LONG

AN UNUSUAL NAME

One of the oddest names I have ever run across was Eplu. When the woman who brought this cat to me as a patient spelled it, I tried to figure out what it might mean, but I could not. Perhaps it was not of English origin, but then I could not even begin to guess from which foreign tongue it might have come. I tried to make sense of it in other ways, such as spelling it backwards, but such mental acrobatics were also of no use. Finally, I asked the owner, "Eplu? Is that the correct name for your cat?"

"Yes, it is." she answered. "It is short for *E Pluribus Unum.*

This did not make much sense either, so I asked for further information. She was delighted to explain. Her parents, it seems, had recently escaped from behind the Iron Curtain. More fortunately, they had been permitted to enter the United States. They valued their freedom here so highly, and have developed such strong feelings of attachment to their adopted country, that they chose to name their cat, whom they also love, with the symbol and slogan of American unity.

THE NAMING OF CATS

T. S. ELIOT

The Naming of Cats is a difficult matter,
    It isn't just one of your holiday games;
You may think at first I'm mad as a hatter
When I tell you, a cat must have THREE DIFFERENT NAMES.
First of all, there's the name that the family uses daily,
    Such as Peter, Augustus, Alonzo or James,
Such as Victor or Jonathan, George or Bill Bailey —
    All of them sensible everyday names.
There are fancier names if you think they sound sweeter,
    Some for the gentlemen, some for the dames:
Such as Plato, Admetus, Electra, Demeter —
    But all of them sensible everyday names.
But I tell you, a cat needs a name that's particular,
    A name that's peculiar, and more dignified,
Else how can he keep up his tail perpendicular,
    Or spread out his whiskers, or cherish his pride?
Of names of this kind, I can give you a quorum,
    Such as Munkustrap, Quaxo, or Coricopat,
Such as Bombalurina, or else Jellyorum —
    Names that never belong to more than one cat.
But above and beyond there's still one name left over,
    And that is the name that you never will guess;
The name that no human research can discover —
    But THE CAT HIMSELF KNOWS, and will never confess.
When you notice a cat in profound meditation,
    The reason, I tell you, is always the same:
His mind is engaged in a rapt contemplation
    Of the thought, of the thought, of the thought of his name:
      His ineffable effable
      Effanineffable
Deep and inscrutable singular Name.

NOTES ON CATS, PEOPLE AND RELATED MATTERS

John Simon

WHAT I AM going to say may seem to be about cats and dogs, but it is really about women and men. However, it is also about cats and dogs, and especially cats. I think that most dogs, regardless of sex, are male; I think that most cats, regardless of sex, are female. I like dogs. I adore cats; unfortunately, I am allergic to them.

Not to love people strikes me as quixotic but understandable; not to love animals is inhuman. Animal lovers, traditionally, break down into two categories: those who, among household pets, prefer dogs, and those who prefer cats. I am not a revisionist in animal lore: I agree with the popular wisdom that holds the primary feature of dogs to be sloppy faithfulness; that of cats, fastidious independence. I do not think that it is a prejudice and stereotype that made dogs into tail-wagging, muck-sniffing sycophants, and cats into aloof, discriminating — and, above all, clean — aristocrats. To be sure, cats are also moody and less than wholly reliable. These stereotypes, however, hold water — unlike those about racial minorities, of whom the majority is leery. No one is afraid that cats or dogs will take over the world or the economy, hence no one goes around fabricating derogatory commonplaces about them.

Dogs mirror certain democratic decencies; not for nothing is American writing, from Jack London to Albert Payson Terhune, full of warm, unshaggy dog stories. Cats epitomize elitist selectivity; appropriately, French literature, from Baudelaire to Colette, is full of tributes to cats. Even England, for all its culture, is foursquare and Anglo-Saxon enough to have more dog literature than cat literature (also known as kitty-*lettres*). Thus that eminent British scholar, the Reverend Montague Summers, when asked what his hobby was, replied: "Talking with intelligent dogs." Alas, he must have led a rather taciturn life, for even the brightest dogs are poor conversationalists. So, too, are cats, but they stimulate the imagination into addressing imposing meditations and monologues to them because — here comes the big difference — they have a mystery. Dogs do not.

Because of the mystery, I have always preferred cats to dogs, and, I suppose, women to men. When I was a child, I had a cat named Bibi (I was not allergic then) and a dog named Bari. Bibi (may the lovely actress Bibi Andersson forgive me) was actually a male, but in many respects wonderfully feminine. When he came home one morning with part of his tail gone, bone projecting and blood dripping from the stump, I was profoundly distressed; I don't recall the serious scrapes Bari used to get into ever upsetting me that much. But don't get me

Ignorant people think it's the noise which fighting cats make that is so aggravating, but it ain't so; it's the sickening grammar they use.

MARK TWAIN

The dog for the man, the cat for the woman.

ENGLISH PROVERB

wrong: I am really fond of dogs, too.

I have found my love of cats, or of a cat, most helpful in understanding women, though — women, whom I have loved and continue to love even more than cats. And I have, over the years, come to divide women into two kinds: cat-women and dog-women. That does not mean women who prefer these or those pets (although there is more than a little correlation along those lines); it means that some women remind me of cats, and some of dogs. Before feminist readers explode — accusing me of equating women with animals — let me make clear that I have no doubt that some such classifying is equally in order for men, only because men interest me less, I leave that job to those better qualified for it — women.

To resume. Dog-women are apt to be wholesome, handsome, pretty or cute; cat-women, beautiful or, at any rate, striking. Dog-women are open, loyal and dependable; cat-women are devious, unpredictable and fickle. Dog-women are intelligent, outgoing, uncalculating; cat-women are self-centered, introverted, selfish. Sometimes they are also shrewd, though more often merely neurotic. Their neuroses can destroy *them* sometimes; *you*, always. (These remarks are addressed to men.) Dog-women remember things, bring you presents, and cook for you. Cat-women accept presents charmingly, forget things, and must be taken out to restaurants. Dog-women are good with children, will mother even their men, and, when they have a little money, will gladly share it with you. Cat-women are not interested in children, are courtesans even to their husbands — though they prefer lovers — and are apt to be very rich or very poor. Either way, they are unlikely to share what they have with you. Some of them are quite careless about money, but they spend it mostly on themselves.

Dog-women age more quickly than cat-women, but are seldom garish when old; old cat-women often are. Cat-women are better at the arts; dog-women, at everything else. Cat-women are inefficient but elegant; dog-women are efficacious but usually cannot or will not achieve true elegance. Cat-women tend to be lazy daydreamers; dog-women, hard workers. (In this area, though, there are frequent exceptions.) The favorite perversion of cat-women is narcissism; that of dog-women, masochism. If a dog-woman is frigid, it takes the form of chastity; if a cat-woman is frigid, the outward form is nymphomania. Of course, even without frigidity, cat-women are much more inclined to be promiscuous. Dog-women love you; cat-women are loved by you. Dog-women have no mystery, but they understand you; cat-women may also understand you if they can be bothered to make the effort, but they are mysteries even to themselves. Dog-women may put in a couple of years in psychotherapy; cat-women either avoid it like the plague, or are in permanent analysis. Dog-women make good wives and friends; cat-women are best as mistresses and enemies. Dog-women are, or try to be, moral; cat-women are amoral and seldom try to be anything else. However, few or no women are entirely cat or dog; but most of them, if not all, are more of one thing or the other.

All this is postgraduate stuff, though: women come later in a young man's education; cats, early on. I remember trying to teach Bibi to answer to his name. Sometimes he did; more often he didn't. When you come right down to it, the number of times he responded was not high enough to make the experiment pass scientific muster. Nevertheless, I was convinced that Bibi did answer to his name. This is how we are: we love the cat for its independence, yet busily pretend to ourselves and others that we have tamed it — made it dependent. We are, of course, deluding ourselves: every two-bit circus has a dog act; how often, however, have you seen a cat act? Oh, lions and tigers, certainly; they are wild beasts and lack the culture and sophistication of a so-called domestic feline, over whose eyes no mere man or woman can pull any wool. You simply will not encounter Professor X and His Talented Tabbies or Madame La Z. and Her Performing Pussies.

True enough, many years ago, I was on unemployment compensation, and often stood in line with Sebastian, who was billed on his luxurious basket in which he dangled from his mistress's arm as *Sebastian, The Performing Cat*. But this portly white Persian who was brought in weekly by said mistress to collect his (her? their?)

Cats, like men, are flatterers.

WALTER SAVAGE LANDOR

unemployment checks remained recumbent in said luxurious basket, and never even performed the simple task of going to pick up his check by himself. I wondered what sort of performer he was, and later, when I became a drama and film critic, hoped to catch up with his act and review it. But Sebastian never came within my critical purview (in cat criticism sometimes called purrview), and the cats I did encounter on stage and screen all clung to their cherished amateur status: they merely permitted themselves to be carried on and off stage, put up with being petted, and sometimes roamed about the stage ignoring both script and director. I distinctly recall a cat in the off-Broadway production *Colette* forsaking the stage and slinking about the auditorium. Very unprofessional behavior, but, considering the quality of the play, not unsound critically.

It is no accident that in literature dogs more often appear in prose, cats in verse. And I do not mean merely light verse, such as that of Don Marquis, which was nevertheless weighty enough to immortalize that archetypal cat, or cat-woman, mehitabel. I mean bona fide poetry. For cats are, to repeat, mysterious creatures, and poetry is better equipped than prose to penetrate to the heart of mysteries. That grave poet T.S. Eliot, who wrote a whole tome's worth (among male chauvinist cats sometimes called Tom's worth) of cat poems, put his finger on it in the very first poem, "The Naming of Cats." Here Eliot expounds that a cat must have three names: an ordinary one, a special one and a wholly individual one:

But above and beyond there's still one name left over,
And that is the name that you never will guess;
The name that no human research can discover –
But The Cat Himself Knows, *and will never confess.*

Some cats in poetry are wicked, like that of the late British poetess Stevie Smith, called "The Galloping Cat." This one gallops about pretending to do good when it is actually doing evil; viciously, it even tries to bite an angel who happens to be standing in its path, and is indignant when its teeth meet "nothing but air." Other cats in poetry are calmly self-sufficient, and only fight back when people shower them with unwanted solicitude — like this cat by the undeservedly neglected American poet Edward N. Horn:

Pussycat sits on a chair
Implacably with acid stare.

Those who early loved in vain
Use the cat to try again,

And test their bruised omnipotence
Against the cat's austere defense.

What is most interesting, though, is how many poetic cats are, in fact, metaphors or symbols for women. I'll just give you one typical example, from Robert Graves's "Cat-Goddesses":

A perverse habit of cat-goddesses . . .
                    . . . is to yield themselves,
In verisimilar love-ecstasies,
To tatter-eared and slinking alley-toms
No less below the common run of cats
Than they above it; which they do for spite,
To provoke jealousy . . .

Still, the predominant poetic tradition is respectful of cats, as when Hilaire Belloc advises children not to be bad:

But so control your actions that
Your friends may all repeat,
"This child is dainty as the Cat,
And as the Owl discreet."

And there has probably never been a more moving tribute to an animal friend than Christopher Smart's to his cat Jeoffrey, included in the long poem "Jubilate Agno." It is true that Smart, who lived from 1722 to 1771, probably wrote the poem in the madhouse, but that has nothing to do with it. The verses addressed to Jeoffrey are numerous and beautiful; I can quote here only one of them: "For he is good to think on, if a man would express himself neatly." I could go on and cite less complimentary things written about felines, too, but I won't. The cat got my tongue.

John Simon, film critic of New York *magazine and drama critic of* The New Leader *and* The Hudson Review, *is the author, most recently, of* Singularities *and* Uneasy Stages.

TEST YOUR CAT'S SANITY

(REMEMBER, HE'S ONLY A REFLECTION OF YOU)

Chris Powers 1976

1. YOUR CAT WOULD RATHER PLAY WITH
   A. A COTTON BALL.
   B. A MUSHROOM.
   C. A RUBBER ERASER.
   D. A COCKROACH.

2. YOUR CAT WOULD RATHER SLEEP
   A. ON THE COUCH.
   B. IN YOUR SHOE.
   C. IN THE BATHTUB.
   D. ON YOUR FACE.

3. YOUR CAT WOULD RATHER EAT
   A. NINE LIVES.
   B. STRING BEANS.
   C. BUGS.
   D. BIRD GUTS.

4. WHEN YOU HAVE GUESTS, YOUR CAT
   A. CLIMBS PURRING INTO THEIR LAPS.
   B. UNTIES THEIR SHOE LACES.
   C. RACES FRANTICALLY FROM ROOM TO ROOM.
   D. LUNGES FOR THEIR JUGULAR.

5. YOUR CAT WOULD RATHER PEE
   A. IN HIS LITTER BOX.
   B. IN THE RUBBER PLANT.
   C. ON THE CLOSET FLOOR.
   D. ON YOUR PORTFOLIO.

6. YOUR CAT GETS STUCK IN THE MIRROR
   A. NEVER.
   B. SOMETIMES.
   C. A LOT.
   D. EVERY DAY.

7. YOUR CAT REACTS TO BEING LEFT ALONE FOR THE WEEKEND BY
   A. READING NEWSWEEK.
   B. STAYING UP PAST HIS BEDTIME.
   C. TEARING THE PLACE TO SHREDS.
   D. TAKING AN OVERDOSE.

SCORE RESULTS —

- 5 OR MORE ANSWERS TO "A" — YOU HAVE A TRUE FELINE DOMESTICUS — CONSTRUCTIVE, WELL-ADJUSTED — CONGRATULATIONS!

- 5 OR MORE ANSWERS TO "B" — ALTHOUGH YOUR CAT IS WELL SOCIALIZED, THIS SCORE INDICATES HE HAS CERTAIN AS YET UNEXPRESSED SUBCONSCIOUS URGES WHICH MAY MANIFEST THEM- SELVES IN THE PASSIVE-AGGRESSIVE BEHAVIOR OF THE NEXT SCORE.

- 5 OR MORE ANSWERS TO "C" — YOUR CAT WALTZES ON THE EDGE OF SCHIZOPHRENIA. TRY TO CONSIDER IN WHAT WAYS YOU THWART HIS INSTINCTS TOWARD SELF-REALIZATION. IF YOUR CAT PLACES IN THIS CATEGORY, YOU MIGHT WANT TO SEEK PROFESSIONAL HELP OR DE-CLAWING.

- 5 OR MORE ANSWERS TO "D" — YOUR CAT IS SEVERELY PSYCHOTIC, IF NOT DOWNRIGHT DEMENTED. HIS ANTI-SOCIAL TENDENCIES MAY EXPLODE INTO VIOLENCE, ENDANGERING YOU AND YOUR LEASE. WITHOUT PROFESSIONAL HELP, HE RUNS THE RISK OF MANIC-DEPRESSION OR CATATONIA.

ASSERTIVENESS TRAINING FOR CAT OWNERS

Mordecai Siegal

CAT TRAINING IS a misnomer. Cat manipulation is more like it. It would not matter if you were Clyde Beatty, Nyoka of the Jungle, or the stage manager of the Circus Maximus, no cat can be made to obey just because it wants to please you. It is only on the simplest level that cats accept the dominant/subordinant idea at all. With the exception of lions, cats in the wild are solitary figures stalking their prey in the lonely shadows of sub-tropical regions of the world. They are occasional eaters who derive 70 percent of their moisture intake from the carcasses of their prey. In other words, the hunt is not always successful and dinner isn't on the table at five P.M. every day. As a hangover from their undomesticated ancestors, cats are always in search of food. They cannot get it into their dear heads that the electric can opener can whirl on a regular basis.

Your little Tabetha is, in a sense, constantly on the hunt. She'll go to almost any lengths to obtain food. She could even be persuaded to obey a command or two as long as there was a reward with a munch factor. What is required is assertion from the cat owner and the will to insist, without backing down or feeling like he is becoming Ivan the Terrible. It is a question of commanding without guilt, of bribery for a higher purpose. Learn to manipulate your cat or she will manipulate you.

Adult humans seldom hear sounds that vibrate over 20,000 cycles per second. Many animals have a hearing capacity far beyond our range. Mice hear at the rate of 100,000 cycles per second, cats fall somewhere between 30,000 and 100,000. They hear much better than do humans but not as well as mice. It is because of this great hearing ability that cats respond better to the higher-pitched voices of women. They are more responsive to higher notes because of their hunting skills. When humans hear the squeeks of mice, they only hear the lower notes. Cats hear higher frequencies and that helps them to become good mouse-finders. Consequently, it is easy to get a cat's attention with a highly pitched sound. One simply feigns a falsetto voice and the feline drops its act and considers leaping into your mouth. Once you've learned how to command your cat's attention without scare tactics, you can forever abandon the whip-and-chair school of cat training. It doesn't work anyway.

There is no command more important to cat owners than COME WHEN CALLED. There are many reasons for this: it facilitates feeding, grooming, going out and moving the animal from one room to another. In suburban and rural areas cats are often allowed to roam the

The cat is "a soft, indestructible automaton provided by nature to be kicked when things go wrong in the domestic circle."

AMBROSE BIERCE

great outdoors and may be far from sight. When such a cat owner wants to use the car, go to bed, leave the house for any of a number of reasons, it is best to have kitty locked safely inside. In order to do so, however, the owner must be able to call the cat and have it come at the sound of the vocal command. And it is precisely at this time that the owner should not be timid in issuing that command.

In teaching a cat to COME WHEN CALLED, one should first get the cat's attention by calling its name in a falsetto voice. When the cat looks up, make it an offer it can't refuse, such as dinner or a snack you know it adores. Most cats will do anything for brewer's yeast tablets. Tap your fingers playfully on the table surface. Once the cat leaps up, give it the treat and tell it what a terrific cat it is. You may even pet or scratch it on the back. From here on it's Pavlov all the way. It is simply a matter of consistent repetition. You call and the cat will salivate and give the desirable response. And please, dear cat person, do not feel guilty if your cat does not come. Cats do not really "obey" you, anyway. They merely respond to their own needs and desires. As long as your manipulations are applied only to cats and not to humans, there is no reason to saddle yourself with feelings of guilt. One must either assert oneself when living with a feline or accept being ruled by a furry fascist who will walk all over you, especially when you're sound asleep. Assert and the world is yours.

Mordecai Siegal is the co-author of Good Dog, Bad Dog *and* Underdog *and the author of the forthcoming* The Good Dog Book.

A CAT TALKS BACK

ROBERT

As I am now seven years old, I have learned how to cope with humans. I would like to pass the information on, but let me warn you that nothing can be done with a bad owner.

Hopeless are all owners who expect cats to behave like dogs. I emphatically refuse to gush, slobber, rush about noisily, knock things over with uncontrollable tail-wagging, or endure the rough handling of children.

Worse yet are all those owners who think nothing of leaving us alone weekends; those who think we can go forty-eight hours without eating; those who feed us in bowls encrusted with last week's discount tuna; those who whack us away from newspapers when we have just settled down for a long afternoon nap; those who are stingy with kitty litter — waiting until the odor is offensive to *them* before cleaning the pan; and those who bring home insufferable wee toys, bonny cat houses, etc.

Good owners can be controlled if you use the right technique. Here are my tips for training a good owner:

1. *The answer to any human complaint.* Even if you have just destroyed a Ming vase, purr. Usually all will be forgiven.

2. *Waking up owners.* The purpose is to get the owner out of bed, with no reprisals, to feed you or pet you. A close-up technique is the best: select an ear and purr into it continually; or, use the wet nose approach, gently tapping the human's ear, nose or cheek with your nose. This is especially effective with soft-hearted humans; avoid using with violent types.

3. *Establishing a hiding place.* Early on in your relationship with your owner, you must find a good hiding place. This rule is of the utmost importance. Not only can you hide there if purring fails but you can also use the place for private naps and for examining forbidden objects. As you become more adept at handling humans, you will soon learn that an exceptionally long stay in the hiding place often guarantees an additional meal. Humans think food will always do the trick when trying to lure cats; do not let pride hinder you from accepting the food. However, if you feel the prize offered is not good enough, stay hidden.

Above all, remember that you are a cat. Don't let anyone get confused about that.

Robert is the cat who owns Lenny Rubenstein.

CAT LOVERS AND CAT ANTAGONISTS

Rose Spiegel, M.D.

THE RANGE OF emotions towards cats is wider than that toward any other animal — certainly more so than toward the dog. The gamut runs from terror, hatred, loathing, fear and wishing to keep one's distance to friendliness and affection — indeed, even to adoration and worship. Both strange powers of malice and uncanny wisdom have been attributed to the cat. More than the dog, the cat has long been obscured in the culture by images, hostile and adoring.

In my work as a psychoanalyst my colleagues and I have encountered clients who have turned cats into personal symbols. For instance a nineteen-year old woman told me she fantasized that she had become my own cat; if she were my cat she would be able to get the affection and petting that she had never received from her mother. Another woman was jealous of my cat; she felt that when I petted it, the cat was receiving the intimacy she herself longed for and was not getting. In both of these cases the cat was an indicator of a deprivation of love. In one instance the cat became a symbol of rivalry; in the other, identification.

Of course there is no reason to seek a pathological explanation for every person's attitude toward cats. Misinformation, ignorance, common prejudices, the traces of superstition, and the accidents of experience influence people in many ways. Extreme examples are helpful in illuminating the range of human reactions more than for identifying typical human responses. Provided they are not destructive, people are entitled to their own preferences and even their prejudices. Some people have subtle negative feelings towards cats — avoidance and dismissal — without ever indulging in cruel or hostile behavior to them.

There are occasionally people who do release violent impulses on helpless creatures, cats and other animals. This cruelty is part of a pathological tendency, often a murderous rage really directed against a parent, or perhaps a brother or sister, who cannot be fought victoriously. And so the innocent cat becomes the victim. This kind of destructiveness, however, belongs in a discussion of psychopathology or psychotherapy more than it does in a general consideration of how people respond to cats.

There is remarkably little formal, organized information or theory on the psychological relationship between people and animals. Freud sets forth the classic position in his book *Totem and Taboo*. Briefly summarized, Freud interprets fear of a particular animal in terms of the Oedipus complex. The child identifies a certain animal with the father and later comes to openly fear the animal for dreads which the child represses when thinking about his father. Freud's ideas have been modified or reconsidered by other psychoanalysts, but they agree that neurotic fears of animals are deep-rooted and appear in adults as well as among children. My own experience confirms these impressions. One client had a fear of cats, saying that their unpredictability and their sensual movements made her uncomfortable. This reaction was because of her own repressed sexuality, her lack of acceptance of her own sensual aspect.

But many people who do not like cats simply do not know them. Information and an open mind is all that is necessary if they want to reconsider the matter. People who do not like or do not trust cats raise a number of questions which ought to be answered.

They remind me of the jungle predators. I'm afraid a cat will jump on me and scratch me. There is much confusion between domestic cats and large predatory felines — tigers, lions, pumas, etc. There is no basis to the fear that cats will leap on people and attack them as the great felines might; cats do not scratch and fight except defensively, when they are cornered and attacked or when their kittens are threatened.

Cats are too silent for me. I don't like the way they lurk and creep up on you. A cat's penchant for retreat into the darkest recesses of a closet does lend itself to bring interpreted as stealth. The silence of cats has long been involved in their inscrutability, but it has a natural explanation. Unlike dogs, who make a great number of sounds, cats depend much less on vocal expression for communication. They signal with their faces, their ears, their body, and by scratching. If you learn to observe these signs, a cat will not seem half so mysterious.

I don't like the predatory nature of cats, the way they hunt birds. The aspect of the cat's predatory instinct which results in hunting down mice probably was one of the first bases for the symbiotic relationship between man and cats. But the hunting of birds, understandably, arouses our antipathy. We are torn by the problem. We recognize that the biological struggle for existance involves animals killing other animals, but it is still troubling to many people to see an attractive, harmless bird slain by a predator. This existential dilemma has no easy solution. Humanity's ethical struggles with its own hostilities, aggressions and violence lead us to interpret the cat's predatory instinct in terms of human morality. Cats cannot be fairly judged or properly understood if we impose our cultural code on their natural conduct.

I agree with Ogden Nash that, "The trouble with a kitten is that / It grows up to be a cat." Amusing, but adult cats do retain their playfulness throughout their lives. Adult cats manifest distinctly different personalities, ranging from whimsicality (my orange cat) to a kind of common-sense quality (as in my smoke-gray cat).

I find dogs are warm; cats seem cold and aloof. Is this, perhaps, related to the difference in the emotional needs of dog lovers and cat lovers? The cat lover generally can play the cat's game of patience. The dog lover expects and gets a quicker and more obvious response from the dog. The person who sees cats as cold creatures has no idea of the cat's capacity for tenderness to people, to each other, and of course to its kittens. I have seen a cat of mine, usually shy in the presence of people, rolling on his back and doing his best to court a relationship with a hyperactive six-year-old boy. I know of another cat who, when her owner was going through a period of distress and was crying herself to sleep, would gently lick her face; another cat helped his owner through a period of loneliness by snuggling and cuddling. The cat's basic need for the physical presence of the owner gives any lonely person a sense of presence — as well as companionship. And by "presence" I mean something quite subtle, more subtle even than companionship. The cat no less than the owner has a need for the sense of presence. Indeed, this craving may manifest itself by the pet's snuggling into the owner's clothes, particularly when the owner is absent.

In this world, where there are so many needy people, I don't think you should give your love and care to an animal. Love comes in great variety; who has the wisdom to limit the capacity and expression of love? The loving intimacy and communication with a creature outside our own kind opens a wider range of engagement in the world of experience. Love of a cat, of any animal, offers a core of closeness that can balance a life of service to others.

Rose Spiegel is a psychiatrist practicing in New York.

WHY I HATE MY CAT

ROBERTA BECK

1. For getting his white hairs on my black pants and his black hairs on my white pants.

2. For chewing the edges off my best typing paper and, when that is done, for sliding off the mounds of papers as though he were in training for the Winter Olympics.

3. For preferring lamb and liver to fish and chicken.

4. For thinking my garbage is the leftovers of the Garden of Eden.

5. For terrorizing and exploiting my dog Tubby.

6. For knowing my threats are empty ones.

Roberta Beck's cat is a lemon.

TROUBLE

THE PHILLIPS COLLECTION, WASHINGTON

The Arena (1930) by Harold Weston.

T**ALK ABOUT NATURAL** antagonists! The cat is surrounded by them. Scampering, scurrying, quixotic little creatures of many sorts lurk, ready to rush away the minute a cat makes a move. It is no accident the cat has an elegantly choreographed wait-it-out-then-pounce instinct. He needs it, because of the animosity he is up against.

Mice, fish, birds — how they do dart about! And how frustrating it is for the cat. Those little creatures, after all, are the most domestic of animals, really no match when you think about it. Tiny, sweet, nothing in size compared to this galoot. While one slap of the paw should be all that is needed, a fine tensing of every muscle is required instead. So huge is the cat in contrast to the prey he chooses that he must not allow so much as a ripple of fur to be seen. Ssh! Just tuck that front paw in the slightest bit for the jump. Just slowly, ever so slowly, adjust the enormous weight of the body, and . . . now! Too bad. He is

seen. Nothing to do but wait it out and start all over again.

Cats have been drowning in bowls of goldfish, suffering coronaries in pursuit of mice, and catapulting into the air after birds since history began. Shameless, they do not see that they make themselves look silly chasing after the small adorable creatures of the universe. On and on they plunder and blunder. Can it really be victory in the sweetest sense to wrestle to the ground the flicker of a firefly, or, indeed of a television screen? Noble, perhaps, this misplaced passion. Windmill-tilting, certainly. A grand, if odd, notion.

Cats who hold mice/fish/birds at bay could easily be called bullies, even in a dog-eat-dog world. Bullies, that is, save for the fact that it is not a dog-eat-dog world — it is a dog-eat-cat world.

Watch the dog approach, with those horrendous and disgusting barks, those fangs, that tongue. Clearly this is no match for the clumsy, paw-swinging cat who cannot even wipe out a single circling mosquito or a passing pair of feet without a struggle.

Ah, but now the situation is different. How the cat does dart about! Up the tree. Safe in escape if not conquest. And while he waits for rescue from that windy, precarious limb, sweet memories of the time that with a single swat he felled a baby mouse/fish/bird mingle with his longings for dignity.

To look like the cat that swallowed the canary.

YIDDISH SAYING

ANATHEMA OF CATS

JOHN SKELTON

On all the whole nacyon
Of cattes wylde and tame;
God send them sorrow and shame!
That cat especyally
That slew so cruelly
My lytell pretty sparowe.

AESOP'S FABLE: THE CAT AND THE BIRDS

A Cat, hearing that the Birds in a certain aviary were ailing, dressed himself up as a physician, and, taking with him his cane and the instruments becoming his profession, went to the aviary, knocked at the door, and inquired of the inmates how they all did, saying that if they were ill, he would be happy to prescribe for them and cure them. They replied, "We are all very well, and shall continue so, if you will only be good enough to go away, and leave us as we are."

Reprinted from Three Hundred Aesop's Fables *translated by the Rev. George Fyler Townsend. London, 1871.*

Serious combat: a cat and a hawk. Illustration by Harrison Weir in Mrs. Surr's Stories about Cats *(London, 1881).*

ODE

*On the death of a favourite cat
Drowned in a tub of gold fishes*

THOMAS GRAY

'Twas on a lofty vase's side
  Where China's gayest art had dyed
    The azure flowers, that blow;
Demurest of the tabby kind,
The pensive Selima, reclined,
    Gazed on the lake below.

Her conscious tail her joy declared;
The fair round face, the snowy beard,
    The velvet of her paws,
Her coat, that with the tortoise vies,
Her ears of jet, and emerald eyes,
    She saw; and purr'd applause.

Still had she gazed; but 'midst the tide
Two angel forms were seen to glide,
    The genii of the stream:
Their scaly armour's Tyrian hue
Through richest purple to the view
    Betray'd a golden gleam.

The hapless nymph with wonder saw:
A whisker first, and then a claw,
    With many an ardent wish,
She stretch'd, in vain, to reach the prize
What female heart can gold despise?
    What cat's averse to fish?

Presumptuous maid! with looks intent
Again she stretch'd, again she bent,
    Nor knew the gulf between.
(Malignant Fate sat by, and smiled)
The slipp'ry verge her feet beguiled,
    She tumbled headlong in.

Eight times emerging from the flood
She mew'd to ev'ry wat'ry God,
    Some speedy aid to send.
No Dolphin came, no Nereid stirr'd:
Nor cruel Tom, nor Susan heard.
    A fav'rite has no friend!

From hence, ye beauties, undeceived,
Know, one false step is ne'er retrieved,
    And be with caution bold.
Not all that tempts your wand'ring eyes
And heedless hearts is lawful prize.
    Nor all that glitters, gold.

THE PET I.Q. TEST

Kathryn Lichter

Our RESEARCH GROUP was bored with the old cat/dog comparisons — which is the better pet, which is more affectionate, independent, faithful, fun, loving, etc. We decided to get down to business — which one is smarter. The following article is not meant to be a conclusive study of dog/cat intelligence. It is merely a scratch on the surface of a fund of knowledge which can be uncovered only if another sort of fund is made available.

The research group was composed of an inter-disciplinary collection of animal investigators, who, after lengthy study and

research, devised the series of questions to be presented in this article. The two (2) subjects, to whom I would like to express my sincere thanks and gratitude for their patience and cooperation, are Spot (dog) and Puff (cat). They were chosen because of their similarities in age, background and family. Following are descriptions of the two (2) subjects who will herein be referred to as Subject C and Subject D.

Description of Subjects

Subject C (Puff)
Color: black with white markings

Breed: ?
Sex: female
Age: two-and one-half years
Health: excellent

Puff is friendly and outgoing; quite verbal; leads a normal life for a city dweller; adapts quickly to group activities; enjoys plant-munching and furniture-scratching; has a good appetite; was adopted from a local animal shelter at age eight (8) weeks; exact time of birth uncertain, but acts like a Libra.

Subject D (Spot)
Color: black, brown and silver mottled
Breed: ?
Sex: female
Age: three years
Health: good

Spot is also friendly and outgoing; popular among her neighbors; takes three (3) walks a day; likes garbage; occasionally goes for ankles; was adopted from an animal shelter at the age of seven (7) weeks; later moved to New York City; also a Libra.

The Test

The test contains eight (8) questions. Subjects were given the easier tasks first to give them a false feeling of confidence and security at the outset. For each test I will describe the task, give the responses and present a score unbiased by my ownership of Subject D.

Part One: The Food In Bowl Test

We chose two (2) bowls for this test. Bowl #1 contained cat food of a choice variety. Bowl #2 contained dog food of an equally choice variety. The subjects were hungry — both had been fasting for thirty-six hours. (A little hunger to further the interests of science is not cruel.) Each subject was held in the arms of a skilled handler. A whistle was blown and the subjects were placed on the floor in the middle of the room equal distances from the two (2) bowls.

Response: Two minutes and twenty-three seconds (00:02:23) after the whistle was blown Subject D finished the contents of Bowl #2, and was almost finished with Bowl #1. Subject C had just arrived at her bowl.

Score: Subject D has a healthy appetite and is not wasteful; however she is gluttonous — 8 points. Subject C is finicky, wasteful, and slow — 0 points.

Cats know how to obtain food without labor, shelter without confinement, and love without penalties.

W. L. GEORGE

Part Two: Manual Dexterity

The criteria for this particular test were not accurate and therefore we cannot present our findings. Subject C, who tested high in slyness, may have cheated.

Part Three: Maturity

Subjects were taken on a shopping trip to a fashionable New York department store.

Response: Subject D walked beside her handler and sat quietly listening to the animated discussion of skin care at a cosmetics counter. Subject C scratched a floor walker and was removed from the premises.

Score: Subject D behaved like a lady but fell for the sales pitch — 8 points. Subject C was even more finicky with snooty floorwalkers than she was with food, and scored low for damages inflicted upon face and hands — 2 points.

Part Four: Speed

Subjects were placed at the end of a city block. The speed test task was described to them while a handler waited at the other end of the block (the finish line). Subjects were released by their handlers.

Response: Subject D arrived at the finish line in twenty-seven seconds (00:00:27). Subject C never made it. She climbed into an apartment through an open window.

Score: Subject D is fast — 10 points. Subject C is slow, easily distracted and unable to follow instructions — 0 points.

Part Five: Agility

Subject C called in sick (although she did not *sound* sick over the phone) so Subject D won by default — 10 points.

MIN MISSES A MOUSE

HENRY DAVID THOREAU

Min caught a mouse, and was playing with it in the yard. It had got away from her once or twice and she had caught it again, and now it was stealing off again, as she was complacently watching it with her paws tucked under her, when her friend, Riorden, a stout cock, stepped up inquisitively, looked down at the mouse with one eye, turning its head, then picked it up by the tail, gave it two or three whacks on the ground, and giving it a dexterous toss in the air, caught the mouse in its open mouth. It went, head foremost and alive, down Riorden's capacious throat in the twinkling of an eye, never again to be seen in this world; Min all the while, with paws comfortably tucked under her, looking on unconcerned. What did one mouse matter, more or less, to her? The cock walked off amid the currant-bushes, stretched his neck up and gulped once or twice, and the deed was accomplished. Then he crowed lustily in celebration of the exploit. It might be set down among the *Gesta gallorum*. There were several human witnesses. It is a question whether Min ever understood where that mouse went to. She sits composedly sentinel, with paws tucked under her, a good part of her days at present, by some ridiculous little hole, the possible entry of a mouse.

Part Six: Body Recognition

Subjects were shown paw prints which had been taken earlier on a piece of paper during a rest period, and requested to identify their own.

Response: Subject D immediately raised her right paw. Subject C exhibited no response except for boredom expressed by a series of blinks. Subject D — 10 points. Subject C — 0 points.

Part Seven: Reasoning Ability (The Open Window Test)

A window was opened and subjects were placed in front of it.

Response: Subject D retired to the hearth. Subject C leapt out the window and did not return.

Score: Subject D reasoned that what goes out may not come in but she showed no curiosity — 7 points. Subject C did not reason at all, but did show lots of curiosity — 2 points.

Part Eight: Curiosity

We were unable to determine the results of this test because we are still waiting for Subject C to return from the Open Window Test.

Total scores were: Subject D — 53 points; Subject C — 6 points. Paradoxically, Subject D scored 883 percent higher than Subject C, while Subject C scored only 89 percent lower than subject D.

Conclusion

Many questions are raised by these initial findings of the research group. Further investigation may, of course, refine the results given above. Ailurophiles seeking more testing are invited to find the rearch group.

Kathryn Lichter is a professional dog trainer and satirist who lives in Greenwich Village with her dog Spot.

TO A CAT

A.C. SWINBURNE

Stately, kindly, lordly friend
            Condescend
Here to sit by me, and turn
Glorious eyes that smile and burn,
Golden eyes, love's lustrous meed,
On the golden page I read.

All your wondrous wealth of hair
            Dark and fair,
Silken-shaggy, soft and bright
As the clouds and beams of night,
Pays my reverent hand's caress
Back with friendlier gentleness.

Dogs may fawn on all and some
            As they come;
You, a friend of loftier mind,
Answer friends alone in kind.
Just your foot upon my hand
Softly bids it understand.

DOGS ARE NOT PURRFECT

ROBERT STEARNS

It is time to settle the cat *versus* dog question, once and for all. Anyone who has ever known a cat needs no instruction on this matter, but there are a surprising number of people with no idea of the proper distinctions between the species.

A study of English reveals the relative status of dogs and cats. Consider such expressions: "I wouldn't put a dog out on a night like this," "dog-tired," "a hang-dog look" and "in the doghouse." Compare those with: "He's a pussycat," "the cat's meow," "the cat's pajamas." Did anyone ever hear of a sex puppy?

There is a ridiculous idea that dogs are superior to cats because cats cannot be trained. A cat will not jump into a lake and bring back a stick; would you? A cat has a terrific sense of humor, but it sees nothing funny or cute parading in doll's clothes. A dachshund, on the other hand, is delighted to be dressed in little lederhosen and an Alpine sweater. If you want a cat to do something out of the ordinary, you must first convince it that there is a reason for the diversion, that dignity will not be sacrificed and that cooperation is to the cat's advantage. Then, the cat will gladly comply — if it feels like it.

Dogs are the first to recognize the superiority of cats. Their frustration is expressed in belligerence that often spells doom for the dog. No dog can handle a full-grown cat by itself. The cat will run, or course, but only until it decides how to dispose of the dog.

Tuffy, a cat of my acquaintance, used to handle its pursuers by leading them at top speed from broad daylight into my darkened garage. There Tuffy would immediately leap to the window sill and perch while the disoriented dog bounded off to stumble over lawn mowers, garbage cans and, on good days, straight into a brick wall.

When it comes to the advantages of cats *versus* dogs as pets, there is no competition. Try going away for a weekend, leaving your German shepherd alone with a bowl of dry food, some water and a litter box. Watch a cat eat, delicately savoring every bite. Watch a dog wolfing down everything in sight, spilling half of it on the floor. And does your dog use a litter pan?

Among animals, cats are the top-hatted, frock-coated statesmen going about their affairs at their own pace. Dogs are the peasants dutifully plodding behind their leaders. A human may go for a stroll with a cat; he has to walk a dog. The cat leads the way, running ahead, tail high, making sure you understand the arrangement. If you should happen to get ahead, the cat will never allow you to think it is following you. It will stop and clean some hard-to-reach spot, or investigate a suspicious movement in the grass; you will find yourself waiting and fidgeting like the lackey you are. But this is not annoying to cat lovers, who understand and appreciate a good joke, even when it is on them. Sharing a home with a cat, earning its love and respect, is a rewarding experience. Since each of us is blessed with only one life, why not live it with a cat?

Robert Stearns is a magazine writer for The Pittsburgh Press.

AESOP'S FABLE: A DOG AND A CAT

Never were two creatures better together than a dog and a cat brought up in the same house from a whelp and a kitten; so kind, so gamesome and diverting, that it was half the entertainment of the family to see the gambols and love-tricks that passed betwixt them. Only it was observed, that still at meal-times, when scraps fell from the table, or a bone was thrown at them, they would be snarling and spitting at one another under the table like the worst of foes.

Reprinted from Fables of Aesop and Others *by Samuel Croxall. London: A. Millar, 1797.*

A REPLY

W.H. HUDSON

It came about by chance that a pup, a very few days old, was sent to the house by a friend, and that the gift of a kitten, whose surprised blue eyes had not long been opened, was received at nearly the same time... Kittie and pup slept together in one bed, fed from the same saucer and plate, and their whole time when they were not sleeping was spent in play...

When Pussy came of age she had an affair on one of her evening strolls, and later, when her time came near, she all at once became excessively anxious as to the proper place for her expected family. Every room in the house, from basement to attic, was visited in turn and minutely examined. The ladies watched her movements with deep interest without interfering except to open closed doors for her when she returned again and again to reinspect any room which had first attracted her. In due time the kittens came, and a day or two latter Pussy came to the conclusion that they were not in the best room for them after all — that there was a better place in a room on the floor above.

Now the queer part of the business comes in: she did not remove nor, so far as they saw, attempt to remove them herself, but immediately trotted off in search of her friend, the dog, and he, well able from long custom to understand her, got up and followed her to the spot where the kittens were lying. Then, when he had looked at them, she started off to the upper room and he after her; but seeing that he was following empty-handed, so to speak, she doubled back and returned to the kittens, and eventually, after two or three more false starts, he understood her and, picking up one of the kittens in his mouth, followed her up the stairs to the new place. That was as far as his understanding went, and she had again to conduct him back to the others and repeat the whole performance, until in the end the kittens were all removed by the dog and she was happy in her new quarters. But only for a day: it was not the ideal spot after all, and another removal had to be made. Again the dog was summoned and did it all again, with less trouble than on the first occasion. And again Pussy became dissatisfied and there was a third removal, and from first to last there were so many removals that the ladies lost count of their number.

W.H. Hudson is best remembered for his romance Green Mansions.

HOW TO TEACH YOUR CAT TO SHAKE HANDS

Ken Von Der Porten

CATS HAVE ALWAYS been avoided by serious students of animal behavior. Not that cats can not be taught to behave but because they usually behave only in the way they *feel* like behaving — which rarely coincides with anything except their immediate desires. At least, that is the assumption of the uninitiated.

Dogs can be taught to dance, even to walk other dogs. Parakeets, it is said, can sometimes be taught to talk. Cats, on the other hand, have gone throughout history largely keeping their own counsel, watching the performances of those other eager-to-please household pets with no small amount of overt disdain.

Some people feel that this hauteur is the cat's greatest appeal. Cats are aloof, "cool." There are people who seem to be quite annoyed by a cat's apparent lack of affection for those who so obviously love him. "How can he be so insensitive?" owners are heard to complain. Some even interpret such aloofness as a lack of intelligence on the cat's part. They reason that the animal who most successfully ingratiates himself *must* be the smartest of all animals. Let me say right now, and I need not dwell on it if you live with a cat yourself, cats are every bit as smart as most other animals. Now, what you interpret as smart, and what I interpret as smart might not be what a *cat* thinks is smart, and opinion will always vary on this subject.

If cats were not smart, I would not have anything to say about the main topic of this article — how to teach your cat to shake hands with you — but cats are very smart and the techniques I will describe have been used with

Reinforce this behavior to teach your cat to sit up and show off. (The Cat Picture Book, *London, 1880.*)

complete success. My able assistant in this demonstration was my faithful cat Butch.

If you are going to teach your cat to press the flesh, the first thing you must understand is the technique psychologists call "shaping." In other words, if you want your cat to engage in

If you are worthy of its affection, a cat will be your friend but never your slave.

THEOPHILE GAUTIER

some form of new behavior, you have got to reinforce (i.e., strengthen) present behaviors that are similar to the new action. As these similar behaviors are strengthened and dissimilar behaviors are ignored ("extinguished" is the technical term), the cat will gradually start behaving more closely to the way you want.

Now the obvious question that arises is: what can you do to strengthen a cat's behavior? A very simple answer was provided by a famous cat psychologist around the turn of the century. E.L. Thorndike's "Law of Effect" was an early attempt to state a behavioral law as certain as the physical laws that govern physical objects. Simply stated, one part of this law says that actions which lead to pleasure are remembered and become habits.

What gives a cat pleasure? Well, that is a question entirely between you and your cat. For Butch, pleasure is being able to stick his head in a container of dry cat food and eat one of the crunchy little morsels.

The shaping procedure can be used with your hungry cat. Watch for the first faint signs of him lifting a front paw (concentrate on the front paws). When this happy moment finally arrives, immediately present him with his food container or offer him a reward. You might also say, "shake hands" when he begins offering his paw more frequently. In this way, he comes to associate the command with the handshake followed by the food. If, after all this, he's still in the mood to play this new game, simply continue reinforcing closer and closer approximations to

a good, unhesitating handshake. It sounds difficult, but cats are smart. Butch caught right on. After only a few minutes of training each day for about a week he was shaking hands on command. He was apparently quite pleased to have discovered how to work the cabinet door by remote control or to produce a piece of food with a mere flick of his little paw. But remember, unless you want your cat offering his paw to everyone he meets, including complete strangers — behavior quite out of keeping with normal cat stand-offishness — he must be reinforced for handshaking only when he hears the command "shake hands," and discouraged from offering his paw spontaneously.

Although your cat should be rewarded in the beginning whenever he shakes hands, once the response has become well established, it is a good idea to begin rewarding only occasional handshakes. This has the effect of actually making the behavior stronger and more resistant to having the command forgotten. Start by rewarding every second, then every fourth, and ultimately randomly at an average of about one reward for every ten handshakes, In this way you will instill a well-learned habit without having a grocery bill that is skyrocketing due to the whim of your suddenly very outgoing cat.

To those of you who are scandalized by this perversion of the cat's "basic nature," I can only say that the cat has been misunderstood. His cool reputation has been largely due to the *expectations* of his owners. Most people have always just assumed that you couldn't teach a cat anything. Cats accepted the role that society gave them, and the myth has been perpetuated. They have a far wider range of behaviors and more ability to interact with humans than we generally give them credit for, if we would only take the time to explore them.

Ken von der Porten is a graduate student in physiological psychology at the University of New Hampshire. He and his wife Nancy have two cats, Butch and Sybil.

CAT TRIVIA GAME

Ed Goodgold

*Score: 5 points for each correct answer;
0–50, do not tell your cat about your score;
55–65; fair; 70–80, good; 85–100, you have been
spending entirely too much time mastering cat trivia.*

Warm-up Questions

1. Who was the rival of Sylvester the Cat?

2. What kind of cat does Alice meet in "Wonderland"?

3. What kind of eater is Morris supposed to be?

4. Who turned owning a cat into being mayor of London?

5. Complete: *The Gingham Dog and the* _____ *Cat.*

Harder Questions

6. What was the name of the cat cherished by "Our Miss Brooks' " landlady, Mrs. Davis?

7. Who sang "The Ballad of Cat Ballou" in the movie of the same name?

8. What was Felix the Cat's favorite mode of transportation?

9. In *Alice in Wonderland* what is Alice's own cat named?

10. Who starred in "Cat People" and "The Curse of the Cat People"?

11. What is the feline language of the Iberian Peninsula?

12. On "Father Knows Best" what was Cathy Anderson's nickname?

13. Match the cat with his mouse:

Courageous Cat   Jerry
Midnight   Minute Mouse
Tom   Squeaky

14. Where does Krazy Kat live?

15. Who starred as "T.H.E. Cat"?

Real Toughies

16. Who drew Felix the Cat?

17. Ralph _____, creator of Fritz.

18. True or false? Maurice Gosfield was the voice of "Top Cat."

19. Who was "The Big Georgia Cat"?

20. What were the nicknames of pitchers Harry Brecheen and Harvey Haddix?

Ed Goodgold is an author, critic, lecturer, and, therefore, an expert on trivia.

Answers

20. The Cat and The Kitten.

19. Johnny Mize.

18. False, he was the voice of Benny.

17. Bakshi.

16. Pat Sullivan.

15. Robert Loggia.

14. Coconino County.

13. Courageous Cat — Minute Mouse, Midnight — Squeaky, Tom — Jerry.

12. Kitten.

11. Catalan.

10. Simone Simon.

9. Dinah.

8. flying carpet.

7. Stubby Kaye and Nat King Cole.

6. Minerva.

5. Calico.

4. Dick Whittington.

3. finicky.

2. Cheshire.

1. Tweety Pie.

GLAMOUR PUSS

There she (or maybe he) is, your ideal, Ms. Cat-America. Every year, Glamour Kitty® kitty litter holds a beauty contest at the Fontainebleau Hotel in Miami Beach, Florida, to select the glamour cat of the year. Entries need have no pedigree. They need not even be female. A quality photo is all that is necessary to become one of the nine finalists.

But don't think this is just a search for a beautiful body. Cat skills — such as fence leaping and maze escaping — are tested, too. Every catestant is interviewed by Chuck Zinc, emcee of the Miss Universe Pageant. (Mr. Zinc would not tell us which contest produces the more intelligent responses to his questions.)

At last comes the moment of supreme tension. The winner is crowned amidst tears of joy and sighs of disappointment. Cameras click. The winner parades down Glamour Ramp and the world is told the news. The 1975 winner was Casper.

HOW TO LIVE SANELY WITH 12 CATS

David Love

RECOGNIZING INDIVIDUALS among a dozen cats may sound like a real problem. Not so. For one thing, we love them, and therefore we want to be able to tell them apart. For another, a particular cat is sometimes easier to identify than a particular human being because a cat always wear the same coat. Find a human being who does that! So the field is immediately narrowed to recognizing a particular cat as, for instance, one of our five black ones.

After a few days, even doubting house guests learn to tell our five black cats apart. One is cross-eyed and crabby; another has a weight problem and sings beautifully; still another has a profile like a banana. Sounds also help to identify which is which. One says "Ngak"; another purrs very, very fast, and we even have one that meows like a proper cat. The feel of a cat helps too. In the middle of the night, our cat with a chopped-off tail is easily distinguishable from our inverted cat who always wants his stomach rubbed.

Taste and smell we leave to the cats. They are better at such differentation anyway.

Naming

If given time, a cat will name itself. We have prematurely named a newcomer, only to have it correct us later. For example, Mouse began life as Fat Minnie. Eventually, she slimmed down and took to bringing us mice or leftover mouse parts in the middle of the night. If you are rigid about names and cannot stand to change your cat's name, the cat won't mind.

Equipment

Our major fixtures for keeping cats are standard, but plentiful.

1. *Litter trays* — seven, placed strategically on the three floors of our home.
2. *Water Bowls* — four and lots of refills all day long.
3. *Accident Traps* — for cats with emotional problems or political statements to make who can't or won't use the litter trays. We deliberately stake out mothballs or those little deodorizers for toilet bowls in favorite target areas; the "deodorizers" smell awful but are better than the alternative.
4. *Food* — cases of canned food and bags of dry — lots of it.
5. *Litter* — We got a great deal on 1,000 lbs. of litter. So at least we are set for a while.

Feeding Time

This is difficult. The performance resembles a dozen sharks attacking a dead whale. Each cat has a bowl and a place, but all crowd into the kitchen to help, offer comments, complain or obstruct during food-dispensing time. A handful of dry food thrown in the right corner can save your sanity.

Toys

Single items are not enough to keep a family of cats happy. Scratching posts are a necessity. We have four. A flower pot of catnip growing on the porch is the family cat community narcotic source. Some sniff, some nibble, and some sit in it.

Cardboard boxes are placed in a row along one kitchen wall — a full ward of cat beds. Size of the box bears no relationship to the occupant; and they do switch off occasionally and sleep in each other's beds.

Society

Although the cats have long lived together under the same

roof, all is not sweetness and
light. They take fiendish
delight in scaring and chasing
each other. The tormentor and
the pursued change regularly.
These disagreements do not
seem serious, but more on the
order of cheap thrills.

Part Time Cats

We have several of these. As far
as we can tell, these visitors do
not have other homes, but split
their time between us and the
wooded hillside near by. We
treat them as our own when

they are with us. When they are
elsewhere, we assume they are
showing us what all cats seem
best able to do: live their lives
on their own terms.

*David Love, an organized scientist,
lives in Berkeley, California.*

EAST COAST CATS VS. WEST COAST CATS

Richard Smith

MANY PEOPLE BELIEVE that the West Coast cat can be distinguished from the East Coast cat only by a darker tan and whiter teeth. New evidence, however, indicates that with the exception of a mutual love for shiny things and string, major differences do exist.

The eminent cat psychiatrist, Milton Tuba, noted that an East Coast cat, when parachuted from a plane over Los Angeles suffered a severe personality disorder upon discovering no candy stores open past 10 p.m.

Another cat specialist, Martin Soup, explains the difference between East and West Coast cats by suggesting that most of the cats who venture out West do so to become movie stars. Unfortunately, they seldom make it and end up as alley cats, car hops, or porno movie queens. Selected excerpts from Soup's latest research efforts follow.

Psychological: Because they are constantly pressured to be neat and well-adjusted, East Coast cats suffer migraines and are more prone to neurotic behavior. Tuba backs this finding in his recent book, "Hideous Delusions of Kitty Cats," citing an instance in which a docile, well-behaved cat, after being reproached for dripping milk from its whiskers on to the carpet, suffered an identity crisis, attempted to bark and begged his owner to call him Lassie. West Coast cats enjoy better mental health, possibly due to their freer lifestyle and a plentitude of good, cheap wine. West Coast cats may experience slight anxiety attacks, but they dispel them easily by cracking their paws and taking tranquilizers.

West Coast cat

East Coast cat.

JACQUELINE KONTAK

JACQUELINE KONTAK

Relationships: West Coast cats maintain that a meaningful, caring, sharing relationship is less important than meeting a cat with a good body. East Coast cats have a healthier attitude; they select their partners on the basis of a good personality, similar interests and the sound principles of astrology.

Feeding: West Coast cats are far more adventurous in their eating habits and welcome new foods such as yogurt, chicken-flavored soda with plenty of fizz, or small pieces of linoleum, especially during an earthquake. A West Coast cat can easily switch from canned cat food to sushi just as long as it is served in a hand-thrown pottery bowl. East Coast cats are less eclectic, preferring your basic candlelight dinner of a saucer of milk and a bird.

Personal habits: Only on the West Coast do cats insist on macrobiotic kitty litter.

Personality: Although West Coast cats appear easy-going and fun-loving, statistics indicate they have a higher suicide rate, perhaps caused by watching too much television, or by their owners' excessive kissing habits. East Coast cats are more serious and believe in God. They are also snobs — New York City cats generally refuse to enter Gucci's unless someone holds the door open.

Appearance: East Coast cats are less concerned about looks, preferring instead to be valued for their minds rather than their bodies. West Coast cats do not mind being regarded as sex objects; many even tease their fur and use deodorants.

As pets: West Coast cats are far more entertaining than their East Coast counterparts. In California it is common to see a Siamese cat walk on its hind legs, roll over, play dead and perform simple card tricks. West Coast cats are also more assertive. Indeed, after a weekend of *est* and Rolfing, one cat made her owner move to an apartment with a terrace. East Coast cats are content to be cats, and tricks such as walking on hind legs and rolling over are usually performed only by their owners. East Coast cats are extremely loyal, and newspapers are constantly filled with stories of faithful cats who drag their owners from burning buildings.

Cat owners: On both coasts they are generally taller than their cats.

Richard Smith is an East Coast humorist who does not even own a cat.

RELATIONSHIPS

ESTHER COHEN

Felix was all bones. A thin, black and white stray, he moved in with me when I was a junior. We were compatible. He liked to jump. He was always hungry, but ate a peculiar, health-oriented diet. He had one friend, a pleasant female named Naimah. She died the middle of my junior year. She was on the floor one morning, smiling in her sleep. Not breathing. My friend Susan buried her with a shovel, in back of our building, before I got up. Felix ran in circles looking for Naimah. He called out to her. I didn't want to tell him. And I knew he would know.

When Naimah disappeared, Felix became restless. He spent a large number of his days on the streets. Felix would leave me alone, for my own familiar search. But he'd find me in the end. I was never the one to find him. I'd think that he'd disappeared forever.

I mourned for him before he was gone.

Ours was a nonverbal relationship. We didn't have much need for recounting, rehashing. Pre-analysis, we lived in a world of spontaneous action.

Sometimes there would be problems. He'd leave for the night, soundless. I'd think he was coming back momentarily. All night. I'd imagine him wandering to Seven-Eleven, a block away. He liked it there. He had friends who spent their nights around the store. At eleven-thirty, when the store shut down, I'd start to worry. Felix, Felix. I'd phone friends and ask if they'd seen him. They inevitably had not. A day or two later, he'd slip next to me on the couch with an ease I never understood too well. I knew I wouldn't question him.

We left each other in June, 1969.

Esther Cohen is a writer in New York City.

THE EDUCATION OF A CAT DOCTOR

Joseph F. Skelley, D.V.M.

FOR THE PAST several years, an ever-increasing number of young men and women have been preparing for careers in veterinary medicine. Veterinary schools throughout the United States are being overwhelmed with applications for admission. Applicants across the country have approximately a 10 percent chance of being accepted to an entering class. Because most schools reserve seats for state residents or residents of states with which contractual relationships have been established, out-of-staters face even longer odds. Admissions committees are compelled to turn away a far greater number of highly qualified applicants than they are able to accept, simply for lack of available space.

There are only twenty veterinary schools in the country today. Several states are in various stages of developing veterinary schools, but the financial resources for facilities and faculty acquisition are not easily obtained. Existing schools have expanded their class size to the fullest possible extent, and further major expansion is unlikely at this time. The existing veterinary schools are concentrating most of their efforts and financial resources on meeting obligations for current operations.

What does the average applicant do when he is not accepted at a veterinary school? In most cases, he may be reluctant to consider an alternate career. Rather, he will strive to improve his credentials by taking additional courses or by accumulating further work experience with veterinarians before applying again. Because of the growing number seeking admission, it is not unusual for an applicant to apply several times before being accepted, but many qualified and dedicated young people will probably never achieve their primary career goal.

Realistically, it is absolutely essential that prospective applicants to veterinary school examine possible alternate careers. Those who are unable to gain admission to veterinary school or who do not wish to spend the necessary six to eight years in study may find fulfilling careers in such veterinary-related fields as animal technology or husbandry, wildlife or marine biology, teaching or research. Recently, a number of colleges have developed two- and four-year veterinary technician programs that prepare their graduates to assist veterinarians in a wide variety of activities. The emergence of the veterinary paramedic opens many new avenues of opportunity for those oriented toward animal medicine.

Admissions requirements of veterinary schools vary, and those who plan a career in veterinary medicine are strongly urged to contact the admissions office of those schools to which they expect to apply in order to obtain specific information. In general, most schools require at least two to three years of college training in a variety of biology, chemistry, physics and math

---

ANIMAL-RELATED CAREERS

Animal psychologist	Breeder
Trainer	Shelter worker
Handler	Boarder
Sitter	Lab researcher
Groomer	Zoo worker
Vet's assistant	Fund raiser
Boutique worker	Cat show organizer

courses, as well as certain nonscience courses. Though not the only requirement, academic excellence is a must for the successful applicant. Many schools require work experience with veterinarians and animals, and some require farm experience. Admissions groups are looking for individuals who are enthusiastic, dedicated and strongly motivated toward a career in veterinary medicine. Personal interviews often play an important role in evaluating qualified candidates for admission.

As with all education, the costs of veterinary medical education have skyrocketed. Costs will vary, however, depending on whether the veterinary school is a state or privately operated school. Scholarships and a wide variety of loan programs are available and, in general, are used extensively by veterinary students.

Once admitted, the qualified student should have little difficulty completing the required four-year course of study in a veterinary school. Attrition rates are very low, and rarely must a student withdraw because of academic deficiency. The graduate is awarded a degree of Doctor of Veterinary Medicine. A wide variety of opportunities is available to the new veterinarian in areas such as private practice, teaching, research, public health and regulatory medicine, military and government service, and private industry. In general, the new veterinarian will earn approximately $12,000 to $15,000 during his first year after graduation. Income can vary according to activities and responsibilities assumed.

There are approximately 29,000 veterinarians in the United States today, and it is estimated by a National Academy of Sciences committee that 42,000 will be required by 1980. Today's veterinarian is becoming increasingly involved in widely diversified areas of health services.

For many years, veterinary medicine was not considered an appropriate career for women. However, this fallacy has been eliminated, and women applicants comprise a substantial segment of most veterinary schools' applicant pools. Currently, approximately 25–40 percent of the entering students in our country's veterinary schools are women.

The curricula of veterinary schools have undergone major changes in the last two decades. As a result of the tremendous growth of knowledge in the field, many veterinary schools have developed in-depth specialties dealing with particular species as well as disciplines such as veterinary pathology and neurology. Students can take elective courses permitting exposure to their areas of special interest. Veterinary medicine may now be regarded as a personalized or customized course of study geared to the individual student's needs and interests in preparing for his or her career in veterinary medicine.

Joseph F. Skelley is the Associate Dean for Admissions at the University of Pennsylvania School of Veterinary Medicine.

SIAMESE COLORING

The elegant coloring of Siamese cats is due to a genetic freak. The pale coat and darker points are a modified form of albinism. Albino animals are unable to synthesize melanin, the pigment that controls all coloring of hair, skin and eyes. The Siamese coloring pattern is governed by the "Himalayan" gene, which is found at the same location on the chromosome as the albino gene. Himalayan animals are able to synthesize melanin only at comparatively low body temperatures. The animal's torso and upper legs are maintained at a higher temperature than the extremities — tail, paws, ears, nose. Melanin can therefore by synthesized in these outer locations but not on the main surfaces of the body. Hence, only those areas are dark-colored.

The blue eyes of the Siamese result from a low distribution of melanin in the iris. Similarly, the eyes of Siamese reflect red rather than green in the dark because of lack of pigmentation behind the retina.

The "Himalayan gene," like the albino gene, is associated with serious abnormalities of vision. Siamese do not have the incapacitating problems of true albinos, but they are well known to be cross-eyed.

THE EDUCATION OF A CAT SITTER

Mary Hoe Love

WHEN YOU SHARE a home with twelve cats to begin with, there is no more perfect or satisfying career than running a cat-sitting agency. Find a partner with her own fifteen cats at home — someone else intensely devoted to animal welfare — and you are in business.

Our goal was to provide cat-sitting care through frequent, regular visits into the cat's own home. While dogs need constant attention when their owners are away and can thrive in a kennel, cats are more vulnerable to change and should be cared for in their own home where they are secure in their routine and safe from the health hazards of an institutional setting.

Through caring for our own brood at home, we knew many veterinarians in our area; when we first opened the cat-sitting agency, we had a head start making contacts. We had business cards printed with our names, phone numbers and services, and we distributed them to all the local veterinary hospitals with the request that they refer all boarding inquiries to us. Few hospitals or veterinarians, in our area, had facilities to board healthy cats.

We tried to get liability insurance but decided against it when the costs proved exhorbitant. Instead, for credibility, we used our veterinarian friends for references.

A standard contract, to be signed in duplicate by both the cat-sitter and the client, with a copy for each party, is essential. Our contract spells out in detail: the names of the owner and the cat; addresses where the owner can be reached; dates the client will be away; emergency phone numbers; the past record and and present condition of the cat's health; explicit instructions for the care and feeding of their pets. It also outlines exactly how much we are to be paid based on the time the owner will be away and allows for trips to the vet and additional food or supplies, which must be bought at the owner's expense. Naturally, all our transportation fees are paid by the client. If the owner does not return as scheduled, we state that we will continue to care for the cat, or cats, and be paid at the same rate until the time the owner actually returns. We have learned through experience that flat tires, accidents, snowstorms and other unforeseen disasters can substantially delay a client's return home.

Our day-to-day responsibilities as cat-sitters are simple, though all are important. We come to the client's home once or twice a day, depending on our instructions or the animal's needs. On each visit, we feed the cat from a freshly cleaned food dish, provide a fresh supply of water, clean out or change the litter in the cat pan and administer any medication, grooming or special attention the individual cat requires. We also take the time to socialize, giving the cat a few valuable moments for play and affection.

Additional services we have provided for clients in our cat-sitting business are watering plants; feeding aquarium fish; taking in mail; turning lights on or off; pulling drapes and opening windows as per instructions. But our main concern is the welfare of the cats. The animals we care for get the best possible attention while their owners are away. All it takes is time, love and gas mileage!

Mary Hoe Love lives with twelve cats in Berkeley, California.

HOW TO TRAIN YOUR CAT

Kathleen Cruzic

IS YOUR CAT guilty of such naughty feline behavior as scratching the furniture, climbing on the dining table, or snuggling down in a forbidden arm chair?

Training is the best answer and the earlier you begin, the easier the job. If you have a new kitten, begin teaching him proper behavior immediately. If you have acquired an older cat, do not despair. He may respond more slowly and require more patience, but he can learn.

In a kitten some misbehavior may be due to uncertainty or confusion. For example, the mother cat may have taught her baby to use the litter tray but sometimes he'll make a mistake. When he does, put him in his tray, and encourage him to watch you dig or take his paw and go through the motions of digging a hole. The tray should always be kept in the same place. Put it in a secluded spot where children or other family members are not apt to interfere or frighten the kitten away from the tray. If your cat becomes bewildered and chooses the wrong spot, pick him up, dump him into his tray and scold, "Sammy, no, no!" Actually, words count less when correcting your pet than the tone of voice. Praise the kitten when he has used the tray. The fundamental lesson will be learned quickly if you do your part in watching the pupil so as to correct each mistake as it occurs. Because many cats hate any loud sudden noise, a week or two of vigilance and loud hand clapping at the opportune moment is often enough to teach a kitten that food-laden tables, refrigerators and stoves are forever forbidden territory.

Another effective way to correct a kitten is to slap a newspaper on the floor as if you are really angry. He will soon learn he has displeased you. Always speak in an authoritative tone of voice so your cat knows you mean what you say.

Coypel's engraving appeared in Moncrif's Les Chats *(Paris, 1727), one of the earliest books about cats.*

A kitten soon learns to avoid such undesirable behavior as leaping on tables, clawing draperies and all the things most kittens become addicted to, unless taught otherwise.

Much misbehavior springs from a cat's desire to play. He may be bored and so looks for something to do. Be sure to provide your cat with sufficient diversions of his own. Continued correction will not result in a "perfectly behaved" cat if you fail to provide permissible amusements.

It is only fair for you to recognize that there are certain cat instincts which must be obeyed. For instance, claws have to be sharpened. For a house-bound cat you should provide a scratching post. Usually, an upright post that is carpeted and set on a firm base is most acceptable. However, some cats will be content with a flat log type. A kitten may be trained to use the carpet-covered post by picking him up every time he claws the rug and placing him in front of the post. At first, you may have to take his paw and show him how to scratch on it. Sometimes, putting catnip on or under the carpeting will help attract the cat to the scratching post.

Clawing drapes, furniture and carpets is behavior that is difficult to control in some cats, even with training. With a persistent clawer, or an older cat that was not properly trained as a kitten, the tips of the claws can be trimmed with nail clippers. Trim only the claws on the front feet, leaving the back paws untouched. This leaves the cat able to defend himself or to climb a tree out of harm's way.

Older cats can be trained, provided they understand and approve of what you want them to do. They hate to be scolded or punished. A stern reprimand like a sharp "ah-ah!" or "bad!" will help them learn. If this is not enough, a fold of newspaper, rolled up and taped at the ends and cracked like a switch on the floor beside them — as compared to the simple fold slapped on the floor for a kitten — will reinforce discipline.

Remember, though, when a chair or sofa is placed off-limits, it must stay that way. You cannot expect to break the rules one time and enforce them the next. Confusion never trained a cat, but it has given them nervous breakdowns.

Some cats are not frightened by noise but are so gentle and sensitive they can not stand even the gentlest form of physical rebuke. One cat owner tells about the first time he caught his Siamese cat, Samantha, on the kitchen table daintily scooping up his scrambled eggs. He picked her up, slapped her very softly twice across the flank and pushed her outdoors. She did not come back for several hours, but never again did she violate the rules of the kitchen.

Some cats do not respond as easily to punishment as correction for misdeeds as do others. Whenever you get a new cat you will have to determine what method is best for that particular cat. Try a sharp "no!" when you find your cat doing something undesirable. If harsh words and praise are not sufficient, you may have to use other means of correction. A squirt from a toy water gun or spray bottle will often work better than more direct punishment. When your cat chews on your plants, gets into the fireplace, climbs on the draperies or does something equally irritating in his explorations, squirt him with water. A few confrontations with the efficiency of the water pistol will usually produce longlasting results in showing your cat what he is *not* to do.

Even the experts, however, have occasional failures, so do not be easily discouraged. One veterinarian tells of his cat who would jump on the table whenever his back was turned, and swipe chicken, chops or steak so fast that by the time he realized what was happening and made a grab for the culprit, he was just in time to see his disappearing tail. All attempts to break him from snitching food from table, counter-top or stove were unsuccessful. He concluded, "he's just a plain hungry cat who was born that way."

Kathleen Cruzic lives in San Jose with two cats, one of whom is well trained.

BEWARE OF CAT TOYS

Many commercial cat toys are good, but be sure to inspect them before assuming they are safe. All toys should be too big to swallow and should be sturdy enough to prevent them from being torn apart and eaten. Avoid string, thread and yarn, if your cat chews on them. Cats often swallow these materials and this can cause serious gastrointestinal problems.

A patch of fresh catnip, catnip toys, paper bags, empty thread spools, stuffed socks and large knuckle bones that can be chewed on but not splintered or swallowed are good inexpensive toys your cat can enjoy. (See Cat Product Review for more information on cat toys.)

CATS AND YARN

WE WERE WONDERING one morning why today one seldom sees pictures of cats entangled in yarn, a motif we remembered.

We pondered and theorized. What could explain the fading image of the cat and its passion for yarn? Were workbaskets containing those balls of yarn not so prevalent any longer? Had leisure and mass-produced manufactured clothing brought us to this point? We phoned a yarn manufacturer to ask what was up.

"People knit and spin and weave these days because they want to, for the satisfaction of it," said the spokesman for the Spinnerin Yarn Co. in New York. "But not because they have to?" we asked. "That's right," she answered, explaining that pride in craftsmanship is what Spinnerin likes to stress in their current advertising. Gone is any implication that it is necessary for women to stay at home, knitting by the fire. *And* — we doped it out with the Spinnerin spokesman — gone is the long-popular depiction of the kitten caught in yarn — symbol of that homey scene which for many women now proves confining.

So, we noted, the former association of cats and tangled yarn is fading. But what of the yarn and thread? If persons are nevertheless displaying proudly the garments and home decorations they have made, there must still be yarn and thread around the house, even

SUSUKI HARUNOBU, GIRL WITH CAT (1766–1770), THE NEWARK MUSEUM.

if they are not as they once were near the hearth.

And what about needles? That subject rose when we got Dr. Jay Luger on the phone. He is a veterinarian at the Forest Hills, New York Cat Hospital. Our investigation took a turn as we talked.

"I'm sorry," Dr. Luger said, "I know you're after a light-hearted article, but the fact is that this yarn business is a very serious issue. In the last four or five months, I must have removed needles or wads of yarn from as many cats. Surgery was often involved. I wish people who are letting their cats play with yarn would supervise them. And I wish they would put the yarn away as soon as the cat loses interest. Just yesterday I took a completely threaded needle out of a cat's throat. Cats, by instinct, try to swallow the yarn they play with." His voice sounded emphatic.

Often a cat owner does not know what is troubling his cat, and takes him to the doctor simply because he is listless, not eating, perhaps coughing a bit. It is then that string, thread, or yarn may be discovered. Sometimes it is bunched up in the intestine. Sometimes it is anchored at the base of the tongue, with a strand pulling from the stomach. When a needle has been ingested, it may be discovered anywhere in the digestive system. If it has already passed through, it may even have perforated the rectum.

"Why do cats chase yarn?" we asked Dr. Luger. "It is just their natural curiosity about anything that moves," he said. "A ball of yarn rolls across the floor and the cat is after it. It is not the color of the yarn that attracts him; cats don't see colors. It's the fact that it's moving. Cats like to explore anything that is different in their environment, and when a ball of yarn moves they will go for it. That's play behavior for them." "Do they think they are attacking the yarn?" we wanted to know. "Yes," replied Dr. Luger. "For cats, attacking is part of play behavior."

We thanked Dr. Luger for his time — he was being called from the phone on hospital business — and we hung up. It had been an edifying morning.

Over lunch, we found ourselves wishing hobbyists, needle-pointers, and other crafts persons would be careful with their tools. We wondered if the old-time knitters-by-the-fire had been careful, remembering to put out of reach when play was through those balls of yarn and spools of thread in which their cats frolicked so prettily.

Late nineteenth century American primitive scene

THE ELASTICIZED CAT

Linda Abrams

Feeling good, I decided to wear my secondhand silk dress to work — the one with the beautiful long sash. When I went to tie it, the sash was gone. It was not torn or cut, just gone, like it had been eaten. Henry sat calmly on the couch and threw me one of those innocent kitten-eyed glances of his.

I took the dress back to the shop where I bought it, and they told me they would have to remake the sash.

I came home and yelled at Henry. He was sitting on the floor, not looking quite so innocent. In fact, he did not look well. He tried to jump onto the couch and missed — strange, since the couch was only a few inches from the floor. He would not eat and he ignored me. Whatever was wrong, it was my fault. I knew Henry liked to eat stringlike things and had tempted him with a long-flowing sash, so much more interesting than thread or yarn. Henry had a refined taste in strings; he liked silk, satin and nylon underwear — shimmering see-through brassieres in particular.

Especially, Henry liked elastic. No doubt about it. He once even ate the straps off my brand-new John Kloss nightgown, a wedding present. And once, after a friend visiting from Tunisia had bought bagfuls of new silky lingerie, we found Henry sitting in her suitcase enjoying a snack of spaghetti straps. Henry's fondness was costing me a fortune in lingerie and veterinary bills. Only six months earlier, doctors had pulled nine inches of brassiere out of Henry's stomach; he was in the hospital for two days recovering. And now my silk sash was missing.

Henry continued to mope around the apartment, never even bothering to jump onto a chair. He was lethargic — a sure sign something was wrong, because Henry was normally fourteen pounds of active feline. It was decidedly out of character for my two-year-old tabby to confine himself to the floor.

So Henry and I made another visit to the vet. They put him on a steel table and took his temperature. It was up. He was kept overnight for observation. They took X-rays. They gave him barium at 4 P.M., and by 6 P.M. everything that could pass through him should have passed, but the X-rays showed a large clump of something still in the stomach. Diagnosis: a foreign body that would have to be removed surgically.

The next morning, Henry went under the knife. They gave him ether, shaved the white fur on his belly, slit open his stomach and removed six inches of antique-green silk sash. He stayed in the hospital for three days.

Poor Henry had big railroad-track stitches on his bald belly. I took him to the country to rest and stopped wearing a bra for the summer. I made sure there were no dangling dress sashes in the closet to entice him, because, the vet said, cats do not learn. He would do it all over again if he had the chance. Worse, once he takes a nibble on anything stringlike he has no choice. Cats, I was told, have tiny little spituals on their tongues that let things pass in only one way — backward — and once the string is on the tongue the cat cannot bring it out again. The string can only go further back into the throat.

Our vet told me he had pulled yards of string, sewing thread and needles out of cats. At Christmas-time, he pulls out tinsel. But never before had he pulled out shimmering elastic bras and silk sashes.

Linda Abrams is a magazine, newspaper and television reporter. Her cat misbehaves.

CALICO CAT

Carolyn Ambuter

Instructions for making the needlepoint Calico Cat are:

Canvas: 10-mesh mono.
Yarn: 3-Ply Persian.
Colors: Many odd colors from leftover yarns are suitable. A simple color pattern is also appealing. I used the following Persian colors: A, #574, green; B, #650, lavender; C, #446, yellow; D, #860, pink; E, #365, dark blue; F, #395, and G, #396, light blue; H, #843, coral red; I, #G54, green; J, #441, and K, #442, yellow; L, #365, M, #334, and N, #330, blends of dark blues.

Stitches: The canvas can be worked entirely in Tent (Diagonal) or in a combination of stitches. I used: vertical rows, Reversed Tent; flower centers and poppy heads (H) in background, Mosaic; J and K tulips, Continuous Mosaic; Straight Gobelin worked horizontally over 2 rows of Tent stitches; rest of canvas, Tent.

Carolyn Ambuter wrote The Complete Book of Needlepoint, *which provides a pattern for the Gingham Dog, and* Needlepoint Celebrations.

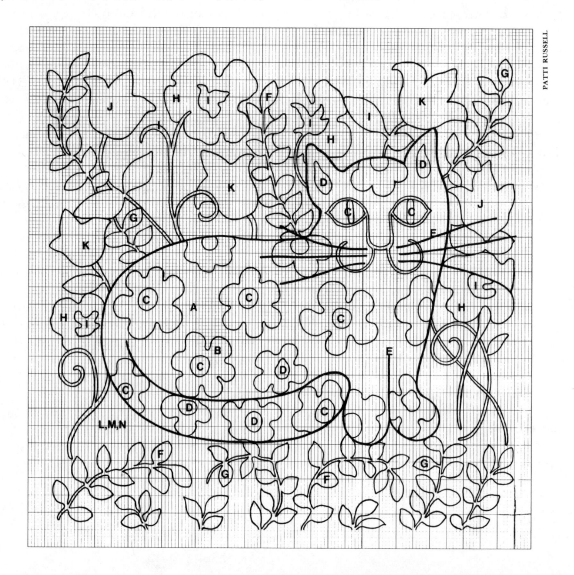

PATTI RUSSELL

HOW TO TRAVEL WITH YOUR CAT

ALICE SU

IF YOU ARE traveling with a cat, or plan to ship one, there are a few general rules to keep in mind. Tag the cat and its box with the cat's name, the owner's name and home address, and the destination.

Stop feeding the cat eight hours before the trip; stop giving water two hours beforehand.

If the trip will take longer than twenty-four hours, make arrangements in your schedule for exercising, watering and feeding. With car and airplane travel, meals are best at the end of the day, to give time for digestion before the journey resumes.

There are also special considerations for each form of travel.

By car

Since many cats are disoriented by motion, owners whose cats will travel in cars throughout their lives (on trips to the vet, trips to cat shows, vacations, etc.) should become used to car travel from a young age. Experts suggest frequent short rides as a way to get used to the car. Tranquilizers to alleviate nausea or any anxieties the cat may have can be prescribed by the vet, but some cats do not react well to such medication and become even more excitable than they would without it.

In the car, it is advisable to keep the cat in a ventilated container — one that is large enough

to allow both standing up and lying down, but one that is small enough to provide a feeling of security. There is no need to furnish water or food; cats can go twenty-four hours without water, and longer without food.

One warning: much long car travel is done in the summer, during hot weather. *If you get out of the car, do not leave the cat locked inside without ample ventilation.* The temperature in a sealed car quickly rises to 20 or 30 degrees above the temperature outside. Beyond the discomfort is the danger of brain damage, which for cats can occur at temperatures of 115°F. and above.

By plane

Call ahead of time, about two weeks beforehand if you can. Each airline has its own requirements, and you will need to know what is particular to the carrier you have chosen. Many companies demand a health certificate and/or record of immunizations from a certified vet.

In addition, you may have to prepare for the special entry regulations for cats in foreign countries (check the consulates) and even in some states. (Hawaii requires a 120-day quarantine, paid in advance; cats must arrive at the airport in Honolulu.)

Some airlines will allow you to take the cat into the passenger area, but only in a case or cardboard carton (sometimes but not always provided free of charge). The cat must stay in its box during the trip. Animals are never considered free baggage on airlines and may be accepted as checked baggage only when the owner is on the same flight (the current cost for this checked-baggage status is around $15). Unaccompanied cats have to be sent as air freight.

By train

Amtrak does not allow a cat to travel without a passenger. Even then, the cat must stay in the baggage compartment — in a well-ventilated box *supplied by the owner.* The minimum charge is currently $3, with the actual total dependent upon the weight of the cat. Call your local Amtrak information office for particulars.

By bus

Neither Greyhound nor Trailways accepts cats. A few regional bus lines do allow cat passengers to travel with you in a "suitable container."

By ship

Arrangements vary. Usually, cats will be accepted if they are kept in a special shipboard kennel area, where they may be visited by their owners. There is an extra charge for taking animals along — often so high that many travelers prefer to leave their cats at home.

Leaving the cat behind

Many cities have special "hotels" where cats can be boarded. Check the Yellow Pages. There are also kennels, friends and relatives who can take in pets. A cat may prefer these alternatives to enduring the rigors of travel. Cat-sitting services are also available.

Cats can take care of themselves if left alone for a weekend. A clean litter pan, a full water bowl and a big dish of food serve perfectly well. Don't worry about your cat — it sleeps about eighteen hours a day anyway, and can occupy itself with eating, running around and staring out the window during waking hours.

XIII.
THE LEGAL CAT

DENNIS CORRIGAN

CAT LAW

Burton Tauber

"If the law supposes that," said Mr. Bumble . . . "the law is a ass, a idiot."

— Charles Dickens, *Oliver Twist*

CATS DO NOT HAVE THE RIGHT TO VOTE, but legislators still have claimed the power to regulate their activities. For example, cats in Idaho are prohibited from joining in a fight between two dogs.

In Dallas, Texas, any cat running in the street after sundown must wear a headlight.

In Lemonine, Montana, the law declares that cats must wear three bells to warn birds of their approach.

In Morrisburg, Louisiana, cats that chase a duck down a city street are in violation of the law.

In Natchez, Mississippi, the law goes to the heart of the problem. Spotting the only reason why a cat would get between two fighting dogs, chase a duck, or go out in the dark without a flashlight, the law simply prohibits cats from drinking any beer whatsoever.

Ancient Law

In earlier times, when the ways of nature and nature's creatures were assumed to be beyond human reach, laws were concerned with encouraging humans to be on guard against problems caused by the presence of cats. The Talmud, for example, enjoins people from going barefoot in a house where there is a cat. This law was a response to the problem that arises when cats kill and eat snakes in houses. The satisfied cat tends to leave snake bones scattered on the floor, where they can hurt people who walk around without shoes. In the modern world of brooms and vacuum cleaners, the danger is much less severe than it was in ancient days.

Among the lawyers of long ago there was a strong appreciation of the cat's utilitarian values. Stepping on snake bones is far better than stepping on a snake, and the Talmudic commentaries speak of laws which forbid people to enter a darkened house that does not contain a cat. The risk of having a snake wind itself about your leg was too strong for wise legislators to ignore.

The ancient Britons felt that the hunting powers of the cat made it a creature of intrinsic value, and the stealing or killing of a cat was a crime subject to fine. Blackstone's *Commentaries on the Laws of England* reported that in the early Middle Ages a person found guilty of killing or stealing a cat that was the king's own property was subject to "a very peculiar forfeiture." As to the nature of that forfeiture Mr. Blackstone kept a discreet silence.

The old legal tradition that a cat is valuable property still survives in the United States. Even if the cat is not used to keep down the pest population, it does not lose its worth in the eyes of the law. The courts have ruled, "A cat which is kept as a household pet may properly be considered a thing of value. It ministers to the pleasures of its owner." So the law is not always a ass, or even a idiot.

Modern Law

The rights of property owners are balanced in law by responsibilities and liabilities. Courts do have a tendency to take the cat's free ways into consideration. An owner is not liable merely because his cat has trespassed on another's property or even if his cat has wandered onto a highway and provoked an accident; however, if you

Cats seem to go on the principle that it never does any harm to ask for what you want.

JOSEPH WOOD KRUTCH

ADLAI STEVENSON ON CATS

Birds are birds and cats are cats and often the twain do meet — frequently to the bird's bitter sorrow. In 1949, when bird lovers in Illinois sought to change this natural law through an act of the state legislature, Governor Adlai Stevenson vetoed the bill and gave the following explanation:

I cannot agree that it should be the declared public policy of Illinois that a cat visiting a neighbor's yard or crossing the highway is a public nuisance. It is the nature of cats to do a certain amount of unescorted roaming. Many live with their owners in apartments or other restricted premises, and I doubt if we want to make their every brief foray an opportunity for a small-game hunt by zealous citizens with traps or otherwise.

I am afraid this bill could only create discord, recrimination, and enmity.

Also consider the owner's dilemma: To escort a cat abroad on a leash is against the nature of a cat, and to permit it to venture forth for exercise unattended into a night of new dangers is against the nature of the owner.

Moreover, cats perform useful service, particularly in rural areas, in combatting rodents — work they necessarily perform alone and without regard for property lines.

We are all interested in protecting certain varieties of birds. That cats destroy some birds, I well know, but I believe this legislation would further but little the worthy cause to which its proponents give such unselfish effort. The problem of cat versus bird is as old as time. If we attempt to resolve it by legislation, who knows but what we may be called upon to take sides as well in the age-old problems of dog versus cat, bird versus bird, or even bird versus worm.

know that your cat has a tendency to cause problems, or, worse, if you have trained your cat to act in a way that causes problems, you can find yourself in trouble with the law, your neighbors and your insurance agent.

An examination of decisions involving cats suggests that there is a kind of enough-is-enough factor at work. For example, in the case *Boudinot vs. the State of Oklahoma* a court ruled that a woman was guilty of creating a public nuisance by keeping forty cats in her home "in a residential area so that a considerable number of persons are disturbed by the stench and noise arising therefrom."

There are, naturally, some citizens who are not at all happy about the free-ranging ways of cats and who lobby for laws to license cats. In Arizona there has even been an effort to permit the killing of any "feral" cat which wanders onto a person's private property. Feral cats on public lands could be shot by people with hunting licenses. (A "feral" cat was defined as a wild cat or any domestic cat not under the control of its owner.) The Arizona bill caused a tremendous uproar when it was proposed, and finally it was withdrawn. Proposals to make the shooting of cats legal are still unusual, but there is a growing national trend to call for the licensing of domestic cats and the altering of strays.

Cat Rights

An encouraging feature of the modern age has been the general recognition that animals do have feelings which must be respected. In Elizabethan times people enjoyed going to a publicly advertised arena to watch bears being tortured. Indeed, such "entertainment" was more popular than Shakespeare's plays. Tormenting or killing animals for show or sport is no longer legal, although it does continue. The basic law of the land which defines the rights of cats and other animals is the *Federal Laboratory Animal Welfare Act of 1966*. This law has been amended a number of times, most recently in a bill signed into law on April 22, 1976. In the opinion of many groups concerned with animal welfare, the existing legislation is still much too limited.

The most controversial aspect of cat welfare concerns the use of cats in scientific experiments. Because the experiments are often part of medical research, the laboratory work has many ardent defenders. Because the experiments often lead to terrible suffering for the animals, the research has many vocal critics. The laws, which are written by people anxious to be reelected, try to steer a compromise course between these two polar opposites. Legislation is generally directed at regulating the housing and transporting of laboratory animals rather than at controlling or limiting the experiments which can be performed on cats and other animals.

Cat Inheritances

There are people whose concern for the needs of cats have led them to remember pet cats in their wills. It has become so ordinary an event that, unless a fortune is left to a cat, newspapers seldom take notice. There is always the danger that a person who wishes to challenge a will can site provision for a cat as proof that the testator, the person who wrote the will, was not of sound mind; however, the courts have recognized that a bequest for the care and protection of a cat can be a valid charitable trust.

The first known will to mention a cat was that of Madame Dupuis, a famous seventeenth-century harpist. Her will caused a sensation

DUMPLING, A FERAL FOUNDLING

CAROL CHAPPELEAR

My husband and I live in Phoenix, Arizona, in the arid region close to Camelback Mountain. We share our surroundings with the usual desert flora and fauna, a few neighbors and a tribe of feral cats.

The cats are indeed wild, managing to exist off the lizards, mice, rabbits, insects and birds on the desert. The only concession the cats make to the humans of Camelback is to take occasional long drinks during the withering days of summer from the swimming pools which dot the landscape here and there.

Life is hard for the Camelback cats, but they endure. Their offspring, however, often die during the torrid temperatures of June, when 115° F. is not uncommon. By the time June arrives with its sweltering heat, the mother cats often have nursed their kittens for three months—twice as long as a house cat—and, just as the kittens' appetites grow, their milk supply is depleted. It is then that the kittens die one by one.

Painful as it was to know the kittens' fate, we never thought we could help, until two summers ago. It was June. I was confined to the house, recuperating from an operation, and my mother came out to visit and help. One day she came to my room filled with excitement.

"I have just seen the fluffiest, most beautiful beige kitten!" she exclaimed.

I told her it was probably one of the wild cats and that we would never see him again.

But with July the beige kitten came stalking into my ken, with mamma cat close behind, both looking painfully undernourished. The kitten was as beautiful as my mother had described it. I found myself putting food out to lure both parents and their beautiful kitten. Day by day the cat family became more accustomed to me. About one month after I began feeding them, I was able to stroke the little one—never the parents. Soon the parents began to spend more and more time away from our house, but the kitten remained.

We called him "Dumpling," for he was actually dumped at our doorstep without our realizing what was happening. Since the disappearance of his parents, Dumpling has never spent a day away from his adopted home. A bit weary from a romp or chase on the mountain, he returns to purr and coo his appreciation of the rest, refreshment and affection we humans provide.

when it was published because of its closing instructions:

Item: I desire my sister, Marie Bluteau, and my niece, Madame Calonge, to look to my cats. If both should survive me, thirty sous a week must be laid out upon them, in order that they may live well.

They are to be served daily, in a clean and proper manner, with two meals of meat-soup, the same as we eat ourselves, but it is to be given them separately in two soup-plates. The bread is not to be cut up into the soup, but must be broken into squares about the size of a nut, otherwise they will refuse to eat it. A ration of meat, finely minced, is to be added to it; the whole is then to be mildly seasoned, put into a clean pan, covered close, and carefully simmered before it is dished up. If only one cat should survive, half the sum mentioned will suffice.

THE CAT MAN OF NEW JERSEY

ALAN CARUBA

My quest to license cats began humbly: I had long been aware of cat attacks on birds visiting my family's feeding stations; but then I noticed that cats were also doing naughty things on the roof of my car.

I called the Maplewood Health Department and asked the Animal Control Officer to come and fetch the stray cats. "Oh no! We can't do that!" "Do you pick up dogs?" "Yes." "Do you pick up raccoons, opossums and such?" "Yes." "Well then, please come and get the pussycats. They may belong to someone." "We don't pick up cats."

It was my first glimpse of the double-standard. While there are ample state and local laws governing nearly every other species of stray animal, cats seem to have immunity.

Taking my case to the Township Committee I pointed out that since my taxes paid the Animal Control Officer's salary, and since a law concerning strays was on the books, cats as well as dogs should be picked up. The committee members laughed me out of City Hall. They stopped laughing when I began returning week after week.

Word spreads swiftly in a small town. Soon my phone was ringing. Other citizens, themselves subject to cat insults, told me horror stories; still other callers, who preferred to remain anonymous,

suggested I move out of town — quickly.

I pursued the matter to the state level. There I discovered that politicians would sooner raise taxes than touch the cat issue. Today, some nine years later, the situation remains the same; in New Jersey stray cats, as well as those with owners, continue to roam and to do what they wish, when they wish. That freedom still includes the top of my car.

There is, of course, another more serious side to this issue. Stray, unwanted pets — dogs as well as cats — are a health hazard; they do property damage; and cats, in their particular way, are irritating with their mating calls, fights and other activities.

If dogs must be licensed, so should cats. To maintain a special status for cats, which differs from dogs, is beyond logic or good sense. Other communities are learning this fact and are now controlling their cats; but I continue my lonely battle to license cats in New Jersey. No doubt I shall go to my grave branded as the infamous "Cat Man of New Jersey."

The label is unfair. I love cats as some of God's most glorious creatures. Loving, wise and mysterious, cats are splendid beyond words. *They* know my heart, even if my fellow citizens do not.

Alan Caruba is the author of several books and is, by most reports, a gentle soul.

But thousands die, without or this or that,
Die, and endow a college, or a cat.

ALEXANDER POPE

Nicole-Pigeon is to take charge of my two cats, and to be very careful of them. Madame Calonge is to visit them three times a week.

Madame Dupuis' will was challenged by her relatives and was broken.

Today it is recognized that the care and feeding of cats cost money, and, if a properly drawn will includes a modest provision for the support of cats, it is unlikely that the testator's sanity will be successfully challenged simply because he loved a cat.

It is also possible to leave money to organizations or foundations specifically concerned with animal welfare. The Morris Animal Foundation in Denver, Colorado, has prepared a small booklet which explains how to go about making charitable bequests. The booklet includes forms to fill out which can help speed matters when you have your will formally drawn up.

In every case it is important that you write your will with the advice of an attorney.

Burton Tauber is a practicing lawyer in New York City.

PUBLIC CAT FIGHTS

The following testimony was given by Jerry Owens, a licensed private investigator working in and around Dallas, Texas. Mr. Owens appeared on September 10, 1975, before a subcommittee of the U.S. House of Representatives Committee on Agriculture to report:

Cat are used for training and entertainment as accurately described in the August 1975 issue of *Texas Monthly* magazine. I quote: "The cat number is traditional at dog fights, much like clowns at a circus or halftime bands at football games. What they do is throw live cats, which they buy for 50 cents a head from the city pound, to assorted dogs who aren't fighting that day but who need exercise, self-confidence, and a show of affection."

Investigations have confirmed that a local humane society in Dallas, Texas, has furnished and is now furnishing dogs and cats for the above purposes, namely, "training" and entertainment at bulldog fighting.

There are a number of reasons why this cruel and inhumane practice is allowed to continue. Among the reasons are (1) apathy and the lack of concern of local citizens, (2) reluctancy of chief law enforcement agencies to enforce animal cruelty laws and other laws related to pit fighting such as gambling and prostitution, (3) the district inability to interpret such laws or his unconcern for the inhumane treatment of animals. Even after grand jury indictments, the defendant is not prosecuted.

CATS IN THE WHITE HOUSE

*Rutherford
B. Hayes
received
the first
Siamese cat
ever sent
to America.
It became a
White House
favorite.*

OFFICIAL WHITE HOUSE PHOTO

*Susan Ford's pet, Shan, maintains the Hayes tradition
of having a Siamese in the White House.*

"Tad" Lincoln had a cat named Tabby. Slippers, a polydactyl, lived with Theodore Roosevelt in Washington.

No matter how much cats fight, there always seem to be plenty of kittens.

ABRAHAM LINCOLN

CATS AND THE AMERICAN WAY OF LIFE

GILBERT GUDE

Tyrants hate cats. Genghis Khan and Napoleon and Mussolini are said to have hated cats.

Who loved cats? America's heroes, that's who. Thomas Jefferson loved cats. There were cats at Mt. Vernon because George Washington liked them too, as did Abraham Lincoln.

Several recent Presidents, of course, have been famous for having dogs. But one had to resign and two others got us bogged down in Vietnam. So maybe in the future we should add one more question to those we ask of presidential candidates. In addition to asking where they stand on Rhodesian chrome and socialized medicine, we should ask them where they stand on cats.

Better still, we should demand to see the cats these candidates say they have raised, just to make sure we are not having the fur pulled over our eyes.

These remarks were made by Congressman Gude (R-Maryland) in welcoming the Cat Fanciers' Association to Washington, June 25, 1976 for its annual meeting and convention.

A cat may look on a king.

JOHN HEYWOOD

SEEING-EYE CATS

BRIAN MCCONNACHIE

In 1968 the Department of the Army began experimenting with the use of "night eyes" or seeing-eye cats. The Army had, for a long time, been quietly impressed with the night vision of cats. The mission of the project was to employ this special ability; harnessed cats were to lead foot-soldiers through the thick jungle during the dead of night.

Certain people in high command had such enthusiasm for the idea that an order was given that night eyes be "field-tested," so the operation was put into use in Viet Nam on an experimental basis. After a month of night maneuvering with the seeing-eye cats, a report was filed with the section on Unconventional Warfare which, in part, stated:

". . . A squad, upon being ordered to move out, was led off in all different directions by the cats.

". . . On many occasions the animals led the troops racing through thick brush in pursuit of field mice and birds.

". . . Troops had to force the cats to follow the direction of the patrol; the practice often led to the animals stalking and attacking the dangling pack straps of the American soldier marching directly in front of the animal.

". . . If the weather was inclement or even threatening inclemency, the cats were never anywhere to be found.

". . . Often when the troops were forced to take cover, the animals took the opportunity to sharpen their claws on the boots of the troops, regardless of the seriousness of the situation.

". . . A number of the troops traded their animals to Vietnamese women for their favors. When questioned about this, the troops claimed that their animals ran away.

The project was suspended.

Brian McConnachie is a humorist who has written for the National Lampoon.

XIV. THE CONSUMING CAT

© 1976 Joseph Pomerance

JOSEPH POMERANCE

THE FASHIONABLE CAT: THE SEASON'S SHOWINGS

Jennifer Carden

O NE THING IS CLEAR from the newest collection of cat fashions: overdressed is definitely out. Not one designer this week was showing the traditional leather hip galoshes popularized by Puss in Boots, or the swirling (some say menacing) velvet capes favored by Dick Whittington's chic cat. Even the delicate embellishments — silver bells to be worn at the throat or baby blue satin ribbons for behind the ear — seem to be gone.

The new fashion words are comfort and ease of movement. Accessories are at a minimum. Fantasy clothing is gone with the sixties. And the hemline debate will not trip up cats *this* season.

Edith Head, for example, has adjusted her tennis dress to fall just below the tail. Unisex walking shorts by the noted costume designer are similarly abbreviated, with the out-of-favor troubador boots now replaced by argyle socks. Her party dress falls in soft flounces — but again, to lengths no longer than the average cat's tutu. Rather than grandiose fashions, suggested wardrobes focus on everyday life, and make the most of the cat's personal features.

Cathy Hardwick was undaunted by the hard fact that cats do not have knees on their front legs, a problem that continues to plague most signature designers. Her collection focuses attention on the cat's pretty face and unusual markings. She frames the face with large nautical collars.

Al Sardella, also taking attention away from the no-knees area, went for the neck, underscor-

Grandville's illustration of Puss in Boots

Victorian with rabbit fur muff

A style for old-fashioned cats only

SOLOMON R. GUGGENHEIM MUSEUM

Marya Anastasievna Chroustchova by Dimitri Kardovsky (1900)

Joan Harris designs for bohemian cats

ing its regally graceful line, its capacity for hauteur. Snoods, chokers, and jewelled necklaces highlight his collection. It is Sardella who has pioneered the rage of the season's showings: the much talked-about "neck belts," which fasten in the back. One style has a heart on which the owner's name may be inscribed; another, a little wallet for mad money or credit cards.

Among the new wave of young designers that includes Sardella, Joan Harris was also accepting the cat's anatomy and true way of life. She sees sunglasses as a way around the cat's frequent blinking and snoozing. Harris' "Greenwich Village" mannequin was dressed in a Mexican workshirt, carried a large leather pouch, and may or may not have been asleep.

One dissenting note was heard throughout the showings. Menswear designer John Weitz leafleted the gatherings with a short essay on why cats should not wear clothes at all. His pronudity statement shocked many in the fashion establishment, and was everywhere discussed. Some took his part. ("After all, they have their fur and that marvelous tail they can do so much with.") Others were indignant. ("Has *John Weitz* ever gone without clothes?")

The fur flew.

Jennifer Carden is a book publicist with a cat named John.

An overdressed woman is like a cat dressed in saffron.

EGYPTIAN PROVERB

Helen Gurley Brown of *Cosmopolitan* magazine confesses: "I have two fourteen-year old Siamese cats. One of them, Gregory, doesn't talk; the other, Samantha, and I have a running dialogue. Samantha's one trick is that she lies on my stomach and pushes the reading glasses off my nose with her paws. That is so we can hug and kiss. That cat is in love with me, but to say that it's 'mutual' doesn't begin to describe *anything*. I'm totally irrational about her. She and I are a *scandal*."

HARRY HARTMAN

EDITH HEAD

Feline Fashions by Edith Head

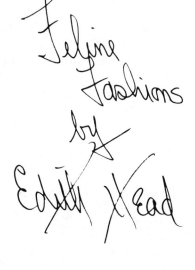

Walking shorts —

Party Dress

Bicentennial Bikini

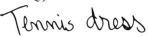

Tennis dress

SARDELLA

JOHN WEITZ

CATS SHOULDN'T WEAR CLOTHES

The trouble with being a designer is you can design clothes, but you can't design people. Clothes can be elegant! Clothes can be graceful! People usually are neither.

Animals are seldom better — after their seventh birthday, most dogs tend to walk on the bias. But cats? Even overweight cats instinctively know the cardinal rule: when fat, arrange yourself in slim poses.

Cats are *always* elegant. They know that the secret of elegance is a combination of several components: *fear* — affection to be given grudgingly and withdrawn on whim; *suspicion* — to create mystery; and *security* — acquired from the ability to run like hell. Cats are also superbly dressed in great colors and fabrics; each possesses one supremely simple outfit which never wears out.

Yes, cats are elegant; I wish I could design for them but that is impossible. That Great Dior in the sky beat me to it.

CATHY HARDWICK

PUSS IN BOUTIQUES

Irma Reichert

AMERICA IS A consumer society, and American cats have become consumers just like the rest of us. Specialty shops that cater to cat needs and cat owners' fancies have spread across the land. Boutiques for cats range from chic shops for spendthrifts to small stores for the wiser consumers who have largely given the lie to the legend of the extravagant cat and overindulgent cat owner. Even in New York City, the modern world's monument to the spending of money, chic is out and service is in for catdom. The best cat boutiques are stores run by people who are serious about cat welfare and are concerned for the reputation of cat owners. Shop around before settling on the best boutique for your cat and budget.

Pet boutiques can also be good places for gaining or exchanging information about cats. Sometimes they provide bulletin boards for people seeking to buy or sell cats and other animals. Store owners can also be a mine of information. They know what brands regularly satisfy their customers, and they learn what characteristics of a product seem to be especially appealing to cats. And they are often good sources of interesting, if useless, cat trivia and gossip. In checking boutiques, it is a good idea to chat with the shopkeepers and find out how much they know or care about cats. Our survey found most store owners to be helpful. Although clerks in pet accessory sections of department stores were helpful, they tended to be limited in their knowledge. Sometimes owners did combine lack of interest with a rude tone of voice. Shopkeepers in Beverly Hills, California, for example, were consistently unhelpful and uninformative.

Stores can be classed as: 1. *Total Cat Shops,* which offer more than you or your cat will ever want or need — but also all that you and your cat *will* need; 2. *General Stores,* which stock a number of practical items but limit the number of more frivolous goods offered; 3. *Health Fooderies,* which stress quality foods — some available only with a vet's prescription; 4. *Butcher Shops* that specialize in cuts and grinds of meat for the particular needs of cats. Our survey did locate examples of every category of pet boutique in New York; however, not all types of stores can be found in all parts of the country.

Cat trapped atop scratching post.

Representatives of the different types of cat boutiques in New York City:

Felines of Distinction, Ltd. *552 Hudson Street, New York, New York   10014*

A Total Cat Shop. You can even get T-shirts with your cat's portrait drawn to order.

Carousel Pet Boutique *261 Third Avenue, New York, New York   10010*

A General Store — carriers, collars and catnip toys. Typical general store wares.

Anima, Inc. *1161 York Avenue, New York, New York*

A Health Foodery with a no-nonsense approach to animal nutrition and care. Considers itself an "animal think tank" on questions of nutrition.

Hound House *168 East 24th Street, New York, New York   10010*

A Butcher Shop for animals, with coarsely chopped lamb and beef for cats.

Some cat boutiques in other parts of the country:

Robinson's House of Pets *135 Maiden Lane, San Francisco, California   94108*

A General Store tending toward the Total Cat Shop. Includes cat trees and "four-story condominiums" with carpeted floors for your cats to climb in.

The Feline Boutique *2418 East Pacific Coast Highway, Long Beach, California   90804*

A General Store for supplies. Also sells, bathes, grooms and boards cats.

Victor's of Hollywood *7513 Santa Monica Boulevard, Los Angeles, California   90046*

A General Store that originally specialized in birds and now includes a typical variety of products for cats.

Kitty's Kritter Korner *2340 East Bell Road, Phoenix, Arizona   85022*

A General Store.

Fifth Avenue Pet Shop *4255 Winfield Scott Plaza, Scottsdale, Arizona   85251*

A General Store tending toward the Total Cat Shop.

Feline Inn *1445 N. Welles, Chicago, Illinois   60610*

A General Store tending toward the Total Cat Shop.

Marshall Field *Pet Accessory Department, Various branches, Chicago, Illinois*

A General Store that includes some extravagant collars and rough-weather clothing.

Friendly Beasties *2319 Wisconsin Avenue, N.W., Washington, D.C.*

A General Store.

Virginia Pet Center *Springfield Tower Shopping Center, Springfield, Virginia*

A General Store that includes ceiling-high scratching posts.

Irma Reichert writes and lives in New York. Her cat, Molly, is well-supplied, but not pampered.

CAT CURRENCY

At some future date the lion is expected to lie down with the lamb. Might there have been an earlier time of peace when at least the cat lay down with the rabbit? Legend on the Isle of Man says yes. The Manx cat which is common to the island is popularly reported to be the result of a crossing between the domestic cat and the rabbit. Since the Manx cat has a hopping run, raised hind quarters, and no tail, it is not hard to see how such a story arose even though the cat seems to be a natural mutation.

To commemorate its unusual animal, the Isle of Man put the Manx cat on its one-crown coins, reputedly the only coin in the world with a cat on it. The Isle of Man is a British-owned island not far from the French coast. In 1840, when the British Empire was reaching its height, the Isle of Man abandoned its local currency in favor of English money, but in 1970, with the British Empire a fading memory, the island again issued a coin of its own. On one side is the face of the foreign sovereign, Queen Elizabeth II; on the other is the Manx cat, a fitting symbol of the island's independent nature.

Collectors can obtain the Isle of Man coin from Spink & Son Ltd., King Street St. James, London, S.W. 1, England.

CAT FUNERALS

Edmund Blair Bolles

WHY ON EARTH would anyone have a funeral for their cat? The short and cynical answer is because they are crazy, but that explanation is unsatisfactory. Sure, there are people who were unable to appreciate their cat for its cat qualities and they cannot be expected to change after the cat dies. But most people who pay to have a cat buried are under no delusions that their cat was human, yet they still want to have their pet buried in a cemetery.

Any relation with another living thing, be it person or pet, will inevitably include some attitude towards death. People with healthy attitudes recognize death as a natural event which ends the physical and growing part of the relationship, but it does not automatically end the emotion felt by the survivor. The death of a friend or loved one does not erase the memories of the living any more than graduation ends our memories of pleasant times we enjoyed with friends in school. Naturally in every human society there arises the question of how to confront the reality of death without degrading the memory that survives; the funeral customs of the world have provided diverse answers to the problem.

Cat owners who have enjoyed a living relationship should not be expected to pretend the loss of a long-treasured cat means little. Such a cold response would be as false and unhealthy as holding a ruinously expensive cat funeral and making tearful, daily pilgrimages to the pet cemetery. For people living in the country or in residential areas where every house has a yard, the solution has long been simple — burial on the owner's property. In this way, the cat's death is faced while the body is treated with enough respect for the surviving memories to go unscarred.

What can people with little or no suitable land do? The dead pet cannot be easily buried and yet the need to confront the totality of death is still with the owner. Many city pets end up in garbage cans or in the curb, but for owners who have lost a much-loved companion, such a callous solution is often unthinkable. Not surprisingly, as a solution to this problem, numerous pet cemeteries and crematoriums have been created.

Some pet cemeteries are very large. The Bide-A-Wee Pet Memorial Park on Long Island, near New York City, and the Bubbling Well Pet Memorial Park at Napa, California, near San Francisco, are bigger than many cemeteries for humans. Several hundred smaller pet cemeteries have also been established throughout the United States to serve the needs of smaller communities. Prices for funerals vary. Gravestones are also available and can include lengthy epitaphs if you are willing to pay the additional cost. Cremation, since it avoids the cost of land and perpetual care, is generally less expensive.

Each cat owner, upon the death of a pet, must decide for himself what is both appropriate

---

EPITAPHS IN A PET CEMETERY

*To mark a friend's remains
These stones arise;
I never knew but one,
And here he lies.*

LORD BYRON

Lovable But Ornery

---

*Oh harried orphan who found tender refuge
in our hungry hearts, sleep now in peace.*

---

*No. Heaven will not ever Heaven be
Unless my cats are there to welcome me.*

BIDE-A-WEE

and practical. For some, a commercial funeral is either unnecessary or impossibly expensive. Those who feel the need of such a service should keep in mind that neither they nor their cat will gain from a funeral which costs more than they can reasonably afford. Religious ceremonies are frowned on by most pet cemeteries. Such services are offensive to many religious beliefs since they cross the line that distinguishes between cat and human. Pet cemeteries do not use hearses; in order to stress that a natural rather than a religious event is taking place one manufacturer of pet coffins produces them in green rather than black.

Burying a cat in a pet cemetery is bound to seem silly to some people and may draw rude or insulting remarks from the unfeeling, but a pet owner whose attitude toward the death of his pet is healthy can look the scoffer in the eye and say, "I know what I am doing. Do you?"

Edmund Blair Bolles has cared for house cats in America and forest cats in Africa.

FROM
LAST WORDS TO A DUMB FRIEND

Housemate, I can think you still
Bounding to the window-sill,
Over which I vaguely see
Your small mound beneath the tree,
Showing in the autumn shade
That you moulder where you played.
THOMAS HARDY

LINES UPON THE DEATH OF A CAT

BOB RUSSELL

Tie Dye was an unusual cat. When most people came by to select among Princess Ming's kittens, Tie Dye ran and hid instead of greeting the visitors. As a consequence of her bashfulness, and perhaps her peculiar coloring (a hodgepodge of grays, white and a bit of red), Tie Dye was the last of the litter and we decided to keep her.

Unlike Ming, her slim lilac-point mother, Tie Dye didn't look Siamese, but when she opened her mouth you forgot her chunky body and yellow eyes. She "talked" Siamese.

Ming washed, wrestled with and educated her sole remaining kitten. In time, Tie Dye grew bigger than her mother. They sometimes stalked one another and pounced with enthusiasm, but when it was rest time they curled up together, each somehow managing to make a headrest of the other.

Tie Dye was an undemanding cat. She was happy with dry cat food out of the bag and never sought special tidbits. She made no unwarranted assumptions: every time she went to the water pan to drink, she first put her paw in to make sure there was water; then, reassured, she drank.

Most cats have a way of glancing sideways at you. Tie Dye, her youthful bashfulness lost or revealed as a shrewdness to avoid adoption, gazed at you directly. She sensed the moods of people, and when my wife was not well Tie Dye gave up her leisure and stayed by her side.

If Tie Dye had a vice, it was loving to be brushed. She came whenever the brush appeared and enjoyed every stroke of it. Brushing Tie Dye made people feel better, too.

At night, when satisfied that all was well, she came to bed and slept with her head on her mistress's ankles.

That about covers Tie Dye. It is difficult to put together now, although we had four years to get acquainted. Last Saturday morning, Tie Dye was run down by a speeding black car a few feet from her home and safety. It could easily have been a person run down, one of the youngsters who skateboard frequently on that corner. But it was Tie Dye, intent upon some cat business which she never got completed.

So please watch the road, even for a fifteen-pound bundle of gray and white and red. It might be someone else's Tie Dye. That animal has a family to enjoy and a life to lead.

Bob Russell, an avid cat lover, writes for the Onslow Herald *in Jacksonville, North Carolina.*

JUAN HOYOS

POOR CAT SEEKING FAVOR OF ENTHRONED FAT CAT

MARTY NORMAN

CATAGENESIS

SUZANNE WEAVER

This is the story of how kitties become human beings in their next life (the natural order of things). First they have to get into kitty heaven. You may not think there is a kitty heaven, but there is. I know for a fact that only dead good little kitties go there. Dead bad little kitties go elsewhere. Human beings are evolved from the souls of good little kitties. Here is an example to illustrate.

Once there was a cat named Terrance who lived with an owner who loved him very much. Terrance was easygoing, ate what was offered, slept the acceptable amount without overdoing it and chose unobtrusive places, purred when petted, didn't shed, left the birds and gerbils alone, never missed the litter box or jumped up on the tables. Terrance watched his owner carefully, thinking in his little kitty brain "how good a human I will make." Terrance was right; he died, went to kitty heaven, was reincarnated as President of the United States.

This is not always the case. There is a sad fact in this world — that is that some kitties do not make it to kitty heaven but in fact go elsewhere. These bad little kitties go to the fiery pit which is hot and a real bummer.

A case in point — Beelzebub, an American shorthair owned by a lady of the manor, got off to the wrong start with her unfortunate choice of his name. This immediately put the workers in the underground retreat on alert.

Needless to say, gadflies from the lesser of the two beyonds pestered Beelzebub his entire lives — four through six mostly — and caused him to behave poorly. Upon death, Beelzebub was summoned to the kitty pits where his soul, greatly flawed, does not repose but works like the devil.

Suzanne Weaver thinks cats are ridiculous.

THE CAT
PRODUCT REVIEW

A very special cat house decorated with sea shells. Designed and executed by Barton Benès.

ALICE SU

To cover all the cat products available would take a book in itself. Here, therefore, we have touched only upon articles that might be considered staples or those that are new or a little different. Frequently, a product will vary insignificantly from manufacturer to manufacturer; in those cases, specific recommendations have not been made, but general information about the product has been given. Some products should not be used without first consulting your veterinarian; these have been pointed out.

The majority of the products mentioned are available from your local retailer. If he does not stock them, he should be able to get them for you. In the event that an item can be purchased only by mail order, the source has been given. Because prices and shipping costs vary, we suggest you write first for a catalog and order form.

Grooming Aids

Nail Trimmers. Trimming your cat's nails can be a painless experience for all involved if done correctly and with the proper equipment. Place the cat on a smooth-surfaced table and gently, but with authority, lift each paw and remove only the curve of the nail, just short of the pink color. Both Millers Forge™ and Felix™ make excellent trimming implements: the former, a small-bladed scissor with a claw-size notch; the latter, a clipper resembling ones used by humans, but, like the Millers Forge™, is notched. Two other types of trimmers to be found in your pet shop are the guillotine and curved blade. The larger size of the opening makes both of these more difficult to manipulate and riskier to use than the notched variety.

Combs. It is important that all cats, long- or shorthaired, be combed frequently (daily, if feasible) — their skin will be healthier and hairballs will not be so much of a problem. A short-toothed metal flea comb is suggested for shorthaired cats and a medium- or long-toothed one for longhairs. Double-sided combs (large teeth on one side, smaller teeth on the other) are good for first getting out major mats and then finer combing. If your cat has a long, thick coat, try the Greyhound comb by Berlina Imports; it is double-sided, with teeth that are considerably longer than those on any other comb we've seen.

Brushes. The brush you use depends on your reason for brushing. If you are grooming for show or are particularly fussy about good coat condition, a pure-bristle brush is a must. For routine brushing after combing or for a cursory removal of surface hair, use a rubber brush. Wire slicker brushes are not recommended; they tend to rip and tear the coat. A plastic brush is fine for occasional brushing; however, frequent use over the long haul will cause the coat to lose its sheen. For those cats that do not need to be indulged in constant coifing, the self-cleaning Pet Brush by Kat-Trene™ (Box 476, Montour Falls, New York 14865) is a unique item; as the brush is twisted, the bristles retract into the cylinder and *presto!* your brush is clean. A great gift idea for your favorite tom.

Shampoos. To shampoo or not to shampoo — it's difficult to find agreement on this question. Some say once a month; some, once every six months; some, never. (If only cats could talk!) Since your veterinarian will ultimately deal with your cat's skin problems, it is probably best to take his advice. As far as what to use is concerned, Ring 5™, Lambert Kay™ and Pulvex™ are tried and true; human baby shampoo is fine and bar Ivory® works as well as anything. These are only recommended for routine Saturday night baths. If your cat has a skin problem, of course, see the vet. Whatever you use, *rinse well!*

Health Aids

Vitamins. Here again, the question of vitamin usage prompts divergent responses. We know some conservative cats who don't let a day go by without popping a vitamin or two; on the other hand, there are those devil-may-care types who have never had a vitamin in their lives. If you're not a gambler, here's a pragmatic approach: vitamins every day until your pet is about a year and a half old; then every second or third day. This presupposes, of course, that your cat has a well-balanced diet. We don't pretend to be nutritionists; ask your veterinarian for food recommendations. One piece of advice: make sure your kitty's diet is low in ash content (canned food under 4 percent and dry food under 12 percent); anything higher enhances the risk of cystitis (urinary tract infection), and that's one problem you and your cat don't need.

P.S.: The vitamin selection is vast, but the "breeders' choice" is Fauve®. And, if your pet is promiscuous, Nata-Fauve® is highly recommended for lactating queens.

Hairball Preparations. Hairballs are caused by the animal's ingestion of hair when grooming itself. The problem is common in longhaired cats and shorthairs too are not immune. Constipation and dry heaving are two strong indicators. Two of the preparations seen most are Femalt® and Petromalt®, and both will do the job. If you're penny-wise, however, some Vaseline® smeared on the paw will also do the trick.

Mineral oil is another home remedy often suggested; used indiscriminately, however, it can cause a roaring case of diarrhea, so unless you're a pro and know how to use it, *don't*.

Worming Compounds. Cats are susceptible to three types of worms: round, tape and hook. Roundworms (ascarids) are characterized by a mucous diarrhea, poor hair coat, loss of weight and, especially in kittens, a distended abdomen. Weight loss and poor hair coat are also symptomatic of tapeworms, but the most telling sign is ricelike particles around the rectum. With hookworms, there will probably be some bloody diarrhea, and the cat may be lethargic and have a hunched-up appearance.

The commercially available worming compounds are all very much the same and are generally successful only against roundworms, so if you suspect your pet has worms, have a veterinarian analyze your pet's stool and determine which parasites are present. He can then advise you about what course of treatment to follow.

Ear Mite Preparations. When your cat scratches his ears and shakes his head frequently, this does not mean he is making an important political decision. Chances are that if you look inside his ears you will find black gook — this is ear mites. Although there may be others, the only across-the-counter preparation we've seen for treatment of this problem is a two-step process *by Dr. Daniels*™ — Effer Wash® and Mitey Ear Drops®. During treatment, it is wise to bathe your cat to get rid of any mites that happen to be outside the ear. A good preventive maintenance program is to swab the inside of the ear once a week with mineral oil on a wet Q-tip®. Don't be afraid of going well into the ear — you won't hit the eardrum. Needless to say, see your veterinarian if the situation persists.

Insecticides

Many brands and methods of protection against fleas and ticks are available (fleas are much more of a problem with cats than ticks), and every cat reacts differently to each particular product. Qualified trial and error is the only means for determining what your pet will tolerate. It is important, however, that you do not use more than one method at a time; using products in combination can be very hazardous. Here are a few general pointers.

Collars. Before putting a collar on your cat, aerate it for a day or so. Fasten it loosely enough so that your finger can fit between the collar and the cat's neck. Also, check frequently for skin irritation; if there are any signs, remove the collar immediately. Remember, too, that this method isn't going to kill the fleas and ticks that prefer your bed to your cat; a spray or bomb will have to be used on those.

Flea Tags. Flea-repellent collars and tags are petroleum-based and not intended to be ingested. If your cat population exceeds one, there is probably a lot of licking and smooching going on, and since your pets may get sidetracked and lick the collar instead of their friends, a flea-repellent tag or pendant is a safer means of protection than a collar because it offers less licking area and comes in contact with less hair. Use one of these tags with a regular collar. Watch to be sure the tag does not dangle in your pet's water bowl; if it does, try another method of flea control.

Sprays. Use only sprays labeled specifically for cats and, of course, don't spray the animal's head. If you own birds, be careful that they do not come in contact with this aerosol.

Powders. In addition to checking fleas on your cat, powders are a good means of eliminating fleas from your pet's bedding. Again, be sure the product you purchase is marked particularly for cats and look for powders that are rotenone-based; they are nontoxic and the most effective of those that are available commercially.

Dips. Be sure the dip you buy is made for cats, and follow the dilution instructions carefully. Shampooing your cat before dipping will allow for better penetration of the skin. If you can't see your cat through the fleas, check with the vet; he can give you something stronger than you can buy across the counter.

Toys

There is a plethora of flimsy toys on the market, so before investing in anything make sure there is nothing in, on or about a toy that can harm your cat. Avoid the following:

1. Toys with bells, pompoms or other ornaments small enough for your cat to be able to chew off and swallow.

2. Toys with stuffing that your cat might eat after ripping them apart.

3. Toys with dangling strings that might be swallowed. Remember, too, that there is little snobbism among cats when it comes to toys, and they can have a good time with a paper bag, a box, a ball (try a ping-pong ball), an old shoe — almost anything you have hanging about the house capable of being batted around or nosed into. A marrow bone makes a great chewing toy, while also prompting strong gums and tartarless teeth.

Here are a few of the more substantial toy offerings:

Felix's Toughie Mouse®. This catnip-scented toy mouse is made of gray felt and will stand hard wear — one of the sturdiest mouse-type toys around.

The Gommelgrabber®. A refreshingly different toy — the cat chases a ball in and out of holes in a circular plastic container. The cats we've spoken to love it.

4-pack sponge balls. Just colored sponge balls, but fully digestible.

Dr. Daniels' Catnip Ball®. A wooden ball with a plugged opening for catnip — our cats had fun with this one. Put the plug back in tightly though.

Cosmic Cat's Dangles®. A take-off on the peacock feather idea (a pompom on a string connected to a stick) — your cat will enjoy chasing this when you dangle it for him. However, don't let him play with it alone; he could swallow the string.

Pic O' The Litter™ Puff Ball. A sturdy, fully digestible, catnip-treated puff ball for your cat to bat around.

Catnip. Catnip is best used in a toy, as some cats become frenetic when it is given in a raw state. To put together a jiffy plaything, wrap tissue paper around some catnip and tie it up in an old sock.

Miscellanea

Carriers. Before investing in a carrier — and they are an investment give some thought to your needs. Consider the following:

1. Size is important; your cat should be

In a cat's eyes all things belong to cats.

ENGLISH SAYING

able to turn around in the enclosure.

2. Weight is a factor; don't buy something you can't comfortably carry.

3. Make sure the case is well-ventilated.

4. The inside surface of the case should be able to withstand repeated washings. An anxious cat frequently has accidents.

5. If you use public transportation, the case should be extra-sturdy — enough to withstand the abuse it will take.

6. If you have a calm cat and the extent of your traveling is an occasional trip to the veterinarian, you can easily get away with an inexpensive cardboard case.

7. For car travel, avoid a bubble-top carrier. It is a very hot enclosure. Also, many cats tend to be less hysterical if they cannot see where they are going.

8. Avoid zipper tops. The case should close very quickly to eliminate the possibility of escape.

9. Wire-top cases with roll-back covers are adaptable to any kind of travel. Do watch, however, for stuck claws.

10. Above all, if you have an uncontrollable cat, no carrier will solve the problem. See your veterinarian about a tranquilizer. The trip will be a lot more pleasant.

11. The Cadillac of carriers? Vari-Kennel®!

(Incidentally, to put your cat in a carrier, pick him up by the scruff of the neck, dump him in the case, and close the top quickly and firmly. He who hesitates may have a lost cat.)

Scratching Posts. Scratching posts appear in many forms — rug, cork, sisal and burlap, upright and wall-mounted. The prices are as variable as the materials, running from several dollars for a disposable cardboard type to $70 or $80 for a very jazzy floor-to-ceiling model made by Wen-Rub™. If money is an object, a simple log is quite effective. There's no telling which kind your cat might take a fancy to, but to wean him from the couch try a little catnip on the new post. The important factor is that, whichever one you choose, it should stand or be mounted high enough so that the cat must stretch up to use it. Also, if you select an upright post, the base should be broad and sturdy enough so that it does not tip over.

A delightful conversation piece can be purchased at the Cat Cottage, 230 W. 82nd St., New York, New York 10024. Called the Cat's Bow-Wow, it's wall-mounted and comes in the shape of a dog. Ah, sweet revenge!

Collars and Harnesses. For a city cat who never leaves the apartment, there really is no need for a collar. If he does go for an occasional stroll, a harness is suggested; he cannot back out of it, nor can his neck be injured by a sudden jerk. There are three types of harnesses to choose from: the "T" (one strap buckles around the neck, another in back of the front legs and around the chest, connected by a strap on top), the figure-eight (around the neck and under the chest, connecting at the top), and the adjustable. If you decide on either the "T" or the figure-eight, measure the animal behind the front legs and under the chest to make sure the halter will fit. The nicest "T" we've seen is the Kindness Cat Halter® (Commodity Sales, P.O. Box 468, Oshkosh, Wisconsin 54901). It is leather and quite amply made, so fit should not be a problem on any normal-sized cat. Our favorite, however, is an adjustable nylon harness made by Pet-Care™. It can be slipped on and off once adjusted, is elasticized for greater comfort and, for you economically minded folks, comes with a matching nylon lead.

For the country cat who is outside, a collar is really necessary for identification. Always — but always — use one that is elasticized; it will be easier for your pet to slip out of should he get hung up on a branch.

Specialty Items

Pet Protector®. A plastic tag that attaches to your cat's collar — one side is a reflector (visible up to 650 feet) and the other side is for identification. An inexpensive way to keep your cat a little safer.

Cat Stamp. If the real paw prints on your kitchen counter aren't enough, here's a rubber stamp in the shape of a paw. (Available from The Kiss Co., P.O. Box 771, Madison Square Station, New York 10010)

Kitty Purr-ch®. There's no reason for your cat not to have his place in the sun. Capable of being attached to any window sill (no, you don't have to be an engineer to figure it out), the Kitty Purr-ch® is a regal roost for your pampered pet and also a place to call his very own. (Kitty Purr-ch, Box 2131, Scottsdale, Arizona 85252)

Pet Door. If you've been getting up in the middle of the night to let your tom in after his late-night dates, look into a FlexPort®. Made of an aluminum ring with plastic in the center, it allows your cat easy ingress and egress. It's not an inexpensive item, but it will save your cat having to explain where he's been, and you won't need as much coffee the next morning. (Turen, Inc., Danvers, Mass. 01923)

Havahart Trap®. We would be remiss if we failed to mention those animals who, through man's indifference, have been left to live in the wild. Allowing these cats to remain feral only adds to an already uncontrollable population problem. They should be caught and offered for adoption or humanely disposed of. The Havahart Trap® allows for capturing these animals without harming them in any way. (Allcock Manufacturing Company, North Water St., Ossining, New York 10562)

The Tail End

Litter. The standard clay variety is the overwhelming favorite. Look for a heavy, ground clay — it will be more absorbent and not as dusty as some of the lighter clays. Poise® is a good one and modestly priced. If you can't find it, try Cat-San®, Chips® or Kitti-Kleen®.

Cedar sawdust material (Katgo®, to name one) is also popular, the only complaint being that it tends to get tracked through the house because of its light weight. The smell is marvelous, though.

Green litter gets a "paws down," with bad reports from cats and owners. Many cats refuse to use it, and some people find the smell objectionable. Rodents, however, love it — to eat, that is (it's alfalfa!).

Pans and Covers. An ordinary plastic pan will do, but there are many more exotic offerings.

For litter-kicking cats, a number of manufacturers offer boxes with snap-on tops that not only help to confine the litter, but also secure a plastic liner, which eliminates the retention of urine odor in the box. Always lift this unit from the bottom, or you'll find the top in your hands and the litter on the floor.

A more sophisticated box is the Tabby Tender®. It has a screen on the bottom, allowing the liquid to filter through and the litter to be aerated. Although not inexpensive, it does add to the life of the litter and keep the odor to a minimum.

If you live in tight quarters and have no place to camouflage a box, an enclosure might solve the problem. There are several cardboard models, but the most elegant is the molded-plastic Kitti-Potti®. If it works (there have been reports that some cats don't want to be bothered coping with portals when there are more important things to be dealt with), it will eliminate litter spillage and prevent undiscerning toms from spraying the wall. (To let your cat know what this apparatus is for, put used litter in the box the first time around.)

Litter Additives. A good litter additive will do a lot toward checking urine odor. Holiday®, Pink Puff®, Litter Fresh® and Odor-Mute® all get good reviews, as does Dr. Una's®, which is an air pump spray, rather than granular or powdered as are the others. Baking soda is also an option, but so much must be added to the litter that the cost is prohibitive. To increase the effectiveness of these products, use a little less additive a little more frequently than called for in the directions

WALTER CHANDOHA

(i.e., a teaspoon a day rather than a tablespoon a week). Don't expect miracles, either; the litter should still be changed on a regular basis.

Mail-Order Houses

Studio B, *Box 4882, Station B, Columbus, Ohio 43202.*

A wide selection of books, diet aids and novelty items, with new products being added all the time. Send for their catalog; they're nice folks to do business with.

The Cat House, *38 Archer Lane, Stamford, Connecticut 06905.*

A unique selection of gift and novelty items for the cat lover, including some particularly interesting cat stamps from around the world and an unusual cat coin necklace. Also, free catnip seeds with every order! Catalog available.

Katnip Tree Company, *416 Smith St., Seattle, Washington 98109.*

A potpourri of fine-quality merchandise made by Felix™ (an old, reliable firm). Catalog available.

The Cat Book Center, *Box 112 Wykagyl Station, New Rochelle, New York 10804.*

A huge selection of cat books, in and out of print. Catalog available for $1.

Felines of Distinction, *552 Hudson Street, New York, New York 10014.*

One of the largest collections of products we've seen assembled under one roof. Not primarily a mail-order house, Felines of Distinction has no catalog, but if you cannot find a particular product in your own locality it is a good bet they carry it — and they'll be glad to send it to you parcel post.

INDEX